MORRIS MEDLEY

**readings
on
economic
sociology**

prentice-hall international, inc., London

prentice-hall of australia, pty., ltd., Sydney

prentice-hall of canada, ltd., Toronto

prentice-hall of india (private) ltd., New Delhi

prentice-hall of japan, inc., Tokyo

readings
on
economic
sociology

Neil J. Smelser
University of California, Berkeley

prentice-hall, inc./englewood cliffs, new jersey

prentice-hall readings in modern sociology series
Alex Inkeles, Editor

preface

My intention in collecting these readings is to add a dimension of depth to my *The Sociology of Economic Life*, published as part of the Prentice-Hall Foundations of Modern Sociology Series. In that essay I attempted to cover the issues of economic sociology as comprehensively as possible. Comprehensiveness, however, necessarily limits any detailed analysis of research. By presenting several dozen original studies now, I intend to compensate for this limitation.

The starting point of analysis in the original essay was the belief that economic behavior—though subject to the specialized discipline of economics—is always embedded in a social context. Economic behavior is empirically understood only by reference to other social variables—familial, political, religious, and so forth. My purpose was to illustrate connections between the economic and noneconomic aspects of social life and to interpret research relevant to these connections, such as how the family, politics, and religion influence economic activity, and vice versa. Now, however, in collecting these more specialized readings, I am able to present some of the original research, rather than pure summary.

Usually a companion volume of readings is subdivided according to the subdivision of the chapters of the text, with several selections for each chapter. I have followed this parallelism to a limited extent. The two Parts of this volume parallel Chapters Three and Four—the two major substantive chapters—of *The Sociology of Economic Life*. Part I begins with the view that the links between the economic and noneconomic aspects of social life are definite and traceable. The headings related to the cultural, political, integrative, and stratificational boundaries of economic life correspond—though in somewhat different sequence —to the subheadings of Chapter Three. "The Economy and Other Social Sub-Systems." In addition, a few selections in Part I illustrate the relations between personality and economic activity. Part II approaches economic sociology from the economic processes themselves—production, exchange, and consumption. This Part contains articles that illustrate how social variables impinge on these economic processes, and vice versa. The headings in this Part exactly parallel the subheadings of Chapter Four, "Sociological Analysis of Economic Processes."

There are no selections that exactly parallel Chapters One, Two, and Five of the essay. Chapter One is entitled "Historical Developments in Economic Sociology." The obvious companion readings would be selections from Adam Smith, Karl Marx, Émile Durkheim, and others, but these would have carried me well beyond the permitted space; and to present a few skimpy excerpts would have added little to the summaries in the text. Therefore I have not included any "classics," though some selections, especially the opening item by Norman Birnbaum, refer to historically significant thought in the development of modern economic sociology.

Chapter Two, "Economics, Sociology, and Economic Sociology," deals with the analytic relations between economics and sociology as academic disciplines. There are no selections in the present volume to parallel this chapter, though some of the authors do refer to the foci of the two fields. The reason I have included no selections here is that the literature yields disappointingly few incisive discussions on the relations between economics and sociology. To have reprinted some of these discussions, I would have added mainly polemical and hortatory sentiments to the points developed in Chapter Two.

Chapter Five concerns "Sociological Aspects of Economic Development." Important as this subject is, space limitations forbade a full section of supplementary readings. I have, however, interspersed a number of selections throughout the volume that deal explicitly with problems of economic and social development. Especially relevant are the articles by Kennedy on the Parsis and Protestant ethic; Bendix on ideologies and economic change; Comhaire and Greenfield on kinship and economic development; Deyrup on labor relations in underdeveloped areas; Hoselitz on patterns of political coordination of economic growth; Firth and Hoselitz on the formation of a labor force in developing countries; and Hoyt on changing patterns of consumption in the early stages of rapid urban-industrial change.

Four working criteria have governed my decisions on including or excluding selections: (1) Each selection should illustrate in depth an idea that could be covered only cursorily in the original essay. On page 82 of the essay, for example, it was possible only to give a listing of the determinants of cliques in office organizations. The selections by Gross, Roy, and Hughes, on the other hand, not only spell out these determinants in greater detail but also give the student a vivid account of how these determinants integrate themselves into the workaday activities of the office. (2) The selections must be directly related to the various headings by which I have chosen to break down the field of economic sociology. (3) The selections must represent the highest quality of research available. (4) In the interests of maximum coverage, the selections must be brief. By applying these criteria in a balanced way, I hope to have given the student a helpful supplement to *The Sociology of Economic Life*.

NEIL J. SMELSER

table of contents

Part 2
sociological
analysis of
economic
processes

readings
on
economic
sociology

Part 1

the relations
between
economic activity
and other
aspects of
social life

culture

one

One of the most debated issues in the past century concerns the role of cultural elements in economic life. A radical spokesman on one side of the debate is Karl Marx, who believed that the economic structure of society determines the general character of its cultural life. Another side of the debate is represented by Max Weber. Basing his case on the comparative analysis of religions, Weber argued that ideas, especially religious ones, exercise an independent influence on a society's economic activity. All the selections in this section concern issues related at least indirectly to this debate. In the opening selection, Birnbaum reviews the Marx-Weber controversy. In the second, Kennedy investigates the applicability of the "Weber thesis" to an Indian setting. The following selection (by Bendix) explores some of the connections between ideologies and economic development in different national settings, while the article by Chinoy analyzes the ideological "rationalizations" held by workers whose careers fall far short of the American success ideal. In the final selection, Halsey shows how universities—major "producers of culture"—have both responded to the needs of advanced economic development and increased their capacity to initiate even further development.

The readings in this section on culture and economic activity should be read in conjunction with pp. 40-44 of *The Sociology of Economic Life*.

The Rise of Capitalism: Marx and Weber

NORMAN BIRNBAUM

The postwar years have witnessed a considerable growth of interest in Max Weber among sociologists in England and the United States. This paper is an attempt to recall some of the polemical origins of a major theme in Weber's work: the function of ideology as an independent variable in social development. Weber struck upon this theme in the course of inquiry into the emergence of capitalism in western society—an inquiry that focused on England. A comparison of Weber's explanation of this phenomenon with that of Marx, whose historical materialism it so drastically challenged, is at once a venture in sociological analysis and a study in intellectual history.

Less than half a century separated Weber from Marx. Perhaps the fullest presentation of the latter's views on the genesis of capitalism in the west appeared in the famous twenty-fourth chapter of *Capital*, published in 1867.[1] Weber's views crystallized as early as 1904, when he first published *The Protestant Ethic and the Spirit of Capitalism*.[2] This was the first of a series of studies Weber undertook on the relationship of religious ideology to social development, studies published in the

Norman Birnbaum, "Conflicting Interpretations of the Rise of Capitalism: Marx and Weber," *British Journal of Sociology*, 4 (1953), 125-141.

Religionssoziologie[3] and later summarized, in a very general way, in the final chapter of the *General Economic History*,[4] which is actually a transcription of Weber's last course of lectures.

Both Marx and Weber were deeply influenced by the historicist tendency of German social thought. This tendency, which found full early expression in the writings of Hegel, held that social existence is process, that each historical epoch and social structure is unique, to be understood by laws referable only to itself. Marx and Weber, each in his way, broke with these postulates. Marx rejected historicism's predominantly idealistic interpretation of the content of social process, asserting that the decisive events were in the realm of social relationships, not in the sphere of the evolution of ideas. And in fashioning a theory which insisted on underlying regularities in social change, Marx also rejected the notion of the total uniqueness of historical epochs and social structures. Yet Marx retained historicism's sense of process and transformation. Weber, especially in the posthumously published *Wirtschaft und Gesellschaft*,[5] attempted to formulate some general categories that would apply to all historical epochs: this, too, constituted a break with historicism, particularly with the late nine-

[1] *Capital*, Samuel Moore and Edward Aveling, trans. (Chicago: C. H. Kerr & Co., 1921). Except where stated, references in this paper to *Capital* are to this edition.

[2] *The Protestant Ethic and the Spirit of Capitalism*, Talcott Parsons, trans. (New York: Charles Scribner's Sons, 1930).

[3] *Gesammelte Aufsätze zur Religionssoziologie* (Tübingen, 1920-1921) .

[4] F. H. Knight, trans. (New York: The Free Press of Glencoe, Inc., 1951).

[5] *Wirtschaft und Gesellschaft*, Vol. III: *Grundriss der Sozialökonomik*, 3rd ed. (Tübingen: J. B. C. Mohr, 1947).

teenth-century versions of it so prominent in the German intellectual climate of Weber's earlier academic years. But Weber's poignant sense of historical contrast surely stems from his historicist background. Thus both Marx and Weber worked in the historicist temper, even if they broke with the central theoretical tendencies of the school, and utilized its notions even when transforming them.

Both thinkers, moreover, labored on problems that had some special immediacy for Germans. Germany had, up to the large-scale introduction of capitalism in the nineteenth century, a curious amalgam of rational-legal and traditionalist political organization (in terms employed by Weber in his typology of authority).[6] We can anticipate a bit at this point: Weber strongly implied [that] these terms are descriptive not alone of authority structures but of the total organization of society.[7] Industrial capitalism, with its intrinsically dynamic qualities, had severely disruptive effects on German society.[8] This rendered capitalism a particular problem to German social thinkers, by contrast with England, where a more gradual development allowed figures like Adam Smith and David Ricardo to treat the capitalist economic processes as more "natural." It is against this background that we can understand the con-

cern of both Marx and Weber with capitalism not as a limited, economic system, but with its effects on society as a whole—on familial structure, political authority, personality organization, and on cultural phenomena like science and art.

Much of Weber's work was a test and modification of Marx's theory. Their conflicting interpretations of the rise of capitalism, then, should be discussed in the context of an analysis of the more general assumptions each brought to bear on this empirical case. We begin, however, by stating their views on the facts of the case: These prove strikingly similar, and so underscore the theoretical differences at issue.

Capitalism

The phenomenon both Marx and Weber wished to explain was the development, unique in world historical perspective, of an economic system in western Europe in which the following attributes were combined. The means of production were concentrated in the hands of a relatively small segment of the population. Labor was performed by a mass of formally free workers selling their services on a market. New social values called for a maximization of efficiency in the means of production through a relentless application of canons of rationality, and prescribed unlimited gain as an end of economic behavior.

This development was all the more remarkable against the feudal background, with its fixed and unfree social relationships, the irrational and spendthrift way of life of the feudal ruling classes, and the magical character of medieval European culture. Both thinkers agreed on the uniqueness of the new economic structure, and both agreed that it could not be treated simply as

---

[6] *Theory of Social and Economic Organization*, A. M. Henderson and Talcott Parsons, trans. (New York: Oxford University Press, 1947), pp. 324-423.

[7] See Talcott Parsons' introduction, *ibid.*, and Edward Shils, "Some Remarks on the Theory of Social and Economic Organization," *Economica*, **15** (1948), 36-50.

[8] See Talcott Parsons' remarkable essay, "Democracy and Social Structure in Pre-Nazi Germany," *Journal of Legal and Political Sociology*, **1** (1942), 96-114. I am indebted to Professor Parsons for this hypothesis on the social context affecting German intellectual concerns in the late nineteenth and early twentieth centuries.

such, that it entailed a new type of society. They also agreed on the enormous productivity of this new society, in cultural as well as material terms: sections of the *Communist Manifesto*, paradoxically, eulogize the bourgeoisie.

Marx and Weber held that the new social values embodied in capitalist economic activity were not "natural"—they were precipitates of historical development. Marx delighted to jibe at bourgeois economists for mistaking attitudes and behavior specific to capitalism for functions of some generic human nature. Weber insisted that the means and ends of action under capitalism were not simply expressions of some universal economic impulse but constituted a definite, socially sanctioned form taken by the more general human demand for want satisfaction.

Weber emphasized the distinction between traditional and rational social values in depicting the sharp contrast between feudalism and capitalism. Traditionalism in economic behavior, for Weber, meant fixation on an immutable standard of concrete preferences. Rationality, on the other hand, entailed a continual weighing of preferences in terms of the relative cost of attaining each. And the injunction to unlimited gain was much more abstract, much more devoid of specific concrete content, than the typically fixed goals of traditionalist economics. Traditionalism also included the transmission of sacrosanct ways of attaining its fixed preferences. Rationality, however, prescribed a perpetual critique of economic means: these were no longer sacrosanct, but subject to the criteria of technical efficiency. Every hitherto fixed way of doing things was now to be examined and, if necessary, replaced. The point Weber made, and in which Marx concurred, was that the canons of rationality no less than the dicta of traditionalism were arbitrary in the sense that both were concrete sets of values,

guiding action that took historically variable form. Thus Weber asserted: "A man does not by nature wish to earn more and more money, but simply to live as he is accustomed and to earn as much as is necessary for that purpose."[9]

The application of the canon of rationality unloosed an intrinsically dynamic force in economic behavior. A given producer was no longer obliged to confine his activities to a limited sphere, if he could maximize gain in another one. The effects of this continuous calculation of means-ends relationships were experienced in all other aspects of capitalist society as well: rationality, so destructive of precedent, could hardly be confined to economic life. It gave a decisive cast to the entire modern cultural ethos. (Weber argued that a rational-legal state was the only political structure that allowed this calculability in economic activity: traditionalist states were much too bound by specific precedent and arbitrary administrative decision. Weber went so far as to make this rational-legal, or bureaucratic, state a precondition for the emergence of capitalism.) Although rationality is a key point in Weber's analysis of the distinctive characteristics of capitalism, Marx was also well aware of it. Witness this passage from the *Communist Manifesto*:

The bourgeoisie cannot exist without constantly revolutionizing the instruments of production. . . . Conservation of the old modes of production was, on the contrary, the first condition of existence for all earlier industrial classes. Constant revolutionizing of production, uninterrupted disturbance of all social conditions, everlasting uncertainty and agitation distinguish the bourgeois epoch from all earlier ones. All fixed, fast-frozen relations, with their train of ancient and venerable prejudices and opinions, are swept away, all new-formed ones become antiquated be-

---

[9] *The Protestant Ethic, op. cit.*, p. 60.

fore they can ossify. All that is solid melts into air, all that is holy is profaned. . . .[10]

To recapitulate, Marx and Weber agreed on the cultural characteristics of capitalist society. Like all other societies, its economic goals are arbitrary in the sense that they are standards of value (in the capitalist case, the injunction to unlimited gain) between any two sets of which choice is a matter of arbitrary preference. The value of unlimited gain was not one found in traditionalist systems, with their injunctions to limited economic gains. Further, capitalism represented a break with traditionalism in economic means as well as economic ends. This does not mean that capitalism was undisciplined, by contrast with sanctified traditional procedures. But it does mean that the specific capitalist economic discipline was that of the maximization of technical efficiency. Marx and Weber both agreed that this had wide consequences for noneconomic activity. Weber argued that this canon is fundamentally incompatible with a magical or sacramental view of the world. Marx, too, recognized the connection between the emergence of capitalism and the banishment of magic from the west: "At the date when, in England, people gave up the practise of burning witches, they began to hang the forgers of bank-notes."[11] As we shall see, Marx and Weber differed on the explanation of this connection, but hardly on its existence.

One more point concludes our discussion of the common problems of Marx and Weber. Both agree that the new capitalist entrepreneurial class did not come from the precapitalist financial or merchant classes, which ruled the urban centers of medieval Europe. Marx emphasized the rapid rise of the new industrial capitalists (as opposed to the gradual development of a class of agricultural entrepreneurs). Although he placed much emphasis on colonial exploitation, he said: "Doubtless many small guild masters, and yet more independent small artisans or even wage workers, transformed themselves into small capitalists; and (by gradually extending exploitation of wage labor and corresponding accumulation) into full-blown capitalists."[12]

Marx described the struggle between these elements and the merchant and financial classes: new manufactures were begun in centers other than the great urban centers of medieval England. Weber agreed with the contention that the capitalist class was a rising class. These were the petty and middle bourgeoisie, who smashed the traditional practices and restrictions of the guilds, and who opposed the state monopolies of the Tudor-Stuart era. For Weber, this stratum was the bearer *par excellence* of that acquisitiveness and rationality which we have just described. In England, above all, this stratum did not immediately fuse with the older merchant and financial groups (as happened in the Italian Renaissance cities). Taking note of this internal differentiation without the class structure of sixteenth- and seventeenth-century England, both thinkers found in it a crucial aspect of the historical transformation under examination. But we shall find Weber asking some questions about the new bourgeoisie for which Marx had only some prefabricated answers.

Marx's Theory

Late in his life, Marx was credited with the observation: "Je ne suis pas

[10] In *A Handbook of Marxism*, Emile Burns, ed. (New York: Random House, Inc., 1935), p. 26.
[11] *Capital*, Eden Paul and Cedar Paul, trans. (London: J. M. Dent & Sons, Ltd., 1928), p. 837.
[12] *Capital* (Moore and Aveling trans.), Vol. I, p. 822.

Marxiste." He expressed, in this way, his repudiation of the overmechanical utilization of his theory by his followers, their lack of specification of the variables he had introduced into sociological analysis. We should be relatively unenlightened as to what Marx meant, were we today to discuss him as an economic determinist or as a historical materialist without defining the meaning of these terms. Marx was *not* an economic determinist in the sense that he thought economic motives [to be] the decisive ones in the social action of individuals. It is, indeed, crucial to our contrast of Marx and Weber that Marx left motivation relatively unanalyzed. It is precisely in the unanalyzed parts of a generally well-elaborated theory (the question to which it gives offhand answers) that we may find its flaws. Marx knew that he had to account for motivation, but did so in terms that are, by contrast with other aspects of his work, strikingly undeveloped.

A brief discussion of historical materialism is a necessary preliminary to a consideration of the Marxist theory of motivation. We may remember that Marx used the term "materialism" in a polemical context: he wished to overthrow the Hegelian notion that ideas, in the form of "spirit," were the essential factors in history, and instead depicted ideas as dependent, in their genesis and functioning, on material factors. These factors are found primarily in a society's economic institutions.

Every society, according to the sociology of Marx, has a set of economic institutions, a social relationship system allocating roles in the production, distribution, and utilization of goods. This system is organized around a society's production technology, and is acutely responsive to changes in technological complexity and efficiency. (Property relations, under this view, are as-pects of this social relationship system, and aspects of a highly variable kind, when viewed in historical perspective.) Roles in the economic system determine roles in the status system; broad strata of the population group together in terms of economic similarities. Taken together, these two systems constitute a class system, and the members of a given class share common interests, values, and a style of life. The allocations dictated by the economic system determine not only differences in status, for they include differences in political power as well. Thus the way to understand the functioning of a total society is to treat its economic institutions as the key variable.

The notion that economic institutions constitute the critical variable in the organization of society is of course especially emphasized in the historical aspects of the theory of historical materialism. All societies are in a continual process of change. Changes in material factors determine the direction of historical change for the society as a whole. Indeed, major processes of historical change are inconceivable without a material basis in the sense of a change in economic institutions.

The Marxist theory of motivation developed within this framework has two components. The first emphasizes the role of purely external pressures on individuals: force, fraud, and compulsion. The second begins with a concept of class interests and involves a theory of ideology: this component is central to the present discussion. For Marx, despite his emphasis on the varieties of coercion, was aware of the fact of consensus in society—that agreement on basic values among all its members, or substantial sections of them, such that individuals want to do what they have to do, and voluntarily, even eagerly, perform their social roles. How, then, did he explain it?

Position in a class endows an individual with a set of interests, a stake in certain present aspects of the society, or a potential for gain should the society undergo changes of a determinate sort. These interests are intuitively or rationally understood by the members of a class or their political leaders. Class interests not infrequently directly dictate social action. But in perhaps the more common case, class interests determine action indirectly and are effective through the medium of an ideology, an elaborated rationalization of a set of class interests. This ideology, in Marxist terms, comprises values as well as belief systems, imperatives as well as world images. We can see that for both sorts of action, that based directly on class interests or that following the imperatives of ideology, Marx inserted the economically determining factor well back in the process, in the genesis of class position. Economic motives were not, for him, the decisive motives in action. Thus the familiar dictum, "religion is the opiate of the masses," clearly states that action would take a different course were the opiate removed.

Although this theory may account for uniformities in the motivation of members of a single class, it had yet to account for consensual phenomena of an interclass sort. To meet this difficulty, Marx advanced the proposition that the class which controlled the means of production could and did impose its ideology on the rest of society. The failure of the members, leaders, or ideologists of a class to comprehend their real interests leads them to accept the ideology of another, opposed stratum and so underlies this imposition. At this point Engels introduced the notion of "false consciousness"—a process by which men incorrectly assess the sources of their beliefs, attributing these to the history of thought, for instance, rather than to their real roots in the system of production.[13] It is in this context that Marxist theory could explain how patriotism and religion unified societies.

What may we say about all of this? Marx recognized the social function of common values and developed his theory of ideology, partially to explain it. But Marx did not explain how class position, effective through class interests, generates ideology. He seemed to assume that this was done mechanically and automatically. But unless one specifies the relationships accounting for observed correlations of social facts, one may overlook more useful explanations for the observed correlations. It was precisely of this lacuna in Marxism that Weber was to make so much.

Marx's failure to specify the mechanisms by which common values are produced left quite implicit another function of such values, and the general ideological systems from which they derive. For such systems have uses other than their functions for society as a whole: they have definite psychological functions for individuals. These systems assure individuals a coherent world image and are an indispensable factor in maintaining psychological stability. Marx left these functions quite implicit: he seemed to assume an infinite sort of plasticity to human nature, such that these functions could be met by *any* ideology and its associated values. Thus Marx did not even pose a problem [that] Weber was to find so important: what values led to given patterns of social behavior?

Again, we may say that if social relationship systems (for example, a class system) determine the behavior of individuals, they may do so through proc-

<hr>

[13] Friedrich Engels and Karl Marx, *Correspondence*, Dona Torr, ed. (London: Lawrence & Wishart, Ltd., 1936), p. 511.

esses not inferable from a narrow description of the system itself. These processes, overlooked, may account for behavior one had mistakenly attributed to the system as narrowly defined. The psychological processes we have just mentioned may play precisely such a role, as may the other mechanisms that translate class position into action—all unspecified by Marx. It was at these points that Weber was to mount his attack on historical materialism. One more point concludes our discussion of Marx. The Marxist theory of the primacy of class position in determining social behavior rested upon the unanalyzed assumptions of the mechanical production of values and of complete psychological plasticity. It also stemmed from a purely arbitrary decision to intersect the historical process at a given point. The notion that class position determines ideological commitment, for instance, can have a purely temporal meaning: given a change in class relations, ideology will change to follow suit. Marx and Engels in their later writings admitted that a given historical process witnessed considerable interaction of factors within its temporal limits, but portrayed these as minor cross currents, of no decisive effect on the major direction of change.[14] This simply casts the issue onto another crux: how do we define the limits of a given historical process? If we say that it begins with a change in class relations, and ends when that change is completed, the very definition of the limits forbids a test of the Marxist hypothesis —for we are defining the problem so as to allow only one answer. We will soon see what Weber did with this methodological difficulty.

Weber's Theory

Weber never presented a statement of his general sociology as complete as

Marx and Engels' *German Ideology*,[15] nor of his entire structure of thought (philosophical and methodological as well as sociological) in the manner of Engels' *Anti-Duhring*.[16] The posthumously published *Wirtschaft und Gesellschaft* is fragmentary: its schematization does not serve as a statement of the components of an articulated theory. Nevertheless, the elements of a general theory are visible in Weber's work: elements bearing directly on critical issues in Marxist thought.

We have said that Weber's typology of political authority structures had implications pointing beyond a concern with government or its equivalent. The characterization of various authority structures as charismatic, rational-legal, or traditional refers to the bases of legitimacy: the values enjoining acceptance of the authority. Weber's analysis made clear, however, that political values can only be separated from the other values of a society with great artificiality. Weber's typology of authority was really a typology of the more general value system endowing a society with consensus. For Weber assumed that social behavior is of a piece: a society traditionalist in economic relationships usually does not possess a rational-legal authority structure. The value system of a society limits the possibilities for institutional variation within it: too much of a shift in the bases of legitimation and the structure of behavior it allows, from one segment of a society to another, can produce severe disruptions in institutional function. We may recall, at this point, Weber's insistence on the connection between rational political administra-

[14] *Ibid.*, p. 477.

[15] Karl Marx and Friedrich Engels, *The German Ideology*, Roy Pascal, ed. (New York: International Publishers Co., Inc., 1930).

[16] Friedrich Engels, *Herr Eugen Duhring's Revolution in Science*, Emile Burns, trans. (London: Lawrence & Wishart, Ltd., 1935).

tion in Europe and the rise of rationalized economic activity.

Weber, however, by no means saw societies as emanations of values. In the final phrases of *The Protestant Ethic*, he specifically renounced the intention of substituting what he termed a one-sided spiritualistic interpretation of history for an equally onesided materialistic interpretation. But in his analyses of stratification and the phenomena associated with it, Weber held that economic institutions were not the only relevant critical variables. Differential prestige distribution, for instance, and variations in style of life might counterbalance the effects of economic factors in the genesis and functioning of a stratification system. Within the context of this view of the bases of stratification, however, Weber was not unaware of the effects of class systems on ideology and values. In his later years he discussed the class basis of religion in the following terms.[17] Religions of privileged, ruling strata emphasize this-worldly values. Members of such strata feel intrinsically worthy because of their present social positions, and their religious beliefs justify the social system that allowed them such elevation. Members of underprivileged and oppressed strata, far from feeling worthy in terms of what they *are*, emphasize the importance of what they will *become*. They emphasize other-worldly values, and their religions depict a future salvation entailing a radical transformation of society's present relationships.

Clearly, religion interpreted in these terms is religion treated as a class ideology. But Weber made explicit what Marx left implicit. He asserted that religion answered the needs of men for some coherent account of their life situation. The raw materials for that account were drawn, for Weber no less than for Marx, from the situation of the various social strata. But the account was an answer to a need described in this way:

Salvation religion and ethical religiosity [have] a source other than the social situation of the negatively privileged and that bourgeois rationality which is conditioned by the practical life situation—the intellect considered of itself, especially the metaphysical needs of the human spirit, which is compelled to struggle with ethical and religious questions, not by material compulsion alone, but through its own inner necessity to comprehend the world as a meaningful cosmos and to know what attitude to take before it.[18]

If, as Weber asserted, religious systems and their associated values meet the individual's general psychological needs, the relationship between these needs and the individual's social position becomes problematical. The connection between the two does exist; but it is not a mechanical one and the sociological analysis of ideology cannot overlook it. The relationship was crucial to Weber's analysis.

Weber, again, cannot be understood as a onesided ideological determinist. He did emphasize the relatively independent development of systems of ideas. He denied that ideas are simply "reflections" of a class position, or that class interests may be understood apart from a class's conception of these interests, its ideology and its values. And he did insist, as we shall see in discussing his substantive analysis of western capitalism, that ideas (taken in conjunction with other factors) can exercise some independent influence on the course of historical development.

We have said that the failure to analyze the properties of the relationship between class position and ideology might lead to faulty interpretation of

[17] "Religionssoziologie," esp. Parts 7-8, in *Wirtschaft und Gesellschaft, op. cit.*, Vol. I, pp. 227-356, esp. pp. 267-301.

[18] *Ibid.*, p. 286 (my trans.).

the observed facts. We have also said that Marx left these properties unanalyzed, and assumed that class position automatically produced an appropriate ideology. Having postulated "the metaphysical needs of the human spirit," Weber could demonstrate that it was precisely this psychological property of the relationship that Marx left unanalyzed. This opened the way for his assertion that this property of the relationship might affect historical development in its own way, and not simply as a derivative of a more basic factor, economic institutions. Thus Weber's interpretation of the observed correlations between class position and ideology took cognizance of the initial facts Marx had noted, but refined and so amended the analysis.

Weber held that ideology had independent effects on behavior, but insisted that these effects could be just as unanticipated as those resulting from material factors. Thus Weber warned: "If one wishes to study at all the influence of a religion on life, one must distinguish between its official teachings and the sort of actual procedure upon which, in reality, perhaps against its own will, it placed a premium, in this world or the next."[19] In the same way, he was to say of the Reformation that its cultural consequences "were predominantly unforeseen and even unwished for results of the labors of the reformers."[20]

We have criticized Marx's theory of ideology for assuming what it had to demonstrate: that ideas are simply reflections of social position and exercise no independent effects on historical development. How did Weber demonstrate his thesis? If Marx intersected the historical process arbitrarily, was not Weber's intersection of it, albeit at a different point, no less arbitrary? Weber solved this difficulty by going outside the process of western history—by undertaking a series of studies we can understand as sociological equivalents to experimentation.

Experimental method has this advantage: if the scientist wishes to test the effects of a single variable, he can hold all other variables constant while altering the one under examination. The reconstruction of a single historical process allows no such control of experimental conditions, although it may be a necessary preliminary to such control. In this sense, we can charge Marx with failure to explore the possibility that, under different conditions, the material factors he saw as decisive in the west might have had results other than the ones he attributed to them.

But Weber took advantage of the fact that history has left us with the record of its own sociological experiments. Several large-scale civilizations have developed in relative isolation from each other: the west, China, and India, among others. By tracing out economic developments in each, Weber attempted to hold constant the material preconditions for western-style capitalism. This enabled him to focus on religious ideology, in each society, to see if it had independent effects. Comparative method, then, may be called a sociological equivalent of experimentation. What Weber did, moreover, was to analyze comparative materials with a very specific hypothesis in mind—a hypothesis derived from his encounter with Marxist theory.

Marx on the Rise of English Capitalism

We have seen that Marx agreed with Weber as to the cultural values of the new capitalist society, its emphasis on rationality. But Marx's account of the

---

[19] *General Economic History, op. cit.,* p. 364.

[20] *The Protestant Ethic, op. cit.,* p. 90.

rise of capitalism in England treated rationality as a consequence of this social development. His explicit emphasis in his depiction of the rise of capitalist society rested heavily on elements of compulsion and external pressure. It was a devastating indictment that this nineteenth-century prophet handed down before the court of history:

> The spoilation of the church's property, the fraudulent alienation of state domains, the robbery of the common lands, the usurpation of feudal property and clan property and its transformation into modern private property, under circumstances of reckless terrorism, were just so many idyllic methods of primary accumulation.[21]

It would be an error to underestimate the justness of Marx's emphasis on the role of force in this development. Least of all would Weber, himself an illusionless student of the uses of power in society, do so. The point, rather, is whether this constitutes a *sufficient* explanation.

Marx treated capitalism as a product of the feudal social system. Wars exhausted the feudal ruling class while its irrational and spendthrift way of life (itself a factor in causing these wars) emphasized consumption and not production. This emphasis gave rise to a wealthy merchant class, and financial powers developed in the medieval cities to assist in these mercantile transactions. Late in medieval times money became the decisive power of feudal Europe. Only in this way could the rural lords convert their desires into commodities. The rise in the price of English wool, a result of the development of a market for it in the Flemish woollen industry, provoked the money-hungry feudal lords to enclosures. These enclosures restricted their lands to sheep pasturage, and either drove the peasants away or severely altered their social position. These changes had, according to Marx, an economic basis. But on this developed a new superstructure: "With the coming of money rent the traditional and customary relations between the landlord and the subject tillers of the soil, who possessed a part of the land, is turned into a pure money relation, fixed by the rules of positive law."[22] (We may again see the empirical agreement with Weber in Marx's acknowledgment of the nontraditional character of capitalist relationships.)

The ousting of the peasantry produced, at once, an army of landless proletarians and a market for commodity production, for this group had formerly produced goods at home for immediate consumption. In the cities, a new class developed: former guild artisans and masters, petty burghers, even former proletarians took advantage of a fluid situation to become entrepreneurs and so rise to wealth. Marx emphasized that this was a new class, the seventeenth-century representatives of which were to wage the English Revolution against older mercantile and financial interests. Marx acknowledged the lack of adaptability of the older interests, but did not explain it—except by telling us that theirs was an unprogressive role (which constitutes no explanation, but a description after the fact). Marx, in the same way, did not tell us why members of the newer bourgeois class, in their original statuses as masters or independent artisans or proletarians, broke with traditionalistic economic standards.

Again, we cannot tax Marx with unawareness of the sorts of values and psychological factors associated with the new system. Discussing a closely related problem, that of proletarian

---

[21] *Capital*, op. cit., Vol. I, p. 805.

[22] *Ibid.*, Vol. III, p. 927.

work discipline in the same period, he said:

It is not enough that the conditions of labor are concentrated in a mass, in the shape of capital, at the one pole of society, while at the other are grouped masses of men who have nothing to sell but their labor power. Neither is it enough that they are compelled to sell voluntarily. The advance of capitalist production develops a working class which by education, tradition and habit looks upon the conditions of that mode of production as self-evident laws of nature.[23]

What was unproblematical for Marx, however, was the nature of the values and psychological processes he summarized under the rubric "education, tradition and custom." Marx's system had a relentless consistency, but its worth seems to lie in its assertion of the existence of historical connections rather than the explication of their full structure. The rationalization of economic life that Marx attributed to the "immanent laws of capitalist development" is precisely what Weber sought to explain in the light of a broader sociological perspective, conscious that what Marx regarded as inextricably forged together could, on other historic anvils, be shaped another way.

Weber on the Rise of English Capitalism

Comparative method allowed Weber to make an estimate of the relative effects of material and ideological factors in the rise of capitalism, not only in the west as contrasted with other societies, but also among Catholic, Lutheran, and Calvinist segments of western society. Population growth and the influx of precious metals were dismissed as the sole inciting causes of the rise of western capitalism by Weber in view

of their effects in India and China, from which capitalism hardly issued. (Capitalism meant something very specific to Weber: the organization of formally free labor in methodical, rational, and disciplined work.) Weber argued that the two factors mentioned above were effective in the west only insofar as the labor relations system allowed. This was a material argument; but we may recall that Weber did not wish to promulgate a onesided interpretation. And Weber emphasized, as we shall see, some of the ideological and psychological dynamics of that labor relations system.

Weber's freedom from the notion of progressive direction in history enabled him to study India and China without treating these societies as "arrested" or "preliminary" variants of capitalism.[24] Marx and his followers, on the contrary, tended to do the latter—and precluded comparative correction of their analyses of the west. The Indian and Chinese studies strengthened Weber's emphasis on the economic consequences of religious belief. The Indian caste prohibition on changing occupations prevented the destruction of Indian guild organization in a western manner. Religion, in the Weberian analysis, meanwhile generates indirect consequences of a no less important sort. The banishment of magic from the world, transmitted to Christianity by Judaism, had to precede the development of rational economic technique. And religious ethics had to take a form other than the duality of treatment sanctioned for brother and stranger before the free market could come into existence. Thus comparative data en-

---

[23] *Ibid.*, Vol. I, p. 809.

[24] Despite occasional passages implying that "Asiatic society" and the "Asiatic mode of production" had an independent evolution, Marx generally treated nonwestern society as precapitalist—very specifically so in the case of Japan. . . .

couraged a closer examination of the association of religious ideas and the rise of western capitalism.

We have already said that Weber portrayed religious ideas as having unanticipated consequences for economic development. Thus he insisted:

We are naturally not concerned with what was taught theoretically and officially in the ethical compendia of the time. . . . We are interested rather in something entirely different: the influence of those psychological sanctions which, originating in religious belief, and the practise of religion, give a direction to practical conduct and hold the individual to it.[25]

It is of some value to emphasize this point; Tawney's valuable work, *Religion and the Rise of Capitalism*, is an attempted refutation of Weber which emphasized what Weber explicitly treated as unimportant; what we could term "formal religious ideology."[26] Tawney, then, hardly refuted Weber, since he did not meet his argument. It is to that argument that we now turn.

Medieval Catholicism provided its believers with an escape mechanism, as it were, from their guilt in the confessional. The sacramental power of the priest was a residue of magical belief. Medieval Catholicism thus allowed relief and prevented rationalization. The Catholic lived morally, in Weber's words, from "hand to mouth"—his life was a succession of acts, each judged by its intention, not a systematized whole. Only a special group, the monks, had an incentive to rationalize their lives. For the layman, this system dispensed grace in a magical way. The absence of harshness and rationalization for the common man produced a

genial and benign acceptance of life. And since the world and its institutions were viewed as lower sections of the supernatural order, traditional standards were created and received a religious sanctification.

Luther, the first heroic figure of the Reformation, rejected the notion that the church possessed magical powers. But his doctrine of *solafideism*, that men could be saved by faith alone, rooted on an indwelling notion of grace. Men were vessels of the divine, and since the divine was incarnate on earth, God had decreed the current social order. This, in its own way, sanctified traditionalism in economics and authoritarianism in politics. Luther did, however, introduce the notion of the calling as applying to all, not only monks: God's injunction to the individual to work in his allotted sphere. We shall see how Calvinism transformed this notion.

Calvin posed an absolutely transcendental God, decreeing salvation or damnation at will. This created a terrible inner isolation for the believer, an intolerable burden of anxiety to know whether he was one of the elect. This anxiety forced the development of Calvinism (after Calvin) in a Puritan direction. One could know one was saved by works, which could not, however, insure one's salvation. Deprived of the relief of the confessional, deprived of the inward conception of grace possessed by Lutheranism (Calvinism distrusted the feelings as chimerical), Puritanism turned outward. A modification of Luther's conception of the calling developed. One had a duty to work in the world, not because God had sanctified one's position, but because that position was an opportunity to honor the glory of God. The absolute transcendence of God resulted in a rejection of the notion that God dwelt in the world—the world was,

---

25 *The Protestant Ethic, op. cit.*, p. 97.
26 R. H. Tawney, *Religion and the Rise of Capitalism* (London: John Murray, Publishers, Ltd., 1926).

rather, an impersonal sphere, a setting for the labors of those who were not vessels of the divine, but its instruments.

Under Catholicism only monks were religious virtuosi. However, Calvinism enjoined upon all the duty of systematic, rational work. One demonstrated one's election by suppressing the natural man, by systematic planning of one's life. In Weber's words:

The religious life of the saints, as distinguished from the natural life, was no longer lived outside the world in monastic communities but within the world and its institutions. This rationalization of conduct within this world, but for the sake of the world beyond, was the consequence of the concept of the calling of ascetic protestantism. Christian asceticism, at first fleeing from the world into solitude, had already ruled the world which it renounced, from the monastery and through the church. But it had on the whole left the naturally spontaneous character of daily life in the world untouched. Now it strode into the marketplace of life, slammed the door of the monastery behind it, and undertook to penetrate just that daily routine of life with its methodicalness, to fashion it into a life in the world, but neither of nor for this world.[27]

The bearers of this Christian asceticism were the new middle classes of England and Holland. The Puritans, under the notion of the calling, were enjoined to make the most of their opportunities in the world, provided they did not relapse into the state of the natural man. One could pile up wealth, for not to do so would be to deny one's duty in one's calling. But one could not use wealth for pleasure. "The idea of a man's duty to his possessions, to which he subordinates himself as an obedient steward, or even as an acquisitive machine, bears with chilling weight

on his life."[28] (Marx speaks of the "fetishism of commodities";[29] here Weber gave this conception a definite ideological source.) The notion of the transcendence of God and the impersonality of the world led the Puritans to reject traditionalism; they thus had a religious sanctification for the destruction of traditionalist restrictions. Meanwhile, "the emphasis on the ascetic importance of a fixed calling provided an ethical justification of the modern specialized division of labor. In a similar way, the providential interpretation of profit making justified the activities of the businessman."[30] Thus the Puritans had religious incentives of the strongest sort to utilize the opportunities attendant upon the disruption of the feudal system. They could not utilize their wealth for spendthrift consumption in the manner of the former ruling classes, for to do so would be to repudiate the ascetic standards they honored. Perforce, they reinvested.

Their religious ideas precluded acceptance of the Tudor-Stuart type of state monopoly and the Anglican conception of a corporate economic life. God worked through the elect; the conviction of election born of business success formed a hard and sober middle-class pride. This pride, which denied to external agencies the obligation or right to intervene in the earthly fate of the individual, combined with the concept of the inner isolation of the believer to produce a Puritan independence and brutality. The general quality of Puritanism was antisensuous and antispontaneous in the extreme: "Asceticism descended like a frost on the life of 'Merrie old England.' "[31]

Rejection of the possibility of the intervention of a church body or a state

---

[27] *The Protestant Ethic, op. cit.,* p. 154.

[28] *Ibid.,* p. 170.
[29] *Capital, op. cit.,* Vol. I, pp. 81ff.
[30] *The Protestant Ethic, op. cit.,* p. 163.
[31] *Ibid.,* p. 168.

in the individual's path to salvation led to a political antiauthoritarianism that Weber contrasted with the social quietism of Lutheranism. He cited the political institutions of Puritan England and America as cases in point, in contrast with those of Lutheran Germany. The Puritan injunction against idolatry of the flesh, Weber adds, has also resulted in an anti-Caesarist tendency in the political life of Puritan countries.

What Weber was saying in all of this was that the institutions of capitalism were no outgrowth of the feudal system in any mechanistic sense. They demanded a specific set of values, and specific psychological qualities, for maximum utilization of their potential. The social history of England and the economic role of the Puritans in British sixteenth- and seventeenth-century society provides European evidence for the role of religious ideas in historical development. Weber also cited as evidence the absence of rationalization in Lutheran Germany and in the Catholic countries, the importation of Calvinists by European rulers desirous of encouraging industry, even early twentieth-century occupational differentiation statistics comparing Catholics and Protestants—well after the secularized development of capitalism had made Puritans of all the children of the west.

Weber really made two points in reference to Calvinism. Its values were such that it sanctified capitalist activity, providing an ideology that set the Puritans onto the restless pursuit of gain. But along with the values the Puritans possessed, they were also organized as personalities to function in this methodical, ruthless way. It was this inner ruthlessness and conviction that led them to break traditionalism, that sustained them against Church and State. The inner development of religious thought to the point of Calvinism and the production of hard Puritan char-

acters had to take place before economic activity could be rationalized in a way that Marx saw as an automatic consequence of the opportunities provided by the inner disruption of the medieval social system. By inserting an ideological and a psychological variable (the latter, to be sure, more implicitly) in historical analysis, Weber showed that the explication of variables relatively implicit in Marxist analysis may alter the conclusions that analysis reached, without essentially altering the facts it considered.

Conclusion

Weber's concern with the independent effects of ideology on social development, then, originated in his polemical encounter with Marxism. This led him to develop at least an implicit general theory to oppose to that of his great nineteenth-century predecessor. The immediate occasion for this development, however, was Weber's concern with the facts of Marx's central empirical case: the rise of capitalism. In analyzing these facts, Weber fairly may be said to have built on Marx's work.

Marx, who treated ideology as a dependent variable in the process of social transformation, formulated this problem more precisely than had his predecessors in the history of social thought. Weber in his turn utilized Marx, not by accepting his hypotheses, but by testing them and amending them. He eschewed the assumption of a mechanical production of values (and of ideology, generally) and made explicit what Marx had left implicit: the psychological functions of belief systems. This explication allowed him to point out that ideology did not derive automatically from social position but was, rather, a means of interpreting that position: a possible function of ideology, under this viewpoint, was to give direction to social change.

In similar fashion, Weber himself may be amended. We have said that he gave the ideological variable an explicit independent status in the analysis of social change, but that he left implicit not the psychological *functions* but the psychological *origins* of an ideology. His discussion of the brutality of the Puritans, however, reminds us of Freud, one of whose major empirical themes was the harshness of the psychological discipline imposed by western culture. Perhaps we can say that the insertion of a viable psychological theory in the analysis of social process is the next step for systematic social theory: if so, this is well under way. This is not to assert ·that Marx and Weber, with their analyses of social structure and ideology, can be superseded. Rather it is to say that their work may be included in a new theoretical synthesis.

The Protestant Ethic and the Parsis

ROBERT E. KENNEDY, JR.

Max Weber's famous essay, *The Protestant Ethic and the Spirit of Capitalism*,[1] has stimulated a host of writings, not all of which have supported his ideas. In presenting still another paper in this area, our purpose is not to defend or to attack Weber's thesis in its entirety. Rather, by abstracting certain specific ideas from both his work and the subsequent work by Merton,[2] and by testing, in a very rough way, the validity of these ideas as they apply to a non-European community, the Parsis of India, we hope to gain more confidence in the suggested high association between the belief in economic and technical values and the actual performance of the tasks of trade and technology.

Robert E. Kennedy, Jr., "The Protestant Ethic and the Parsis," *American Journal of Sociology*, **68** (1962-63), 11-20. This article, as well as all other articles from the *American Journal of Sociology*, is reprinted by permission of The University of Chicago Press.

[1] *The Protestant Ethic and the Spirit of Capitalism*, Talcott Parsons, trans. (New York: Charles Scribner's Sons, 1958).

[2] R. K. Merton, "Puritanism, Pietism and Science," in *Social Theory and Social Structure* (New York: The Free Press of Glencoe, Inc., 1957), pp. 574-606.

Since Puritan and Parsi beliefs differ on the specific level of terminology in ritual and scripture, a linguistic bridge must be constructed at a slightly higher level of generalization to span the gap between the two value systems and give us an abstract language in which to describe the relationships between value and behavior we hope to find. To meet this semantic problem, we have used a stylistic device based on Weber's concept of varying rationalities.

Values Associated With Economic Activity

Acquisitive Rationalities

As Weber pointed out, "When the limitation of consumption is combined with the release of acquisitive activity, the inevitable practical result is obvious: accumulation of capital through the ascetic compulsion to save."[3] This statement contains two specific notions: the idea that the acquired goods are to be accumulated and saved rather than consumed and "used up" and the belief in acquisitive activity as opposed to a more passive attitude toward mate-

[3] *The Protestant Ethic, op. cit.*, p. 172.

rial goods. Viewed in this way, it is possible to formulate two distinct values: *the desire to accumulate rather than to consume material goods* and *the desire to maximize one's material prosperity.*

The two values are similar, yet the important difference lies in the meanings the acquired goods have as reflected in the uses to which they are put. On the one hand, the desire to accumulate material holdings need not be related to the absolute level of one's material prosperity. Savings can occur among both the rich and the poor. On the other hand, as Deusenberry has pointed out,[4] efforts spent in increasing one's material prosperity need not lead to increased accumulation of wealth if there is a corresponding increase in consumption. It is possible for the two types of behavior to exist independently of each other.

Financial Rationality

When the two acquisitive values are found within one system of rationality, they may balance and complement each other, and in this combination could be thought of as "financial values." Accumulated wealth is used (invested) in the pursuit of increased prosperity, and the increased riches are not consumed but are saved for further use in the never-ending quest for greater income, more accumulated wealth. The financial values may be held for religious (as with the Puritans), political, or cultural reasons, but in each case we would expect members of such groups holding the values to tend—given the opportunity[5]—to select financial vocations in favor of other possible pursuits.

In other words, we would expect the members to be favorably biased toward financial activity.

Rationality of Work

Weber described the attitude toward work among the early Protestants in the following way: "the valuation of the fulfillment of the duty of worldly affairs as the highest form which moral activity of the individual could assume . . . gave everyday worldly activity a religious significance."[6] The net result of this belief was that "for the Puritan . . . mundane toil becomes itself a kind of sacrament."[7] We can reformulate this value in a more secular sense to read: *a belief that material work is intrinsically good.* If we accept Weber's descriptions of the belief of the early Protestants not only in the two previously discussed financial values, but also in the *intrinsic value of material work*, then we would expect the early Protestants to be favorably biased not only toward financial activities, but also toward those vocations involving more physical work, including, perhaps, the buying and selling, the storage and shipping of the material goods of commercial trade.

Values Associated With Scientific Pursuits

Having briefly set forth three values among many that Weber said were associated with economic activity, let us move on to discuss two of the values Merton said were associated with scientific pursuits.

Scientific Rationality

Merton said that one Puritan belief, the assumption of an *underlying order in nature*, was also a basic value of science. In saying this, he followed that

---

[4] J. S. Deusenberry, *Income, Saving and the Theory of Consumer Behavior* (Cambridge: Harvard University Press, 1952), p. 22.
[5] Given not only the material opportunity, but also the absence of conflicting values within the beliefs of the group which would counterbalance the effect of the two values being discussed.

[6] *The Protestant Ethic, op. cit.,* p. 80.
[7] *Ibid.,* p. 166.

school of philosophy that argues that the scientist believes the random impressions received through his senses can be made orderly through human arrangement.[8] This belief is in turn based upon the assumption that the diverse phenomena can be grouped under general laws which will reveal what Einstein called the "pre-established harmony."[9] The "ultimate given" in this system of scientific rationality is the basic assumption of what Whitehead called the *order in nature*.[10]

However, as Merton has pointed out, the assumption of an *underlying order in nature* is not the only ultimate given in the scientific rationality.[11] Another criterion is needed to sort the various impressions into the meaningful and the meaningless, those accepted and those rejected. What is needed is some standard of verification which can be used to establish the "reality" of the assumed *order in nature*. Merton and others have suggested that empiricism was the standard used in the search for evidences of the regularities of the universe. In spite of the various uses of the term, all systems of scientific empiricism make the assumption that it is possible to know the world through the senses. This dependence of science "upon the agreement of sense impressions for verification of its observations"[12] can be expressed as the belief in a *sensate standard of verification*. Merton argues that the Puritan assumption of an *underlying order in nature* and the Puritan acceptance of a *sensate standard of verification* favorably biased the members of that religion toward scientific pursuits.[13]

When science is applied through material work to the physical world for practical purposes, it becomes, by definition, technology. In performing the tasks of technology, the technician may have a greater tolerance than the abstract scientist for the material work involved. It is possible that the belief in the *intrinsic worth of material work* may be more widely held among technicians than among "pure" scientists. Following this line of conjecture, one could say that the "rationality of work," discussed above, could also be one of the distinguishing features between the basic attitudes of the scientist and those of the technician.

Having briefly described five abstract values suggested by the works of Weber and Merton, we shall now turn to their formulation in the religion of the Parsis —Zoroastrianism. The reader should understand that our purpose is to relate certain values with certain behavior patterns and not to discuss the role of religion *as such* in economic or technical behavior. The point is that if other ideologies—religious, political, economic, philosophical, cultural, or any other—also accept and believe in the five values delineated here, then we would also expect the members of those groups, given the opportunity, to be favorably biased toward the relevant pursuits. Keeping this point in mind, let us examine the Zoroastrian expression of the five abstract values.

The Values as Expressed in Zoroastrianism

Zoroastrianism is considered to be one of the great religions of the world

[8] J. Bronowski, *The Common Sense of Science* (New York: Modern Library, Inc., n.d.), p. 58.

[9] J. W. N. Sullivan, "The Values of Science," in *The Limitations of Science* (New York: Mentor Books, 1949), p. 166.

[10] A. N. Whitehead, *Science and the Modern World; Lowell Lectures, 1925* (New York: New American Library, 1948), p. 11.

[11] "Puritanism, Pietism and Science," *op. cit.*, p. 579.

[12] W. J. Goode and P. K. Hatt, *Methods in Social Research* (New York: McGraw-Hill Book Company, 1952), p. 20.

[13] "Puritanism, Pietism and Science," *op. cit.*, p. 574.

even though its followers today number only about 150,000. It was established as a systematic body of belief by Zoroaster in Persia around 600 B.C. From that time until the seventh century, when Persia was conquered by the Muslims, Zoroastrianism was the official state religion of the Persian Empire.

While the primary source for the Zoroastrian statements reflecting the abstract values of our opening discussion will be the ancient Gathas,[14] other sources are used to indicate that the religion of the Gathas was still basically the religion of the Parsis in the period relevant to this paper. The five values are found in the Zoroastrian ideology in a systematic way based primarily upon what we have called the assumption of an *underlying order in nature*.

Underlying Order in Nature

This belief is of such importance in Zoroastrianism that it has been given its own term: it is called *"asha."* Asha and its derivatives are mentioned in at least 185 of the 256 existing verses of the Gathas.[15] According to Jackson, *asha* "represents the divine law and moral order in the world, together with good works, purity, truth, and holiness, in short all that is meant by the Sanskrit cognate *rta*."[16] The Indian scholar Dhalla describes the Indo-Iranian meaning given to *rta*:

Despite the casual freaks and caprices, the laws governing the movements of nature seem to be immutable. This unfailing regularity of nature led the Indo-Iranians to discern the fact that a stable order prevailed in the universe which insured its existence. They called it *rta*. They emulated this universal order and introduced it in all their human activities.[17]

For example, the critical question of what is "good" is made clear in terms of this order in nature to every Zoroastrian. From infancy they are taught the holy aphorism, called *"Ashem Vohu,"* which may be rendered: "Order or holiness is the best good. Hail, Hail is to him who is the best holy one by way of holiness."[18] Upon the three injunctions of purity and order in thought, word, and deed is built the entire structure of Zoroastrian morality. Or as Jackson has said, the three goals of good thoughts, good words, and good deeds are the "quintessence of the moral and ethical teachings of Zoroaster."[19]

Given this belief in a spiritual order to the universe, how do Zoroastrians recognize the divine order as it exists in the mundane world? Is it described in all its particulars by the priests, the scripture, or the traditional rituals? Does Zoroastrianism delineate a specific creed which gives an explanation of every possible facet of the divine law of order?

Sensate Standard of Verification

In partial answer to these questions, Zoroaster teaches that the revelation of the divine order is found in nature itself and not in any one man's doctrine (*Ha* 43:10).[20] He says that the perfect as-

---

[14] The Gathas contain the oldest parts of the Zend Avesta and concern the establishment of the ethics of the religion. Later works dealt with ceremonies, rituals, and specific theological practices. . . .

[15] *The Holy Gathas of Zarathustra*, B. T. Anklesaria, trans. (Bombay: Shahnamah Press, 1953).

[16] A. V. W. Jackson, *Zoroastrian Studies* (New York: Columbia University Press, 1928), p. 49.

[17] M. N. Dhalla, *History of Zoroastrianism* (New York: Oxford University Press, 1938), pp. 46-47.

[18] E. S. D. Bharucha, *Zoroastrian Religion and Customs* (Bombay: D. B. Taraporevala Sons & Co., 1928), p. 45.

[19] *Zoroastrian Studies, op. cit.*, p. 134.

[20] This and all of the following quotations from the Gathas will use Anklesaria's translation and transliteration. The citation will either be mentioned in the text or will be

pect of religious grace is found among those who "seek the splendour of the Law divine," so that they may know the universe (*Ha* 51:4,5).

As we have seen in our opening discussion, some philosophers consider a questioning mind, curious about the possible regularities in nature, as one of the qualities of the scientist. If we take this Zoroastrian insistence on a questioning mind as one aspect of a sensate standard of verification, we might expect certain regularities to have been discovered by Zoroaster or his followers. In other words, if Zoroastrianism has two of the values of science, then we could reasonably expect a historical record of Zoroastrian science. If such a body of knowledge existed, it would present another indirect evidence of the existence within the religion of a sensate standard of verification.

Among the ancient Greeks, Zoroaster was perhaps as well known for his works determining certain regularities in nature as he was for his other religious teachings. The Macedonian conquest placed the Greeks in direct contact with the writings of Zoroaster, and the "works catalogued under the name of Zoroaster in the library of Alexandria contained two million lines."[21] These works have been lost to the world, but they may have been the missing books of the Avesta which were reportedly wholly scientific in their contents.[22]

We would have much more confidence in the religious acceptance of a sensate standard of verification if we could find explicit instructions to the faithful to verify their beliefs through their senses. We have been able to find

---

given in parentheses thus: *Ha* 43:10, meaning Chap. 43, v. 10.

[21] Franz Cumont, *Oriental Religions in Roman Paganism* (New York: Dover Publications, Inc., 1956), pp. 138-139.

[22] A. V. W. Jackson, *Zoroaster, The Prophet of Ancient Iran* (New York: Columbia University Press, 1898), pp. 95-96.

only two such very specific instructions. In one, Zoroaster teaches his followers that knowledge acquired through the sense of sight is for the praise of Ahura Mazda through the Law immutable (*Ha* 50:10). In the second instance, he clearly states that each man is to accept only those beliefs he himself believes to be true after hearing different sages and by listening and looking, instructing himself about the nature of the universe:

Do you listen with your own ears, do you look with the best inspiring divine intelligence,
At the creed of your own choice, each man for himself,
In order to instruct himself through our sages before the magnific events (*Ha* 30:2)?

These fragments and traces, while in no way conclusive, do permit us to operate on the reasonably well-grounded assumption that the sensate standard of verification was indeed the standard used by Zoroaster to determine the evidences of the divine order in the material world.

Material Work Is Intrinsically Good

The Zoroastrian quest for empirically verified knowledge of the underlying order in nature was not simply for the sake of knowledge. The wisdom of the law immutable, *asha*, was to be *used* to construct the Kingdom of Ahura Mazda in the mundane world (*Ha* 44:6). Zoroaster asks Ahura Mazda to declare that the "real progressive spiritual life" is won by the "best Words and Works . . . of praise by the Good mind and by the divine Law . . ." (*Ha* 34:15). The Zoroastrian insistence on good deeds done in the material world is a more concrete formulation of the abstract value, a belief that material work is intrinsically good.

The establishment of the Kingdom of Perfect Order was the ultimate goal of this work in the material world. Zoroaster passionately asks his faithful not to waver, not to be staggered by the formidable magnitude of the task, "but to aspire and work and struggle and fight for it with body and mind, heart and soul:"[23]

Therefore does Zarathustra dedicate even his own life
And that of his Good Mind as the first offering to Mazda.
And the Inspiration and Kingdom of Work and that of Word to Asha (Ha 33:14).

It is through these great exertions to establish the Kingdom of Order that faithful Zoroastrians win their salvation. Bharucha says that every Zoroastrian "will have to be judged, rewarded, or punished solely according to his deeds in this world irrespective and independent of the merits of any intervening medium or savior."[24]

This Zoroastrian belief in the intrinsic worth of material work has not escaped the notice of several scholars. Jackson wrote that the "Iranian, by influence of his creed, was characterized by action, exertion, and practical views of life. . . ."[25] Cumont argued that the Persian view of the world as a great struggle between the forces of Good and Evil was "peculiarly favorable for the development of individual effort and human energy. . . ."[26] Max Weber gave Zoroastrianism as an example of those religions whose devout believe they are God's tools accomplishing God-willed action.[27] Tilgher said that Zoroastrian-

ism prized labor and gave it an ethical value.[28]

Maximization of Material Prosperity

Since the Kingdom of Order was to be constructed in the mundane world with material goods, such goods were highly valued. Furthermore, the increasing material wealth of the Zoroastrian faithful is believed to be an increasing glorification of Ahura Mazda. The following verse is repeated *sixty* times throughout the Gathas, testifying to the central importance of directing one's efforts toward ever-greater prosperity:

The excellent Law immutable is prosperity; it is uprightness; the Law immutable is weal for him who is for the excellent Law immutable
In the name of God.
May the eminent glory of the prospering Lord Ahura Mazda increase!

It might be reasonable to argue that this prosperity is of an other-worldly type, had not Zoroaster made clear what he meant by the term. In unusually plain language, the prophet asks for the rewards of both worlds:

I who go around you, O Omniscient Lord! with the Good Mind
To gain for me the rewards of the two lives, of the corporeal and that of the mental,
With the Law divine whereby to the aspiring ones prosperity may be given (Ha 28:2).

The religious idea of using the Law immutable to increase one's wealth is very near to the social idea that when one's wealth is increasing one must be following *asha*, and conversely, when one's wealth is decreasing one must be failing to meet the standards of the reli-

[23] Dhalla, *op. cit.*, p. 56.
[24] *Op. cit.*, p. 25.
[25] *Zoroastrian Studies, op. cit.*, pp. 132-133.
[26] *Op. cit.*, p. 157.
[27] "The Social Psychology of the World Religions," in H. H. Gerth and C. W. Mills, trans., *From Max Weber: Essays in Sociology* (New York: Oxford University Press, 1958), pp. 284-285.

[28] Andriano Tilgher, *Work, What It Has Meant to Man Through the Ages*, D. C. Fisher, trans. (London: George G. Harrap & Company, Ltd., Publishers, 1931), p. 21.

gion.[29] This idea is expressed in the Gathas in that to the noble who "associate with Asha," "Mazda Ahura will give him spiritual life, / Will with the Good Intelligence increase properties for him" (Ha 46:13). But for the wicked there is no prosperity, instead there is only injury and adversity (Ha 30:11).

Accumulation Rather Than Consumption of Material Goods

To shift our attention away from the religious reasons for increasing one's wealth to the meaning acquired wealth has for Zoroastrians is only to look at the same religious reasoning from a slightly different point of view. By keeping the wealth one has won through hard work, the successful Zoroastrian, in effect, preserves the fruits of his past religiosity. For example, Zoroaster asks not only to acquire, but also to maintain wealth: "Verily I desire the immutable Law to maintain; give me through Perfect Devotion that / Reward acquired by following the path of Asha, which is the life of the Good Mind" (Ha 43:1). The idea of gaining and maintaining wealth is also found in certain aspects of the Zoroastrian marriage ceremony, the initiation ritual, and in some proverbs.

In our description of the ethics of Zoroastrianism, we have limited ourselves to those religious values which appeared to be similar to the theoretically defined values of our opening discussion. We have not attempted to describe the total system of the religion, nor are we saying that these are the only Zoroastrian attitudes which are conducive to economic and technical pursuits. In fact, the Zoroastrian emphasis on honesty, education, human welfare, and the national pride among Zoroastrians today in their great Persian heritage, all are probably factors promoting an active, knowledgeable approach toward attaining desired ends.

In the preceding pages we have attempted to identify values in Zoroastrianism which have a theoretical relevance for certain types of behavior. If our thinking has been correct, then present-day Zoroastrians—the Parsis of India—would tend to pursue these activities once they are given the opportunity to do so.

The Behavior of the Parsis

The Zoroastrians of India are called "Parsis" after Persia, the land of their origin. The ancestors of the contemporary Parsis came to India in the eighth century as religious pilgrims fleeing from the persecutions of the Muslims in their homeland. The Hindus allowed them to settle, and by 1931 the Parsis were the most urban (89 per cent),[30] and the most literate in English (50.4 per cent, almost twice that of the next highest native group, the Jews, who had 26.4 per cent).[31] Yet they had remained one of the smallest religious communities in India, having a population of only 102,000 persons in 1921.[32] These demographic variables are important and should be kept in mind as likely factors contributing to the Parsi activity in trade and finance. However, our attention here is focused only on other possible variables—including the presence of the relevant values.

---

[29] Weber emphasized this "social" effect of similar religious ideas in early Protestantism. Good works and the wealth resulting from such efforts were the means "not of purchasing salvation, but of getting rid of the fear of damnation" (The Protestant Ethic, op. cit., p. 115).

[30] Kingsley Davis, The Population of India and Pakistan (Princeton: Princeton University Press, 1951), p. 185.
[31] Ibid., p. 159.
[32] Statistical Abstract of British India, 57 (1912-13/1921-22), Tables 8 and 9.

Since we are following Weber's ideas on the influence of certain beliefs on economic behavior, we would expect that the economic values of accumulation, rather than consumption of material goods, a desire to increase one's material prosperity, and a desire to work in the material world, would tend to lead Parsis—given the opportunity—into commercial ventures. Of course the "capitalism" of Weber's thesis did not exist in India before European domination, but other forms of commercial behavior did. The question is not whether the Parsis were "Weberian capitalists," but simply whether the Parsis took a proportionately greater part than others in the economic activities of their time and place.

Parsi Commercial Pursuits

It is believed that as early as the close of the eleventh century, Parsis were one of the chief classes of traders in Cambay. In 1534 a Portuguese doctor visited Cambay, and in his book published in 1563, he mentions that there were merchants in Cambay, "Gentios who come from Persia" who were called "Esparcis."[33] Another European traveler visited Surat in 1638 and observed that the Parsis were engaged in various pursuits including trading and banking.[34] These early accounts are valuable since they show a Parsi interest in trade long before major European commerce came to India.

However, with the arrival of the Europeans, the Parsi traders now had the opportunity to extend their activities by using the larger ships of the Europeans. In the first half of the eighteenth century, Parsis opened new native trade routes to Burma, Calcutta, Persia, Arabia, and China. Perhaps the greatest of the Parsi China merchant princes was Sir Jamshedji Jijibhai. An idea of the wealth he made from his trading activities can be gathered from the amount of his wealth that he gave away. From 1822 to 1847, he gave away more than £221,981 to various schools, public works, and charities.[35]

The first occupational statistics indicating Parsi activity in trade appeared in 1858. However, this report is not considered to be very reliable since it listed the total population of Bombay Parsis as 110,544 in 1858 (the total number of Parsis in all India did not reach this figure until the census of 1931). While the total numbers may be misleading, perhaps something can be gained from Dosabhoy's comment: "the largest number, or more than one half of the whole Parsee population, follow the avocation of merchants, bankers, or brokers, which fact furnishes a clear proof of the commercial bent of the Parsee mind."[36]

The argument advanced in this paper is that this "commercial bent of the Parsee mind" is similar to the capitalistic bent of the Puritan mind in Weber's study. As Weber did, we stress the point that values are only one factor in the total behavior pattern. Any analysis of a particular group must also include the *opportunity* it had to pursue its interests. The fact that the Parsis prospered under British rule was in no small way related to the British establishment of the right of private property for its sub-

[33] Garcia da Orta, *Colloquies on the Simples and Drugs in India*, Sir Clements Markham, trans. (1913), p. 445, as quoted in R. B. Paymaster, *Early History of The Parsees in India: From Their Landing in Sanjan to 1700 A.D.* (Bombay: Society for the Promotion of Zoroastrian Religious Knowledge and Education, 1954), p. 37.

[34] Albert de Mandelslo, *Les Voyages du Sieur Albert de Mandelslo*, p. 180, as quoted in Paymaster, *ibid.*, pp. 42-43.

[35] Framjee Dosabhoy, *The Parsees: Their History, Manners, Customs, and Religion* (London: Smith, Elder & Co., 1858), pp. 181-183.

[36] *Ibid.*, p. 152.

jects. As one author has expressed it, under British rule the Parsis, "began for the first time to reap the fruit of their own industry."[37]

On the other hand, one must remember that the Parsis were active in commercial pursuits with not only the British, but also the Dutch, the French, the Portuguese, and the native governments of the region. For example, one can consider the Parsi activity in the office of *desai*, or tax farmer, of India. The first recorded Parsi who held this position did so for the native government of Gujarat beginning around 1450. The Parsis of Navsari maintained this position for more than three hundred years, until at least 1779. An indication of the wealth controlled by Parsis in this pursuit can be seen in the case of the Vikajis family, which made direct advances to the native government of the Nizam of Hydrabad of £1,080,000 during the period 1835-45. The Parsis did not limit their tax-collecting activities to native governments, however. The first Parsi to arrive in Bombay came there in 1640 to handle the tax collection in the city for the Portuguese. Later the English took over the city, but we find from a public document dated in 1834 that the Parsis managed the work of tax collection in Bombay for at least 165 years.

The Parsis showed their willingness to follow new vocations in the pursuit of material gain when the English and the Dutch established "factories" in Surat in 1613 and 1618. Just seven years after the opening of the English trade center, the first English account of the Parsis' religion and history was made, "by the interpretation of a Persee, whose long employment in the Company's service had brought him to a mediocrity in the English tongue."[38] By the middle of the seventeenth century, Parsis were acting as agents and brokers, not only for the English but also for the Dutch, the French, and the Portuguese. Toward the end of the nineteenth century, reliable statistics are available on the occupation of *dubash*, or commissioned agent for a European firm. The tentative conclusion of Parsi commercial interest drawn from the historical cases is supported by the rather impressive statistical fact: according to the census of 1881, of the 159 *dubashes* listed in Bombay, 146 were Zoroastrian.

Assuming this all too brief treatment of the Parsi mercantile operations sufficiently indicates Parsi behavior in this field, let us move on to the second part of our thesis: Merton's ideas concerning the relation of the belief in an underlying order in nature, a sensate standard of verification, and the intrinsic worth of material work to the pursuit of scientific and technological activities.

Parsi Technical Pursuits

Parsi activity in trade was matched by Parsi interest in the construction of the means of trade. The fame of the Parsi shipbuilders was recorded by Europeans as early as 1716. Parsi achievements in the technological field of shipbuilding include the following: the establishment, under British auspices, of the Bombay Dockyard in 1735; the first community in India to build ships up to 1000 tons without the aid of any European shipbuilders; the construction in 1804 of the first English man-of-war built in India; and in the first 149 years of the Bombay Dockyard, the con-

---

[37] *Ibid.*, pp. 138-139.

[38] Henry Lord, "A Discovery of Two Foreign Sects in the East Indies, viz., the Sect of the Banians, the Ancient Natives of India, and the Sect of the Parsees, the Ancient Inhabitants of Persia," in *Voyages and Travels*, John Pinkerton, ed. (London: Strahan & Preston, 1811), Vol. VIII, p. 279.

PRENTICE-HALL, INC. P.O. BOX 21X, ENGLEWOOD CLIFFS, N. J. 07632

BILL NUMBER

328698P   1   0000000 0

C 014 0006

19 059

BILLING DATE

12/06/66

A
C
C
O
U
N
T

MR H F SHARP
DEPT OF ZOOLOGY
UNIV OF GA
ATHENS GA

30601

**PLEASE ENCLOSE THIS COPY
WITH YOUR PAYMENT.**

QTY.	TITLE AND EDITION OF BOOK	TITLE CODE		PRICE PER BOOK	TAX	POSTAGE & HANDLING	TOTAL
1	READINGS IN ECOLOGY	1	75586	3.83	.11	.40	4.34
	ED PURP						

328698P

WE NEED THIS NUMBER ➔
WHEN YOU PAY, WRITE OR RETURN.

 PAY

struction of 335 new vessels, in addition to repairing "innumerable ships."[39]

The Parsis also took part in the construction of the railways of India. One of the great Parsi railroad builders and civil contractors was Jamshedji Dorabji, a man with no formal education. By 1882, this self-taught Zoroastrian had constructed ninety miles of railway for the Great Indian Peninsula Railway in addition to building mills, public buildings, and so forth, costing nearly £1,000,000. Of course Dorabji's case was unusual, but the general Parsi interest in technological fields is indicated by the occupational statistics of the census of 1881. Twenty-six of the forty-six shipbuilders, and thirty-three of the eighty-four civil engineers listed in Bombay at that time were Zoroastrian.

Some Parsi merchants demonstrated their concern with science by founding scientific societies and schools. One of the earliest was established in 1831 in the city of Broach by the eldest son of a rich Parsi merchant. But perhaps the greatest Parsi contribution to scientific education in India was made by the Parsi industrialist, Jamsetji Nusserwanji Tata. He gave not only the unusually large sum of £200,000, but also his time and insight to help found the Indian Institute of Science at Bangalore in 1898.

As an indicator of the general Parsi interest in science and technology, we can turn, just as Weber and Merton did with the Protestants, to the "prevocational" attitudes expressed in school records. Fortunately, a record of the college and university degrees taken by religion was made by the Indian census for 1920-21 and 1921-22. While the Parsi population at that time was only 102,-000 persons, or 0.03 per cent of the 316,128,000 total population of India,

they took 6.8 per cent of the engineering degrees; 4.7 per cent of the degrees in medical fields; 1.7 per cent of the degrees in science (bachelor's, master's and doctor's degrees in science); and 1.4 per cent of all "western" degrees granted in India. The Parsis were not only overrepresented in the colleges and universities of India during this period, they were extremely overrepresented in the scientific and technical fields.

Another way of looking at this same set of data is to say that of the 238 degrees taken by Parsis during this period, 37.4 per cent were in scientific or technical fields. This compares with the percentage of degrees taken in these fields by each of the other native Indian groups: Indian Christian, 26.7 per cent; Buddhist, 19.8 per cent; others, 17.5 per cent; Hindu, 14.2 per cent; and Muslim, 5.6 per cent. Again there clearly appears to be an unusually high degree of interest among Parsi students in the more technical fields of study.

The question can be raised as to whether this Parsi interest in the early 1920's was a long-term phenomenon or a more recent development. During the thirty-nine years following the opening of the first school of modern medicine in western India in 1845, "a very large number of Parsis qualified themselves as physicians and surgeons. Fourteen entered the Indian Medical Service by successfully passing the competitive examination in London."[40] More complete data for other technical fields [are] available concerning the degrees taken from Bombay University by Parsis from 1901 through 1937. During this period, the Parsi students took roughly one third of all their degrees in the fields of science, engineering, and medicine. It seems reasonable to conclude that the early Parsi interest in technological pursuits was continued and reflected in

---

[39] Karaka, *History of the Parsis* (London: Macmillan & Co., Ltd., 1884), Vol. II, pp. 60-62.

[40] *Ibid.*, Vol. I, p. 298.

their choice of school topics when formal western education came to India in the nineteenth century.

Conclusion

We have treated the twin Parsi interests in trade and technology in one article to gain the advantage of explaining two different types of behavior with one set of variables and using one methodology. Specifically, the commercial values suggested by Weber's work are a great help in understanding the Parsi record of trade; and the values suggested by Merton's work are useful in giving meaning to the technical pursuits of the community, since in both cases the relevant abstract values of commerce and technology were expressed in Zoroastrianism. On the other hand, the case of the Parsis gives us more confidence in the reliability of the suggested positive association between the acceptance of commercial and technological values and the appearance of commercial and technological behavior. Methodologically, the historical techniques used by Weber and Merton still are fruitful if one succeeds in finding those instances in the recorded history of the world which lend themselves to the analysis of issues of current sociological interest.

There is another useful idea which results from this dual treatment—that of "industrial rationality." When the values of commerce are "combined" with the values of technology, in other words, when all five values mentioned . . . are considered to be part of a single rationality, then the resulting "mixture" can be thought of as the rationality of the industrial entrepreneur. . . .

Industrialization, Ideologies, and Social Structure

REINHARD BENDIX

Since World War II American social scientists have become preoccupied with the industrialization of underdeveloped areas. Considering the recent history of our disciplines, this is a relatively novel undertaking insofar as it involves the study of social change in complex social structures on a comparative basis. One approach to such a study consists in the selection of a social problem encountered in several societies but resolved differently in each. In a recent publication I used this approach by examining the authority relationship between employers and workers and the ideologies of management which justify that authority.[1] The present paper considers some implications of this analysis.

The first part of this essay summarizes the changes of ideology that have occurred in Anglo-American and in Russian civilization over a 200-year period. The second part deals with the historical significance of ideologies of management, and the third part with the theoretical implications of a study that treats such ideologies as an index of social structure. In the fourth part I turn to the problem of bureaucratization and to the difference between to-

Reinhard Bendix, "Industrialization, Ideologies, and Social Structure," *American Sociological Review*, 24 (1959), 613-623.

[1] Reinhard Bendix, *Work and Authority in Industry* (New York: John Wiley & Sons, Inc., 1956).

talitarian and nontotalitarian forms of subordination in industry.

Changes in Ideology

At the inception of industrialization in England an ideology of traditionalism prevailed; John Stuart Mill called it the "theory of dependence." According to this view the laboring poor are children, who must be governed, who should not be allowed to think for themselves, who must perform their assigned tasks obediently and with alacrity, who must show deference to their superiors, and who—if they only conduct themselves virtuously—will be protected by their betters against the vicissitudes of life. This interpretation of authority is self-confirming and self-serving.[2] But it sets up the presumption that the dependence of the poor and the responsibility of the rich are the valid moral rules of the social order. In the course of industrial development these ideas were gradually modified. As the responsibility of the rich was increasingly rejected by the advocates of laissez faire, the dependence of the poor was turned from an inevitable into a self-imposed fate. As it was "demonstrated" that the rich cannot care for the poor without decreasing the national wealth, it was also asserted that by abstinence and exertion the poor can better their lot. The same virtues which in the eighteenth century were extolled so that the lowly [would] not aspire above their station were praised by the middle of the nineteenth century because they enable a man to raise himself by his own efforts.

In England, and even more in Amer-

ica, this praise of effort led toward the end of the nineteenth century to an apotheosis of the struggle for existence. The militant language of an ethics of the jungle was applied to the relations between employers and workers. Riches and poverty merely reflect differences of ability and effort. The employer's success is evidence of his fitness for survival, and as such justifies his absolute authority over the enterprise. This assertion of authority has a clear-cut meaning only as long as most managerial functions are in the hands of one man. The idea becomes ambiguous as the use of expertise in the management of enterprises increases and the managerial function becomes subdivided and specialized. Yet the idea of the employer's absolute authority over his enterprise coincided with the "scientific management" movement which sought to give him expert advice on what to do with that authority. It may be suggested, therefore, that the doctrines of Social Darwinism gradually lost their appeal, in part because changes in industrial organization gave rise to a changing imagery of men in industry. From the Gilded Age to the 1920's, workers and managers were self-evident failures or successes in a struggle for survival, in which they were the recalcitrant objects or the exasperated originators of managerial commands. Today they have become individuals-in-groups whose skills must be improved and allocated systematically and whose productivity must be maximized by appropriate attention to their psychological makeup. Thus over the past two hundred years, managerial ideologies in Anglo-American civilization have changed from the "theory of dependence" to laissez faire, to Social Darwinism, and finally to the "human relations" approach.

In the Russian development we also find the assertion of paternal authority and of childlike dependence, and in

2 The laboring poor are asked to prove their virtue by their obedience, but they are also told that their dependence results from a natural inferiority. Similarly, the ruling classes are said to be responsible for the deserving poor, and if they do not meet this responsibility, it is only, they say, because the poor who suffer are not deserving.

much the same terms as in England. But in Russia this ideology of traditionalism was a very different thing from what it was in England because of the tsar's assertion of supreme authority over all the people. This authority remained intact regardless of how many privileges the tsar granted to the landlords and regardless of how rarely he interfered in fact with the use and abuse of these privileges. Ideologically the tsar maintained his pre-eminence through repeated assertions concerning his paternal care and responsibility for all of "his" people. Through repeated petitions and sporadic revolts the people used this tsarist claim in order to obtain redress for their grievances against landlords and employers. Finally, because of the early centralization of authority under the Muscovite rulers, the whole distribution of wealth and rank among the aristocracy turned upon the competition for favors at the Court and hence reinforced the tsar's supremacy.[3]

During the second half of the nineteenth century this pattern of tsarist autocracy had far-reaching consequences. The dislocations incident to the emancipation of the serfs (1861) and the development of industry brought in their train assertions of absolute authority by the employers, efforts of the workers to organize themselves, and sporadic attempts of the government to regulate the relationship between

[3] In Russia the landed aristocracy never succeeded in making itself the unavoidable intermediary between the ruler and the people, in contrast with western Europe, where the ruler's administrative and juridical authority in effect ended at the boundaries of the estate, though this contrast merely states the end result of protracted struggles over the division of authority. See Max Weber, *Wirtschaft und Gesellschaft* (Tübingen: Mohr, 1925), Vol. II, Chap. 7, esp. pp. 720-723, and Otto Hintze, "Weltgeschichtliche Bedingungen der Repräsentativverfassung," *Historische Zeitschrift*, **143** (1931), 1-47.

them. Although ostensibly acting on an equitable basis, the government in fact supported the employers against the workers. Much of this is again broadly familiar from the English experience; but Russia's historical legacies prevented the shift in ideology which has been described for England. As long as tsarist autocracy remained intact, neither the rejection of responsibility by the tsar and the ruling strata nor the demand for the self-dependence of the workers developed. Instead, the tsar and his officials continued to espouse the ideology of traditionalism. Quite consistently, tsarist officials sought to superintend both employers and workers in order to mitigate or suppress the struggles between them. That is, the officials aided *and* curbed the employers' exercise of authority as well as the workers' efforts to formulate grievances and organize protest movements.

Tsarist autocracy was overthrown in the Russian revolutions of 1905 and 1917. Although vast differences were brought about by the revolution, the managerial ideology of tsarism lived on in a modified form. In theory, tsarist officials had regarded employers and workers as equally subject to the will of the tsar; loyal submission to that will was the mark of good citizenship. In theory, Lenin believed that all workers were equal participants in the management of industry and government; their loyal submission to the Communist party represented their best interest and expressed their sovereign will. The logic of Lenin's as of the tsarist position is that under a sovereign authority the same person or organization can and should perform both subordinate and superordinate functions. For example, Soviet labor unions approach the ideal of workers' control of industry when they are called upon to participate in the management of industry. But they also function in a managerial capacity when they inculcate labor discipline among their members under the authoritative direction of the Communist party.

Ideologically this position is defended on the ground that the party represents the historical interests of the proletariat against the short-run interests of individuals and factions. In this orientation one can still see survivals of tsarist autocracy, since all wisdom and responsibility reside in a small group or indeed in one man, who, like the tsar, knows better than private persons what is the good of all, and cannot but wish the well-being of the people. But there is also an important difference. The leaders of the Russian revolution were faced with the task of developing self-discipline and initiative among workers if a suitable industrial work force was to become available.[4] They proceeded to inculcate these qualities by the direct or indirect subordination of everyone to the discipline of the Communist party. This policy continued the tsarist tradition by making all matters the object of organizational manipulation rather than of personal striving; but it also represented a break with the past in that it was no longer restricted to personal submission. . . .

Historical Significance of Ideological Change

What are the historical implications of this analysis of managerial ideologies? Ruling groups everywhere, including the rulers of developing industrial societies, justify their good fortune as well as the ill fortune of those subject

[4] Lenin's statement that "the Russian is a bad worker" and his advocacy of the Taylor system and of electrification as the road to socialism are indicative of the fact that the problems of complex industrial organizations came to the fore at once.

to their authority. Their self-serving arguments may not appear as a promising field of research; in fact, the whole development of industrialization has been accompanied by an intellectual rejection of such ideologies as unworthy of consideration. Yet the fact is that all industrialization involves the organization of enterprises in which a few command and many obey; and the ideas developed by the few and the many, I believe, may be considered a symptom of changing class relations and hence as a clue to an understanding of industrial societies.

Historically, ideologies of management became significant in the transition from a preindustrial to an industrial society. The authority exercised by employers was recognized as distinct from the authority of government. This was a novel experience even in western Europe, where there was precedent for such autonomy in other institutions, because the industrial entrepreneurs were "new men" rather than a ruling class buttressed by tradition. This was also the period during which the discipline of sociology originated. Under the impact of the French revolution society came to be conceived in terms of forces that are independent from, as well as antagonistic to, the formal institutions of the body politic. Some early elaborations of this key idea enable us to see the historical significance of ideologies of management.

The authority of employers rests on the contractual acquisition of property, which the eighteenth-century philosophers made the conceptual basis of the social order. In Rousseau's view, that order can be and ought to be based on a general will which presupposes that the individual acts for the whole community. In such a society, as George Herbert Mead has pointed out, ". . . the citizen can give laws only to the extent that his volitions are an expression of the rights which he recognizes in others, . . . [and] which the others recognize in him. . . ."[5] This approach provides a model for a society based on consent so that the power of rule making is exercised by all and for all. This foundation of society upon a "general will" was directly related to the institution of property. As Mead has stated:

If one wills to possess that which is his own so that he has absolute control over it as property, he does so on the assumption that everyone else will possess his own property and exercise absolute control over it. That is, the individual wills his control over his property only in so far as he wills the same sort of control for everyone else over property.[6]

Thus the idea of a reciprocal recognition of rights specifically presupposed the equality of citizens as property owners.

This implication gave pause to some eighteenth- and nineteenth-century philosophers. They noted that the reciprocity of rights among property owners based on freedom of contract does not apply to the relations between employers and workers. As early as 1807 the German philosopher Hegel formulated the problematic nature of this relationship in a manner which anticipates the modern psychology of the self, just as Rousseau's "general will" anticipates the sociological analysis of interaction. Hegel maintains that men come to a recognition of themselves through a process whereby each accepts the self-recognition of the other and is in turn accepted by him. That is, each man's sense of identity depends upon his acceptance of the identity of others and upon their acceptance of himself. In Hegel's view this reciprocity is lacking in the relation between master and servant. The master does not act toward himself as he acts toward the servant; and the servant does not do toward others what his servitude makes him do against himself. In this way the mutuality of recognition is destroyed and the relations between master and servant become onesided and unequal.[7]

In western Europe this inequality of the employment relationship coincided with the ideological and institutional decline of traditional subordination. Yet while the old justifications of subordination crumbled and new aspirations were awakened among the masses of the people, their experience of inequality continued. According to Tocqueville this problem had a differential impact upon masters and servants. In the secret persuasion of his mind the master continues to think of himself as superior; but he no longer recognizes any paternal responsibilities toward the servant. Still, he wants his servants to be content with their servile condition. In effect, the master wishes to enjoy the age-old privileges without acknowledging their concomitant obligations; and the servant rebels against his subordination, which is no longer a divine obligation and is not yet perceived as a contractual obligation.

Then it is that [in] the dwelling of every citizen . . . a secret and internal warfare is going on between powers ever rivals and suspicious of each other: the master is ill-natured and weak, the servant ill-natured and intractable; the one constantly attempts to evade by unfair restrictions his obligation to protect and to remunerate, the other his obligation to obey. The reins of domestic government

---

[5] G. H. Mead, *Movements of Thought in the Nineteenth Century* (Chicago: University of Chicago Press, 1936), p. 21.

[6] *Ibid.*, p. 17.

[7] G. W. F. Hegel, *Phänomenologie des Geistes* (Leipzig: Felix Mainer, 1928), pp. 143, 147. My paraphrasing attempts to convey Hegel's meaning without use of his language. The relevant passages are readily accessible in C. J. Friedrich, ed., *The Philosophy of Hegel* (New York: Modern Library, Inc., 1953), pp. 399-410.

dangle between them, to be snatched at by one or the other. The lines that divide authority from oppression, liberty from license, and right from might are to their eyes so jumbled together and confused that no one knows exactly what he is or what he may be or what he ought to be. Such a condition is not democracy, but revolution.[8]

In the nineteenth century men like Hegel, Tocqueville, and Lorenz von Stein pointed out that the spread of equalitarian ideas was causing a transition in the relations between masters and servants. This transition may be called a crisis of aspirations. In Tocqueville's words the servants "consent to serve and they blush to obey. . . . [They] rebel in their hearts against a subordination to which they have subjected themselves. . . . They are inclined to consider him who orders them as an unjust usurper of their own rights."[9] As a consequence most European countries witnessed the rise of a "fourth estate" which struggled against existing legal liabilities and for basic civil rights, above all the right to suffrage. In a parliamentary debate on Chartism, Disraeli remarked that this struggle was invested with a degree of sentiment usually absent from merely economic or political contests. To the extent that such complex movements can be characterized by a common denominator this sentiment referred, I think, to the workers' quest for a public recognition of their equal status as citizens. Where this and other civil rights became accepted, such recognition compensated for the continued social and economic subordination of the workers and thus assuaged the crisis

of aspirations. Moreover, the political utilization of these civil rights could lead to a recognition of basic social rights which today is embodied in the institutions of social welfare characteristic of many western democracies. The initial crisis of aspirations continued, on the other hand, where civil rights were rejected or where their acceptance was postponed for too long, leading either to an eventual revolutionary upheaval, as in tsarist Russia, or to a more or less damaging exacerbation of class relations, as in Italy and France.

My hypothesis is that the break with the traditional subordination of the people gave rise to a generic problem of many industrial societies. The question of nineteenth-century Europe concerned the terms on which a society undergoing industrialization will incorporate its newly recruited industrial work force within the economic and political community of the nation. Ideologies of management are significant because they contribute to each country's answer to this question. In England the workers were invited to become their own masters, if they did not wish to obey; in Russia they were told that their subordination was less onerous than it seemed, because their own superiors were also servants of the almighty tsar.

Theoretical Significance of Ideologies

What are the theoretical implications of this approach? Ideologies of management may be considered indices of the flexibility or rigidity with which the dominant groups in the two countries were prepared to meet the challenge from below. This "preparedness" or collective tendency to act is analogous to the concept of character structure in the individual: it may be defined as an "inner capacity" for recreating similar lines of action under more or

[8] Alexis de Tocqueville, *Democracy in America* (New York: Vintage Books, Inc., 1945), Vol. II, p. 195. Some phrases in the preceding paragraph are also taken from this chapter of Tocqueville's work.
[9] *Ibid.*

less identical conditions.[10] The ideologies of management, which reflect this "inner capacity," naturally provoke new challenges, and these in turn lead to new managerial responses, so that at the societal level there is a replication of the action-reaction process so typical of interaction among individuals.

An analysis of this process must deal with those explicitly formulated ideas that are as close as possible to the collective experience of employers and workers. This social philosophizing of and for the ordinary man as a participant occurs at a level somewhere between his attitudes as an individual and the sophisticated formulations of the social theorist. Such philosophizing is exemplified by what Andrew Ure wrote in his *Philosophy of Manufactures* or by what the publicity men for General Motors say in their pamphlet *Man to Man on the Job*. However, the serious analysis of such documents is at variance with the prevailing tendency to dismiss them as obviously biased and hence unworthy of consideration on their own terms. Marx, it may be recalled, reserved some of his choicest invective for his characterization of Ure's book, and in this respect Marx was a forerunner of the intellectuals born in the 1850's and 1860's. Freud, Durkheim, Pareto, and others shared with

Marx the search for some underlying principle or force that could explain the manifest beliefs and actions making up the external record of individual and collective behavior. Many writers of this generation were less interested in what a man said than in why he said it. Accordingly, ideologics of management might be dismissed because they *merely* express a class interest, or because they do not reveal the *real* attitudes of the employers, or because they disguise *actual* exploitative practices, or because all this talk tells us nothing about man's behavior or about his personality structure. These various objections have in common an intellectual preoccupation with covert forces that can explain the manifest content of the social world.

Modern social science owes to this intellectual tradition many important insights, but also many of its aberrations. Where the phenomena of the social world are treated merely as the reflection of "hidden forces," speculation easily becomes uncontrolled, with the result that observable evidence is dismissed from consideration as being "irrelevant" or "uninteresting" on theoretical grounds. The difficulty is familiar in Marx's theory of history, which encouraged him to treat whole series of facts as epiphenomena, such as the "false consciousness" of the workers that was bound to be superseded in the course of history. Similarly, the Freudian approach tends to devalue a behavioristic study of social life because it deals with the appearance rather than the underlying motivations of social action. Again, the use of organic analogies in the study of society treats all actions as dependent adjustments to other actions (or environmental conditions); consequently this approach devalues all deliberate and all innovative activity, since upon analysis such activity will be revealed as yet an-

[10] The quoted phrase occurs in Burckhardt's definition of the objective of culture history, which "goes to the heart of past mankind [because] it declares what mankind *was, wanted, thought, perceived,* and *was able to do.* In this way culture history deals with what is constant, and in the end this constant appears greater and more important than the momentary, a quality appears to be greater and more instructive than an action. For actions are only the individual expressions of a certain inner capacity, which is always able to recreate these same actions. Goals and presuppositions are, therefore, as important as events" [Jacob Burckhardt, *Griechische Kulturgeschichte* (Stuttgart: Kroener Verlag, 1952), Vol. I, p. 6].

other dependent adjustment. In inexpert hands all of these approaches lead to a cavalier construction of the evidence which can always be more easily imputed to the "underlying determinants" than analyzed in detail on its own ground.

Yet human experience occurs at this phenomenological level—and the study of ideologies of management illustrates that it can also provide an approach to our understanding of the social structure.[11] The managerial interpretations of the authority relationship in economic enterprises together with the workers' contrast conception concerning their collective position in an emerging industrial society constitute a composite image of class relations which has changed over time and which also differs from country to country. This aspect of the changing social structure may be studied by examining each ideological position in terms of its logical corollaries as these relate to the authority of the employers and in a wider sense to the class position of employers and workers in the society. Where these corollaries create major problems for the complacent self-interest of the group, one may expect the development of tensions, and perhaps of change, ideologically and institutionally.[12]

Such ideologies, and this is a second level of analysis, are in part expediential rationalizations for the problems confronting the entrepreneur and in part the result of historically cumulative response patterns among social groups In this way ideologies are formulated through the constant interplay between current contingencies and historical legacies. As Marx put it, "men make their own history," but they do so "under circumstances directly given and transmitted from the past." Marxian dogmatism consistently sacrificed the first to the second part of this generalization.[13] Accordingly, ideologies of management can be explained only in part as rationalizations of self-interest; they also result from the legacy of in-

---

industry brought to the fore experts who worked out methods for the exercise of authority. Again, the tsar's assertion of authority over all the people inadvertently encouraged the peasants to appeal to the tsar for redress of grievances. This procedure is adapted from that used by Max Weber in his sociology of religion.

[13] The sentence immediately following this quotation reads: "The tradition of all the dead generations weighs like a nightmare on the brain of the living" [Karl Marx, *The 18th Brumaire of Louis Bonaparte* (New York: International Publishers Co., Inc., n.d.), p. 13]. I do not accept this polemical exaggeration, since traditions are enabling as well as disabling, but the emphasis upon the impact of cultural tradition on current ideologies is more in line with the facts than the effort to explain the latter solely in terms of the problems the businessman encounters in his work. Such an interpretation leads to an elimination of ideological changes, and of differences between ideologies, since all ideologies are in this sense responses to the strains endemic in modern society. See F. X. Sutton, et. al., *The American Business Creed* (Cambridge: Harvard University Press, 1956), where the change of business ideologies over time is denied and where these ideologies are explained in exactly the same terms as nationalism and anticapitalism. See also the comments of Leland Jenks, "Business Ideologies," *Explorations in Entrepreneurial History*, **10** (October, 1957), 1-7.

---

[11] By "ideologies" I do not refer to attitudes of the type that can be elicited in a questionnaire study, but to the "constant process of formulation and reformulation by which spokesmen identified with a social group seek to articulate what they sense to be its shared understandings" (Bendix, *op. cit.*, p. xxii). I call these articulations "ideologies" in the specific sense of "ideas considered in the context of group action." All ideas may be analyzed from this viewpoint; hence I depart from the identification of "ideologies" with false or misleading ideas.

[12] For example, at the turn of the century American employers asserted their absolute authority over the workers, but this assertion lacked content until the bureaucratization of

stitutions and ideas which is "adopted" by each generation much as a child "adopts" the grammar of his native language. Historical legacies are thus a part of the social structure: they should not be excluded from a discipline that focuses attention upon the persistence of group structures. . . .

Ideologies, Industrial Bureaucracy, and Totalitarianism

Since the eighteenth century, Anglo-American and Russian civilizations have witnessed a growing managerial concern with the attitudes as well as the productivity of workers. It is possible to relate this change of ideology to a large number of the developments which comprise the transition from an early to a mature industrial society. The changing structure of industrial organizations was only one of these developments. Yet the bureaucratization of economic enterprises is of special importance for any attempt to "interpret the difference of fact and ideology between a totalitarian and nontotalitarian form of subordination in economic enterprises."[14] Bureaucratization is also especially suitable for a comparative study of authority relations in industry, since it involves processes that are directly comparable in two such different civilizations as England and Russia. This choice of focus deliberately eschews a comprehensive theory of society in favor of selecting a problem which, if suitable for comparative analysis, will also lead to an analysis of social structures. For if comparable groups in different societies confront and over time resolve a common problem, then a comparative analysis of their divergent resolutions will reveal the divergence of social structures in a process of change.[15]

Problems of a systematic management of labor come to the fore where the increasing complexity of economic enterprises makes their operation more and more dependent upon an *ethic of work performance*. This ethic involves a degree of steady intensity of work, reasonable accuracy, and a compliance with general rules and specific orders that falls somewhere between blind obedience and unpredictable caprice. Where personal supervision is replaced by impersonal rules, the efficiency of an organization will vary with the degree to which these attributes of work performance are realized, and this realization is part of the ongoing bureaucratization of economic enterprises. That is to say, management subjects the conditions of employment to an impersonal systematization, while the employees seek to modify the implementation of the rules as their personal interests and their commitment (or lack of commitment) to the goals of the organization dictate. As everyone knows, there is no more effective means of organizational sabotage than a letter-perfect compliance with all the rules and a consistent refusal of the employees to use their own judgment. "Beyond what commands can effect and supervision can control, beyond what incentives can induce and penalties prevent, there exists an exercise of discretion important even in relatively menial jobs, which managers of economic enterprises seek to enlist for the achievement of managerial ends."[16] In the literature on or-

---

[14] Bendix, *op. cit.*, p. xx.

[15] Here again I am indebted to the work of Max Weber, although more to what he did in his own studies than to what he wrote about them in his methodology. See my *Max Weber, An Intellectual Portrait* (New York: Doubleday & Co., Inc., 1960), Chap. 8.

[16] Bendix, *Work and Authority, op. cit.*, p. 251. To avoid a possible misunderstanding, I add that this assertion, which is elaborated in *ibid.*, pp. 244-251, is in my judgment compatible with the endeavor to put managerial decision making on a more scientific basis. The substitution of machine methods for manual operations is obviously an ongoing process that has greatly curtailed the areas of

ganizations this exercise of discretion by subordinates is known by a number of terms. Veblen called it the "withdrawal of efficiency"; Max Weber referred to it as the bureaucratic tendency toward secrecy; Herbert Simon might call it the "zone of nonacceptance." I have suggested the phrase "strategies of independence" so as to get away from the negative connotations of the other terms, since the exercise of discretion may serve to achieve, as well as to subvert, the goals of an organization.

Now the great difference between totalitarian and nontotalitarian forms of subordination consists in the managerial handling of this generic attribute of all authority relations. The historical legacies of some western countries have encouraged management to presuppose the existence of a common universe of discourse between superiors and subordinates, and this presupposition is related to the successful resolution of the crisis of aspirations. From the evangelism and the tough-minded laissez faire approach of eighteenth-century England to the latest refinement of the "human relations" approach, managerial appeals have been addressed to the good faith of subordinates in order to enlist their cooperation. Whether such good faith existed is less important than that such appeals were made, though it is probable that in England and the United States large masses of workers in one way or another accepted managerial authority as legitimate even if they were indifferent to, or rejected, the managerial appeals themselves. In Russia, on the other hand, historical legacies did *not* encourage management (under the tsars) to presuppose the existence of a common universe of discourse between superiors and subordinates. From the time of Peter the Great to the period of rapid industrial growth in the last decades preceding World War I, managerial appeals were addressed to the workers' duty of obedience toward all those in positions of authority. Whether or not the workers actually developed a sense of duty, the appeals presupposed that they had not. Accordingly, officials and managers did not rely on the good faith among their subordinates, but attempted instead to eliminate the subordinates' strategies of independence.

This managerial refusal to accept the tacit evasion of rules and norms or the uncontrolled exercise of judgment is related to a specific type of bureaucratization which constitutes the fundamental principle of totalitarian government. In such a regime the will of the highest party authorities is absolute in the interest of their substantive objectives. The party may disregard not only all formal procedures by which laws are validated, but also its own previous rulings; and where norms may be changed at a moment's notice, the rule of law is destroyed. Totalitarianism also does away with the principle of a single line of authority. Instead of relying on an enactment of laws and on the supervision of their execution from the top, totalitarian regimes use the hierarchy of the party in order to expedite and control at each step the execution of orders through the regular administrative channels. This may be seen as the major device by which such regimes seek to prevent officials from escaping inspection while compelling them to use their expertise in an intensified effort to implement the orders of the regime. A totalitarian government is based, therefore, on two interlocking hierarchies of authority. The work of every factory, of every governmental office, of every unit of the army or the

possible discretion, although machine methods also create new opportunities for discretionary judgments. But while these methods and organizational manipulations may curtail and reallocate the areas in which discretion is possible or desired, and may in this way achieve greater efficiency, they cannot, I believe, eliminate discretion.

secret police, as well as every cultural or social organization, is programed, coordinated, and supervised by some agency of government. But it is also propagandized, expedited, criticized, spied upon, and incorporated in special campaigns by an agency of the totalitarian party, which is separately responsible to the higher party authorities.

The rationale of this principle of a double government can be stated within the framework of Max Weber's analysis of bureaucracy. An ideally functioning bureaucracy in his sense is the most efficient method of solving large-scale organizational tasks. But this is true only *if* these tasks involve a more or less stable orientation toward norms which seek to maintain the rule of law and to achieve an equitable administration of affairs. These conditions are absent where tasks are assigned by an omnipotent *and* revolutionary authority. Under the simulated combat conditions of a totalitarian regime the norms that govern conduct do not stay put for any length of time, although each norm in turn will be the basis of an unremitting drive for prodigies of achievement. In response, subordinates will tend to use their devices of concealment for the sake of systematic, if tacit, strategies of independence. They will do so not only for reasons of convenience, but because the demands made upon them by the regime are "irrational" from the viewpoint of expert knowledge and systematic procedure.[17]

The party, on the other hand, seeks to prevent the types of concealment that make such collective strategies possible by putting every worker and official under maximum pressure to utilize their expertise to the fullest extent. This is the rationale of a double hierarchy of government, which places a party functionary at the side of every work unit in order to prevent concealment and to apply pressure. The two hierarchies would be required, even if all key positions in government and industry were filled by party functionaries. For a functionary turned worker or official would still be responsible for "overfulfilling" the plan, while the new party functionary would still be charged with keeping that official under pressure and surveillance.

In this way totalitarianism replaces the old system of stratification by a new one based on criteria of activism and party orthodoxy. The ethic of work performance on which this regime relies is not the product of century-long growth as in the West, but of material incentives and of a political supervision that seeks to prevent evasion from below as well as from above. For example, the collective "bargaining" agreements of Soviet industry are in fact declarations of loyalty in which individuals and groups pledge themselves publicly to an overfulfillment of the plan, while the subsequent organization of public confessionals, the manipulation of status differences between activists and others, the principle of collective leadership, and further devices seek to maximize performance and prevent the "withdrawal of efficiency." The individual subordinate is surrounded almost literally. Aside from ordinary incentives he is controlled by his superior and by the

---

[17] Hence they will do so even for the purpose of achieving the objectives of the party itself. See Joseph Berliner, *Factory and Manager in the USSR* (Cambridge: Harvard University Press, 1957), which documents that the most successful Soviet managers use the systematic subversion of authoritative commands for the purpose of realizing the ends of these commands as well as for their personal convenience. This fact suggests that "good faith" can be inculcated in many ways, even by the systematic distrust of all sub-

ordinates, provided of course that the distrust has a higher rationale, such as the utopian and nationalist ideology of Russian Communism.

party agitator who stands at the side of his superior; but he is also controlled "from below" in the sense that the social pressures of his peer group are manipulated by party agitators and their agents. This institutionalization of suspicion and the consequent elimination of privacy are justified on the ground that the party "represents" the masses, spearheads the drive for Russian industrialization, and leads the cause of world Communism.

Summary

The purpose of this paper is to state the case for a comparative analysis of social structures, which pays attention to the historical continuity of societies as well as to the concatenation of group structures and deliberate, self-interested action in the process of social change. In lieu of abstract considerations I have tried to make this case by analyzing some implications of ideologies of management in the course of industrialization.

The change of ideologies of management during the last two centuries in Anglo-American and in Russian civilization was similar insofar as it can be characterized as an increased managerial concern with the attitudes of workers that presumably account for their differential productivity. This over-all similarity coincides, however, with a fundamental divergence. In western civilization the authority relations between employers and workers remained a more or less autonomous realm of group activity even where the "human relations" approach has replaced the earlier individualism. In Russia, the employment relationship has been subjected throughout to a superordinate authority which regulated the conduct of employers and workers and which could transform superiors into subordinates or (more rarely) subordinates into superiors, when governmental policies seemed to warrant such action.

This comparison of ideologies of management is significant for specific historical reasons in addition to the fact that authority relations in economic enterprises are a universal attribute of industrialization and hence lend themselves to a comparative analysis. Ideologies of management became significant when the equalitarianism of property owners, brought to the fore by the French revolution and by the legal codifications which followed, was contrasted with the inequality of the employment relationship. A heightened awareness of this inequality coincided with the decline of a traditional subordination of the lower classes and hence with a rise of aspirations for social and political as well as for legal equality. In England these demands for equal rights of citizenship on the part of the lower classes eventuated in a painful but peaceful reconstitution of class relations; in Russia, the same demands were rejected and finally led to the revolutions of 1905 and 1917.

The comparative study of ideologies of management is of theoretical as well as of historical interest. Such ideologies may be considered indices of a readiness to act, which, together with the ideological responses of other groups, can provide us with a clue to the class relations of a society. Ideologies, it is assumed, are an integral part of culture, which should be analyzed on its own terms as an index of the social structure, much as the neurotic symptoms of an individual are analyzed as an index of his personality. It is further assumed that such ideologies are expediential rationalizations of what are taken to be the material interests of a group, but that such rationalizations tend to be circumscribed by the historical legacies which are a part of a country's developing social structure.

Although ideologies of management can be treated as a clue to class relations, it is also worthwhile to relate them to other aspects of the social structure. One such aspect, which is especially suitable for a comparison of totalitarian and nontotalitarian regimes, is the fact that all industrial enterprises undergo a process of bureaucratization and all bureaucracy involves the use of discretion in the execution of commands. Comparison between the Anglo-American and the Russian tradition reveals that in the two cases managerial appeals have differed in terms of whether or not they have presupposed the good faith of subordinates. Where that supposition has not been made, the drive for industrialization takes the specific form of a double hierarchy of government which is designed to apply maximum pressure on subordinates and to forestall their evasion of commands by supplementing executive with political controls at every point in the chain of command.

Both [Anglo-]American and Russian industrialization have been marked by bureaucratization, and bureaucratization certainly threatens the development of initiative. But the Soviet case also illustrates that this threat may provoke countermeasures. One might speak of an institutionalization of initiative in the totalitarian party, and one can speculate that the dynamic drive of the Soviet regime might be jeopardized by too much relaxation of a Cold War which appears to justify that drive. This is, I submit, the new context in which the comparative study of ideologies of management will continue to be an intellectual challenge.

Opportunity and the Aspirations of Automobile Workers

ELY CHINOY

The United States is widely pictured as the "land of promise," where golden opportunities beckon to everyone without regard to his original station in life. The Horatio Alger sagas of "little tykes who grow into big tycoons," it is asserted, "truly express a commonplace of American experience."[1] School children learn early of humble Americans whose careers fulfilled the promise, and the occasional new arrival at the top of the success ladder is publicly acclaimed as a fresh illustration that opportunity is open to all.[2]

Based on some concrete facts plus a substantial admixture of myth and optimism, the tradition of opportunity which has been a sprawled folk gospel deeply imbedded in the American character has now also become a consciously manipulated dream only partially related to the changing conditions of American life. Large corporations, rendered defensive by the events of the post-1929 decades, and the conservative press have tried to bolster their version of free enterprise by energetically fos-

Ely Chinoy, "The Tradition of Opportunity and the Aspirations of Automobile Workers," *American Journal of Sociology*, **57** (1951-52), 453-459.

[1] Eric Johnston, *America Unlimited* (New York: Doubleday & Co., Inc., 1944), pp. 5-6.

[2] The American Schools and Colleges Association, for example, annually presents "Horatio Alger Awards," with much fanfare to businessmen whose "rise to success symbolizes

tering the belief that, to quote one newspaper advertisement, "there are more opportunities in this country than ever before."

The American experience has indeed been distinctive in the opportunities it offered to able and ambitious men. The expansion across a rich, unpeopled continent of a population that roughly doubled every twenty-five years between 1790 and 1914 enabled farm boys, bookkeepers, prospectors, peddlers, clerks, and mechanics to rise significantly in the world, to become in some cases captains of industry and titans of finance.

But with the closing of the frontier, the leveling of the rate of population growth, and the concentration of industry, upward mobility by men starting at the bottom has become more difficult. In this era of big business, with its heavy capital requirements for independent enterprise and its demands for specialized managerial and technical skills in industry, factory workers, with whom we are centrally concerned, are severely handicapped. "It is widely recognized," declared the authors of a report prepared for the Temporary National Economic Committee in 1940, "that substantial opportunity does not exist for a large proportion of workers in either small or large corporations. . . . Most of them, therefore, must look forward to remaining more or less at the same levels, despite the havoc this might visit upon the tradition of 'getting ahead.'"[3]

Industrial workers, therefore, face in their occupational lives a palpable disparity between the exhortations of the tradition and the realities of their own experience. On the one hand, they are

the tradition of starting from scratch under our system of free competitive enterprise."

[3] M. Dimock and H. K. Hyde, *Bureaucracy and Trusteeship in Large Corporations*, Temporary National Economic Committee Monograph No. 11 (Washington, D.C.: U.S. Government Printing Office, 1940), p. 55.

encouraged to pursue ambitious goals by the assurance that anyone with ability and determination can, by his own efforts, "get ahead in the world"; on the other hand, only limited opportunities are open to them.

This paper, which is a partial summary of a larger investigation, is an attempt to explore what opportunity looks like to a group of automobile workers in a middle-sized midwestern city. What are the goals of men who are caught between the promises of the culture and the exigencies of their workaday world? What, if anything, does "getting ahead" mean to them?

Automobile workers were chosen for this investigation because they work in an industry which poses sharply the problems related to opportunity. Automobile manufacturing is a glamorous, relatively new industry whose spectacular growth dramatized and gave new substance to the American success story but whose present characteristics—giant plants, an extremely high degree of mechanization, and specialized corporate bureaucracies—make it difficult for the men who operate its machines to rise from the industrial ranks.

The research for the study was done over a period of fourteen months, from August, 1946, to July, 1947, plus the summer months of 1948. The bulk of the data was secured in seventy-eight prolonged interviews with sixty-two men employed in one large automobile plant. Since the problem of aspirations takes a somewhat different form among Negroes and, perhaps, among immigrants and second-generation Americans, interviews were confined to white workers who, with few exceptions, were at least third-generation citizens. All but six were married. In age they ranged from twenty to sixty-three, with no marked concentration at any age level and a mean age of thirty-eight. Thirty-five men had been employed in the plant prior to the outbreak of the war, fifteen had been hired during the war, and the rest were postwar employees. The group included fifteen skilled workers, ten machine operators, nine assembly-line tenders, and twenty-eight others who held various semiskilled jobs. Most types of work in the plant were represented. The data drawn from interviews were supplemented by several weeks of work in the factory by the investigator, by reports from informants, and by innumerable hours of casual conversation and informal social participation with men from the plant.

The aspirations of the automobile workers who were thus studied represent a constant balancing of hope and desire against the objective circumstances in which they find themselves. Recent research has tended to picture industrial workers as creatures of feeling and sentiment whose "social logic" contrasts sharply with the "rational logic" of managers and engineers.[4] But as our data clearly show, the aspirations of these men are controlled by a reasonably objective appraisal of the opportunities available to them. Given the unreliable picture presented by the culture, they are remarkably rational in their selection of goals. By and large they confine their aims to those limited alternatives which seem possible for men with their skills and resources.

With few exceptions, they see little chance of ever rising into salaried positions in the large corporation in which they work. To them the admonition to "think of the corporation as a pyramid of opportunities from the bottom toward the top with thousands of chances for advancement"[5] has little meaning. They are clearly aware that engineering and management have become so highly selective as to exclude them almost completely. Not one of these workers ever suggested the possibility of moving into the top-salaried ranks. Only foremanship, which itself rarely leads to better managerial posts,[6] remains as an obvious escape hatch from wage labor on the factory floor. And even this seemed to hold little promise for most of the workers who were interviewed.

In normal times only eight or ten openings on the supervisory level occur each year in this plant of almost 6000 workers. To many of them, therefore, it seems as though, in the words of one disillusioned toolmaker with fifteen years' seniority: "They'll have to die off in my department before anybody could get to be a foreman."[7] Since forty of the sixty-two men inter-

---

[4] The major sources for this point of view are F. J. Roethlisberger and W. J. Dickson, *Management and the Worker* (Cambridge: Harvard University Press, 1939), and Elton Mayo, *Human Problems of an Industrial Civilization* (New York: The Macmillan Company, 1933) and *Social Problems of an Industrial Civilization* (Cambridge: Harvard University Press, 1945). See also the approaches of B. B. Gardner, *Human Relations in Industry* (Chicago: Richard D. Irwin, Inc., 1945) and O. Collins, M. Dalton, and D. Roy, "Restrictions of Output and Social Cleavage in Industry," *Applied Anthropology*, **5** (Summer, 1946), 1-14.

[5] Alfred P. Sloan, *Adventures of a White Collar Man* (New York: Doubleday & Company, Inc., 1941), p. 153.

[6] Two discontinuous ladders of promotion seem to have emerged in modern industry. One ladder, open to workers, is short, with few rungs, usually ending at best—for only a handful of men—with foremanship. The other, open to those who start as technicians or white collar employees in the office, is longer and may eventually lead to the top levels of industry.

[7] This pessimism was probably particularly strong at the time the research was done because of the fact that in the preceding year, just after the end of the war, employment in the plant had been cut from almost 12,000 to less than 6000 and over 200 men who had been foremen were returned to wage jobs in the factory. To a large extent, management was drawing upon this reservoir of experienced personnel as new openings occurred.

viewed had not completed high school, their chances of gaining promotion were further contracted, as they can readily see, by management's increasing preference for men with substantial educational qualifications.[8]

Even in these circumstances, however, a few workers with only limited education still manage to become foremen, and their example might provoke a good deal of hope and effort, were it not for uncertainties in the selection process. Since new foremen are chosen on the basis of recommendations by foremen, the crucial question for workers seeking advancement is: What qualities and actions will bring us to the favorable attention of our supervisors? According to management, only merit and ability are taken into account when considering men for promotion. But because the criteria used to define merit and ability remain unspecified, workers tend to stress "pull," "connections," and various personal techniques for gaining favor—"buddying up to the foreman," "running around squealing on everybody," sending the foreman a Christmas card, or getting one's name in the union paper.[9] The rich variety of invidious terms applied to many of these techniques, however—"boot licking," "brown nosing," "sucking around" —indicates how workers feel about them. And in any case, there was no consensus as to which methods were effective, no guide lines to direct men's efforts.

It is not surprising, therefore, that only five of the sixty-two men interviewed expressed any real hope of ever

becoming foremen.[10] While seven others had given up the hopes they had once had, fifty said that they would not want to be foremen[11] or that they had never thought of the possibility. Given the obstacles to advancement into supervision, it is easy to imagine the buildup of verbal objections to foremanship as a rationalization against the likely disappointment of any hopes men might secretly entertain. Or, alternatively, men may protect themselves against the prospect of failure by disclaiming any interest in the goal.

Yet it is not unlikely that the disparagement of foremanship and the lack of interest are in many cases genuine. There are those who, for various reasons, are unwilling to assume responsibility. And the difficulties in the foreman's position which have been documented by numerous academic investigators are clearly evident to the men in the shop.

It is interesting to note that the five men who had hopes of becoming foremen were all still relatively young and that they had done fairly well for themselves in the plant. One was thirty-five, the others between twenty-nine and thirty-two. Three were skilled workers, two of whom had moved up from semiskilled labor during the war. One was a former line tender who had become an inspector, a more pleasant if not a bet-

---

[8] According to the plant's personnel manager: "We try to get the fellows from State College [located in an adjoining town] and from our own technical school into supervision."

[9] Many men felt that management paid careful attention to the contents of the union's weekly paper.

[10] In a *Fortune* poll of factory workers in 1947, only 12 per cent thought that they would someday become foremen [*Fortune* (May, 1947), p. 10].

[11] This finding is consistent with the *Fortune* poll . . . , in which 58 per cent of the sample said that they would not care to be foremen, and with E. W. Bakke's conclusion from his study of unemployed workers in New Haven: "Inasmuch as foremanship was the highest status in the shop to which most workers might aspire, it was a bit surprising to find a rather general lack of enthusiasm for such promotion" [*The Unemployed Worker* (New Haven: Yale University Press, 1940), pp. 51-52].

ter-paying job; one was a group leader in the shipping department, who had started there as an unskilled laborer. The seven men who had given up hope were, on the average, older and had not moved ahead in the shop. Only two were under thirty-five, while the others were thirty-eight or older. Only one had gained any personal advancement, a toolmaker who had finally become a group leader—after thirteen years in the plant. Two had been moved down after the war from skilled to semiskilled work, and the others were all on about the same level on which they had begun in the plant anywhere from five to sixteen years earlier. These facts suggest the possibility that, unless industrial workers gain some evidence while still young that advancement is possible, they are likely to confine their aspirations to modest objectives.

But the advancement which might encourage hope for foremanship or other substantial objectives is hard for these men to secure. Constant mechanization of automobile production has left most automobile workers as semiskilled operatives who can be moved about easily from one job to another. There were relatively few unskilled workers in the work force of almost 6000, while only 300 were skilled craftsmen.

For the semiskilled workers who constitute the great majority in the plant, the obvious line of advancement would be into the few remaining skilled jobs, which represent the top of the wage hierarchy. But the leveling of skill makes it impossible for the plant to provide any sequence of progressively more demanding tasks which might lead toward the skilled occupations.

In the years before recognition of the union it was sometimes possible to learn enough as a helper to be able to pass oneself off as skilled. Now that the union insists that men work only within their job classifications, this possibility has been virtually eliminated; a helper cannot try to do the work of a journeyman, even under the latter's guidance. With this informal route closed—at least in this plant—apprentice training has become the only way to acquire a trade. Admission to apprentice training, however, is limited to high school graduates not over twenty-one years old, stipulations which exclude most of the workers studied.[12] Only during the war, when there was an acute shortage of skilled labor, were semiskilled men—"upgraders," as they were called—trained by journeymen to do at least part of a skilled job.

Thus to practically all the semiskilled workers interviewed, entry to the skilled trades seemed to be completely closed. Only two veterans whose war service exempted them from the age limitation on apprentice training were planning to enter the trade through this route. And one former upgrader who had been returned to semiskilled work after the war still had hopes that he might someday be recalled to a skilled job.[13]

With both foremanship and skilled work out of reach, the best that most workers can see for themselves in the factory is a series of isolated small gains —transfer to a job that pays a few cents more per hour or to one that is easier, steadier, or more interesting. Substantial wage increases for individual workers are almost out of the question, however, since wage rates for semiskilled jobs are highly compressed. In 1947, in the production, inspection, and material-handling divisions of the plant, for example, maximum wage rates[14] for

12 The number of apprentices is also limited to one for each ten journeymen.
13 Five other upgraders who were interviewed felt that their recall to skilled work was most unlikely.
14 Maximum rates, which are ten cents above the starting rates, are reached by two

240 of 280 job classifications fell within a nine-cent range, from $1.41 to $1.50 per hour, while only seven classifications brought as much as $1.64 per hour.

The achievement of even those small monetary gains which are possible has been taken out of the hands of individual workers by the impersonal seniority rule which provides that promotion to better-paying jobs should go to the men with the longest service.[15] For the most part, therefore, higher wages and other economic benefits are now achieved through gaining and holding standardized agreements, a collective effort in which the union rather than the individual plays the central role.

As a result, the factory is not a place where men can do much as individuals to gain personal advancement. If they have worked in the plant long enough to "know the ropes," they may be able to secure a transfer to an easier, steadier, or more interesting job; otherwise they are exposed to the chance job shifts occasioned by constant changes in technology. The traditional imperatives for success—hard work and inventiveness—play an insignificant role in the context of carefully timed jobs and organized scientific research. Nor are "character" and "personality"—the other important traditional requisites for advancement —of much value to men who work with things rather than with people.

Despite the fact that they saw few opportunities for advancement in the factory, most of the workers studied could see no other future for themselves. Although forty-eight of the sixty-two answered "yes" to the question "have you ever thought of getting out

of the shop?" only eight had gone past wishful thinking or escapist dreams. Five of these were planning to buy a small farm or to go into some kind of small business. One had applied for a position on the local police force. And the other two—one a twenty-year-old single man, the other a twenty-nine-year-old veteran who could receive governmental assistance—were planning to go to college. The other forty who answered "yes" quickly qualified their desire to leave with reasons why they could not do so or confessed that they had only vague, unfocused desires. Much as many of these men would like to gain independence and to escape from the factory, they soon recognize that they have neither the financial resources nor, in some cases, the educational and personal qualifications that are needed.

Nevertheless, the possibility of leaving the shop forms a staple topic of conversation on the job. A dozen men spontaneously observed that "everybody" or "almost everybody" talks about getting out of the shop. This endless discussion, though unrelated in most cases to feasible plans or substantial hopes, serves an important psychological function. As one assembly-line tender put it: "It makes the time go quicker and easier if I keep thinking about that turkey farm I'd like to buy." A few minutes later he admitted that he could never hope to save enough money to buy the farm. Even though hopes shrivel when put to the test of reality, however, the talk and daydreams they generate soften the harsh reality of the moment.

To summarize our findings thus far: Of the sixty-two men interviewed, only eight felt that they had a promising future outside the factory. Within the factory, five men had real hope that they might someday become foremen, while only three semiskilled workers felt that it might be possible to move into

---

five-cent increases, one thirty days after being hired, the other after ninety days.

[15] According to the union contract, seniority is supposed to apply only when "ability, merit, and capacity are equal," but in practice seniority is almost automatically applied.

the ranks of skilled labor. The remaining forty-six, both skilled and nonskilled, could see little room for personal advancement and hence restricted their ambitions to small goals.

Despite their limited aspirations and their pessimism regarding opportunity for themselves, these men have not given up the success values of American society. "Everybody wants to get ahead," said a machine operator, and none of his fellows would contradict him. But if they accept the success values and yet see little opportunity for themselves, how do they explain their failure to move up in the economic order? How do they reconcile their limited aspirations with the cultural admonition to aim high and to persevere relentlessly?[16]

The tradition of opportunity itself provides a readymade explanation for failure which is accepted by some of these workers. Responsibility is placed squarely upon each individual. Failure cannot result from lack of opportunity but only from lack of ambition or ability, from unwillingness to make the necessary sacrifices, or from defects in one's character and personality. "I guess I'm just not smart enough," said one worker. "It's my own fault," said another. "Sometimes," he went on, "I look at myself in the mirror and I say to myself, 'Pat, you dumb so-and-so, you could have been somebody if you'd only set your mind to it.'" By thus focusing criticism upon the individual rather than upon its institutions, society protects itself against the reactions of those who fail.

16 Maintenance of a high level of aspiration not only is encouraged by the assurance that perseverance must eventually lead to success, but is also required as evidence of full participation in American life. "Failure" is defined as withdrawal from the race, as well as the inability to cross the finish line a winner. "Failure is ceasing to try! 'Tis admitting defeat," writes Edgar Guest.

But the self-blame thus engendered is obviously painful, and men therefore seek other ways of reconciling their small ambitions with their acceptance of success values. This they do primarily by redefining the meaning of advancement in terms closer to the realities of their own experience, and to a lesser degree by fostering ambitious hopes for their children and by verbally retaining the illusion of out-of-the-shop ambitions.

By labeling the small goals they pursue in the shop as "getting ahead," these workers maintain for themselves the appearance of sustained effort and ambition. Then if they manage to secure a job that pays five cents an hour more or one that is less exacting or more interesting, they seem to be advancing. "I'll be getting ahead all right," said a discontented line tender, "if I can just get off the line." But as men reach the low ceiling imposed on this kind of advancement or as they come to the conclusion that they are in dead-end jobs, they must turn to other meanings if they are to avoid admission of failure.

Since there are few opportunities for occupational advancement, they shift their attention toward security, on the one hand, and toward the acquisition of material possessions, on the other, identifying both as "getting ahead." Security, which has always been a crucial concern for automobile workers because of the erratic employment pattern in the industry, is now equated with advancement. Questions which tried to elicit from these workers the relative importance assigned to security as over against opportunities for advancement proved to be virtually meaningless. They could see no difference between the two. "If you're secure, then you're getting ahead," explained one worker with many years of seniority.

As with wages, security has taken on a collective character. Protection against arbitrary layoffs and assurance of recall after a shutdown are provided by the seniority rule incorporated in the union contract. In 1950, pensions were gained via collective bargaining, and the union has now set its sights on a guaranteed annual wage. Only in the accumulation of personal savings, which is itself defined as advancement, does security retain an individual character. "If you can put away a couple of hundred dollars, then you're getting ahead," said a worker struggling to make ends meet. If one can pay one's bills and meet the instalments on the house, the car, or a new refrigerator and still save a little money, then one is moving forward.

The visible evidence of advancement in this world of anonymous jobs and standardized wage rates, however, is the acquisition of material possessions. With their wants constantly stimulated by high-powered advertising, they measure their success by what they are able to buy. A new car standing in front of one's own home—this is the prevailing symbol of advancement, with a new washing machine, living room furniture, and now probably a television set as further confirmation that one is "getting ahead." This shift in the context of advancement from the occupational to the consumption sphere is justified whenever possible by stressing the potential economic returns from a large purchase, particularly in the case of a home and a car.

Even if men can see little hope for personal advancement in the present, they may still maintain their identification with the tradition of opportunity by focusing their aspirations upon their children's future, a practice strongly encouraged by the culture. "What sustains us as a nation . . . ," wrote Eleanor Roosevelt in one of her daily columns, "[is] the feeling that if you are poor . . . you still see visions of your children having the opportunities you

missed." "I never had much of a chance," said a semiskilled laborer whose entire working life had been spent in this one large plant, "but I want my kid to go to college and do something better than work in a factory." All of the twenty-six men with sons not yet old enough to work felt that their children could do better than factory work; none of them wanted their sons to go into the factory, except perhaps as skilled workers. But with their limited income and lack of knowledge, these fathers can provide little financial assistance or occupational guidance. Yet they all felt that, if their sons would exert the necessary effort and make the requisite sacrifices, they could move up in the economic order. By thus placing responsibility upon their sons, however, they protect themselves against the disappointment they are likely to experience.

Finally, men seek to maintain the illusion that they themselves are still striving by constantly talking about their intention to leave the shop, even though, as we have seen, they admit when pressed that they would probably never do so. Stimulated both by the still lively small-business tradition and by their urgent desire to escape from factory jobs, many of these workers continue to believe that at least modest success as a small entrepreneur is possible for the hard-working, personable man with ideas and initiative. They therefore verbally entertain, in usually disorderly succession, various business ambitions which are critically scrutinized and rejected as impractical or are mulled over, dreamed about, vaguely examined, and eventually permitted to fade away because there is little likelihood of their immediate realization.

From our analysis it seems evident that these automobile workers have to a large extent retained the form but lost the substance of the American tradition of opportunity. It is of course difficult to gauge how often and under what conditions these men see through their fabric of rationalization and self-justification to the fact that they are confined to their working-class status despite the promises of the culture. But as long as they can "get ahead," even on their own terms, they are unlikely to question seriously the validity of the tradition of opportunity.

Universities in Advanced Industrial Societies

A. H. HALSEY

Introduction

The main thesis of this essay concerns the relation of higher education to social structure and involves the notion of a type of society—the technological society—toward which western industrial countries are more or less rapidly moving. The mark of the educational institutions of a technological society is that they are in a special sense crucial to its maintenance and, through the institutionalization of technological research, to its further development.

In the medieval and industrial periods the history of the universities in relation to the economy is one of imperfect and usually belated adaptation to the occupational demands of a culture gradually increasing in its complexity. In the technological society the system of higher education no longer plays a passive role: it becomes a determinant of economic development and hence of stratification and other aspects of social structure. However, the stage reached and the speed of advance toward the technological society is conditioned by the strength of the earlier traditions of higher learning in any given industrial country.

A. H. Halsey, "The Changing Functions of Universities in Advanced Industrial Societies," *Harvard Educational Review*, **30** (1960), 118-127.

Universities and Social Structure

The basic function of education is the preservation and transmission of culture. In this broad sense all societies are educative. Sociologists of education, however, confine their studies largely to those societies in which there is a sufficiently complex culture to require its preservation and transmission by specialized agencies. Higher education is such a specialized agency charged with the conservation of the most highly prized beliefs and intellectual skills in the cultural heritage.

Accordingly, organizations of higher education must be seen as partially independent of, but functioning in relation to, such other aspects of social structure as government, the economy, and religious and military organizations. The existence of the higher learning presupposes certain social conditions, notably a level of economic and political development that affords the possibility of "idleness" for a scholarly class.[1] Indeed, universities always play a role in stratification because, controlling access to highly valued cultural elements, they are intrinsically inegalitarian. As Durkheim pointed out, "to find an ab-

[1] More strictly, in the incipient phase of the development of higher learning, a "vicarious leisure class." See Thorstein Veblen, *The Theory of the Leisure Class* (London: George Allen & Unwin, Ltd., 1924), p. 367.

solutely homogeneous and egalitarian education, it would be necessary to go back to pre-historic societies in the structure of which there is no differentiation."[2]

An adequate analysis of contemporary university developments therefore requires a theory of change involving multiple causes, conditions, and consequences. But the crucial connection, in this context, is with the economy. This is basically because development of knowledge is always likely to issue from its conservation and, in fact, has done so intermittently throughout the history of higher learning. More particularly it is so because, in response to the demands set up by modern industrialism and scientific warfare, research has become institutionalized in universities. The universities have therefore become an established source of instability to the technology and hence to the economy. And at the same time they are the training institutions for the skilled manpower required by a complex technology.

Universities and the Emergence of Industrialism

The present linkage of the university to the economy in industrial society is direct and obvious through the market for professional manpower and through research activities in the applied sciences. It was not always so. Richard Hofstadter has contrasted the present situation with the period before the American Civil War:

In the middle of the twentieth century, the American student of the history of higher education will find it hard to understand why college teaching responded so slowly to social change unless he realizes that the old-time colleges were not organically knit into the fabric of economic life.[3]

The European universities were, in their medieval origins, an organic part of religious rather than economic life, and this was true even of the much later American foundations, where, until the early years of the eighteenth century, the majority of graduates became clergymen.[4] The subsequent development of new economic functions for the universities with the rise of industrialism is only one aspect, though an important one, of the broader process of secularization of learning which spread with the Renaissance and which, through the teaching of Wyclif, Ockham, and Duns Scotus, had already disturbed Oxford in the fourteenth century. A negligible proportion of the alumni of modern western universities enters the ministry.[5]

However, the typical transition of universities from their earlier functional emphasis was not a simple story of extension in provision for secular professional training as a response to the demands of developing industrialism. On the contrary, there was an overlapping and, in England at least, still observable phase in which the universities were dominated by their function as preserves of the aristocratic and gentry classes. Indeed, the history of European and

[3] Richard Hofstadter and C. P. Hardy, *The Development and Scope of Higher Education in the United States* (New York: Columbia University Press, 1952), p. 21.

[4] Seventy per cent of the first few years of Harvard graduates (in the 1640's) became clergymen and nearly 73 per cent of Yale graduates between 1701-19. See Hofstadter., *op. cit.*, pp. 6-9.

[5] At Yale it was reduced to 6 per cent by 1900. In 1955 2 per cent of those admitted to Oxford and Cambridge went to read theology, the figure for the modern British universities being 0.4 per cent [R. K. Kelsall, *Applications for Admission to Universities* (London: Association of Universities of British Commonwealth, 1957), Table 1].

[2] Emile Durkheim, *Education and Sociology*, S. D. Fox, trans. (New York: The Free Press of Glencoe, Inc., 1956), p. 69.

American universities in the age of coal and steam industrialism is one of successful resistance, by ideological and other elements in the "superstructure," to the pressures set up by economic change. Max Weber's view of education as a differentiating agency, socializing individuals into the total style of life of the strata for which they are destined, has to be used as if in application to an aristocratic "structure of domination" up to the Second World War. In this sense higher education has been essentially a phenomenon of status rather than class, a process directed "against the market."[6]

Traditionally the university has rightly been seen as primarily devoted to the education, moral and physical as well as intellectual, of the "cultivated man,"[7] with its emphasis on "character," "service," poised and rounded personality, and an easy amateur command of the nonspecialist skill appropriate to a ruling class in a world of steam navigation, gunpowder, and manuscript.[8]

For the lower strata the educational equivalent in Europe has been a simple literacy heavily imbued with ideas of docility, piety, and nationalism.

Vocationalism was resisted in the European universities long after the religious domination of curricula had been overcome and long after secular universities had been founded on the basis of state and industrial patronage. Thus the creation of the University of Berlin in the early years of the nineteenth century, which set the tone for much of the subsequent modernization of universities in Europe and America, "was intended primarily to develop knowledge, secondarily, and perhaps as a concession, to train the professional and the official classes."[9] In America the landgrant colleges created after the Morrill Act of 1862 failed, despite the lead given by Wisconsin to create a comprehensive link between higher education and agriculture, through either research or teaching, until after the First World War. In England the great champion of the modern universities, T. H. Huxley, asserted before the Cowper Commission of 1892 that "the primary business of the universities is with pure knowledge and pure art—independent of all application to practice, with progress in culture not with increase in wealth."[10]

The emergence of the modern British universities as undergraduate professional schools, though it begins with the foundation of the University of

---

[6] Though access to it, in accordance with Weber's general definition of status, is in the long run determined by access to market opportunities.

[7] Weber points out that " 'the cultivated man,' rather than the 'specialist' has been the end sought by education and has formed the basis of social esteem in such various systems as the feudal, theocratic, and patrimonial structures of domination: in the English notable administration, in the old Chinese patrimonial bureaucracy, as well as under the rule of demagogues in the so-called Hellenic democracy." H. Gerth and C. Mills, *From Max Weber* (London: Routledge & Kegan Paul, Ltd., 1948), p. 242.

[8] "In the eighteenth century, while the gentry ruled, the country [England] had practically no officials; the Church and the Law were allied powers. . . . The Universities accordingly developed on lines convenient to the ruling caste, as seats in which the youth of the country could acquire a modicum of classical learning; they gave an intellectual sanction to the domination of the gentry and brought up the young men to be gentlemen, accepting and exemplifying the ideals of a

class. And such, despite the far-reaching reforms of the nineteenth century, Oxford and Cambridge remain to this day to a very large extent." W. Dibelius, *England*, M. A. Hamilton, trans. (London: Jonathan Cape, Ltd., 1929), p. 409.

[9] Abraham Flexner, *Universities: American, English, German* (New York: Oxford University Press, 1930), p. 312.

[10] Quoted in C. Bibby, "T. H. Huxley's Idea of a University," *Universities Quarterly*, **10** (August, 1956).

London, is largely a twentieth-century phenomenon and even then is explicable primarily in terms of the continued command held by Oxford and Cambridge over the avenues of entry into the national élites. Even in America, where the absence of an indigenous aristocracy made professional and technological training more acceptable, it was absorbed into the universities more by their extension into graduate schools than by revision of undergraduate curricula.

The aristocratic domination of universities which was typical of Europe in the eighteenth century, with its American equivalent in the education of ministers and lawyers as community leaders, continued despite the shifting class basis of power in the nineteenth and early twentieth centur[ies]. However, this did not preclude the more limited function of higher education as an agent of social mobility, of assimilation into élite groups, or "resocialization" for a selected minority of able boys from the lower strata. The nineteenth-century American colleges and the German universities both recruited from the middle and lower classes. And in England with the beginning of expansion of professional and administrative employment in the second half of the century, "the old and the new middle classes needed avenues of employment which would provide both prestige and relatively high income for their sons."[11] But the working classes were scarcely touched by these developments.[12]

In any case, as Hofstadter says of the American college, "Education was for gentlemen, it was designed to create among them a core of central knowledge that would make of them a community of the educated."[13] And even Veblen's bitter classic, though directed against "the conduct of universities by businessmen" and the perversion of scholarly values by the predatory ethics of business, describes an example of the ideal university man as one striving for "lifelike imitation of a country gentleman."[14]

Universities and Technological Society

A new relationship is now discernible. In general, whereas both Weber and Veblen saw the university as a corporate structure in process of adaptation (Veblen thought betrayal) to industrial society, W. H. Whyte,[15] writing forty years, later had to see it as an integral part of the organization of a technological society. Development in this direction has its origins in the nineteenth-century application of science to industrial processes, the "invention of invention," and the slow subsequent development of technological profes-

---

[11] D. V. Glass, "Education" in M. Ginsberg, ed., *Law and Opinion in the Twentieth Century* (London: Stevens & Sons, Ltd., 1959), p. 326.

[12] D. V. Glass in *ibid*. Of the generation of working-class boys born between 1910 and 1929, only 1.4 per cent went to a university. For the best available statistical description see J. E. Floud, "The Educational Experience of the Adult Population of England and Wales as at July, 1949," in D. V. Glass, ed.,

Social Mobility in Britain (New York: The Free Press of Glencoe, Inc., 1954). Writing of the German universities in 1929, Flexner (*op. cit.*, p. 337) states, "It has been estimated that at this moment not exceeding 3 per cent of the university students come from the working classes, and the number was formerly even smaller." In the American system of higher education, initial access has traditionally been more open, but selection *within* the system ("dropout") has been more severe and along class lines. . . .

[13] Hofstadter, *op. cit.*, p. 11.

[14] Thorstein Veblen, *The Higher Learning in America* (New York: The Viking Press, Inc., 1918), p. 164. He goes on: "the incumbent had no distinguishing marks either as a teacher or a scholar, and neither science nor letters will be found in his debt."

[15] W. H. Whyte, *The Organization Man* (London: Jonathan Cape Ltd., 1957).

sions in agriculture, chemistry, metallurgy, mechanical and electrical engineering, and so on. However, it begins to become clear as a direct relationship of economic organization to the higher learning only with escape from the economic depressions of the 1930's and the search for high productivity of the war and postwar years. Both as research organizations and as training establishments, the institutions of higher education in this period have been drawn more closely into the economy either directly or through the state. The exchange of ideas, people, and contracts between university departments and research institutes and their counterparts in private industry and government agencies is such as to merge these organizations and to assimilate the life styles of their staff.

Basically, the new functions reflect a new stage in the development of the means of production in which, as Drucker puts it, "the highly educated man has become the central resource of today's society, the supply of such men the true measure of its economic, military and even its political potential."[16] The class formation appropriate to the new means of production is one in which educational institutions play a crucial role. The search for talent to man the economy implies democratization of access to education and the development of selective processes. Schools, colleges, and universities become the agencies through which "achievement" in the occupational role is largely determined and in which the forces of "ascription" and "achievement" contend to determine the life chances of individuals.

The educational characteristics of a technological society are clearest where they are most advanced—in America.

The explosive expansion which has taken place there in the demand for high scientific manpower has not only created conditions of chronic shortage of supply; it has also transformed the universities. In 1900 the percentage of American eighteen to twenty-one year olds enrolled in institutions of higher education was 4.0. It doubled in the next twenty years and again in the following twenty years to 15.6 in 1940. Since then expansion has been even more rapid until in 1956 the figure was about one third. Under these circumstances the function of universities as nurseries for élite groups is overlaid by their new function as a mass higher education service in an emergent technological society. The "community of the educated" similarly tends to disappear.[17] Meanwhile it should be noticed that the structure of higher education has adapted itself to the new conditions by forming itself into a status hierarchy or "academic procession"[18] with graded access to "achievement" and power in the stratification system.

Russia is the same kind of society in the sense that higher education is geared closely to the economy, which, in this case, is controlled centrally in the interests of maximizing economic growth. At first glance the U.S.S.R. appears to be educationally underdeveloped. It has proportionately only half as many secondary school graduates

[16] P. F. Drucker, *The Landmarks of Tomorrow* (London: William Heinemann, Ltd., 1959), p. 87.

[17] It was once maintained in part by the role of two or three major universities as training institutions for all university faculty. But with expansion this integrating factor operates less and less. The minor universities are forced to become self-recruiting. Thus the status exclusiveness of the high prestige universities is preserved though the distribution of academic talent may be widening. See T. Caplow and R. J. McGee, *The Academic Market-Place* (New York: Basic Books, Inc., 1958), pp. 211ff.

[18] David Riesman, *Constraint and Variety in American Education* (New York: Doubleday & Co., Inc., 1958), Chap. 1.

as the U.S.A. and only sixteen per 1000 of its people have had higher education compared with the American figure of forty-four.[19] But the essential feature of the Russian case is that the sharp break with earlier social traditions, which was made possible by the revolution, resulted in the development of a system of higher education adjusted directly to the demand for technological manpower. Thus in the supply of professional and scientific workers to agriculture, medicine, engineering, and so on, the Russian system is as far advanced as the American. For example, in engineering and science the number of graduates per 1000 of the population is nine in [the] U.S.S.R. and ten in the U.S.A.

The different points reached by these two countries in their advance toward the technological society is indicated by the fact that in Russia the percentage of science and engineering graduates to all graduates is 55, whereas in America it is 21. This certainly does not mean that in America the higher learning either already is or is becoming less closely geared to the economy. On the contrary, there is a strong tendency for business to increase its influence over the content of American higher education, as is indicated by the decline of the fundamental disciplines and the rise of applied subjects, especially those connected with business administration and commerce. The "extra" output of American graduates in the humanities and social sciences mainly reflects the professionalization of the tertiary sec-

tors of American industry and may be viewed as an adornment of the affluent society, which Russia has yet to become.

The British case is instructive as one in which the medieval and aristocratic traditions of the universities have hitherto acted as a powerful break against movement toward the technological society. British university life has been dominated by Oxford and Cambridge since the defeat of the migration to Stamford in 1334. In the fourteenth century Oxford and Cambridge, backed by royal power, established themselves as national institutions with a monopoly over the higher learning. The monopoly was challenged frequently but unsuccessfully until the rise of the universities in the great industrial cities of the nineteenth century, and even then monopoly only gave way to pre-eminence. The challenge of industrialism and nonconformity was met partly by reform and expansion of the ancient foundations, partly by assimilation of the sons of successful businessmen through the colleges and the "public schools" which supply them, and partly by sending staff to the newly created universities.

As a result, a two-tier structure emerged in the early twentieth century. Oxford and Cambridge were national universities connected with the national élites of politics, administration, business, and the liberal professions. The rest were provincial, all of them, including London, taking most of their students from their own region and training them in undergraduate professional schools for the newer technological and professional occupations created by industrialism, such as chemistry, electrical engineering, state grammar school teaching, and the scientific civil service.

Since the war, as may be seen from Table 1, a new wave of expansion, with

---

[19] For this and the following figures, see N. DeWitt, "Basic Comparative Data on Soviet and American Education," *Comparative Education Review*, **2** (June, 1958). See also his *Soviet Professional Manpower* (Washington, D.C.: National Science Foundation, 1955), esp. pp. 254-258, where a comparison is made of the supply of professional manpower in [the] U.S.S.R. and U.S.A.

some emphasis on science and the technologies, has been taking place.

TABLE 1   Percentage Distribution of Fulltime University Students by Faculties in the United Kingdom in 1938-39 and 1956-57

Faculty	1938-39 (N = 50,002)	1956-57 (N = 89,866)
Arts	44.7	43.1
Pure Science	15.3	22.2
Medicine, Dentistry	26.8	17.4
Technology, Agriculture	13.2	17.3
Total	100.0	100.0

Source: *University Development 1952-57*, H.M.-S.O. Cmd. 534.

But the pace of expansion is much slower than in the U.S.A. or the U.S.S.R. The élite conception of the university continues to dominate development plans. Oxford and Cambridge are again expanding to assimilate the rising technological élite through the Cavendish Laboratories and Churchill

TABLE 2   Geographical Origins of University Students in English Universities, 1908-56

University	Per cent students drawn from within thirty miles		
	1908-09	1948-49	1955-56
Birmingham	—	56	38
Bristol	87	39	26
Leeds	78	60	40
Liverpool	75	62	55
Manchester	73	59	48
University College, London	66	53	43

For the United Kingdom as a whole, including Oxford and Cambridge, the proportion of university students living at home fell from 41.7 per cent in 1938-39 to 34.6 per cent in 1951-52 and further to 26.6 per cent in 1956-57 (*University Development 1952-57*, H.M.S.O. Cmd. 534).

College. A scrimmage for precedence on the second tier is taking place among the modern universities and the newly emancipated university colleges; and, in the process, the provincial universities are being nationalized. An indication of this trend may be had from the proportion of students drawn from within thirty miles of the university. In Table 2 some examples have been calculated from the returns from Universities and University Colleges to the University Grants Committee.

Meanwhile, a third tier in the structure of higher education is being formed by Colleges of Advanced Technology and Teacher Training Colleges offering courses of three years' duration. The creation of this new level in the hierarchy is to the emerging technological economy what the provincial universities were to large-scale industrialism.

Conclusion

Throughout the period of emerging industrialism in Europe and America the principal social function of the universities has been that of status differentiation of élites with some assimilation of students from the lower strata. But the progressive secularization of higher learning since medieval times has increased the potential of the universities as sources of technological and therefore of social change until now they are beginning to occupy a place as part of the economic foundation of a new type of society. In this new technological society educational institutions are expanded not only to exercise research functions, but also to play a central role in the economy and the system of stratification as agencies for selection, training, and occupational placement of individuals.

Movement toward this state of affairs is uneven among the western industrial countries. A comparison of America, Russia, and Britain shows that it is furthest advanced in America where professionalization has entered the tertiary sectors of industry and has resulted in far-reaching modifications of the content of university studies. It is fastest in Russia, where the supply of graduates is closely attuned to the needs of a fast-developing economy. It is slowest in Britain, where the legacy of the traditional status-differentiating function of Oxford and Cambridge persists and where the response to technological change is most strongly contained within an educational hierarchy corresponding to the power and prestige pyramid of the wider society.

personality: psychological aspects of economic activity

two

The postulate of economic rationality has held a prominent place in the tradition of economics. A simple version of this postulate is the following: If an individual's tastes, his income, and the prices of products in the market are known, it can be postulated that he will allocate his income rationally so as to maximize his satisfactions. Applying this postulate to various economic agents—businessmen, laborers, consumers—economists have constructed models of economic processes that rest on the assumption that every agent maximizes his economic position. Work in allied social sciences suggests, however, that economic motivation is much more complicated than this simple picture. This section contains two samples of this work. In the first, Parsons argues that economic rationality is itself an institutionalized value, varying greatly from one social context to another. In the second, Henry explores some of the underlying motivational patterns—such as acquisitiveness, achievement, and uncertainty—that commonly characterize businessmen.

The student should read these two selections in conjunction with pp. 34-35 of *The Sociology of Economic Life*.

The Motivation of Economic Activities

TALCOTT PARSONS

Specialization is, without doubt, one of the most important factors in the

Talcott Parsons, "The Motivation of Economic Activities," *Canadian Journal of Economics and Political Science*, **6** (1940), 187-203.

development of modern science, since beyond a certain level of technicality it is possible, even with intensive application, to master only a limited sector of the total of human knowledge. But some modes of specialization are, at the same time, under certain circumstances, an impediment to the adequate treatment of some ranges of problems.

The principal reason for this limitation of the fruitfulness of at least some kinds of specialization lies in the fact that the specialized sciences involve a kind of abstraction. They constitute systematically organized bodies of knowledge, and their organization revolves about relatively definite and therefore limited conceptual schemes. They do not treat the concrete phenomena they study "in general," but only so far as they are directly relevant to the conceptual scheme which has become established in the science. In relation to certain limited ranges of problems and phenomena this is often adequate. But it is seldom, after such a conceptual scheme has become well worked out, that its abstractness does not sooner or later become a crucial source of difficulty in relation to some empirical problems. This is apt to be especially true on the peripheries of what has been the central field of interest of the science, in fields to which some of the broader implications of its conceptual scheme and its broader.generalizations are applied, or in which the logically necessary premises of certain of these generalizations must be sought.

This has been notably the case with economics, precisely because, of all the sciences dealing with human behavior in society, it was the earliest to develop a well-integrated conceptual scheme and even today has brought this aspect of its science to a higher level of formal perfection than has any other social discipline. More than a century ago, however, economists began to be interested in the broader implications of their system and of the facts it had succeeded in systematizing. Perhaps more than in any other direction these "spec-ulations" have concentrated on the range of problems which have been involved in the idea of "laissez faire," of the functioning of a total economic system of "free enterprise" untrammelled by controls imposed from without and without important relations to elements of human action which played no explicit part in the conceptual armory of economic theory.

Once the attention of the economist has extended to problems as broad as this, the problem of the motivation of economic activities, whether explicitly recognized or not, has inevitably become involved by implication. The equilibrating process of a free economy was a matter of responsiveness to certain types of changes in the situation of action, to the prices, the supplies, and the conditions of demand for goods. The key individual in the system, the businessman, was placed in a position where money calculations of profit and loss necessarily played a dominant part in the processes of adjustment, when they were analyzed from the point of view of why the individual acted as he did. In a certain empirical sense it has seemed a wholly justifiable procedure to assume that he acted to maximize his "self-interest," interpreted as the financial returns of the enterprise, or more broadly, he could be trusted to prefer a higher financial return to a lower, a smaller financial loss to a greater.

From these apparently obvious facts it was easy to generalize that what kept the system going was the "rational pursuit of self-interest" on the part of all the individuals concerned, and to suppose that this formula constituted a sufficient key to a generalized theory of the motivation of human behavior, at least in the economic and occupational spheres. It is important to note that this formula and the various interpretations that were put upon it [were] not the result of intensive technical economic observation and analysis in the sense in which the theory of value and of distribution have been, but of finding a plausible formula for filling a logical gap in the closure of a system. This gap had to be filled if a certain order of broad generalization [was] to be upheld. Such current doctrines, outside the strictly economic sphere, as psychological hedonism, seemed to support this formula and to increase confidence in the universal applicability of the economic conceptual scheme.

In the meantime a good deal of work has been going on in other fields of the study of human behavior, which has for the most part been rather rigidly insulated from the work of economists, but which bears on the problem of motivation in ways which are applicable, among others, to the economic sphere. This has been true of social anthropology, and of parts of sociology and of psychology. Though there have been some notable examples of individual writers who, like Pareto, Durkheim, and Max Weber, have brought out various aspects of the interrelations of these fields with the problems of economics directly, on the whole they seem to have remained insulated, so that it can scarcely be said that a well-rounded analysis of the problem, which takes account of the knowledge available on both sides, is, even in outline, well established as the common property of the social sciences. An attempt to present the outline of such an analysis is the principal object of the present paper.

On the economic side the impression has been widespread that a predominantly "self-interested" or "egotistic" theory of the motivation of economic activities was a logical necessity of economic theory. It can be said with confidence that careful analysis of the methodological status of economic theory as an analytical scheme demonstrates conclusively that this is not the case. There are, to be sure, certain necessary assumptions on this level. They are, I think, two. On the one hand, economic analysis is empirically significant only insofar as there is scope for a certain kind of "rationality" of action, for the weighing of advantages and disadvantages, of "utility" and "cost," with a view to maximizing the difference between them. Insofar, for instance, as behavior is purely instinctive or traditional it is not susceptible of such analysis. On the other hand, its significance rests on there being an appreciable scope for the treatment of things and other people, that is, of resources, in a "utilitarian" spirit, that is, within limits, as morally and emotionally neutral means to the ends of economic activity rather than only as ends in themselves. In both respects there is probably considerable variation between individuals and between societies.

But this does not necessarily have anything to do with "egoism" in the usual sense. It has already been pointed out that the immediate goal of economic action in a market economy is the maximization of net money advantages or more generally of the difference between utility and cost. Choices, so far as they are, in the immediate sense, "economically motivated," are, in the first instance, oriented to this immediate goal. It certainly is not legitimate to assume that this immediate goal is a simple and direct expression of the ultimate motivational forces of human behavior. On the contrary, to a large extent its pursuit is probably compatible with a considerable range of variation in more ultimate motivations. Indeed, it will be the principal thesis of the subsequent analysis that "economic motivation" is not a category of motivation on the deeper level at all, but is rather a point at which many different motives may be brought to bear on a certain type of situation. Its remarkable constancy and generality [are] not a result of a corresponding uniformity in "human nature" such as egoism or hedonism, but of certain features of the structure of social systems of action which, however, are not entirely constant but subject to institutional variation.

The theoretical analysis of economics is abstract, probably in several different senses. This is crucial to the argument because it is precisely within the area of its "constant" data or assumptions that the problems of the present discussion arise. To describe the kind of abstractness which is relevant here, perhaps the best starting point is a formula which has been much discussed in economics, but which can be given a much more specific meaning in modern sociological terms than it has generally had in economic discussions. It is that economic activity takes place within the "institutional" framework of a society; economic behavior is concretely a phase of institutional behavior.

Institutions, or institutional patterns, in the terms which will be employed here, are a principal aspect of what is, in a generalized sense, the social structure. They are *normative* patterns which define what are felt to be, in the given society, proper, legitimate, or expected modes of action or of social relationship. Among the various types of normative patterns which govern action there are two primary criteria which distinguish those of institutional significance. In the first place, they are patterns which are supported by common moral sentiments; conformity with them is not only a matter of expediency, but of moral duty. In the second place, they are not "utopian" patterns which, however highly desirable they may be regarded, are not lived up to except by a few, or by others in excep-

tional circumstances. Thus the extreme altruism of the Sermon [on] the Mount or extreme heroism are very widely approved, but the ordinary individual is not *expected* to live up to them. When, on the other hand, a pattern is institutionalized, conformity with it is part of the legitimate expectations of the society, and of the individual himself. The typical reaction to infraction of an institutional rule is moral indignation of the sort which involves a feeling of being "let down." A person in a fiduciary position who embezzles funds, or a soldier who deserts is not doing what others feel they have a *right* to expect them to do.

Institutional patterns in this sense are part of the social structure in that, so far as the patterns are effectively institutionalized, action in social relationships is not random, but is guided and canalized by the requirements of the institutional patterns. So far as they are mandatory, they in a sense directly "determine" action, otherwise they set limits beyond which variation is not permissible and sets up corrective forces.

Seen from this point of view, institutional structure is a mode of the "integration" of the actions of the component individuals. There are, it may be suggested, three principal ways in which it is functionally necessary that such a social system should be integrated if it is to remain stable and avoid internal conflicts which would be fatal to it. In the first place, the different possible modes of action and of relationship become differentiated. Some are socially acceptable and approved, others reprehensible and disapproved or even directly prohibited. But in any case this system of differentiated actions and relationships needs to be organized. Stability is possible only if within limits people do the right thing at the right time and place. It is furthermore exceedingly important that others should know what to expect of a given individual. Thus in all societies we find institutional definitions of *roles*, of the things given people are expected to do in different contexts and relationships. Each individual usually has a number of different roles, but the combinations of different roles vary with different "social types" of individuals.

Secondly, it is inherent in the nature of society that some individuals should be in a position to exercise influence over others. Again it is necessary that there should be a differentiation between those modes of influence which are held permissible or desirable, and those which should be discouraged or even forbidden. Where the lines will be drawn will differ with the social roles of the persons concerned. The compulsion exercised by police officers will not be permitted to private individuals, for instance. Certain modes of influencing others, often regardless of the willingness of the others to be influenced, are often necessary to the performance of certain roles. Where such modes of influence are institutionally legitimized they may be called "authority." On the other hand, it is often socially necessary or desirable that some or all individuals should be protected from modes of influence which others would otherwise be in a position to exert. Such institutionalized protection against undesirable or unwanted influence may be called "rights." An institutionalized structure of authority and rights is a feature of every integrated social system.[1]

Finally, action generally is teleologically oriented to the attainment of goals and to conformity with norms. It is inherent in its structure that acts, qualities, achievements, and so on, should be valued. It makes a difference on a

scale of evaluation what a person is and what he does. This necessity of evaluation implies in turn the necessity of ranking, in the first place, qualities and achievements which are directly comparable; thus if physical strength is valued, persons will insofar be ranked in order of their physical strength. Secondarily, this means that persons, as such, will be evaluated, and that where a plurality of persons are involved, they will, however roughly, be ranked. It is of crucial importance that the standards of ranking and their modes of application should, in the same social system, be relatively well integrated. This third aspect of institutional structure, then, is *stratification*. Every social system will have an institutionalized scale of stratification by which the different individuals in the system are ranked.

This institutional structure is found in social relationships generally and is as important in the sphere of economic activities as in any other. Every function at all well established in the economic division of labor comes to involve institutionally defined roles such as those of "banker," "business executive," "craftsman," "farmer," or what not. In connection with such a role there is a pattern of institutionally defined expectations, both positive and negative. Certain of these economic roles involve institutional authority such as that of an employer in the role of supervisor over his workers. Again, in various respects, persons in economic roles are subject to the authority of others, notably of public officials in matters of taxation, labor legislation, and many other fields. They are institutionally expected to obey and usually recognize this authority. Persons in economic roles, further, enjoy certain institutionally protected rights, notably those we sum up as the institution of property, and in turn are institutionally expected to respect certain rights of

---

[1] Whether they are legally enforceable is secondary for present purposes.

others, to refrain, for instance, from co-
ercing others or perpetrating fraud upon
them. Finally, each of them has a place
in the system of stratification of the
community. By virtue of his occupation
and his status in it, of his income, of his
"reputation," and various other things,
he is ranked high or low as the case
may be.

So far an institutional structure has
been described as an "objective" entity
which as such would seem to have little
to do with motivation. The terms in
which it has been described, however,
clearly imply a very close relation. Such
a structure is, indeed, essentially a relatively stable mode of the organization
of human activities and of the motivational forces underlying them. Any considerable alteration in the latter or in
their mutual relations would greatly
alter it.

When we turn to the subjective side,
it turns out that one principal set of
elements consists in a system of moral
sentiments. Institutional patterns depend, for their maintenance in force, on
the support of the moral sentiments of
the majority of the members of the society. These sentiments are above all
manifested in the reaction of spontaneous moral indignation when another seriously violates an institutional pattern.
It may, indeed, be suggested that punishment and sanctions are to a considerable extent important as expressions
of these sentiments and as symbolizing
their significance. The corresponding
reaction to violation on the actor's own
part is a feeling of guilt or shame which,
it is important to note, may often be
largely repressed. On the positive side
the corresponding phenomenon is the
sense of obligation. The well-integrated
personality feels an obligation to live up
to expectations in his variously defined
roles, to be a "good boy," to be a "good
student," an "efficient worker," and so
on. He similarly has and feels obliga-

tions to respect legitimate authority in
others, and to exercise it properly in his
own case. He is obligated to respect the
rights of others, and on occasion it may
be a positive obligation from moral motives to insist on respect for his own
rights. Finally, he is obligated to recognize the status of others with respect to
stratification, especially, but by no
means wholly, of those superior to himself. The element of obligation in this
sense is properly treated as "disinterested." It is a matter of "identification"
with a generalized pattern, conformity
with which is "right." Within comparatively wide limits his personal interests
in the matter in other respects are irrelevant.

The prevailing evidence is that the
deeper moral sentiments are inculcated
in early childhood and are deeply built
into the structure of personality itself.
They are, in the deeper senses, beyond
the range of conscious decision and
control, except perhaps in certain critical situations, and even when consciously repudiated, still continue to exert their influence through repressed
guilt feelings and the like. In situations
of strain these may well come to be in
radical opposition to the self-interested
impulses of the actor; he is the victim
of difficult conflicts and problems of
conscience. But there is evidence of a
strong tendency, the more that people
are integrated with an institutional system, for these moral sentiments to be
closely integrated with the self-interested elements, to which we must now
turn.

If the above analysis is correct, the
fact that concretely economic activities
take place in a framework of institutional patterns would imply that, typically, such disinterested elements of
motivation play a role in the determination of their course. This is not in the
least incompatible with the strict requirements of economic theory, for that

requires only that, as between certain alternatives, choice will be made in such a way as to maximize net money advantages to the actor, or to the social unit on behalf of which he acts. Both in the ultimate goals to which the proceeds will be applied and in the choice of means there is no reason why disinterested moral sentiments should not be involved. But there is equally no reason why, on a comparable level, elements of self-interest should not be involved also. Indeed, the distinction is not one of classes of concrete motives, but of types of element[s] in concrete motives. In the usual case these elements are intimately intertwined.

There is furthermore no general reason to assume that "self-interest" is a simple and obvious thing. On the contrary, it appears to be a distinctly complex phenomenon, and probably the analytical distinctions to be made respecting it are relative to the level of analysis undertaken, hence to the problems in hand. Only such distinctions will here be made as seem essential to the main outline of a theory of motivation of economic activity.

The most general term which can be applied to this phase of motivation is, perhaps, "satisfaction." There is an interest in things and modes of behavior which yields satisfactions. One of the important components of this is undoubtedly "self-respect." So far, that is, as moral norms are genuinely built into the structure of personality, the individual's own state of satisfaction is dependent on the extent to which he lives up to them. This is above all true with respect to the standards of his various roles, particularly, in our context, the occupational role, and to the place he feels he "deserves" in the scale of stratification.

Closely related to self-respect, indeed in a sense its complement, is what may, following W. I. Thomas, be called "recognition." To have recognition in this sense is to be the object of moral respect on the part of others whose opinion is valued. To be approved of, admired, or even envied, are flattering and satisfying to any ego. As the works of Mead and others have shown, the relations of self-respect and recognition are extremely intimate and reciprocally related. The loss of respect on the part of those from whom it is expected is one of the severest possible blows to the state of satisfaction of the individual.

Third, there is the elements which lies closest to the pattern of economic analysis, the fact that we have an interest in a given complex of activities or relationships for "what we can get out of them." That is, they are, to a certain extent, treated as a means to something altogether outside themselves. This is the classic pattern for the interpretation of the significance of money returns. The pattern involves the assumption that there are certain "wants" which exist altogether independently of the activities by which the means to satisfy them are acquired. Though unjustified as a general interpretation of economic motivation, such a dissociation does, on a relative level, exist and is of considerable importance. In this, as in many other respects, the prevailing economic scheme is not simply wrong, but has not been properly related to other elements.

Fourth, there is another element which has played a prominent part in the history of economic thought—"pleasure." This may be conceived as a relatively specific feeling tone which is subject to interpretation as a manifestation primarily of particular organic states. Of course pleasure may be one of the "ulterior" ends to which economic activities are means—it is certainly not, as the hedonists would have it, the sole one. It may also be present, and often is, in the actual activities performed in the pursuance of economically significant roles; most of us actually enjoy a good deal of our work. One fact, however, is of crucial significance. Pleasure, or its sources, is not, as the classical hedonists assumed, a biologically given constant, but is a function of the *total* personal equilibrium of the individual. It does seem to have a particularly close connection with organic states, but undoubtedly these in turn are greatly influenced by the emotional states of the individual, and through these, by the total complex of his social relationships and situation. Hence pleasure, as an element of motivation, can only in a highly relative sense be treated as an independent focus of the orientation of action.

Finally, there is still a fifth element in "satisfactions" which, though perhaps less directly associated with the economic field than with others, should be mentioned. Men have attitudes of "affection" toward other human beings, and somewhat similar attitudes toward certain kinds of inanimate objects. The "aesthetic emotion" very likely contains in this sense a component which is distinguishable from pleasure, by which one, for instance, can say "I am exceedingly fond of that picture." In the case of other human beings, however, this affectional attitude is often reciprocal and we may speak of a genuine egotistic interest in the affectional "response" of another, again to use Thomas's term. It is true that the institutional patterns governing economic relationships are, in our society, largely "impersonal" in a sense which excludes response from direct institutional sanction. It does, however, come in in at least two important ways. On the one hand, it is very prominent in the uses to which the proceeds of economic activity are put, constituting for one thing a prominent element of family relationships. On the other hand, on a noninstitutional level, response relationships are often of great importance, concretely in the occupational situation and motivation of individuals. Thus a very important motive in doing "good work" may be its bearing on friendship with certain occupational associates.

In all these respects there is a further fundamental aspect of the motivational significance of a great many things which the traditional economic analysis does not take into account. Many of the most important relations of things to action lie in the fact that they are associated with one or more of these elements as symbols. An excellent example is that of money income. From the point of view of valuation it is probably fair to say that the most fundamental basis of ranking and status in the economic world is occupational achievement and the underlying ability. But for a variety of reasons it is difficult to judge people directly in these terms alone. Above all, in view of the technical heterogeneity of achievements it is difficult to compare achievements in different fields. But in a business economy it is almost inevitable that to a large extent money earnings should come to be accepted as a measure of such achievements, and hence money income is, to a large extent, effectually accepted as a symbol of occupational status. It is hence of great importance in the context of recognition.

Once the institutional pattern in question comes to be thoroughly established, though it continues to be in part dependent on the moral sentiments underlying it, its maintenance by no means depends exclusively on these. There is, rather, a process of complex interaction on two levels at once, on the one hand between the disinterested and self-interested elements in the motivation of any given individual, on the other between the different individuals. The first aspect of interaction has already been outlined in discussing the content of the concept "self-interest." The general tendency of the second process, so far as the institutional system is integrated, is to reinforce conformity with the main institutional patterns through mechanisms which work out in such a way that, in his relations with others, the self-interest of any one individual is promoted by adhering to the institutional patterns.

It has already been pointed out that the normal reaction of a well-integrated individual to an infraction of an institutional rule is one of moral indignation. The effect of this is to change an otherwise or potentially favorable attitude toward the individual in question to an unfavorable one. There are of course many different variations of degree between the various possible effects of this. It may be a matter simply of lessened willingness to "cooperate" in the achievement of the first person's ends in ways in which the second is useful or necessary as a means. In the more extreme instances it may involve positive obstruction of his activities. It will certainly mean a lessening of the respect which is involved in recognition; again in the more extreme cases it may mean positive action to belittle and run down the offender's reputation and standing, dismissal from positions, withdrawal of honors, and the like.

It would be unusual, except in very extreme cases, for direct pleasures to be involved, certainly in a physical sense. But in various subtle ways the disapproval of others, especially when it is intense enough to be translated into direct action, affects the sources of pleasure to which an individual has become accustomed. Finally, so far as people on whom he counts for response share the moral sentiments he has offended, this response, notably in "friendship," is likely to be lessened. In the extreme case again a friendly attitude may be transformed into a directly unfriendly one, indeed on occasion into bitter hatred.

Thus even without taking account of the possible internal conflicts which violation of his own moral sentiments brings about, it can be seen that a very substantial component of the individual's own self-interest is directly dependent on his enjoying the favorable attitudes of others with whom he comes into contact in his situation. Even if he continues to "make money" as before, his loss from the point of view particularly of recognition and respect may be of crucial importance, and in the long run probably his income is (the better integrated the situation the more so) bound up with his maintenance of good relations with others in this sense.

It is now possible to bring out what is, in many respects, the most crucial point of the whole analysis. It is true that it has been argued that it is impossible to treat the self-interested elements of human motivation as alone decisive in influencing behavior, in the economic sphere or any other. But it is not this thesis which constitutes the most radical departure from a kind of common sense view which is widely accepted among economists, as among other normal human beings. It is rather that the *content* of self-interested motivation itself, the specific objects of human "interests," cannot, for the purposes of any broad level of generalization in social science, be treated as a constant. That is, not only must the fact that people have interests be taken into account in explaining their behavior, but the fact that there are variations in their specific content as well. And these variations cannot, as economic theory has tended to do, be treated at random relative to the *social* structure, including in a very important sense that of the economic sphere of society itself. For it is precisely around social institutions that, to a very large extent, the content of self-interest is organized. Indeed, this organization of what are the otherwise, within broad limits, almost random potentialities of the self-interested tendencies of human action into a coherent system may be said, in broad terms, to be one of the most important functions of institutions. Without it, society could scarcely be an order, in the sense in which we know it, at all. It thus depends on the standards according to which recognition is accorded, on the specific lines of action to which pleasure has become attached, on what have come to be generally accepted symbols of prestige and status, what, in concrete terms, will be the *direction* taken by self-interested activity, and hence what its social consequences will be. Again this applies to what are ordinarily thought of as "economic" interests just as it does to any others.

The most convincing evidence in support of this thesis is to be derived from a broad comparative study of different institutional structures. Such a comparative study can go far to explain why, for instance, such a large proportion of Indian Brahmans have been interested in certain kinds of mystical and ascetic religious behavior, why so many of the upper classes in China have devoted themselves to education in the Confucian classics looking toward an official career as a mandarin, or why the members of European aristocracies have looked down upon "trade" and been concerned, if they have followed an occupational career at all, so much with the armed forces of the state, which have counted specifically as "gentlemen's" occupations. There is, unfortunately, no space to go into this evidence.

It may be useful, however, to cite one conspicuous example from our own society, that of the difference between business and the learned professions.

There are important differences between the institutional patterns governing these two sectors of the higher part of our occupational sphere, and perhaps the most conspicuous of these touches precisely the question of self-interest. The commonest formula in terms of which the difference is popularly expressed is the distinction between "professionalism" and "commercialism." Now in the immediately obvious sense the essence of professionalism consists in a series of limitations on the aggressive pursuit of self-interest. Thus medical men are forbidden, in the codes of medical ethics, to advertise their services. They are expected, in any individual case, to treat a patient regardless of the probability that he will pay, that he is a good "credit risk." They are forbidden to enter into direct and explicit price competition with other physicians, to urge patients to come to them on the ground that they will provide the same service at a cheaper rate. It is true that, in all this, infraction of the professional code would, in general, permit the physician to reap an immediate financial advantage which adherence to the code deprives him of. But it does not follow that, in adhering to the code as well as they do, medical men are actually acting contrary to their self-interest in a sense in which businessmen habitually do not.

On the contrary, the evidence . . . points to a quite different conclusion, which is that a principal component of the difference is a difference on the level of the institutional pattern, rather than, as is usually thought, a difference of typical motivation.[2] In both cases the

[2] This is by no means meant to imply that there are no differences of typical motivation. Such differences could be accounted for either on the ground that the two occupational groups operated selectively on personality types within the population, or that they influenced the motivation of people in them.

self-interest of the typical individual is on the whole harnessed to keeping the institutional code which is dominant in his own occupational sphere. It is true that by advertising, by refusing to treat indigent patients, or in certain circumstances by cutting prices, the individual physician could reap an immediate financial advantage. But it is doubtful whether, where the institutional structure is working at all well, it is from a broader point of view to his self-interest to do so. For this would provoke a reaction, in the first instance among his professional colleagues, secondarily among the public, which would be injurious to his professional standing. If he persisted in such practices his professional status would suffer, and in all probability various more tangible advantages, such as habitual recommendations of patients by other physicians, would disappear or be greatly lessened. It is not suggested that the average physician thinks of it in these terms; for the most part it probably never occurs to him that he might consider deviating from the code. But the underlying control mechanisms are present nonetheless.

In business the "definition of the situation" is quite different. Advertising, credit rating, and price competition are, for the most part, institutionally accepted and approved practices. It is not only not considered reprehensible to engage in them, but it is part of the institutional definition of the role of the "good" businessman to do so.

It is true that in the professions

money income is one of the important symbols of high professional standing. The more successful physicians both charge higher fees and receive larger total incomes. But there is still an important difference. There are in the first place important exceptions to the regularity of this relationship. There is probably nothing in the business world to correspond to the very high professional prestige of the "full-time" staff of the most eminent medical schools, even though their average income is markedly lower than that of the comparably distinguished men in private practice. There are probably very few resident physicians or surgeons in the teaching hospitals associated with such institutions as the Harvard Medical School who would refuse an opportunity to go on the full-time staff in order to enter private practice, even though the latter promised much larger financial returns.

But, beyond this, in business money returns are not only a symbol of status, they are to a considerable extent a direct measure of the success of business activities, indeed, in view of the extreme heterogeneity of the technical content of these, the only common measure. This situation is, however, being rapidly modified by the large-scale corporate organization of the business world. There "profit" applies only to the firm as a whole, for the individual it is primarily his office and his salary which count. This development is greatly narrowing the gap, in these respects, between business and the professions.[3]

The essential point is that the treatment of the concrete differences of behavior as direct manifestations of differences of ultimate motivation alone is clearly illegitimate in that it fails to take account of the institutional factor. It is quite possible that the institutionalization of financial self-interest does, however, tend to cultivate a kind of egoism and aggressiveness in the typical businessman which is less likely to be created in a professional environment.

[3] This development involves a major change in the institutional setting of the problem of self-interest. Even though, as will be noted presently, in individual market competition, profit is an institutionally defined goal rather than a motive, it makes a considerable difference whether, as the older economists assumed, the consequences of a business decision will react directly on the

It is thus suggested that the much talked of "acquisitiveness" of a capitalistic economic system is not primarily, or even to any very large extent, a matter of the peculiar incidence of self-interested elements in the motivation of the typical individual, but of a peculiar institutional structure which has grown up in the western world. There is reason to believe that the situation with respect to motivation is a great deal more similar in this area to that in other parts of our occupational structure which are not marked by this kind of acquisitiveness than is generally supposed.

Our occupational structure is above all one in which status is accorded, to a high degree, on the basis of achievement, and of the abilities which promise achievement, in a specialized function or group of functions. One may, then, perhaps say that the whole occupational sphere is dominated by a single fundamental goal, that of "success." The content of this common goal will of course vary with the specific character of the functional role. But whatever this may be, it will involve both interested and disinterested elements. On the disinterested side will be above all two components, a disinterested devotion to "good work" which

must be defined according to the relevant technical criteria, and a disinterested acceptance of the moral patterns which govern this activity with respect to such matters as respecting the rights of others. On the side of self-interest, in most cases the dominant interest is probably that in recognition, in high standing in the individual's occupational group. This will be sought both directly and through various more or less indirect symbols of status, among which money income occupies a prominent place. Part of the prominence of its place is undoubtedly a result of the fact that a business economy has become institutionalized in our society.[4]

The traditional doctrine of economics that action in a business economy was primarily motivated by the "rational pursuit of self-interest" has been shown in part to be wrong, in part to cover up a complexity of elements and their relationships of which the people who have used this formulation have for the most part been unaware. It may be hoped that the above exposition has, schematic as it has been, laid the foundations, in broad outline, of an account of the matter which will both do better justice to some of the empirical problems which confront the economist and will enable him to cooperate more fruitfully with the neighboring sciences of human behavior instead of, as has been too much the tendency in

---

personal pocketbook of the person making the decision, or only on that of the organization on behalf of which he decides. The position of the business executive thus becomes to a very large extent a fiduciary position. There is little difference between the considerations which will influence the manager of an investment trust, especially of a conservative type, and the treasurer of a university or a hospital, even though one is engaged in profit-making business, the other is a trustee of an "altruistic" foundation. In both cases the individual concerned has certain obligations and responsibilities, and unless the situation is badly integrated institutionally, it will on the whole, though perhaps in somewhat different ways, be to his self-interest to live up to them relatively well.

[4] To avoid all possible misunderstanding it may be noted again that no claim is made that there are no important differences of motivation, above all that the business situation may not cultivate certain types of "mercenary" orientation. The sole important purpose of the present argument is to show that the older type of discussion, which jumped directly from economic analysis to ultimate motivation, is no longer tenable. The institutional patterns *always* constitute one crucial element of the problem, and the more ultimate problems of motivation can only be approached through an analysis of their role, not by ignoring it.

the past, insulating himself from them in a kind of hermetically sealed, closed system of his own.

It would, however, be unfortunate to give the impression that this account is by any means a complete one, suitable for all purposes. In closing, a further aspect of the problem which is of great empirical importance, but could not receive full discussion in the space available, may be briefly mentioned. The above analysis is couched in terms of the conception of an institutionally integrated social system. It is only in such a case that the essential identity of the direction in which the disinterested and the self-interested elements of motivation impel human action, of which so much has been made in this discussion, holds. Actual social systems are, in this sense, integrated to widely varying degrees; in some cases the integrated type is a fair approximation to reality, in others it is very wide of the mark. But even in developing a theory which is more adequate to the latter type of situation the integrated type is a most important analytical starting point.

There is a very wide range of possible circumstances which may lead individuals, in pursuing their self-interest, to deviate from institutionally approved patterns to a greater or less degree. Sometimes in the course of his life history a far from perfect integration of personality is achieved, and the individual has tendencies of self-interest which conflict with his institutional status and role. Sometimes the social structure itself is poorly integrated, so that essentially incompatible things are expected of the same individual. One of the commonest types of this structural malintegration is the case where the symbols of recognition become detached from the institutionally approved achievements, where people receive recognition without the requisite achievements and, conversely, those with the achievements to their credit fail of the appropriate recognition. The result of all these various failures of integration is to place the individual in a conflict situation. He is, on the one hand, in conflict with himself. He feels urged to pursue his self-interest in ways which are incompatible with the standards of behavior in which he himself was brought up and which have been too deeply inculcated for him ever to throw off completely. On the other hand, objectively he is placed in a dilemma. For instance, he may live up to standards he values and face the loss of recognition and its symbols. Or he may seek external "success," but only by violating his own standards and those of the people he most respects. Usually both internal and external conflicts are involved, and there is no really happy solution.

The usual psychological reaction to such conflict situations is a state of psychological "insecurity." Such a state of insecurity in turn is well known to produce a variety of different, more or less "neurotic" reactions by which the individual seeks to solve his conflicts and re-establish his security. One of the commonest of these is an increased aggressiveness in the pursuit of personal ambitions and self-interest generally.

It has been maintained that the institutionalization of self-interest accounts for one very important element of what is usually called the "acquisitiveness" of a capitalistic society. But it is far from accounting for all of it. Ours is a society which in a number of respects is far from being perfectly integrated. A very large proportion of the population is in this sense insecure to an important degree. It is hence suggested that another component of this acquisitiveness, especially of the kind which is most offensive to our moral sentiments, is essentially an expression of this widespread insecurity. Elton Mayo[5] coined an appropriate phrase for this aspect of the situation when he inverted Tawney's famous title and spoke of the "Acquisitiveness of a Sick Society." But it should be noted that this is an element which, along with the institutionalization of self-interest, is not adequately taken account of by the formula of the "rational pursuit of self-interest."

Many other points could doubtless be raised to show the incompleteness

---

[5] Elton Mayo, *Human Problems of an Industrial Civilization* (New York: The Macmillan Company, 1933). This type of element is probably prominently involved in the widespread complaints about the prevalence of "commercialism" in medicine.

of the above outline of this problem. There is no doubt that in a great many respects its formulation will have to be altered as well as refined as our knowledge of the phenomena accumulates, as is the fate of all scientific conceptual schemes. In addition to whatever merit it may possess as a solution of this particular range of empirical problems, it is important for another reason. So far as it is substantiated it will help to demonstrate that many problems can be more fruitfully attacked by collaboration between the various social disciplines on a theoretical level than they can by any one of them working alone, no matter how well established its theoretical scheme may be for a certain range of problems.

The Business Executive

WILLIAM E. HENRY

The business executive is a central figure in the economic and social life of the United States. His direction of business enterprise and his participation in informal social groupings give him a significant place in community life. In both its economic and its social aspects the role of the business executive is sociologically a highly visible one. It has clearly definable limits and characteristics known to the general public. These characteristics indicate the function of the business executive in the social structure, define the behavior expected of the individual executive, and serve as a guide to the selection of the novice.

Social pressure plus the constant de-

William E. Henry, "The Business Executive: The Psychodynamics of a Social Role," *American Journal of Sociology*, **54** (1948-49), 286-291.

mands of the business organization of which he is a part direct the behavior of the executive into the mold appropriate to the defined role. "Success" is the name applied to the wholehearted adoption of the role. The individual behaves in the manner dictated by the society, and society rewards the individual with "success" if his behavior conforms to the role. It would punish him with "failure" should he deviate from it.

Participation in this role, however, is not a thing apart from the personality of the individual. It is not a game that the person is playing; it is the way of behaving and thinking that he knows best, that he finds rewarding, and in which he believes. Thus the role as socially defined has its counterpart in personality structure. To some extent, too, the personality structure is reshaped to be in harmony with the social role. The extent to which such reshaping of the adult personality is possible, however, seems limited. An initial selection process occurs which reduces the amount of time involved in teaching the appropriate behavior. Persons whose personality structure is most readily adaptable to this particular role tend to be selected, whereas those whose personality is not already partially akin are rejected.

This paper describes the personality communalities of a group of successful business executives. The research upon which it is based explored the general importance of personality structure in the selection of executive personnel. Many aptitude tests have been employed in industry to decrease the risk involved in the hiring of untried personnel and to assist in their placement. These tests have been far less effective in the selection of high-level executive personnel than in the selection of clerical and other nonadministrating persons. Many business executives have found that persons of unquestioned high intelligence often turn out to be ineffective when placed in positions of increased responsibility. The reasons for their failure lie in their social relationships. No really effective means has yet been found to clarify and predict this area of executive functioning. It is to this problem that our research[1] was directed.

From the research it became clear that the "successful"[2] business executives studied had many personality characteristics in common. (It was equally clear that an absence of these characteristics was coincident with "failure" within the organization.) This personality constellation might be thought of as the minimal requirement for "success" within our present business system and as the psychodynamic motivation of persons in this occupation. Individual uniqueness in personality was clearly present; but, despite these unique aspects, all executives had in common this personality pattern.

Achievement Desires

Successful executives show high drive and achievement desire. They conceive of themselves as hard working and achieving persons who must accomplish in order to be happy. The areas in which they do their work are clearly

---

[1] The research . . . involved the study of over one hundred business executives in various types of business houses. The techniques employed were the Thematic Apperception test, a short undirected interview, and a projective analysis of a number of traditional personality tests. The validity of our analyses, which were done "blind," rested upon the coincidence of identical conclusions from separately analyzed instruments, upon surveys of past job performance, and upon the anecdotal summary of present job behavior by the executive's superiors and associates. . . .

[2] Success and failure as here used refer to the combined societal and business definitions. All our "successful" executives have a history of continuous promotion, are thought to be still "promotable" within the organization, are now in positions of major administrative responsibility, and are earning salaries within the upper ranges of current business salaries. Men in lower supervisory positions, men who are considered "failures" in executive positions, and men in clerical and laboring jobs show clear deviations from this pattern. This suggests of course that this pattern is specific for the successful business executive and that it serves to differentiate him from other groupings in industry.

The majority of these executives come from distributive (rather than manufacturing) businesses of moderately loose organizational structure in which cooperation and teamwork are valued and in which relative independence of action is stressed within the framework of a clearly defined, over-all company policy. In organizations in which far greater rigidity of structure is present or in which outstanding independence of action is required, it is possible that there will be significant variations from the personality pattern presented here. . . .

different, but each feels this drive for accomplishment. This should be distinguished from a type of pseudo-achievement drive in which the glory of the end product alone is stressed. The person with this latter type of drive, seldom found in the successful executives, looks to the future in terms of the glory it will provide him and of the projects that he will have completed—as opposed to the achievement drive of the successful executive, which looks more toward the sheer accomplishment of the work itself. The successful business leader gets much satisfaction from doing rather than from merely contemplating the completed product. To some extent this is the difference between the dreamer and the doer. It is not that the successful executives do not have an over-all goal in mind or that they do not derive satisfaction from the contemplation of future ease or that they do not gain pleasure from prestige. Far more real to them, however, is the continual stimulation that derives from the pleasure of immediate accomplishment.

Mobility Drive

All successful executives have strong mobility drives. They feel the necessity of moving continually upward and of accumulating the rewards of increased accomplishment. For some the sense of successful mobility comes through the achievement of competence on the job. These men struggle for increased responsibility and derive a strong feeling of satisfaction from the completion of a task. Finished work and newly gained competence provide them with their sense of continued mobility.

A second group relies more upon the social prestige of increased status in their home communities or within the organizational hierarchy. Competence in work is of value and at times crucial.

But the satisfactions of the second group come from the social reputation, not from the personal feeling that necessary work has been well done. Both types of mobility drive are highly motivating. The zeal and energy put into the job [are] equal in both instances. The distinction appears in the kinds of work which the men find interesting. For the first group the primary factor is the nature of the work itself—is it challenging, is it necessary, is it interesting? For the second group the crucial factor is its relation to their goals of status mobility—is it a step in the direction of increased prestige, is it appropriate to their present position, what would other people think of them if they did it?

The Idea of Authority

The successful executive posits authority as a controlling but helpful relationship to superiors. He looks to his superiors as persons of more advanced training and experience, whom he can consult on special problems and who issue to him certain guiding directives. He does not see the authorities in his environment as destructive or prohibiting forces.

Those executives who view authority as a prohibiting and destructive force have difficulty relating themselves to superiors and resent their authority over them. They are either unable to work smoothly with superiors or indirectly and unconsciously do things to obstruct the work of their bosses or to assert their independence unnecessarily.

It is of interest that to these men the dominant crystallization of attitudes about authority is toward superior and toward subordinates, rather than toward self. This implies that most crucial in their concept of authority is the view of being a part of a wider and more final authority system. In contrast, a few executives of the "self-made," driving type characteristic of the past of business enterprise maintain a specific concept of authority with regard to self. They are the men who almost always forge their own frontiers, who are unable to operate within anyone else's framework, and to whom cooperation and teamwork are foreign concepts. To these men the ultimate authority is in themselves, and their image does not include the surrounding area of shared or delegated power.

Organization and Its Implications

While executives who are successful vary considerably in their intelligence test ratings, all of them have a high degree of ability to organize unstructured situations and to see the implications of their organization. This implies that they have the ability to take several seemingly isolated events or facts and to see relationships that exist between them. Further, they are interested in looking into the future and are concerned with predicting the outcome of their decisions and actions.

This ability to organize often results in a forced organization, however. Even though some situations arise with which they feel unfamiliar and are unable to cope, they still force an organization upon it. Thus they bring it into the sphere of familiarity. This tendency operates partially as a mold, as a pattern into which new or unfamiliar experiences are fit. This means of course that there is a strong tendency to rely upon techniques that they know will work and to resist situations which do not readily fit this mold.

Decisiveness

Decisiveness is a further trait of this group. This does not imply the popular idea of the executive making quick or final decisions in rapid-fire succession, although this seems to be true of some of the executives. More crucial, however, is an ability to come to a decision among several alternative courses of action—whether it be done on the spot or after detailed consideration. Very seldom does this ability fail. While less competent and well-organized individuals may become flustered and operate inefficiently in certain spots, most of these men force their way to a conclusion. Nothing is too difficult for them to tackle and at least try to solve. When poorly directed and not modified by proper judgment, this attitude may be more a handicap than a help. That is to say, this trait remains in operation and results in decision-making action regardless of the reasonableness of the decision or its reality in terms of related facts. The loss of this trait (usually found only in cases in which some more profound personality change has also occurred) is one of the most disastrous for the executive: his superiors become apprehensive about him. This suggests an interesting relationship to the total executive constellation. The role demands conviction and certainty. Whenever a junior executive loses this quality of decisiveness, he seems to pass out of the socially defined role. The weakening of other aspects of the ideal executive constellation can be readily reintegrated into the total constellation. The questioning of the individual's certainty and decisiveness, however, results in a weakening of the entire constellation and tends to be punished by superiors.

Strong Self-Structure

One way of differentiating between people is in the relative strength or weakness of their notions of self-identity, their self-structure. Some persons lack definiteness and are easily influenced by outside pressures. Some, such as these executives, are firm and well defined in their sense of self-identity. They know what they are and what they want and have well-developed techniques for getting what they want. The things they want and the techniques for getting them are of course quite different for each individual, but this strength and firmness [are] a common and necessary characteristic. It is of course true that too great a sense of self-identity leads to rigidity and inflexibility; and while some of these executives could genuinely be accused of this, in general they maintain considerable flexibility and adaptability within the framework of their desires and within the often rather narrow possibilities of their own business organization.

Activity and Aggression

The executive is essentially an active striving, aggressive person. His underlying motivations are active and aggressive—not necessarily is he aggressive and hostile overtly in his dealings with other people. This activity and aggressiveness are always well channeled into work or struggles for status and prestige—which implies a constant need to keep moving, to do something, to be active. This does not mean that they are always in bodily movement and moving physically from place to place (though this is often true), but rather that they are mentally and emotionally alert and active. This constant motivator unfortunately cannot be shut off. It may be part of the reason why so many executives find themselves unable to take vacations at leisure or to stop worrying about already solved problems.

Apprehension and the Fear of Failure

If one is continually active and always trying to solve problems and ar-

rive at decisions, any inability to do so successfully may well result in feelings of frustration. This seems to be true of the executives. In spite of their firmness of character and their drive to activity, they also harbor a rather pervasive feeling that they may not really succeed and be able to do the things they want to do. It is not implied that this sense of frustration comes only from their immediate business experience. It seems far more likely to be a feeling of long standing within them and to be only accentuated and reinforced by their present business experience.

This sense of the perpetually unattained is an integral part of this constellation and is part of its dilemma. It means that there is always some place to go, but no defined point at which to stop. The executive is "self-propelled" and needs to keep moving always and to see another goal ever ahead, which also suggests that cessation of mobility and of struggling for new achievements will be accompanied by an inversion of this constant energy. The person whose mobility is blocked, either by his own limitations or by those of the social system, finds this energy diverted into other channels. Psychosomatic symptoms, the enlargement of interpersonal dissatisfactions, and the development of rationalized compulsive and/or paranoidlike defenses may reflect the redirection of this potent energy demand.

Strong Reality Orientation

Successful executives are strongly oriented to immediate realities and their implications. They are directly interested in the practical, the immediate, and the direct. This is of course generally good for the immediate business situation, though the executive with an overdeveloped sense of reality may cease to be a man of vision; for a man of vision must get above reality to plan and even dream about future possibilities. In addition, a too strong sense of reality, when the realities are not in tune with ambitions, may well lead to a conviction that reality is frustrating and unpleasant. This happens to many executives who find progress and promotion too slow for their drives. The result is often a restlessness rather than an activity, a fidgetiness rather than a well-channeled aggression, and a lack of ease that may well disrupt many of their usual interpersonal relations.

The Nature of Their Interpersonal Relations

In general the mobile and successful executive looks to his superiors with a feeling of personal attachment and tends to identify himself with them. His superior represents for him a symbol of his own achievement and desires, and he tends to identify himself with these traits in those who have achieved more. He is very responsive to his superiors—the nature of this responsiveness of course depends on his other feelings, his idea of authority, and the extent to which he feels frustrated.

On the other hand, he looks to his subordinates in a detached and impersonal way, seeing them as "doers of work" rather than as people. He treats them impersonally, with no real feeling of being akin to them or of having deep interest in them as persons. It is as though he viewed his subordinates as representatives of things he has left behind, both factually and emotionally. Still uncertain of his next forward step, he cannot afford to become personally identified or emotionally involved with the past. The only direction of his emotional energy that is real to him is upward and toward the symbols of that upward interest, his superiors.

This does not mean that he is cold and that he treats all subordinates casually. In fact he tends to be generally sympathetic with many of them. This element of sympathy with subordinates is most apparent when the subordinate shows personality traits that are most like those of the superior. Thus the superior is able to take pride in certain successful young persons without at the same time feeling an equal interest in all subordinates.

The Attitude Toward His Own Parents

In a sense the successful executive is a "man who has left home." He feels and acts as though he were on his own, as though his emotional ties and obligations to his parents were severed. It seems to be most crucial that he has not retained resentment of his parents, but has rather simply broken their emotional hold on him and been left psychologically free to make his own decisions. We have found those who have not broken this tie to be either too dependent upon their superiors in the work situation or to be resentful of their supervision (depending of course upon whether they are still bound to their parents or are still actively fighting against them).

In general we find the relationship to the mother to have been the most clearly broken tie. The tie to the father remains positive in the sense that he views the father as a helpful but not restraining figure. Those men who still feel a strong emotional tie to the mother have systematically had difficulty in the business situation. This residual emotional tie seems contradictory to the necessary attitude of activity, progress, and channeled aggression. The tie to the father, however, must remain positive—as the emotional counterpart of the admired and more successful male figure. Without this image, struggle for success seems difficult.

The Nature of Dependency Feelings and Concentration Upon Self

A special problem in differentiating the type of generally successful executive is the nature of his dependency feelings. It was pointed out above that the dependency upon the mother image must be eliminated. For those executives who work within the framework of a large organization in which cooperation and group and company loyalty are necessities, there must remain feelings of dependency upon the father image and a need to operate within an established framework. This does not mean that the activity-aggression need cannot operate or that the individual is not decisive and self-directional. It means only that he is so within the framework of an already established set of over-all goals. For most executives this over-all framework provides a needed guidance and allows them to concentrate upon their achievement and work demands with only minimal concern for the policy making of the entire organization. For those executives who prefer complete independence and who are unable to work within a framework established by somebody else, the element of narcissism is much higher and their feelings of loyalty are only to themselves rather than to a father image or its impersonal counterpart in company policy. These feelings differentiate the executives who can cooperate with others and who can promote the over-all policy of a company from those who must be the whole show themselves. Clearly there are situations in which the person highly concentrated upon self and with little feeling of dependency loyalty is of great value. But he should be distinguished in advance and be placed in only situations in which these traits are useful.

The successful executive represents a crystallization of many of the attitudes and values generally accepted by middle-class American society. The value of accumulation and achievement, of self-directedness and independent thought and their rewards in prestige and status and property, are found in this group. But they also pay the price of holding these values and of profiting from them. Uncertainty, constant activity, the continual fear of losing ground, the inability to be introspectively leisurely, the ever-present fear of failure, and the artificial limitations put upon their emotionalized interpersonal relations—these are some of the costs of this role.

integrative groupings

three

Two features of an advanced industrial society are likely to blind us to the fact that diffuse integrative groups—such as families and ethnic groups—are intimately related to the structuring of economic activities. The first feature is the institutional fact that business enterprises and households are structurally segregated; the productive family unit, except for the family farm, is rare in our society. The second feature is the American value of universalism, which holds that a man's family and ethnic "connections" should not matter in his occupational career. When we look closely at our society, however, and even more when we take a comparative perspective, it is possible to observe the interplay between integrative groups and economic activities. The first two selections in this section concern the family and economic activity. Nimkoff and Middleton take a broad comparative look at how types of family structures are correlated with types of economic activities in several hundred cultures. Then, in a broad comparative essay, Greenfield questions just how closely urbanization and industrialization are correlated with a given family type. In the next two selections, Gross and Roy inquire into the characteristics and consequences of intimate friendship groups in economic enterprises. The final two articles concern ethnic status. Hughes shows how racial factors infiltrate the social organization of business firms, while the Handlins present a broad historical overview of the experiences of different ethnic groups in the American economy.

The articles in this section should be read in conjunction with pp. 57-64 of *The Sociology of Economic Life.*

Types of Family and Types of Economy

M. F. NIMKOFF   **RUSSELL MIDDLETON**

The simplest type of family is a unit consisting of a married man and woman with their offspring, the type familiar

M. F. Nimkoff and Russell Middleton, "Types of Family and Types of Economy," *American Journal of Sociology*, **66** (1960-61), 215-225.

to us in the West. Because the accent is on the husband-wife relationship, it has been referred to as the *conjugal* family. It has also been called the *nuclear* family, being the basic unit of all more complex forms.

A more complex family form may

be produced by uniting two or more nuclear families through a common husband or wife, as in polygyny or polyandry, respectively; Murdock has designated such families *compound* families. A different type of family can be produced by uniting families of individuals between whom there is a blood tie, that is, either siblings or parents and children. Thus two or more brothers with their wives and offspring may form a corporate unit. Or the family may comprise the father, mother, their unmarried children, and their married sons or daughters, their spouses, and children. Because the emphasis here is on the blood ties, these have been designated *consanguine*. They vary in size, from the largest (normally comprising the families of procreation of at least two siblings or cousins in each of at least two adjacent generations) to those of intermediate size (normally consisting of the families of procreation of only one individual in the senior generation but of at least two individuals in the next generation) to those of smallest size (usually consisting of only two related families of procreation, other than polygamous unions, of adjacent generations). Murdock calls these *extended* families, *lineal* families, and *stem* families, respectively. But since he describes lineal families as "small extended families," and stem families as "minimal extended families," in the present study we combine all three into the single category, *extended* family. These we contrast with *independent* families, defined as familial groups which do not normally include more than one nuclear or polygamous family. A family system is independent if the head of a family of procreation is neither subject to the authority of any of his relatives nor economically dependent upon them.

It is assumed here that the family is a function of the social order, which is a complex of religious, political, economic, aesthetic, and other activity. In this paper we examine the relationship between the family and economy and specifically consider the subsistence patterns associated with the two basic family types, the independent and the extended. Such an examination, it is hoped, will shed light on social conditions associated with them and, therefore, on some of the factors that give rise to them.

TABLE 1   Subsistence Patterns of Societies in the Sample

Subsistence Pattern	Number of Societies	Percentage of Total
Agriculture dominant	341	62.1
Animal husbandry dominant	42	7.6
Fishing, shellfishing, and marine hunting dominant	40	7.3
Hunting and gathering dominant	72	13.1
Agriculture and animal husbandry codominant	18	3.3
Agriculture and fishing codominant	18	3.3
Agriculture and hunting-gathering codominant	3	0.5
Animal husbandry and fishing codominant	1	0.2
Fishing and hunting-gathering codominant	14	2.6
Total	549	100.0

The statistical data are from a world ethnographic sample, selected by Murdock, covering 565 cultures said to be representative of the entire known range of cultural variation.[1] Data on

[1] G. P. Murdock, "World Ethnographic Sample," *American Anthropologist*, **20** (August, 1957), 664-687. The original data are revised in accordance with a list of additions and corrections issued by Murdock in mimeographed form on October 14, 1957. Two other corrections have been made for this study: The Chenchu appear to have an independent rather than an extended family system, and the Timbira have a subsistence pattern which is predominantly agricultural,

subsistence patterns are available for all the cultures, but data as to family type are not reported for sixteen societies, leaving a sample of 549 societies for purposes of this study.

The societies are classified by Murdock according to major types of food-getting activities: agriculture; animal husbandry; fishing, shellfishing, and marine hunting; and hunting and gathering. Each activity is rated as dominant, codominant, important, unimportant, or absent. The 549 societies in the sample are distributed among these subsistence patterns as shown in Table 1. Of the 549 societies, 301 or 54.8 per cent are characterized by the extended family system and 248 or 45.2 per cent by the independent family system.

Subsistence Patterns and Type of Family

Information regarding family type as related to subsistence pattern is presented in Table 2. The null hypothesis was tested that the type of family system is independent of variations in the subsistence pattern. A chi-square value was computed from a 6×2 table. The eleven subsistence pattern categories of Table 2 were reduced to six and placed in rank order according to their theoretical productivity and stability. The resulting categories were as follows: (1) agriculture and animal husbandry codominant; (2) agriculture dominant or codominant with other subsistence patterns; (3) fishing or animal husbandry dominant or codominant with hunting and gathering; and (4)-(6) identical with the last three categories of Table 2. The computation yielded a chi-square value of 35.01, which, with

---

hunting and gathering being important and fishing and animal husbandry absent or unimportant. The Timbira were earlier classified as a solely hunting and gathering people.

five degrees of freedom, is significant beyond the .001 level. Consequently, the null hypothesis was rejected, and it appears that there is a rough relationship between the type of family system and the subsistence pattern ordered according to productivity and stability.

Table 2 shows that: (1) the independent family is most common in "pure" hunting and gathering cultures, that is, those in which hunting and gathering are dominant and other subsistence patterns either absent or unimportant; (2) the independent family is more common than is the extended family in "mixed" hunting and gathering cultures (those in which hunting and gathering are dominant but in which one of the other subsistence patterns is important); (3) the extended family and the independent family occur with equal or about equal frequency in societies where fishing and hunting are codominant or where animal husbandry is either dominant or codominant with fishing; (4) the extended family is the prevailing type in societies where fishing is dominant; (5) the extended family is the prevailing type in all classes of society in which agriculture is dominant; (6) the extended family is more common in societies where agriculture is codominant with one of the other subsistence types than it is in societies with agriculture dominant; (7) the greatest frequency of the extended family occurs in societies with agriculture and animal husbandry codominant.

How is the association of the independent family with hunting culture, and the extended family with dominantly fishing or agricultural society, to be accounted for?

The advantages of the extended family have been admirably set forth by Linton, who, however, minimizes the disadvantages almost to the point of

TABLE 2   Family Type and Subsistence Pattern

	FAMILY TYPE			
Subsistence Pattern	Independent		Extended	
	N	Per Cent	N	Per Cent
Agriculture and animal husbandry codominant	2	11.1	16	88.9
Agriculture and fishing codominant	4	22.2	14	77.8
Agriculture and hunting codominant	1	33.3	2	66.7
Fishing dominant	15	37.5	25	62.5
Agriculture dominant, animal husbandry important	72	39.8	109	60.2
Agriculture dominant, animal husbandry absent or unimportant	73	45.6	87	54.4
Animal husbandry dominant or codominant with fishing	21	48.8	22	51.2
Fishing and hunting codominant	7	50.0	7	50.0
Hunting and gathering dominant; agriculture or animal husbandry important	10	55.6	8	44.4
Hunting and gathering dominant; fishing important; agriculture or animal husbandry absent or unimportant	22	73.3	8	26.7
Hunting and gathering dominant; agriculture, animal husbandry, and fishing absent or unimportant	20	83.3	4	16.7

neglect.[2] The extended family capitalizes the asexual associations of siblings; the independent family capitalizes the sexual attraction between adults. The paramount advantages of the extended family are economic. The efficiency of the household is not impaired by the removal of both son and daughter at marriage as it is in the individual family system. In the latter a husband and wife must start married life with little experience and limited resources, whereas the parental household is a going concern. In the extended family the members have the advantage of long association and familiarity with one another—circumstances useful in economic cooperation. There is more security, too, for the individual in the extended family in times of economic deprivation and other crises. Thus death or divorce is not so serious as in the conjugal family, for the removal of one parent from the home does not deprive the children of association with other adults of the same sex as the

missing one. There is also a possible social or recreational advantage in the more ample fellowship of the extended family. Although some nuclear families are larger than some extended families, on the average in any society extended families are likely to be larger.

When a sample of persons in Pakistan was asked what they considered to be the advantages of the joint family, they mentioned chiefly economy in expenses, security against illness and other calamities, and the fun of living in a big family.[3] When asked what they regarded as the disadvantages, they said only that the joint family may foster idleness and discourage initiative. Other critics of the joint family mention the possibility of friction between father and son, brother and brother, mother-in-law and daughter-in-law; the fact that leadership is based on age, not

[2] Ralph Linton, *The Study of Man* (New York: Appleton-Century-Crofts, Inc., 1936), Chap. 10.

[3] A. F. A. Husain, *Human and Social Impact of Technological Change in Pakistan*, a report on a survey conducted by the University of Dacca and published with the assistance of UNESCO, Vol. I (Pakistan: Geoffrey Cumberlege, Oxford University Press, 1956), pp. 77-78.

necessarily on ability; and the lack of privacy, especially between husband and wife.

These observations indicate that the ties that bind the members of the extended family may be weakened by tensions that threaten the integration of the group. The desire for economic independence and the desire for privacy, among other things, may dispose the young adults to establish independent households. On the other hand, where the interpersonal relationships are pleasant, the sentiment regarding blood ties makes the extended family popular.

A point worth noting is that either type of family can perform the major functions required of it by society. Legitimate reproduction is performed solely by the conjugal units, whether organized independently or as part of an extended family unit; its frequency, however, may be affected by the presence or absence of the extended family. Rearing the young, especially the very young, is mainly a function of the nuclear family, whether organized separately or not. But in the extended family, relatives give the parents much assistance with the socialization of their children. In a society with independent families, the responsibility for child nurture resting on the parents is correspondingly greater, except in a society like the United States with a highly developed auxiliary structure for formal education.

Since the frequency of different family types varies with type of economy, we look to the economic situation for clues as to what favors the one type or the other. Three economic factors seem especially relevant: the size of the food supply, the degree of spatial mobility involved in subsistence activities, and the kind and amount of family property.

In general, the size of family seems to be a function of the food supply. Since the supply of food is usually less stable and abundant in hunting than in agricultural societies, hunting does not encourage the extended family as much as does agriculture. Hunters generally cannot feed the members of the extended family so well, or so advantageously utilize their labor, as can agriculturalists.

This general point has been explored previously by Steward, who stresses the importance of the size and composition of the family as adjustive factors in the exploitation of the environment.[4] When game and wild plants are limited and dispersed, the members of a hunting or gathering society will generally scatter to achieve their optimal exploitation. Steward sees the existence of the independent family in hunting societies as one aspect of the low population densities generally associated with hunting. Among the western Shoshone, who are primarily gatherers of wild vegetable foods and lower forms of animal life, the fragmented family, he argues, is closely determined by their subsistence patterns. Participation of many persons in seed- and root-gathering generally not only fails to increase the per capita harvest but decreases it.

The nature of the subsistence pattern and food supply may also have a more indirect relation to type of family. Barry, Child, and Bacon maintain that in societies that store food before using it the child-rearing patterns differ from those in societies which consume food as soon as it is procured.[5] In societies which lack techniques for preserving and storing food a greater emphasis is

[4] J. H. Steward, *Theory of Culture Change: The Methodology of Multilinear Evolution* (Urbana: University of Illinois Press, 1955).

[5] H. Barry, I. L. Child, and M. K. Bacon, "Relation of Child Training to Subsistence Economy," *American Anthropologist*, **57** (January, 1959), 414-463.

placed on self-reliance and training in achievement than in societies with a high accumulation of food resources. The resulting personality type might thus be more congenial to the independent family system, which provides greater scope for the expression of individualism and independence.

The production of household arts is generally more highly developed under agriculture than hunting. Thus the handicrafts provide in the former instance a greater market for labor and so encourage the extended family.

The nomadic nature of hunting also militates against the large extended family, as suggested by the folksaying that he travels farthest who travels alone. Murdock provides information on the settlement patterns of the societies in the ethnographic sample, and it is possible to examine the relationship of family type to the local degree of spatial mobility. As is shown in Table 3, the extended family system is found least often among purely nomadic or migratory bands and is most common among sedentary peoples with a fixed residence. Seminomadic societies, whose people lead a migratory life only during certain seasons of the year, are intermediate with regard to the frequency of the extended type of family.

It must be recognized, however, that mobility patterns do not constitute an independent variable; rather, they tend to be an integral part of the general pattern of subsistence. There are relatively few agricultural societies which are nomadic or seminomadic, and few societies in which animal husbandry or hunting and gathering are dominant that are sedentary. Thus when general subsistence patterns are partialed out in the analysis, there is no significant relationship between mobility and family type. It is only in the case of fishing societies that the migratory pattern is not determined largely by the general nature of the subsistence activity. Of the fifty-three societies in which fishing is dominant or codominant with hunting and gathering, twenty-eight are nomadic or seminomadic, and twenty-five are sedentary. The extended family is present in 80 per cent of the sedentary fishing societies but in only 39.3 per cent of the nomadic or seminomadic fishing societies. This, in itself, may be taken as further evidence that the extended family system is dependent upon a more plentiful and stable food supply, for a sedentary fishing economy is possible only where fish occur in relative abundance.

TABLE 3   Societies with Extended Family Systems by Degree of Spatial Mobility

Degree of Spatial Mobility	Number of Societies	Per Cent
Nomadic or migratory	61	27.9
Seminomadic (nomadic only during certain seasons of the year)	78	51.3
Sedentary	410	60.0

$x^2 = 22.75$; d.f. $= 2$; $P < .001$.

Property, Stratification, and Type of Family

Among hunters, private property is recognized in certain privileges, such as names, songs, dances, emblems, religious objects and rituals, and memberships in sodalities. Property of this kind may be transmitted through the family line but would not seem to influence greatly the type of family. In the case of movable property, individual rights are generally recognized, but, again among hunters, the amount of movable property is usually not great. Ownership of livestock intensifies the idea of individual ownership and helps to buttress the extended family, which occurs more often among herders than among hunters.

The concept of the ownership of land

appears to have a considerable bearing on type of family. Hunters probably seldom have a notion of ownership of land, although rights to the use of an area for hunting purposes are common. These rights are usually tribal or communal in scope, rarely individual or familial. Mobility makes individual or family ownership difficult. For herders, land is meaningful mainly as pasturage, and, if it is scarce, notions of individual or family property in it may develop. But land acquires special significance where, as in stable agriculture, the group remains rooted to it over a long time, unlike the situation in shifting cultivation, where it is difficult to develop the idea of permanent ownership.

TABLE 4   Societies with Extended Family Systems by Degree of Social Stratification

Degree of Social Stratification	Number of Societies	Per Cent
Little or none*	173	37.0
Moderate †	44	54.5
Considerable‡	295	64.1

$x^2 = 32.19$; d.f. $= 2$; $P < .001$.

* No slavery; little or no other stratification.
† No slavery, but wealth distinctions of importance based on possession or distribution of property, without definite crystallization into hereditary social classes.
‡ Slavery and/or relatively great stratification among free men.

Among stable agriculturists, ownership of land is a highly important source of pride, prestige, and power. The family becomes attached to the land, well adapted to working it, and reluctant to divide it. If division results in many small pieces, each member of the family owning and working his own piece, the system become relatively unproductive. There is a disposition under the circumstances to hold the family land intact and to add to it if possible. In highly developed form, as in classical Japan, this practice leads to the idea that the current generation is only the custodian and the family head only the trustee of the estate.

The disposition to hold the family land intact and to increase it if possible was seen in pre-Communist China, where surveys in certain regions showed a correlation between size of farm and size of family. It appears that the family tries to stretch itself by adding new members in order to cultivate more land. The family can increase its size by reproduction, by adoption, and/or by adding relatives, via extended family.

Supporting evidence of the relationship between amount of property and type of family is provided by India, where the frequency of the joint family is positively correlated with caste positions. The upper castes, which own more property—especially land—than the lower, have more joint families, whereas the very poor outcastes have the largest proportion of independent families.

The relationship of property to family type can be tested by additional data from Murdock's world ethnographic sample. It is assumed that societies with appreciable stratification will generally have more family wealth than those with little or no stratification. The null hypothesis was tested that the type of family system is independent of the degree of stratification of societies (Table 4). The chi-square value was significant beyond the .001 level, and the null hypothesis was rejected. Thus it appears that the greater the degree of social stratification, the greater is the tendency for the extended rather than the independent family system to become established.

Even when the subsistence pattern is partialed out as a factor, there continues to be a striking difference between those societies with a relatively little and those with a relatively great degree of social stratification (Table 5). The hypothesis that a greater proportion of

TABLE 5   Societies with Extended Family Systems, by Subsistence Pattern
and Social Stratification

Subsistence Pattern	GREAT STRATIFICATION		LITTLE STRATIFICATION	
	N	Per Cent of Total	N	Per Cent of Total
Agriculture dominant or codominant*	274	62.8	90	51.1
Animal husbandry dominant or codominant with fishing or hunting and gathering*	29	62.1	14	28.6
Fishing dominant or codominant with hunting and gathering†	31	83.9	20	20.0
Hunting and gathering dominant*	16	50.0	57	22.8

* Difference between societies with little stratification and societies with great stratification in the presence of the extended family system significant beyond the .05 level, one-tailed test.
† Difference significant beyond the .001 level.

societies with relatively great stratification have extended family systems than societies with little stratification was tested for each of the four groups of subsistence patterns by computing chi-square values corrected for continuity from 2 × 2 contingency tables. The chi-square values were significant with a one-tailed test beyond the .05 level for three of the groups of subsistence patterns and beyond the .001 level for the group of societies in which fishing is dominant or codominant with hunting and gathering. We may conclude, then, that there is a tendency for more highly stratified societies to have an extended family system, even when the subsistence level is held constant through partialing techniques.

Deviant Cases

In the preceding paragraphs we have sought an explanation for the association between the independent family and hunting culture and between the extended family and agriculture, especially where animal husbandry and fishing are also of importance. The addition of herding or fishing may result in an increase in the food supply and the demand for labor; herding, in particular, increases the potentialities for accumulated wealth.

The association of type of family and subsistence pattern is, however, far from

perfect. There are exceptions, as shown in Table 2 and in Table 6, which list twenty-one hunting cultures with the extended family as given in Murdock's sample. We looked in these negative cases for evidence of the size of the food supply, mindful of the fact that it may vary greatly in hunting cultures. While, in general, the level of subsistence is lower in hunting than in agricultural societies, there are hunting cultures which enjoy a greater food supply than do some societies of planters. Planting societies range from very simple hoe cultures to advanced plow cultures. Then, too, there may be cooperative hunting beyond the scope of the independent family and an extensive specialization of subsistence activities requiring the concerted efforts of several adults. Of crucial significance for our purposes are the cases in Category III of Table 6: societies with the extended family system in which hunting and gathering are dominant and agriculture, animal husbandry, and fishing are absent or unimportant. These societies are, so to speak, the "pure" hunting societies, in which we might have the highest expectation of finding the independent family.

The mountain Maidu of California, the first case, were dependent primarily upon hunting and gathering, although they did engage in some fishing. The Maidu hunted birds and insects, gath-

TABLE 6   Hunting and Gathering Societies with Extended Family Systems

Subsistence Pattern	Society and Location
I. Hunting and gathering dominant; agriculture or animal husbandry important	Kiowa—American Plains Comanche—American Plains Blackfoot (Siksika)—American Plains Cheyenne—American Plains Western Apache—American Southwest Motilon (Iroka)—Venezuela Siriono—Interior Amazonia Caduveo—Gran Chaco
II. Hunting and gathering dominant; fishing important; agriculture or animal husbandry absent or unimportant	Pomo (Clear Lake)—California Shasta (Eastern)—California Yana—California Wappo—California Hukundika—American Great Basin and Plateau Lengua—Gran Chaco Yukaghir—Arctic Asia Tiwi—Australia Vedda—Ceylon
III. Hunting and gathering dominant; agriculture, animal husbandry, and fishing absent or unimportant	Maidu (Mountain)—California Chiricahua Apache—American Southwest Bororo—Mato Grosso Dorobo—Upper Nile

ered seeds, and hunted deer and rabbits, cooperatively. The yield, we are told, was plentiful, an evidence of which is the fact that the Maidu furnished their chief with food for entertaining visitors.

In the second negative case, that of the Chiricahua Apache of the American Southwest, the food supply is said to have been precarious, and as such would appear to have favored a type of economic organization based on the small individual family. In explanation, Opler reports that "the wild seeds and mescal must be gathered, prepared and stored when they ripen and the cooperation of a number of men and women is needed at such times."[6] The extended family probably served to minimize friction during such critical periods when cooperative group work was vital.

As to the Bororo of Mato Grosso in South America, there is some uncer-

tainty regarding the nature of the economy. Murdock classifies them as predominantly hunters and gatherers, with other subsistence patterns absent or unimportant, but Lowie says that they are "predominantly hunters, gatherers and fishermen," implying that fishing is not unimportant, an impression supported by the fact that the fish are caught in nets or weirs as well as shot with arrows or drugged.[7]

Another source differentiates the western Bororo (the Bororo da Campahna) and the eastern Bororo.[8] The western Bororo, with only a few natives left and acculturation far advanced, are said to have been extremely poor. The eastern Bororo, who are more numerous and less acculturated, are reported as engaged mainly in "fishing, the cultiva-

[6] M. E. Opler, "An Outline of Chiricahua Apache Social Organization," in Fred Eggan, ed., *Social Anthropology of North American Tribes*, 2nd ed. (Chicago: University of Chicago Press, 1955).

[7] R. H. Lowie, "The Bororo," in J. Steward, ed., *Handbook of South American Indians*, Vol. I, Bureau of American Ethnology Bulletin No. 143 (Washington, D.C.: Smithsonian Institution, 1946), 419-434.

[8] V. M. Petrullo, "Primitive Peoples of Matto Grosso," *Museum Journal* (University of Pennsylvania), **23** (1932), 83-184.

tion of manioc, and hunting." If this is the order of importance of the sources of subsistence, then the Bororo are incorrectly classified and should not be considered a deviant case. Apart from the question of the importance of fishing and agriculture among them, however, it appears that there was extensive cooperation in hunting activities. Bororo men went on communal hunting expeditions, sometimes lasting several weeks, to hunt peccaries, tapirs, jaguars, rabbits, and birds.

Regarding the fourth and final society of the category under discussion, the Dorobo of Kenya and Tanganyika, we are told that their traditional hunting life began to disappear about 1925, when the government forced them to leave the forests and settle in an open agricultural area.[9] They are now in the process of shifting to an agricultural economy and are even beginning to graze cattle. In earlier times, however, they depended almost entirely upon hunting, gathering, and trade with the Nandi. In wet weather, buck were caught in traps; in the dry season, wild pigs of various kinds and several species of monkeys were hunted by parties of from two to eight men. The hunter was responsible for meat not only for his own elementary family, but also for his father, mother, and wife's father, suggesting economic ties of the extended family. Under the old system a man had hereditary rights over a piece of forest, which included hunting, trapping, beekeeping, and food-gathering rights. Presumably, the food supply was sufficient for the extended family.

The remaining hunters and gatherers in Table 5 are those who derive important support and sustenance from agriculture, animal husbandry, or fishing. An abundant food supply was provided

9 G. W. B. Huntingford, "The Social Organization of the Dorobo," African Studies, 1 (September, 1942), 183-200.

by the large herds of buffalo hunted by the Kiowa, Comanche, Blackfoot, and Cheyenne. Prior to the advent of the horse, the buffalo were also hunted communally, a large number of men cooperating to drive the buffalo over cliffs or into pounds. Communal drives disappeared after the 1850's when horses became abundant, but large hunting parties were still well adapted to hunting big game that moved in herds, since a single hunter rarely killed more than two buffalo before the herd got away.

Among the Plains Indians, especially the Comanches and Blackfoot, war or raiding reinforced the joint family, since both in assault and in defense there is an advantage in numbers. Moreover, a consequence of war is widows and orphans: Blackfoot women outnumbered the men two or three to one. One adjustment is the extended family to provide for dependents; another is in polygamy, and, in actuality, more than 50 per cent of the Blackfoot men had at least two wives.

The Hukundika or Promontory Point Shoshone, living north of the Great Salt Lake in Utah and southern Idaho, resembled the Plains Indians in their subsistence pattern and differed from the western Shoshone who did not have horses and who lived in the desert where game was scarce. The Hukundika had some horses and hunted buffalo, and there were communal drives in hunting antelope, rabbits, ducks, and deer. There was also communal fishing for salmon with weirs.

The Yukaghir of Siberia in earlier times were like the Plains Indians and the Hukundika in that they had easy access to herds of big game. The Yukaghir hunted elk and reindeer, both of which ranged in large herds and were easily killed to provide an abundant food supply. By the 1900's, however, the elk had almost disappeared and the reindeer were decimated, causing famine. It seems likely that the extended family system became established during the period of abundance and has persisted in spite of, rather than because of, the more recent economic conditions facing the Yukaghir.

Among the California hunters and gatherers listed in Category II of Table 5—the Pomo, Shasta, Yana, and Wappo—there was an abundant supply of acorns, which constituted the staple of their diet. The gathering of acorns, in conjunction with the gathering of other fruits and vegetables, the hunting of deer, bear, and birds and other small animals, and fishing with weirs and nets for salmon, seems to have provided an entirely adequate food supply to support the extended family system.

The traditional Veddas of Ceylon were almost purely a hunting and gathering society, but we are told that their area was rich in game, and their diet was supplemented by the collection of honey and the digging of yams. The Coast Veddas were primarily fishermen, and the Village Veddas cultivated grain crops, but both of these groups had become relatively acculturated at an early date.

Although they are primarily hunting and gathering societies, agriculture would appear to have provided some stability to the food supply and residence patterns of the western Apache of the American Southwest, the Caduveo and the Lengua of the Gran Chaco region of South America, and perhaps the Motilon of Venezuela. Agriculture accounted for a considerable portion of the food supply among the western Apache, and local organization was oriented around the farm sites controlled by the matrilocal extended family. The hunting and gathering territory was also centered around the agricultural plots. Stability of residence, then, was an additional circumstance making possible extended family organization, since a

highly nomadic life militates against the development of large families. The Lengua depend largely upon hunting and fishing in a swampy environment, but they also have small gardens in which they cultivate pumpkins, sweet potatoes, maize, manioc, and tobacco. The Caduveo have only a rudimentary agriculture, but they acquire agricultural products from subject peoples, from whom they also collect other tribute; booty, slaves, and women. Wealth, in this instance buttressing an extended family system, derives from a source other than their own subsistence techniques. Finally, although the Iroka subtribe of the Motilon is classified as a predominantly hunting and gathering society, other subtribes within the Motilon group appear to be dependent primarily upon fishing or agriculture.

In the final case, the Siriono of the Interior Amazonia region of South America, we find that what is classified as an extended family has minimal functions. The Siriono house a band of sixty to eighty persons in a single hut, a crude affair that takes only one hour to build. When the whole band or settlement is housed together, the extended family is of course included, but its functions are not great. The nuclear family is the regular work unit, but the extended family helps to plant, gather, and hunt on certain occasions. It is as if a society had a choice of maintaining an independent family system with occasional demands on relatives for special labor or maintaining an extended family but utilizing the extra labor potential only occasionally.

These negative cases of hunting societies with extended family systems upon closer examination generally support the generalization that type of family is a function of the size of the food supply and the corresponding demand for cooperative labor beyond that of the independent family.

types of family and types of economy   83

Modern Industrial Society

The world ethnographic sample which furnishes the statistical data for this study includes only a very few cases of industrial society. The subsistence base of an industrial society is of course mainly agriculture, although herding and fishing may be important. But a significant characteristic of industrial society is the relatively small percentage of the population engaged in agriculture: in the United States in 1950 only 12 per cent of the total active population [was] engaged in agricultural occupations. In England and Wales in 1951 the corresponding figure was 5 per cent—the lowest in the world.[10]

The censuses which have been taken in industrial societies give us data for families, by households. In the United States in 1956, 96.7 per cent of all married couples maintained separate dwelling places.[11] While it is possible for extended families to exist with separate dwellings for the component conjugal units, nevertheless the family in most industrial societies is in fact, as field studies indicate, organized along independent, not extended, lines.

The association of the independent family with industrial society is usually accounted for mainly by characteristics of industry itself. One is the small demand for family labor. Unlike the situation in simpler economies, employment in industrial society is provided by nonfamily agencies on the basis of individual competence, not family membership. Payment is in money, which is individualizing in its effects, whereas earlier labor was unpaid family labor, unifying in its influence. The modern industrial scene is also characterized by high rates of physical mobility, which separates the members of families and makes interaction more difficult.

The modern industrial society, with its small independent family, is, then, like the simpler hunting and gathering society and in part apparently, for some of the same reasons, namely, limited need for family labor and physical mobility.[12] The hunter is mobile because he pursues the game; the industrial worker, the job.

Property is more highly developed in modern industrial society than in the earlier agricultural society, but property is mainly in money, individually acquired, not in family-owned land.

To sum up, the independent family is associated with hunting and the extended family with agriculture. Family type is influenced by type of subsistence through the food supply, demand for family labor, physical mobility, and property. The food supply, the demand for family labor, and property are more highly developed in agricultural than in hunting societies.

These findings are generalizations based on many societies. In a given society the causative situation may be highly complex, and various factors, some of which have been identified, may offset the influence of the type of subsistence. The reliability of the findings depends of course upon the accuracy of classification of the family and subsistence patterns of the 549 cultures which form the basis of this study.

---

[10] Yearbook of Food and Agriculture Production, 1957, Vol. II (Rome: Food and Agriculture Organization, 1958).

[11] Statistical Abstract of the United States (Washington, D.C.: U.S. Government Printing Office, 1957), p. 46.

[12] A notable exception is highly industrialized Japan, where virtually all men and women marry and live in a consanguineously related household [Irene Taeuber, The Population of Japan (Princeton: Princeton University Press, 1958)]. It is reported, however, that a person entering employment in a Japanese factory tends to make it a lifelong commitment. [J. G. Abegglen, The Japanese Factory: Aspects of Its Social Organization (New York: The Free Press of Glencoe, Inc., 1958)].

Industrialization and the Family

SIDNEY M. GREENFIELD

I

The small nuclear family found in western Europe and the United States is generally viewed in sociological theory as a consequence of the urban-industrial revolution. The present paper questions the hypothesis and suggests alternative lines of thinking.

As western society continues to disseminate its distinctive technology to the remainder of the world, both theoretical and practical consideration must be given to the changes in social organization that accompany the introduction of the machine and the market-exchange economic system. The specific task of the sociologist and cultural anthropologist here is to seek empirically founded generalizations about cultural process, causality, and functional interdependence. For policy makers and administrators in foreign affairs and international relations have been applying ill-founded generalizations uncritically: they reason that, if certain types of social organization and urban-industrial technology and the market-exchange economic system are interrelated, they must inevitably accompany western technology, and as a consequence, they support action programs designed to establish and foster these forms.

The dominant sociological hypothesis relating technology and social organization postulates a functional interdependence between industrialization and urbanization, the technoeconomic system, with the small nuclear family as the unit of social organization. Hypotheses of functional interdepend-

Sidney M. Greenfield, "Industrialization and the Family in Sociological Theory," *American Journal of Sociology*, 67 (1961-62), 312-322.

ence, however, take several forms, each with different implications. As Nagel has pointed out, statements phrased in functional terms are the equivalent of those phrased in nonfunctional terms, and any statement in one terminology can be translated into the other: "The difference between a functional and a nonfunctional formulation," he states, "is one of selective emphasis; it is quite comparable to the difference between saying that B is the effect of A, and saying that A is the condition (or cause) of B."[1]

There are, however, two contrasting ways of conceptualizing sociocultural phenomena that result in significantly different meanings for statements of functional relationships. In one formulation the functional statements have approximately the same meaning as conventional causal statements, while in the other a special type of causal implication is rendered. The most widely adopted formulation of functionalism found in social science is based upon the organic analogy. Sociocultural systems are likened to living organisms in being goal-directed, self-righting systems in which all of the parts "function" to maintain the whole in a state of equilibrium. As phrased by Radcliffe-Brown:

The concept of function involves the notion of a *structure* consisting of a *set of relations* amongst *unit entities*, the continuity of the structure being maintained by a *life process* made up of the *activities* of the constituent units.

Such a view implies that a social system (the total structure of a society together with the totality of social usages in which the structure appears and on which it depends for its continued existence) has a

[1] Ernest Nagel, "A Formulation of Functionalism," in *Logic Without Metaphysics* (New York: The Free Press of Glencoe, Inc., 1956), p. 251.

certain kind of unity, which we may speak of as functional unity. We may define it as a condition in which all parts of the social system work together with a sufficient degree of harmony or internal consistency, i.e., without producing persistent conflicts which can neither be resolved nor regulated.[2]

Maintenance of the state of equilibrium, then, is likened to the continuance of life in the organism; the destruction of the equilibrium is analogous to death. The system is closed, and change in the total configuration is ruled out by the basic assumptions. The state of equilibrium is based upon the efficient integration of all of the parts, each of which functions to maintain the continuing existence of the whole. As long as the system continues, then, each part is necessarily functional and its relationship vis-à-vis any other part is one of functional interdependence—all of the parts operating to achieve the goal or purpose of the whole: maintenance of the state of equilibrium. Given this self-maintaining system, we can say that both parts and whole are functionally interrelated and interdependent. By varying our perspective, however, we may view each as a functional consequence of the other, that is, any part is a functional consequence of the operation of the total system, or the whole is a functional consequence of the operation of all the parts.

In the terminology of cause and effect there may also be two perspectives: Starting from the parts, we may say that they are the cause of the whole, which is the effect of their activity, since they maintain the totality in a given state. On the other hand, however, the whole is also the cause of the

parts, since the latter operate in accord with the pattern of the former, thereby becoming its effect. In this formulation, however, no causal statements can be made about relations among the parts themselves; that is, one part cannot be the cause of any other since all, taken cumulatively, are either the cause of, or are caused by, the whole. The only relationship that can exist among the parts of a self-regulating, functionally integrated equilibrium system is that of functional interdependence.[3]

The alternative formulation of functional theory in social science modifies the assumption of equilibrium and discards the organic analogy. To those who hold this position, the empirical evidence suggests the conclusion that sociocultural systems are never in a state of complete equilibrium. They are always changing and, consequently, equilibrium is a state relative to a given period of time and, at best, only approximated. In the long run, all sociocultural systems appear to be in continuous flux, and both the parts and the whole can and do change. Adherents of this opinion, then, do not generally conceptualize sociocultural systems as self-regulating and goal directed; consequently, the specialized set of functional statements used to analyze self-regulating systems are not necessary. Functional statements in this formulation are thus the direct equivalent of causal statements, and a causal relationship is implied whether the terms "functional consequence" or "functional interdependence" are used. The term "functional consequence,"

[2] A. R. Radcliffe-Brown, *Structure and Function in Primitive Society* (New York: The Free Press of Glencoe, Inc., 1952), pp. 180, 181.

[3] Associated with the notion of functional interdependence of parts is that of functional alternatives. This refers to a limited range of parts that can perform the same function as the given part in the total system and consequently may be considered as substitutes for the given part since the equilibrium will still be maintained after the exchange.

however, may be read as necessary and sufficient cause, while "functional interdependence" is the equivalent of sufficient cause alone.

In accord with this view, the possible relationships between part and whole and part and part differ from those possible in the prior formulation. Since equilibrium is not assumed, the cause of the total system['s] being maintained in its given state is not the functioning of the parts, nor is the cause of the operations of the units taken to be the achievement of the goal of the whole. Here the total system tends to be viewed as resulting from a process of change and adjustment among the parts. Thus one part can and does, as the interpretation is made, exert a causal effect on the other parts and by implication on the whole. It is only after the parts have had their effect on the other units that the parts may be thought of as being functionally interrelated—the term being taken to mean operating in a state of harmony with each other for a given time. So conceptualized, the locus of the causal nexus is the part-part relationship rather than the part-whole relationship, as is the case in the alternative formulation.

II

Many students in both Europe and the United States have studied the historical conditions that have produced the distinctive modern form of the family. We select Ogburn and Nimkoff because they present the generally accepted point of view. They distinguish three basic types—the consanguine, the stem, and the conjugal family in that temporal order. "The consanguine family and the clan," they state, "tended to break up in the course of time. . . . The family [then] took on the pattern found in historical Europe and colonial America. The consanguine

family tended to disappear, especially in the western world, and the conjugal family became the predominant type." The stem family is seen as a transitional form. "With increasing industrialization," however, it "tends to be superseded by the conjugal family."[4]

For the United States, the base line used in the study of the family is the nineteenth century and the focal type is the rural farm family.

The American family is not a European institution transplanted to a new environment and slightly changed by this transferring. Instead it represents an original development which so reconstructed the contributions of European culture as to bring forth a family type in its characteristics clearly distinctive from the original European institution.[5]

The industrial revolution, starting in the nineteenth and going into the twentieth century, is seen as the force that changed the farm family and is basically responsible for the "modern American family." Industrialization had several immediate consequences:

Industrial organization eventually outgrew the family. The trend was in this direction as the inventions used in handicrafts manufacture multiplied and the use of windmills increased. But with cheaper iron and steel, and the use of streams as a source of power applied to tools, more space was needed and more workers were required than were to be found in the household. The steam boiler was too big for the home and the power generator required more space for the machine. The factory instead of the homestead became the unit of production. The factory was too large to be manned by even a very large family.[6]

[4] William Ogburn and M. F. Nimkoff, *Sociology* (Boston: Houghton Mifflin Company, 1950), p. 469.
[5] Ernest Groves and Gladys Groves, *The Contemporary Family* (Philadelphia: J. B. Lippincott Co., 1947), p. 140.
[6] Ogburn and Nimkoff, *op. cit.*, p. 473.

Thus the adoption of the machine resulted in sweeping changes in social organization: factories needed laborers who could be more readily obtained in cities than on farms; urbanism and industrialization worked hand in hand to change the structure of American society; industry needed laborers and the cities grew to provide them.

In addition to ecological and demographic changes, there were significant structural-functional changes in the social system, primary among them being the expansion of the industrial factory system to assume most of the tasks formerly handled by the isolated farm family. At first, industry was only a new technoeconomic system transforming methods of production. But along with the new technology there developed a set of social relations with its own specific principles of organization and stratification, and its own way of patterning interaction between individuals, into which rural people were assimilated as they moved into the cities to work. One aspect of all this was the small nuclear family with its distinctive form and means of social articulation.

The argument here is concerned with social and cultural change, and a state of equilibrium is therefore not assumed. In fact, it precludes the existence of a self-regulating system since the family is being analyzed in terms of change occurring in it, in the total system, and in the other parts of the system. In formal terms the argument is that the small nuclear family found in the United States takes its present form because of the national industrialization and urbanization. Within a system in a state of change then, one part is the cause of the new form taken by another part.

Once the change is completed, however, and all of the causal factors achieve their effects, a new equilibrium in the total system is commonly assumed. For the present, scholars tend to view the small nuclear family as being in a state of functional interdependence with industry and the other parts of what may be loosely called the American form of western civilization. The family now is functional in that it operates to maintain the new equilibrium.

In Europe, the best example of this line of thinking is presented by Max Weber, who, in his *General Economic History*, for example, states the reasons for viewing the changes in the family as a function of its changing economic position that in turn is a function of the changes in the total society that stemmed from the industrial revolution. The concluding paragraph of Part I of the book summarizes a part of the argument:

With the dissolution of the manors and of the remains of the earlier agrarian communism through consolidation, separation, etc., private property in land has been completely established. In the meantime, in the course of the centuries, the organization of society has changed . . . , the household community shrinking, until now the father with his wife and children functions as the unit in property relations. Formerly, this was simply impossible for physical reasons. The household has at the same time undergone an extensive internal transformation, and this in two ways; its function has become restricted to the fields of consumption, and its management placed on an accounting basis. To an increasing extent, the development of inheritance law in place of the original complete communism has led to a separation between the property of the men and the women, with a separate accounting. This twofold transformation was bound up with the development of industry and trade.[7]

---

[7] Max Weber, *General Economic History*, F. H. Knight, trans. (New York: The Free Press of Glencoe, Inc., 1950), p. 111.

A fuller reading of this and his other works completes the presentation which, though more scholarly and sophisticated, is the same in theory as is argued in the United States. Though Weber seems to imply functional interdependence of the small family and industrialization, the conceptual formulation he uses in explaining the changes in the family is the one in which parts in a dynamic system may be construed to have a causal impact on other parts. It is only after industrialization is accomplished and the new whole is created that he postulates an equilibrium in which the causal nexus is between part and whole and the parts are only interdependent.

III

In a recent paper Erwin H. Johnson questioned the hypothesis that the small nuclear family is caused by industrialization and urbanization. After examining the data from modern Japan, he concludes that the stable stem family, which is at least 400 years old there, "is sufficiently generalized in its nature to conform to the needs of the changing technology of Japan." He then goes on to say that the traditional family, in fact, had not and "does not have to give way under . . . urban or industrial influences."[8]

Modern Japan, then, provides us with a case of both urbanization and industrialization with a family other than the small nuclear form. Garigue reports extensive kinship networks among urbanized, industrialized French-Canadians in Montreal. These extended networks of "urban French Canadian kinship," he writes, "are no new devel-

opment, but seem to have been in existence since the period of New France." He concludes:

The collected evidence indicates no trend toward transformation of the present French-Canadian urban kinship system into the more restricted system reported for the United States. While difficulties were reported in maintaining a united domestic family or an integral kin group, there is no reason to suppose that these difficulties were caused primarily by urban living. Moreover, many cases were reported where the kin group re-formed after a period of disunity. There are many reasons for believing that the present system will continue. Far from being incompatible, kinship and urbanism among French-Canadians seem to have become functionally related.[9]

In a recent paper on Luso-Brazilian kinship patterns, Wagley, after examining data on the *parentela*—a bilateral kindred—from seven Brazilian communities, writes: "It is evident from the data provided . . . that kinship plays an important role in social, economic, and even political affairs."[10] The *parentela*, he adds, operates in both rural and urban areas. In the cities, kinsmen tend to purchase apartments in the same building to facilitate the working out of kinship obligations. The studies by Firth, Young, Shaw, and Townsend in London show further evidence of the extension of kinship in urbanized, industrialized areas.[11]

Additional evidence is presented here

[8] E. H. Johnson, "The Stem Family and Its Extensions in Modern Japan," paper presented at the Annual Meeting of the American Anthropological Association, Minneapolis, Minnesota (1960), 13.

[9] Philip Garigue, "French Canadian Kinship and Urban Life," *American Anthropologist*, 63 (December, 1956), 1098-1099.

[10] Charles Wagley, "Luso-Brazilian Kinship Patterns," unpublished manuscript (1960).

[11] Raymond Firth, *Two Studies of Kinship in London* (London: Athlone Press, 1957); Michael Young, "Kinship and Family in East London," *Man*, 54 (September, 1954), 137-139; L. A. Shaw, "Impression of Family Life in a London Suburb," *Sociological Review*, 3 (December, 1955), 175-195.

to question the hypothesis of functional interdependence and implied causality between urban-industrial technology and the small nuclear family, challenging that part of the generally accepted hypothesis in which the diachronic formulation of sociocultural events is used. The position which assumes a static equilibrium in which functional interdependence within a closed, stable system is assumed a priori will not be argued other than to stress that even here there may be a range of family forms that can serve as functional alternatives to the small nuclear family in urbanized, industrialized systems. The additional evidence is found in an analysis of the family on the island of Barbados, where the small nuclear family and fragmented kindred are present in the same form and functionally articulated with the larger society in the same way as in industrialized western society, but without industry and machines.

We shall, then, have examples from the ethnographic record in which urbanization and industrialization are present without the small nuclear family and fragmented kindred, and the nuclear family is found in the same form and with the same functions as in industrialized western society, but without industrialization and urbanization. Taken together, these combinations seriously question a hypothesis that has received general acceptance in sociological theory before being tested by the comparative evidence.

IV

Barbados is a small, densely populated island, twenty-one miles long and fourteen miles wide, located in the Caribbean Sea at the eastern rim of the Lesser Antilles. It was first colonized by Great Britain at the beginning of the seventeenth century, and, in contrast with her other Caribbean possessions, has remained a British colony from the time of its settlement until 1956, when, with nine other English Caribbean dependencies, it became part of the Federation of the West Indies.

Today, Barbados is not a folk or peasant society. On the other hand, it is not highly mechanized and industrialized. Its economy, which is based upon agriculture, is best not considered underdeveloped since the application of additional capital has not, and, at present, cannot lead to a profitable expansion of productivity and employment opportunities for its very large population.

At present, Barbados—only 166.3 square miles in area—is one of the most densely populated areas in the world: its inhabitants numbered approximately 230,000 at the end of 1956—a density of almost 1380 persons per square mile —and were increasing at a rate of about 2 per cent per year. Overpopulation has long been recognized as a major problem on the island.

How is this myriad of human beings supported? While its economy is based upon agriculture, in contrast with most of the world's densely populated rural areas where subsistence as well as cash crops are raised, Barbados is almost exclusively dependent upon a single cash crop—sugar. As emphasized in a recent national accounts study of the economy of Barbados,[12] agriculture, in which the growing of sugar cane predominates over all other forms of agricultural activity, is the most important contributor to the island's gross domestic product, in which the processing of sugar and molasses accounts for more than half the total contribution of manu-

[12] Jeanette Bethel, "A National Accounts Study of the Economy of Barbados," *Social and Economic Studies*, 9 (June, 1960), 127-128.

facturing. Sugar, to quote the authors of Barbados' ten-year development plan, is truly "the blood of the island."[13]

Barbadians, then, are not subsistence farmers. The island's agricultural activities are organized around the production of sugar, which is cultivated because it provides more revenue per acre than any other crop which could be grown on the island and for which a world market exists. Individuals earn their livelihood in the form of wages; they produce very little for their own consumption.

Barbados, as has already been mentioned, is not an industrialized society in the general sense of the term. The concept of industrialization, however, as it is used in sociological discussions is ambiguous. The specific referent is technological—machines and factories. In general, however, it refers also to the system of social relations that organize human populations in the management of the machines. The use of one term to refer to both the technology and the social structure is regrettable since it leads to thinking of the two as inseparable: that is, the student finds it difficult to think of machine technology without the specific social patterns that have developed in western civilization. This double referent, however, reveals more of the causal assumptions made by the early students of industrialization: the causal impact of machine technology was considered to be so great that the social relations governing the use of the machines were conceptualized as a necessary consequence of it. Both referents of industrialization must be considered independently, at least until some evidence is presented to demonstrate that there is only one way to organize a population in the use of machines.

13 A *Ten-Year Development Plan for Barbados, 1946-56* (Bridgetown, Barbados: Advocate Press, n.d.), p. 11.

This inadequate conceptualization is crucial, however, in the analysis of the data from Barbados since many of its social structural forms are those generally associated with machine technology in North America and Europe, although there are few factories and machines are little used except for a handful of instances in the sugar industry. This situation, itself, however, provides an additional challenge to the hypothesis which claims that industrialization—which at the beginning, at least, was purely technological—is the cause of social organization, since the consequence is present without the cause.

V

The elementary family in Barbados, as in most of the islands of the West Indies, takes two basic forms—one conjugal or nuclear, the other subnuclear and generally matrifocal. As used here, matrifocality refers to the form of the family in which the mother-child relationship is stronger and more durable than the conjugal (husband-wife) bond. It is characterized by (1) a marginal role for the husband-father, (2) high percentages of female heads of households, (3) easy adoption and high ratios of children per household, (4) high rates of illegitimacy (by European and American standards), and (5) low rates of "legal" marriages. The conjugal or nuclear family, on the other hand, is based upon the husband-wife relationship and is characterized by the converse of the features of the matrifocal family.

The household, which generally contains at least one of the elementary kinship units, is variable. Ideally, it is composed of an isolated nuclear family which lives in a separate shelter, usually provided by the adult male. This, however, is rarely achieved by most of the population. When not composed of an isolated nuclear family, the household may consist of a number of alternative forms. The first is a nuclear family in which a mature child, invariably a daughter, has begun to have a family—often she is unmarried—before establishing a firm conjugal relationship in a separate dwelling. This extended family group, or "multifamily" household, is of three generations and is composed of one nuclear family plus one or more matrifocal units of unwed mother and children, all sharing the same house. An alternative appears when a woman and her children become established in an independent dwelling unit without an adult male. This occurs either when the members of the conjugal group separate—the male leaving—or when a woman obtains a dwelling, usually through inheritance, and occupies it with her children but without a mate. An infrequent variant of this denuded family occurs when a man is left alone with his children in a household without an adult female. These denuded family households can become extended when the children mature and begin to have offspring while they are still living at home. Here we find a three-generation unit which, generally, is composed of a woman and her children, including mature daughters and their offspring. This form, which is found throughout the Caribbean, is usually referred to as the "grandmother family." A household, then, can consist of one of four alternative forms which are found distributed in the same frequencies in both the rural and urban areas: (1) a nuclear family, (2) a nuclear extended family, (3) a denuded or subnuclear extended family (male or female, but usually female-centered), and (4) a denuded or subnuclear extended family (male or female, but again usually female-centered).

In form and functional integration with the total society—an at least temporary state of equilibrium is assumed for the purpose of analysis—the ideal nuclear group found in Barbados is very similar to the nuclear family found in the United States and described by Parsons.[14] The tendency toward structural and spatial isolation appears in both places; the importance of the mother in the process of the child's socialization and in the development of his personality are similar; the role of the adult male within the family as "breadwinner," responsible for supporting the entire group, is likewise analogous. More significantly, even the relationship between the individual and the larger society is the same. Individuals are all members of families linked to the larger society through the adult male who occupies a place in the local occupational system, and in both cases, the position of the latter member in the occupational system is a primary determinant of the position of the others in the social hierarchy.

Other similarities can be found in patterns of descent: Both systems are bilateral. In Barbados, where illegitimacy is common, it is usual for parents to leave wills bequeathing their property to all of their children. Relations with ascending and descending generations show no tendency toward structural bias in favor of any one line of descent. Both Barbados and the United States, therefore, can be described as symetrically multilineal.

In both cases, the tendency toward structural isolation is reinforced by the relationship between the family and

14 Talcott Parsons, "The Kinship System in the Contemporary United States," *American Anthropologist*, 45 (January, 1943), 22-38. See also Talcott Parsons and Robert Bales, *Family, Socialization and Interaction Process* (New York: The Free Press of Glencoe, Inc., 1955).

the occupational system, particularly with reference to social mobility. Each nuclear family is ascribed a place in the system of stratification which is based upon the social class of the family of orientation of its adult male subject to the mobility he may achieve in his occupational pursuits. Mobility is a driving force in both societies. Kinship relationships are generally divorced from the occupational system, thus permitting conjugal units to be socially mobile, independent of kinship ties. Nuclear families striving for mobility are often best able to do so by almost total denial of kinship claims, which of course leads to the isolation of the conjugal family. In Parsons' terms, then, both the Barbadian and American nuclear families can be characterized as "bilateral, structurally isolated, open, multilineal, conjugal systems."[15] The alternative forms of the household discussed above are all variants of the isolated nuclear unit produced by factors relating directly to the integration of family and society.

The primary functions of Barbadian society are performed through a highly stratified system of occupational statuses; the hierarchically ranked positions, however, provide their occupants with wages that vary considerably. The insular system of social stratification is tied directly to these ranked occupational positions since they are the primary determinant of an individual's social class. Families are articulated with the larger society through adult males, who are members of both a family and the occupational system simul-

taneously: the male role is defined in terms of supporting women and children; he is also expected to hold a position in the occupational system. In the latter system he holds one of a series of ranked positions from which he receives money and prestige; in the family he holds a position that calls for the contribution of income obtained in the occupational world. Women and children, who, in the ideal, are outside the dominant institutional complex, are linked to it through reciprocal role obligations to a male within the family. Satisfactory performance of the adult male role within the family requires an individual to hold a position in the occupational system that provides him with income sufficient to support a family.

The occupational system in Barbados, however, is so constituted that many, if not most, of the positions at the lower end of the hierarchy provide neither the prestige nor the income necessary for the support of a family. The occupants of these low-ranked positions are not able to fulfill the role expectations of adult male within the family, and if they cannot improve their occupational status after a period of time they tend to leave the household, thereby creating a denuded, subnuclear, matrifocal, or mother-oriented, group. The extended family households, both nuclear and denuded, appear when the fathers of the children born to girls living in parental households have not been able to attain an occupational position with rewards sufficient to purchase a house and to establish the new family as an isolated nuclear group.

The importance of a man to his family and his relationship to the others, therefore, will vary directly with the income and status he earns in the occupational world. Consequently, we may expect both the family and the house-

[15] The most significant differences between the Barbadian and the American nuclear family is size. This difference, however, most critically affects the socialization and personality development of the children and not the form of the family or its articulation with the larger society (Parsons and Bales, *op. cit.*, p. 18). It is, therefore, excluded from the present comparison.

hold to take different forms at varying socioeconomic levels. Whether the unit is nuclear or matrifocal is, therefore, a function of the system of social stratification and the way in which adult males link the family to society. Where adult males hold positions that provide rewards sufficient for the support of a nuclear family, the nuclear group is isolated in a separate household; where not, a subnuclear, matrifocal group appears, causing the household to take one of the forms outlined above.

On the tiny sugar-growing island of Barbados, then, we find the same small nuclear family, articulated with the larger society in precisely the same way as we find in industrialized western society, but without urbanization and industrialization. The industrial revolution, in fact, has not yet come to the island.

The existence of an industrialized and urbanized society in Brazil, French Canada, England, and Japan with an extended family, and the small nuclear family—identical in form and function to the nuclear family of industrialized western society—in Barbados without industrialization or urbanization provides evidence to question the hypothesized causal relationship between urban-industrial technology and the family. The explanation for the similarity in family form and function in Barbados and in industrialized western society, however, may provide us with a new perspective with which to re-analyze the historical data used to support the old hypothesis.

VI

Barbados was settled by colonists who came in family groups from Great Britain. Though African slaves were later introduced to work on the sugar plantations, significant numbers of English and Irish families remained and

their descendents are still there today. The institutionalized form of family now found in Barbados was brought to the island by the first settlers and later adopted by the Negroes when integrated into the larger society through the occupational system immediately following emancipation.[16]

The small nuclear family, the *famille particulariste* of Le Play, which is native to North Europe,[17] is known to have existed in England in the seventeenth century, prior to the colonization of the New World. Specialists in the culture of the Old World (Europe, Mediterranean, Middle East), in fact, believe it to be much older, "as old as the Vikings or older" according to Arensberg.[18] If this is the case, it ante-

[16] It is significant to note that the family form has remained the same even though it has been transferred from one ethnic group to another.

[17] Frederic Le Play, Focillon, and DeLaire, *L'Organisation de la famille* (Tours: A. Marne et Fils, 1884). See also Edmond Demolins, *Comment la Route Crée de type social* (Paris: F. Didet, n.d.), 2 vols., and C. C. Zimmermann and Merle Frampton, *Family and Society* (New York: D. Van Nostrand Company, Inc., 1937), pp. 97ff.

[18] C. M. Arensberg, "Discussion of Methods of Community Analysis in the Caribbean by Robert Manners," *Caribbean Studies: A Symposium* (Mona, Jamaica: Institute of Social and Economic Studies, 1957), p. 97. An example of what might have happened in the total society is found at the upper end of the occupational ladder where a given individual can earn enough to support more than one family.

With the acquisition of great wealth and property, we find the development of extended families, with the income-earning property accumulated by one generation providing support and prestige for several other generations. These extended families, usually patrilineages in Europe, North America, and the West Indies, develop around family property that provides income and status to all who can establish a valid genealogical connection therein.

At the lower end of the occupational scale, jobs do not provide sufficient income for a man to support even one family, and the

dates both urbanism and machine technology in England and the United States. Perhaps its contemporary place in modern, urban, industrialized society is related to its temporal priority to machine technology.

If, at the very beginning of the urban industrial revolution, the inventors of machine technology already lived in small nuclear families, it is no small wonder that this form became functionally integrated with industrial technology as a new equilibrium was achieved. As North European man developed the social forms to go with the machine, it is quite probable that he reworked the social institutions with which he was already familiar. If so, the relationship between the small nuclear family and industrialization is better interpreted as one of the temporal priority of the former and not a necessary functional consequence or cause and effect in which the latter is the determinant. Further investigation of the historical material, then, may indicate that the two are related because the small nuclear family was there first. Subsequent social institutions, such as the occupational system, that went with

prestige rating is so low as to deny status either for himself or his family. It is here that women and children must enter the labor force to help out. The jobs available to them, however, are also at the bottom of the hierarchy. As the primary feature of the division of labor is destroyed, so is the strength of the conjugal bond. It is then that the subnuclear, matrifocal family appears.

The close functional adjustment between the isolated nuclear family and this form of stratified occupational system is related to the organization of the latter system. Since most jobs pay enough to support one family, the total system functions best when one wage earner links one family to the social system through his wage contribution. His income and status are identified with the members of the nuclear group until the children are old enough to establish their own nuclear families, each with its own adult male wage earner.

the machine were probably adapted to, and therefore fitted with, a society organized in small families. One wonders what organizational forms urban industrialized society might have today if these early North Europeans lived in extended families.

Some might argue that wage labor more than machine technology is the cause of the distinctive western family. If one uses the equilibrium formulation, there is no doubt that wage labor and the small family are functionally interrelated and interdependent. The question, however, is whether a system of wage labor is a necessary and sufficient cause for the small family when an entire sociocultural system is in the process of change.

The crucial relationship between wage labor and the form of the family concerns the scale of remunerations. In the systems of North America, Europe, and Barbados, with the exception of the relative few who hold positions at the top of the hierarchy, workers earn only enough for the support of a nuclear group. While variability in wages is considerable, we rarely find a job paying enough to support more than one nuclear family. Since men are the principal wage earners—this probably being based upon a prior cultural definition of the sexual division of labor in North Europe—they are expected to provide money for the kinship unit. The degree of possible extension of the kin group is thus related to the income earned by men. Since each nuclear unit also is expected to have its own wage earner, it is economically independent, which brings about a weakening of reciprocal relations between members and kinsmen outside the group. Within the nuclear family, however, there is relative equality, each member having a right to a share of the income of the adult male or the goods or services it can buy.

Were the occupational system so organized as to pay one individual enough to support a larger group or to enable him to provide employment for such a unit, extended families might arise to engulf or submerge the nuclear group. Perhaps if extended families had existed in England when the complex took its present form, the remuneration scale of modern industrial society would be very different.

In the United States, industrialization started in the Northeast, a section appropriately called New England. With reference to the family in New England, Arensberg writes, "The brittle, easily split 'nuclear' or 'democratic' ('Eskimoan') family, . . . came with [the] Yankees from England and fitted well with their egalitarian, unstratified farmer-artisan towns."[19] The small nuclear family, then, was brought to the United States from Great Britain by its earliest settlers. Therefore, it was present before the industrial revolution began in the United States. We suggest that it was reworked, as it had been several centuries earlier, in England, to provide the foundation for the

———
[19] C. M. Arensberg, "American Communities," *American Anthropologist*, **57** (December, 1955), 1149.

new system of social organization that developed and spread with the industrial revolution. Here again, it was not the industrial revolution that produced the small nuclear family; in fact, the opposite may be true. The prior existence of the small nuclear family as the basic kinship unit of the people who industrialized both Great Britain and the United States may have been responsible for the very forms of social organization that developed along with the machines.

Furthermore, the data from Barbados demonstrates that the small nuclear family can diffuse without urbanization and industrialization just as the latter seems to be able to diffuse without the small nuclear family.

In conclusion, then, an examination of both the comparative and historical evidence indicates that, developmentally, there is no necessary and sufficient causal relationship, whether expressed in terms of necessary functional interdependence or consequence, between the small nuclear family and urbanization and industrialization. Any relationship that exists most probably results from the presence of the small family in North Europe prior to the industrial revolution.

Cliques in Office Organizations

EDWARD GROSS

The present research is an attempt to examine the significance of cliques in work behavior under the special conditions presented by an industrial office. The locus of research was the head

Edward Gross, "Characteristics of Cliques in Office Organizations," *Research Studies of the State College of Washington*, **19** (1951), 131-136.

office of a firm in Chicago, which manufactured plastic items, belts, jewelry, and other products. The firm has one head office and four branches in other cities. In Chicago, it has four factories and at the time of the research employed approximately 1600 persons in Chicago, of whom approximately one hundred were in the head office. The latter are the subjects of the present study. Research was carried out over a two-year period, which included nine months of intensive study throughout the working day and week of the employees. The subjects were studied mainly through personal interviews and observations. Personnel file data were also used. Research took place on the job, at lunch, on the twice-daily "passes" of the workers, and in their homes. At the conclusion of the research, comparative data were gathered on two other firms—one a large mail-order house, and the other a book-publishing company. The latter procedure was employed to guard against the possibility that the firm being studied was atypical of office structures.

Characteristics of the Office Organization

Research revealed that the office had the following major characteristics, which appear to be typical of office organizations:

Nature of the Work

It is customary to refer to office workers as "staff" and "control." At the firm under investigation, three distinctive functions were performed by personnel: coordination of business records (supervised by the treasurer), coordination of the internal structure of the company, and coordination of company relations with the outside world. The head office thus controls the whole company. It is engaged in vital work, and its personnel is well aware of it.

Shortness of "Line"

An important contrast between office and shop organizations is the official distance that separates the bottom from the top. In the office, everyone is "close" to top management, both physically and officially. Immediately below top

management (the president, two vice presidents, and the treasurer) are department heads and an office manager. These are the executives, all of whom have secretaries. Seven department heads have assistants. The rest of the office is organized into these departments, and there are no further authority levels besides those mentioned. Thus even the lowliest clerk may be only two steps, or at most three steps from top management. The worker is very much aware of this proximity, and, as we shall see, his behavior is a function of it.

Elaboration of the Division of Labor

All work structures exhibit a division of labor, but office work is characterized by a truly staggering amount of detail. The tasks themselves are simple, often involving merely the copying of figures from one form onto another. But each figure, invoice, order, copy, and so forth, is used again and again by a multiplicity of persons in different ways. Forms pass from person to person, changes are made, data drawn off; then forms are returned for further treatment and interpretation. Each worker is a specialist, but each in turn performs *many* specialized tasks. It should be noted that this work requires a great deal of physical movement, such as getting forms, checking data, comparing letters, and consulting.

These three features were felt to be the major distinctive characteristics of the office. There were others which are of significance for certain kinds of problems—namely, mode of payment (the salary), "cleanliness" of the occupation ("white collar"), smallness of their numbers (in comparison with the numbers of factory workers in the same firm), and location (close proximity to one another—in this firm, on one and one-half floors in the same building).

The Office Cliques

A total of eleven cliques, composed of thirty-seven persons, were identified. Examination revealed that members of a given clique had a striking factor in common: not one member was a competitor of any other in his clique. Competitors are defined as persons who have the same supervisor and do similar work. When such is the situation, workers are in a position to be compared with one another and to be evaluated by the supervisor. It is difficult for persons who work for different supervisors, or who do different work, to orient themselves competitively to one another. Of course they can, but in fact they did not.

Clique members were next examined from the point of view of their places in the formal structure. Each worker is a part of two formal groups—a supervisor-subordinate group and a work group. It was found that in nine of the eleven cliques, the members came from different supervisor-subordinate groups. For the work groups, it was found that in five of the cliques, none of the members were of the same work group, but in the remaining six, some persons were part of the same work group, though never the whole clique, and never more than two persons in a clique. That is, we find that cliques cut across the formal structure.

It was noted, finally, that the cliques were little more than congenial groups. They engaged in behavior in common and spent much of their time in talk. They were highly undramatic, even dull, to the observer. Members did not seem to "step out of line," and there were few controls on behavior.

The Functions of the Office Cliques

It is the first proposition of the writer that office cliques function as media, or foci, of communication. The condi-tions for, and characteristics of, such communication are, in turn, a function of the special characteristics of offices discussed above.

From the discussion of the nature of the work of the office, it will be recalled that this work is vital and operates to control the whole business and its relations with the outside world. The office is the place where important decisions are made. But the worker below top management and the executives does not himself partake of these decisions. He supplies information or analyses which *others* use for decision making. He is aware of the uses to which his information may be put, and even often anticipates the decision that may result. He is, therefore, in a kind of Cassandra-like position of possessing knowledge without the authority to put that knowledge to use in decision making. But he can do *one* thing with it— namely, communicate it to fellow workers in exchange for similar information on their part. And this he does.

The second characteristic of offices— the shortness of the line—produces a similar effect. Not only are workers engaged in vital control work, but they are very close to the decision makers in these areas. Besides, they are not subordinated to the decision makers in a strict line relationship, but are, in fact, extensions of them—they *assist* the decision makers to perform their work. The fact that such is the situation means that the knowledge they come to possess is not hearsay or rumor; it is eminently reliable and accurate and worth paying attention to.

The ability of the worker to interpret his knowledge, however, is made difficult by the third characteristic of offices—namely, the elaborate division of labor. Each worker possesses vital, reliable knowledge, but only about a small segment of the work. It is meaningless unless related to other knowledge possessed by persons in other work segments.

It is here that the communicative functions of the cliques come into action, for it will be recalled that clique membership *cuts across* both the authority and division of labor substructures. Thus the clique member finds himself in informal contact with persons in other parts of the structure. It is here, therefore, that reliable knowledge of forthcoming decisions may be put forth, compared, and interpreted. Furthermore, it is not only interpreted, but conclusions reached provide the basis for taking steps to anticipate what is coming. The worker is thus protected from unforeseen actions which may affect his welfare. A worker who is not a clique member is without this protection.

The special characteristics of offices have a second effect which sheds further light on the clique findings: that of tending to destroy the meaning of work. In their performance of the vital control work of the office, the workers are in touch with matters which are important, but over which they have almost no control. The situation is comparable to the bank clerk who handles thousands of dollars daily but himself draws forty-two dollars a week salary. The worker appreciates the significance of his work, though it gives him little personal satisfaction. The shortness of the line, as already discussed above, makes the situation especially frustrating. One is so close, yet so far. The shortness of the line has the further effect that promotion is rare, if not impossible. The private secretary to the president will almost certainly never be president. The lowly filing clerk is only two or three steps from top management, but the closeness is entirely illusory. Indeed, the opportunities for upward movement are better in the factory than in the office.

But work itself tends to lose its meaning because of the minuteness of the division of labor. This phenomenon has been the subject of comment by many writers from Veblen through Durkheim to Elton Mayo. On the whole, the evidence seems to support the proposition that when the division of labor becomes elaborated without concurrent coordination, the individual loses his ability to comprehend the whole and his place in it. It becomes routine and devoid of meaning. Coordination itself is difficult when the division of labor is very complex.

These considerations lead the writer to believe that work in an office has less meaning to the worker than in a factory. The factory worker can at least see the completed assembly on which he has worked; he can *see* in flight the airplane to which he has made a small contribution. But an office worker's labors may result, indirectly, in the sale of two dozen belts to Frank's Sport Shop in Punxsutawney, Pennsylvania. The worker will probably never see the belts, the store, or the town. They are simply names on a ledger card.

The near meaninglessness of office work provides a potent motivation for clique formation, for it is in the clique that the worker secures personal response and satisfactions. It is here that he finds himself surrounded by persons who value and need him as a *man*. It is here, also, because workers come from different segments of the work structure, that work takes on some increment of meaning. The worker can, at least to some extent, see the relationship of his work to the whole.

The triple clique functions of communication, congeniality, and the provision of meaning to work thus may be seen to be entirely consistent with the special characteristics of offices—the vital work, the short line, and the elaborated division of labor. There remains the problem of a control group.

For this purpose, we may draw upon the now classic Western Electric research. It is not a perfect control, but it can serve. Roethlisberger and Dickson found that the major function of their cliques was that of enforcing restriction of output.[1] In this paper, I have nowhere referred to this phenomenon. It was indeed present, but it was *not meditated or controlled by the cliques*. This singular difference has significance.

The reason for this is that the office cliques were made up, as pointed out above, of noncompetitors. The office cliques were congenial groups, and it thus was entirely consistent that persons should be selected as cliquemates before whom one could feel at ease, before whom one could relax, and above all, before whom one felt free to communicate secret information about one's work—in other words, before noncompetitors. Note further that the fact that cliques cut across the formal structure contributed even more to the cliquing of noncompetitors. The chances are high that one's cliquemate will not only do different work from oneself and have a different supervisor, but he will probably be from another work group or even department.

Now restriction of output is, above all, a device to *control* competition. But it is obviously unnecessary to control it in cliques if the clique members do not compete with one another. And this is precisely why the office cliques were not concerned with restriction of output.

Competition among members *could not arise*. This approach also helps explain the fact that the office cliques had little of the drama of the Western Electric cliques. They were "flat" organizations. But this will inevitably be the situation if cliques do not try to control their members. The Western Electric cliques were faced with the task of controlling their members and invoking sanctions against rate busters. The "drama" of such cliques lies squarely in watching this control process in operation. In the office, the very makeup of the cliques makes such controls unnecessary. A factor in this connection is the size of office. This is not crucial but permits the analysis of the structural type under discussion.

We return to the problem posed at the start—that of generalization. One case, no matter how "normal," does not prove anything. The case, however, represented a type where the relationship of certain conditions to social organization could be studied. We conclude as follows: If workers are engaged in vital control and staff work, if they are close to decision makers, and if their work is minutely elaborated, then an informal organization of cliques composed of representatives of differential work segments will take shape. These cliques will have the functions of cross-segmental communication and the provision of personal satisfactions which operate to give meaning to work.[2]

[1] F. J. Roethlisberger and W. J. Dickson, *Management and the Worker* (Cambridge: Harvard University Press, 1948), Chap. 18.

[2] The research suggests the possible utility and fruitfulness of further typological research to test the effect of other work conditions on informal behavior.

Intergroup Relations in a Piecework Machine Shop

DONALD F. ROY

As part of a broader examination and appraisal of the application of piece-work incentive to the production line of an American factory, this paper essays the simple but largely neglected task of exploring the network of inter-group relations in which the work activity of machine operatives is imbedded. Exploration will be restricted to a limited sector of the total web of interaction in one shop; description will center upon those relationships that provide support to the operator group in its resistance to and subversion of formally instituted managerial controls on production. It is hoped that observations reported here not only will bear upon the practical problem of industrial efficiency, but will also contribute to the more general study of institutional dynamics.

This could be considered the third in a series of attempts to make more careful discriminations in an area of research that has been characteristically productive of sweeping generalizations, blanket conceptualizations, or algebraic gymnastics that tend to halt inquiry at the same time that they lay a fog over otherwise easily discerned reality. Data for all three papers were acquired in an investigation of a single work situation by a single technique of social inquiry, participant observation. The writer was employed for nearly a year as radial-drill operator in one of the machine shops of a steel-processing plant, and he kept a daily record of his observations and experiences relating to work activity and social interaction in the shop. His major interest lay in the phenomenon of restriction of output, or "systematic soldiering," the practice of which various sociological soundings have revealed in the lower depths of our industrial organization. To complete the analogy: the writer donned a diving suit and went down to see what it looked like on the bottom.

One conclusion has already been set forth,[1] namely, that the usual view of output restriction is grossly undifferentiating. Different kinds of "institutionalized underworking" were practiced, each with its characteristic pattern of antecedents and consequences. The blanket term "restriction" was found to cloak all-important contrarieties of work behavior. Machine operatives not only held back effort; sometimes they worked hard. The very common failure to note such contrarieties has tended of course to impede the progress of research by checking consideration of the specific conditions under which differences in behavior occur.

A second finding was the discovery of complexity where simple lines of relationship had generally been assumed to exist.[2] When inconsistencies in the operator's behavior seemed to contradict the hypothesis that variations in application of economic incentive could account for the variations in work effort,

---

Donald F. Roy, "Efficiency and the 'Fix': Informal Intergroup Relations in a Piecework Machine Shop," *American Journal of Sociology*, **60** (1954-55), 255-266.

[1] D. F. Roy, "Quota Restriction and Gold-bricking in a Machine Shop," *American Journal of Sociology*, **57** (March, 1952), 427-442.

[2] D. F. Roy, "Work Satisfaction and Social Reward in Quota Achievement: An Analysis of Piecework Incentive," *American Sociological Review*, **18** (October, 1953), 507-514.

a more intensive examination of response to piecework was undertaken. This disclosed that piecework incentive was not equivalent to economic incentive and that attainment of piecework "quotas" afforded machine operators a complex of rewards in which the strictly economic might or might not play a part.

The third set of observations, to be here discussed, again exhibits complication in a picture that has come to be accepted as simple in design. Here the focus of interest is the structure of "informal" intergroup connections that bear directly upon work behavior at the machine level. The material will not deny the hypothesis that the willingness of operatives to put forth effort is a function of their relationship with management or the widely held affirmation that this relationship is mediated by the organization of operatives into "informal groups." It will indicate, however, that further advances in the understanding of work behavior in the factory may involve attention to minor as well as major axes of intergroup relations. It will show that the relevant constituents of problematic production situations may include "lateral" lines of interaction between subgroups of the work force as well as "vertical" connections between managerial and worker groups.

It will be seen, in other words, that the interaction of two groups in an industrial organization takes place within and is conditioned by a larger intergroup network of reciprocal influences. Whyte has called attention to the limitations of studying groups in "isolation," without regard for the "perspectives of large institutional structures."[3]

A second warning might be: The larger institutional structures form networks of interacting groups.

As a bona fide member of an informal group of machine operatives the writer had an opportunity to observe and experience management-work group conflict in its day-to-day and blow-by-blow particulars. Also, he participated in another kind of social process, intergroup cooperation. Not only did workers on the "drill line" cooperate with each other as fellow members of a combat team at war with management; they also received considerable aid and abetment from other groups of the shop. This intergroup cooperation was particularly evident when operators were trying to "make out," or attain "quota" production, on piecework jobs.

It has been noted in another connection that machine operators characteristically evinced no reluctance to put forth effort when they felt that their group-defined piecework quotas were attainable.[4] It might seem, at first glance, that the supporting of operators during intensive application to "getting the work out" would represent cooperation *with* and not *against* management. However, the truth is that operators and their "allies" joined forces in certain situations in a manner not only unmistakably at variance with the carefully prepared designs of staff experts, but even in flagrant violation of strongly held managerial "moral principles" of shop behavior. In short, machine operators resorted to "cheating" to attain their quotas; and since this often involved the collusion of other shop groups, not as mere "accessories after the fact," but as deeply entangled accomplices, any managerial suspicion that swindling and conniving, as well as loafing, were going on all the time was well founded. If the workers' conviction

[3] W. F. Whyte, "Small Groups and Large Organizations," in *Social Psychology at the Crossroads*, J. R. Rohrer and Muzafer Sherif, eds. (New York: Harper & Row, Publishers, Inc., 1951), pp. 297-312.

[4] Roy, "Work Satisfaction," *op. cit.*

that the echelons of management were packed with men addicted to the "dirty deal" be additionally considered, it might appear that the shop was fairly overrun with crooks. Since a discussion of "contrast conceptions"[5] cannot find a place within the limited scope of this paper, it must suffice at this point merely to declare that the kind of effort made by operators and their aids to expedite production, when they did try to expedite it, was actually in many respects conflict with management.

One belief, universally accepted in the work group, may be phrased thus: "You can't 'make out' if you do things the way management wants them done." This gem of shop wisdom thus negatively put is hardly a prescription for action, but its obverse, "You've got to figure the angles," gave all hands plenty to do.

According to Al McCann (all names used are fictitious), the "Fagan" of the drill line, "They time jobs to give you just base rates. It's up to you to figure out how to fool them so you can make out. You can't make any money if you run the job the way it's timed."

We machine operators did "figure the angles"; we developed an impressive repertoire of angles to play and devoted ourselves to crossing the expectations of formal organization with perseverance, artistry, and organizing ability of our own. For instance, job timing was a "battle all the way" between operators and time-study men. The objective of the operators was good piecework prices, and that end justified any old means that would work. One cardinal principle of operator job tim-

5 See L. Copeland, "The Negro as a Contrast Conception," in *Race Relations and the Race Problem*, E. T. Thompson, ed. (Durham: Duke University Press, 1939), and S. K. Weinberg, "Aspects of the Prison's Social Structure," *American Journal of Sociology*, 47 (March, 1942), 717-726.

ing was that cutting tools be run at lower speeds and "feeds" than the maximums possible on subsequent production, and there were various ways of encouraging the institution of adequate differentials. Also, operators deemed it essential to embellish the timing performance with movements only apparently functional in relation to the production of goods: little reachings, liftings, adjustings, dustings, and other special attentions to conscientious machine operation and good housekeeping that could be dropped instanter with the departure of the time-study man.

However, the sophistication of the time-study men usually matched the strategy employed against them. The canniest operators often gave of their best in timing duels only to get "hopeless prices" for their pains:

Gus Schmidt was timed early in the evening on a job, and given a price of one dollar per one hundred for reaming one hole, chamfering both sides of three holes, and filing burrs on one end of one hole. All that for one cent!

"To hell with them," said Gus.

This is not to say that the "hopeless price" was always truly hopeless. Since the maintenance of an effective control over job timing and hence price setting was an uncertain, often disheartening matter, operators were forced to develop skills for turning bad into good. Under the shaping hands of the "angle applicators," surprising metamorphoses sometimes took place. Like the proverbial ugly duckling that finally feathered out into a beautiful swan, piecework jobs originally classified in operator vernacular as "stinkers" came to give off the delightful aroma of "gravy." Without going into the particulars of the various types of operation, one might say that jobs were "streamlined." This streamlining was of course at times "rough on the tools" and adverse in its effects on the quality of output. The jettisoning of quality called, necessarily, for a corresponding attention to ways and means of shielding supervisors and inspectors from discovering the sacrifices, and consequently brought into further play the social graces of equivocation, subterfuge, and prestidigitation.

Still, the adroitness of the machine operators, inventing, scheming, and conniving unto themselves to make quotas attainable, was not enough. Many "stinkers" would not yield before the whitest heat of intelligence or the most cavalier disregard for company property. An appreciable incidence of failure should not be surprising when it is kept in mind that the black arts of "making out" were not only responses to challenge from management, but also stimulations, in circular interaction, to the development of more effective countermagic in the timing process. It would be hard to overestimate the wizardry of the time-study men with pencil and paper in computing "angle-tight" piecework prices. During the latter months of his employment, months that marked the peak of his machine performance, the writer was able to achieve quota earnings approximately half the time that piecework jobs were offered. If this experience is roughly representative of the fortunes of the drill-line group, the battle with the stop-watch men was nip and tuck.

It is to be expected that a group of resourceful operatives, working with persistent intent to "make out" at quota levels, and relying heavily upon illegal practices, would be alert to possibilities of assistance from groups that were able and willing to give it and would not hesitate at further flouting the rules and regulations in cultivating it. It is also to be expected that the upholders of a managerial rational and moral order would attempt to prevent corruptive connections and would take action

to stamp out whatever subversive organization did develop. During the eleven-month study, machine operators, including the drill-line men, were enjoying the cooperation of several other shop groups in an illegal facilitation of the "makeout" process. This intergroup network effectively modified certain formally established shop routines, a too close attachment to which would handicap the operators. The "syndicate" also proved adequate in circumventing each of a series of "new rules" and "new systems" introduced by management to expurgate all modifications and improvisations and force a strict adherence to the rules.

The shop groups that conspired with the operators were, namely, the inspectors, the tool-crib men, the time checkers, the stockmen, and the setup men. With a single exception, these "service" groups stemmed from lines of authority distinct from the one for which the operators formed the base. The one exception was the setup group; it was subordinate to the same set of officials in the "production" line of authority that controlled the operataors. A brief description of the duties of each of these service groups and a rough tracing of the sequences of interaction involved in the prescribed work routine of the drill men will indicate the formal pattern of intergroup relations within which informally instituted variations were woven.

The Setup Men

A chief function of the setup men was to assist machine operators in the "setting up" of jigs and fixtures preparatory to operation of machines in the processing of materials. It included the giving of preliminary aid and advice at the beginning of the production process, at which time the setup men would customarily "run the first piece" to show operators how to do it and to indicate that the setup was adequate to meet work specifications. The duties of the setup men also included "troubleshooting" on occasions when operators encountered difficulties that effected a lowering of the quality of output below inspection standards or a reduction of the rate of output unsatisfactory to operators or supervisors.

The Inspectors

The chief function of the inspectors was to pass judgment on the quality of the output of the machine operators, either accepting or rejecting work turned out, according to blueprint specifications. Their appraisals came at the beginning of operations, when especially thorough examinations of the first pieces processed were made, and subsequently at varying intervals during the course of a job.

The Tool-Crib Men

The tool-crib attendants served the operators as dispensers of jigs, fixtures, cutting tools, blueprints, gauges, and miscellaneous items of equipment needed to supplement basic machinery and operator-owned hand tools in the processing of materials. They worked inside a special inclosure conveniently located along one of the main arterials of shop traffic and did most of their dispensing across the wide sill of a "window," an aperture which served, incidentally, as locus of various and sundry transactions and communications not immediately relevant to tool dispensing. There were two other openings into the crib, a door, two steps from the window, and a wide gate, further down the corridor.

The Stockmen

The stockmen were responsible for conducting a steady flow of materials to the machines for processing. Their work called for the removal of finished work as well as the moving up of fresh stock and involved a division of labor into two specializations: "stock chasing" and "trucking." The chief duties of the stock chasers were to "locate" unprocessed materials in the various storage areas, when operators called for stock, and to direct the activities of the truckers, who attended to the physical transportation.

The Time Checkers

The time checkers worked in another special inclosure, a small "time cage," from which they distributed to the operators the work orders "lined up" by the schedulemen of the planning department and within which they registered the starting and completion times of each job. There were four time-registering operations for every work order. First, upon presenting an operator with a work-order slip, the checker would "punch" him "on setup" by stamping a separate order card with a clocking mechanism that registered the hours in tenths. Later, when the operator would call at the cage window to announce completion of all preparatory arrangements for the actual processing of materials, the checker would punch him "off setup" and "on production." Finally, following another operator announcement, the checker would clock the termination of the machining process with a fourth punch. At the time of his terminal punch the operator would report the number of "pieces" completed on the job just concluded and would receive a new work order to start the cycle over again. And since the terminal punch on the completed job would be registered at the same time as the initial punch on the new one, hours on shift would be completely accounted for.

Operator Interaction with Service Groups

The machine operator's performance of each individual job or order assigned to him involved formal relationships with service groups in well-defined sequences or routines.

First, the operator would receive his work order from the time checker. Next, he would present the work order to a tool-crib attendant at the crib window as a requisite to receiving blueprints, jigs, cutting tools, and gauges. At the same time, that is, immediately before or after approaching the crib attendant, sometimes while waiting for crib service, the operator would show his work order to a stock chaser as a requisite to receiving materials to work on. The stock chaser, after perusing the order slip, occasionally with additional reference to the blueprint, would hail a trucker to bring the necessary stock to the operator's machine. If there were no delay in contacting a stock chaser or in locating and moving up the stock, a load of materials would await the operator upon his arrival at his machine with equipment from the tool crib.

Upon returning to his machine, the operator would proceed with the work of "setting up" the job, usually with the assistance of a setup man, who would stay with him until a piece was turned out whose quality of workmanship would satisfy an inspector. In appraising a finished piece, the inspector would consult the blueprint brought from the crib for work specifications and then perform operations of measurement with rules, gauges, micrometers, or more elaborate equipment. The inspector might or might not "accept" the first piece presented for his judgment. At any rate, his approval was requisite to the next step in the operator's formal interactional routine, namely, contacting the time checker to punch "off setup" and "on production."

The operator would ordinarily have further "business" contact with a setup man during the course of production. Even if the job did not "go sour" and require the services of a "troubleshooter," the setup man would drop around of his own accord to see how the work was progressing. Likewise, the operator would have further formal contact during the course of his job with inspectors and tool-crib attendants. Each inspector would make periodic "quality checks" at the machines on his "line"; and the operator might have to make trips to the tool crib to get tools ground or to pick up additional tools or gauges. He might also have to contact a stock chaser or truckers for additional materials.

Upon completion of the last piece of his order the operator would tear down his setup, return his tools to the tool crib, and make a final report to the time checker. Should the job be uncompleted at the close of a shift, the operator would merely report the number of pieces finished to a checker, and the latter would register a final punchout. The setup would be left intact for the use of the operator coming in to work the next shift.

Major Job Categories

Certain variations in types of jobs assigned to operators are pertinent to a discussion of intergroup collusion to modify formal work routines. These variations could be classified into four categories: (1) piecework, (2) time study, (3) rework, and (4) setup.

Each piecework job carried a price per one hundred pieces, determined by the timing operations mentioned earlier. Time-study and rework jobs carried no prices. The time-study category included new jobs that had not yet been timed and jobs that had once carried a piecework price. As the label indicates, rework jobs involved the refinishing of pieces rejected either by inspectors or in the assembly process but considered salvageable by reprocessing.

Since time-study and rework jobs carried no piecework prices, operators engaged in these two types of work were paid "day rate," that is, according to an hourly base rate determined in collective bargaining. The base rates represented minimal wage guarantees that not only applied to "day work," but also covered piecework as well. If an operator on piecework failed to exceed his base rate in average hourly earnings on a particular job on a particular day, he would be paid his base rate. Failure to produce at base rate or above on the first day of a piecework job did not penalize an operator in his efforts to earn premium pay on the second day; nor did failure to attain base rate on one piecework job on a given day reduce premiums earned on a second job performed that day.

Not a fourth type of job, but measured separately in time and payment units, were the setup operations. Piecework jobs always carried piecework setups; failure to equal or exceed base rate on setup did not jeopardize chances to earn premium on "production," and vice versa. Time-study jobs frequently carried piecework setups; rework never.

Obviously, these formal work routines may easily be modified to fit the perceived needs of machine operators. Possibilities for the development of "makeout angles" should be immediately apparent in a work situation characterized by job repertoires that included piecework and day-work operations, minimum wage guarantees uniform for all work done, and separate payment computations by jobs and days worked. If, for instance, time formally clocked as day work could be used to gain a "head start" on subsequent piecework operations, such a transferral

might mean the difference between earning and not earning premiums on doubtful piecework jobs. Similarly, time on "hopeless" piecework jobs might be applied to more promising operations; and the otherwise "free time" gained on "gravy" jobs might be consumed in productive anticipation of the formal receipt of ordinarily unrewarding piecework. Especially lush "gravy" jobs might even contribute extra time enough to convert "stinkers" into temporary "money makers." Realization of such possibilities in any given case would necessarily involve obtaining, without a work order, the following: (1) identification of future operations as listed in sequence on the schedule board inside the time cage; (2) jigs, blueprints, and cutting tools appropriate to the work contemplated; (3) stock to work on; (4) setup help and advice; (5) inspection service; and (6) "troubleshooting" assistance as needed. Obviously, this sequence of accomplishments would call for the support of one or more service groups at each step. That the required assistance was actually provided with such regularity that it came to be taken for granted the writer discovered by observation and personal experience.

The following diary recording of interaction between the writer and a time checker may be indicative of the extent to which service-group collaboration with the operators in perverting the formal system of work routine had become systematized:

When I came to punch off the rework, the time-cage girl said, "You don't want to punch off rework yet, do you?"—suggesting that I should get a start on the next job before punching off rework.

Even line foremen, who, in regard to intergroup collusion preferred the role of silent "accessory after the fact," became upset to the point of actual attempted interference with formal rules and regulations when the naïve neophyte failed to meet the expectations of his own informal system.

Art [foreman] was at the time cage when I punched off the day work of re-reaming and on to the piecework of drilling. He came around to my machine shortly after.

"Say," he said, "when you punch off day work onto piecework, you ought to have your piecework already started. Run a few; then punch off the day work, and you'll have a good start. You've got to chisel a little around here to make money."

Acceptance of such subversive practices did not extend, however, to groups in management other than local shop supervision. The writer was solemnly and repeatedly warned that time-study men, the true hatchet men of upper management, were disposed to bring chiselers to speedy justice.

Gus went on to say that a girl hand-mill operator had been fired a year ago when a time-study man caught her running one job while being punched in on another. The time-study man came over to the girl's machine to time a job, to find the job completed and the girl running another.

New Rules and New Systems

During the near-year that he spent in the shop the writer felt the impact of several attempts to stamp out intergroup irregularities and enforce conformity to managerial designs of procedure. He coincidentally participated in an upholding of the maxim: *"Plus ça change, plus c'est la même chose."*

Attempts to tighten controls came into a series of "new rules" or "new systems" promulgated by bulletin-board edicts. How far the beginning of the series antedated the writer's arrival is not known. Old-timers spoke of a "Golden Age" enjoyed before the installation of the "Booth System" of production control; then operators "kept their own time," turning in their work orders as they saw fit and building "kitties" on good jobs to tide them over rainy days on poor jobs.

The first new rule during this study went into "effect" less than two months after the writer was hired. It was designed to tighten controls in the tool-crib sector, where attendants had not only been passing out setups ahead of time, but allowing operators or their setup men to enter the toolroom to make the advance pickups themselves. An aim of the new rule was also to curb the operators' practice of keeping "main setups" at the machines instead of turning them in at the completion of operations.

A new crib ruling went into effect today. A memorandum by Bricker [superintendent] was posted on the side of the crib window. Those who check out tools and jigs must sign a slip in triplicate, keeping the pink one and turning it in with the tools in exchange for the white original, which would constitute proof that the tools had been returned. No new setups would be issued until the old ones had been turned in.

An optimistic perception of the new procedures was expressed by young Jonesy, a tool-crib attendant and otherwise willing conniver with the operators: "Tools are scattered all over the shop. This way we'll have them all in order in the crib, and the fellows can get them anytime they need them."

But multiple-drill operator Hanks, old-timer on the line, drew upon his lengthy experience with managerial efficiency measures and saw the situation differently:

Hanks commented unfavorably on the new ruling. He and the day man [his machine partner on the other shift] had been keeping the tools for their main setups at their bench, or, rather, under it. This practice, according to Hanks, was to insure their setting up promptly without inordinate waste of time and to insure their having all the tools needed. Hanks said that on a previous occasion he was told to turn in one of his main setups, which included over a dozen drills, reamers, taps, and so forth, of varying sizes. He did so, but, when he needed this setup again, the crib man couldn't locate all the tools. He asked Hanks to come back in the crib and help him find them. Hanks refused. After several hours of futile search, Hanks was finally induced to "come back and find his tools." He did so on condition that it would not be on his own time. The foreman agreed to this.

"The same thing is going to happen again," predicted Hanks. "And I'm not going back there to find my tools they scatter all over, on my own time."

Though the operators went through the formality of an exchange of slips when they exchanged setups, the new procedures did not modify the practice of getting setups from the crib ahead of time. Appreciable effects of the new ruling included making more paperwork for crib attendants at the same time that more work at assembling setups was thrust upon them. Jonesy's happy prediction did not materialize: the tools were not "always in order." Subsequent events confirmed Hanks's gloomy forebodings:

It took Paul [setup man] and me several hours to get set up for the sockets, as the setup given was incomplete.

Some time was spent in looking for an angle plate that was specially made for the job. Both Paul and Steve [superintendent] were irritated because the crib men could not find the plate.

We spent an hour setting up because we could not find the jig.

Included in the new ruling was a stipulation that blueprints and gauges be turned in by the operators at the end of each shift, though setup paraphernalia other than prints and gauges were to be left at the machines as long as jobs were in operation. Calling for prints and guages at the beginning of the shift, waiting at the crib window in the line that naturally formed, even when these items were "located" immediately, consumed operator time.

Owing to the new crib ruling, he [Joe Mucha, the writer's machine partner on another shift] turned in the tap gauge. I spent twenty minutes trying to get it back again. The crib man could not find it and claimed that Joe had not turned it in. Joe stayed after 3:00 to help me get it, countering the arguments of the crib with the slip that he retained as evidence. Finally the gauge was located in the crib.

I started out a half-hour late on operation 55 on the pedestals, due to delay at the crib waiting to check out the print and gauge that Joe had just turned in.

Four months later the new crib ruling was modified by another that canceled the stipulation regarding the turning in of blueprints and gauges and called for changes in the paperwork of operator-crib attendant relations. These changes were featured by a new kind of work order, duplicates of which became involved in tool-crib bookkeeping. The change reduced the waste of operator time at the start of shifts, but to the burden of the crib attendants paperwork irritations were now added.

When I punched in on the rework and asked Walt [crib attendant] for a print, he fumed a bit as he sought a duplicate of my new-type yellow work order in a new file of his.

"I haven't been able to find more than one in five duplicates so far," he said. "And there's supposed to be a duplicate for every one."

Walt said tonight, when I presented him with a work order card for tools, "That makes the twelfth card I've had and no duplicate!"

The tool crib under the new system is supposed to have duplicate work orders in their file of all jobs given operators. These duplicates are to be put in the toolroom files as soon as they are put on the board; and the operators are to sign these duplicates when checking out setups.

The "new system" did operate to handicap operators in that they were not to receive new setups from the crib until they received the new yellow work orders from the time cage to check with the duplicates in the crib. However, setup men roamed at will in the toolroom, grinding tools and fixing jigs, and were able to help the operators by picking up setups ahead of time for them. Their detailed knowledge of the various setups made it possible for them to assemble the necessary tools without the use of setup cards.

"This is a good job," I said to McCann [now setup man]. "I wish I could get it set up ahead of time, but I guess it's no use trying. I can't get the setup now from the toolroom until I get the new work order from the time girls."

McCann thought a moment. "Maybe I can get the jig and tools out of the crib for you."

McCann did get the jig and tools, and I got a half-hour's head start on the job.

The writer had found Ted, a stock chaser, and his truckers, George and Louie, willing connivers in the time-chiseling process. They moved up stock ahead of time, even after the new system made presentation of the new work order to the stock chaser a prerequisite to getting stock. Contrary to first impressions, for all practical purposes the situation was unchanged under the new system.

I could not go ahead with the next order, also a load of connecting rods, because the new ruling makes presentation of a work order to the stock chaser necessary before materials can be moved up. So

I was stymied and could do nothing the rest of the day.

About an hour before I was to punch off the connecting rods, I advised Ted that I would soon be needing another job. He immediately brought over a load of reservoir casings.

The new system also included complication of operator-inspector relations. Inspectors were now to "sign off" operators from completed jobs before new work orders could be issued at the time booth. The "signing-off" process included notation by the inspector of the time of operation completion, a double check on the time checker's "punch out." This added of course to the paperwork of inspectors.

Drill-man Hanks's first response to this feature of the new system was "individualistic":

Hanks commented on the new system tonight. He thinks that its chief purpose is to keep the operators from getting ahead on an operation and starting the next job on saved time. He said that the inspector checked him off a job tonight at 4:40, and he was not due to punch in on the next one until 6:10. He changed the time recorded by the inspector on his work slip to 6:10 and went ahead as usual. If he had not done so, there would have been a "gap" of an hour and a half unaccounted for in the records.

The writer found himself "stymied" at first but soon discovered that the new obstacle could be overcome without engaging in such a hazardous practice as "forging."

It was 10:00 when we were ready to punch off setup, and Johnny [setup man] asked Sam [inspector] to sign me off setup earlier, so that I could make out on setup.

"Punch me off at 9:00," I said, not expecting Sam to check me off earlier, and purposely exaggerating Johnny's request.

Sam refused. "I can't do that! If I do that for you, I'll have to do it for everybody!"

Sam seemed somewhat agitated in making the refusal.

A few minutes later he said to Johnny, "Why did you ask me to do that when Hanks was standing there?"

Hanks had been standing by my machine, watching us set up.

"I can't take you off an hour back. Go find out when you punched in on this job in the first place."

Johnny consulted the time-cage girl as to the time I punched on the job, later talked to Sam at Sam's bench while I was working, and came to me with the announcement that it was "fixed up" so that I made out on setup and was credited with starting production at 9:30. This gave me an hour and a half of "gravy."

By the time the "new system" was a month old, Sam was not only doing this for everybody but actually taking the initiative:

When I punched off setup for the eight pieces, Sam asked me if I wanted him to take me off setup at an earlier time in order that I might make out on the setup. I refused this offer, as it wasn't worth the trouble for me to stop to figure out the time.

Instead of looking at the clock when an operator asks to be taken off setup, Sam usually asks the operator, "When do you want to be taken off?"

No sooner had the shop employees adjusted to this "new system" and settled down to normal informal routine than they were shocked by a new pronunciamento that barred admittance to the toolroom to all save superintendents and toolroom employees:

A new crib ruling struck without warning today. Typewritten bulletins signed by Faulkner [shop manager] were posted on the toolroom door, barring admittance to all save the toolroom employees and the two departmental foremen [superintendents], Bricker and Steve. Other foremen and setup men are not to be admitted without permission from Milton, toolroom supervisor.

Hanks predicts that the new ruling won't last out the week.

Stimulated by Hanks's prediction, the writer kept an eye on the toolroom door. The rule seemed to be enforced.

On one occasion tonight Paul [setup man] asked Jonesy to let him into the crib; he was in a hurry about something. But Jonesy shook his head, and Paul had to wait at the crib window with the rest of us.

Johnny, the setup man, predicted that the new ruling would be "tough on" the tool-crib employees, not on setup men.

Johnny says that the new rule is going to be tough on grinders and crib attendants, because setup men and foremen have been doing much of the grinding and have made it easier for them by coming in to help themselves to tools, jigs, and so on.

Johnny says that the new rule suits him fine. Now he can just stand at the window and holler and let the toolroom employees do the work.

The line foremen seemed to take offense at the new "exclusion act" and threatened reprisals to the crib attendants.

At quitting time I noticed Gil [line foreman] talking to Walt at the crib window. Gil seemed very serious; Walt was waving his arms and otherwise gesturing in a manner indicating rejection of responsibility. I didn't catch any words but gathered that Gil was voicing disapproval or warning, and after Gil left I said to Walt, "Looks like you're behind the eightball now!"

I noticed that Walt's hair was mussed, and he looked a little wild. He denied that he was in any trouble whatsoever; nor was he worried about anything whatsoever.

"I'm just working here!" he exclaimed. "I just go by the cards, and beyond that I've got no responsibility!"

I was curious as to what Gil had told him and asked Johnny later, on the way home. I had noticed that Johnny was standing nearby when Gil was talking to Walt. Johnny said that Gil was telling Walt that from now on the crib was going to be charged with every minute of tool delay to the operators—that if there was any waiting for tools, Gil was going to make out allowance cards charging these delays to the crib.

Contrary to Hanks's prediction, the new rule did "last out the week," and crowds milled around the crib window.

The boys seemed very much disgusted with the slow service at the tool crib. They crowd around the window (always a crowd there) and either growl or wisecrack about the service.

It was at this time that Jonesy, erstwhile optimist and regarded by shop employees as the most efficient of the crib attendants, decided that he had "had enough." He transfered to the quiet backroom retreat of tool grinding. But several days later, just ten days since the new rule was promulgated, the sun began to break through the dark clouds of managerial efficiency. Hanks's prediction was off by four days.

While I was waiting for tools at the crib window tonight, I noticed the jockey [turret-lathe man] dash into the tool crib through a door that was left ajar; he was followed soon after by Gil. Later, when the door was closed, Paul shook it and shouted to the attendant, "Let me in!" He was admitted.

Steve [superintendent] called out, "Hey!" when he saw the jockey go into the crib. When the jockey came out, he spoke to him, and the jockey joshed him back. Steve did not seem to be particularly put out about it.

Soon the boys were going in and out of the crib again, almost at will, and setup men were getting setups ahead of time for operators, ignored by the crib attendants.

I noticed that Johnny and others seemed to be going in and out of the crib again, almost at will.

I noticed tonight that Johnny got into the tool crib by appearing at the door and saying to the attendant, "Let me in!"

So much for Faulkner's order—until he makes a new one!

When I asked Walt for some jaws to fit the chuck I had found, he said, "We've got lots of jaws back here, but I wouldn't know what to look for. You'd better get the setup man to come back here and find you some."

Walt said to me, "I break the rules here, but not too much—just within reason to keep the boys on production."

Faulkner's order still hangs at eye level on the crib door.

"So much for Faulkner's order!" The "fix" was "on" again, and operators and their service-group allies conducted business as usual for the remaining weeks of the writer's employment.

Conclusion

This rough sketch of the operation of one shop "syndicate" has been no more than indicative of the existence of intergroup cooperation in the lower reaches of factory social structure. No attempt has been made here to account for the aid extended by service groups, though suggestion that this assistance might be part of a larger system of reciprocal obligations has been implicit. It is apparent, for instance, that tool-crib attendants benefited from their practice of admitting operators and setup men to the toolroom to seek and pick up equipment.

A more complete picture of intergroup relations would include conflict, as well as cooperation, between operators and the various service groups. It could be shown, if space permitted, that changes in relationship accompanied, in cyclical fashion, changes in basic conditions of work.

Furthermore, attention has not been drawn to intragroup role and personality variations in intergroup relations. Such additional discriminations and the questions that they might raise in regard to the study of institutional dynamics must be left for future discussion.

As for their possible bearing on practical industrial administration, materials presented here seem to challenge the view held in some research circles that the "human" problem of industrial efficiency lies in faulty communication between an economically "rational" or "logical" management and "nonrational" or "nonlogical" work groups. While nothing has been offered to deny linkage between communication and efficiency, observations reported here suggest examination of the stereotypes of the two parties. And questioning the fitness of the stereotypes may lead to a more fruitful conceptualization of the process that is reputedly in need of attention: communication.

Do we see, in the situation studied, an economically "rational" management and an economically "nonrational" work group? Would not a reversal of the labels, if such labels be used, find justification? Docs it not appear that operatives and their allies resisted managerial "logics of efficiency" because application of those "logics" tended to produce something considerably less than "efficiency"? Did not worker groups connive to circumvent managerial ukase in order to "get the work out"? Did not Walt, for instance, break the rules "to keep the boys on production"? May not the common query of industrial workers, "What in the hell are they trying to do up there?" be not merely reflective of faulty communication, but also based on real managerial inadequacy, quite apart from a failure in "explanation"? May

it not be assumed that managerial inefficiency is and has been for some time a serious problem to those who labor?

If managerial directives are not the guides to efficient action that they are claimed to be, then perhaps "logics of efficiency" would be better designated as "sentiments of efficiency." When failure to "explain" is additionally considered, perhaps bulletin-board pronunciamentos might properly be classified with the various exorcisms, conjurations, and miscellaneous esoteric monkey business of our primitive contemporaries.

If we conceive of "logical" behavior not as self-contained ratiocinative exercises but as intellectual operations in continuous reciprocal interplay with concrete experience, machine operators and their service-group allies would appear the real holders of "logics of efficiency." Like big-city machine politicians, they develop plans for action that, under given conditions of situational pressures, "work."

But this rejection of commonly held stereotypes cannot lead to mere reversal of invidious distinctions; the situation is far too complex for that. The group life that the writer shared was by no means devoid of "sentiments." To the contrary, operator interaction was rich in shared feelings, attitudes, and practices not only of doubtful bearing on getting the work out but often undeniably preventing production maximization. Nor can it be maintained that management, in applying its "sentiments of efficiency," was always ineffective. Perhaps solution to the human problem of industrial efficiency would best be expedited by abandoning altogether the use of contrasted caricatures handed down to us from a preindustrial social class structure. Instead of concerning ourselves with such blind-alley issues as who is "rational" and who is not, we might recognize with

John Dewey that both intellectual and emotional activity are essentials of goal-directed behavior[6] and that the development of effective communication focusing on production goals is a matter of instituting interactional processes that engender ideas, sentiments, and plans for action held in common.

[6] *Art as Experience* (New York: G. P. Putnam's Sons, Inc., 1934), p. 55.

Racial Groups in Industry

EVERETT C. HUGHES

Elton Mayo has . . . given the name "rabble hypothesis"[1] to the assumptions which, he claims, still guide not merely many managements in dealing with workers, but also many of those who investigate industrial behavior. He refers to the belief that an industrial organization is an aggregation of individuals each seeking his own gain without reference to other persons, and consequently each capable of being induced to greater effort by devices focused upon this desire for advantage. To this assumption Mayo opposes the view that a working force normally consists of social groups, whose members are highly responsive to each other's social gestures and identify their fates with those of their fellows; social groups which, further, are related to others in the larger system of social relations in and about industry. Mayo argues that a state of good cooperation is dependent upon the existence of such groups, even though one of their functions may be some restriction of individual production. He believes, finally, that the "solitary," the person who does not feel himself part of any such group, is actually somewhat disorgan-

Everett C. Hughes, "The Knitting of Racial Groups in Industry," *American Sociological Review,* **11** (1946), 512-519.

[1] *The Social Problems of an Industrial Civilization* (Boston, 1945), Chap. 2, *et passim.*

ized, and not likely to function well in the long run.

The theme of my remarks is that a fruitful way of analyzing race relations in industry is to look at them against whatever grid of informal social groupings and of relations within and between such groups exists in the industries, departments, and jobs in which Negroes or other new kinds of employees are put to work. Recent experience suggests that this grid of relationships and the manner in which Negroes are introduced into it are more significant in the success of a policy of hiring Negroes than are the generalized racial attitudes of the white workers concerned.

Polling of white workers to find whether they favor the hiring of Negroes as their equal and close fellow workers would almost anywhere result in an emphatic "no." Workers generally prefer not to have any new kinds of workers introduced among and equal to themselves. But Negroes have been successfully employed among white workers; and many other new kinds of workers have been introduced among older kinds of workers who were not enthusiastic about them. Polling of attitudes, on this simple basis, gives little clue to the probable behavior of the old workers to the new. The simple "no" of the workers to many proposals of management is not to be taken at face value, for industry has not been run by majority vote of the workers, and a "no" is often no more than a demonstration of protest. In fact, workers more or less expect each other to object to changes proposed by management.

It does not follow that racial preferences and dislikes have no bearing on the question whether the races will work well together. Racial attitudes themselves take on new dimensions when looked at in the framework of the human relations prevailing in industry. It is characteristic of industry that groups of workers who have knit themselves into some kind of organization in and about their work develop some set of expectations, considered little short of rights, that their jobs and their work fellowship should be limited to persons of some certain kind —as to age, sex, race, ethnic qualities, education, and social class. . . . Orvis Collins[2] . . . shows how the management of a New England factory got itself into an impasse by violating the expectation that certain kinds of jobs should belong to Irishmen. We could do with a good deal more investigation of what workers in various jobs and industries consider the proper kind of fellow worker, what they think are their own rights in the matter, and of the devices which they use to expel newcomers not of the kind they want and of those which management and unions have used to get the newcomers accepted. Such expectations are not likely to be stated formally; they may not even be admitted informally. Defense of the breach of them is likely, as in the case reported by . . . Collins, to be hidden by indirection of various kinds. It is also probable that some of the so-called noneconomic behavior attributed to people new to industry— erratic changing of jobs, failure to re-

spond to wage incentives, quitting industrial work entirely and returning home to farms—may be due not merely to unfamiliarity with the ways of industry. It may be a reaction to rejection by those among whom they have been put to work.

I used the expression "grid of informal relations." By this I mean simply the pattern of grouping which prevails in a place of work. The factory cafeteria, shown in Fig. 1, exhibits such a grid; this is the pattern which renews itself every day at noon, when there are the most and the greatest variety of people there. The employees sort themselves according to their rank, sex, and race, and to their places in the office or out in the plant. The observers found also that while it was seldom possible for all of the workers who belonged to a given close circle to come to the cafeteria and find places at the same table, they did—so far as possible—eat together.

The individual thus finds his table in a grid of rank, sex, race, and personal relations. At a union picnic the unit of the pattern was the table, each serving as headquarters for one or two family parties. The management families were in one corner of the grounds; the mass of the Negro families were concentrated toward the opposite corner. In the middle zone were some tables at which a Negro family party and a white family party sat, but so grouped that Negro faced Negro and white faced white. Near the platform used for announcements, dancing, and contests were the only tables with racially mixed parties. These were the union leaders in charge of the picnic. Thus in this grid, the family—which is by American definition not racially mixed—and rank within the factory worked together to form a pattern, which the union slightly disturbed by drawing a few people away from the family and away from factory rank to

[2] Orvis Collins, "Ethnic Behavior in Industry," *American Journal of Sociology*, **51** (January, 1946), 293-298.

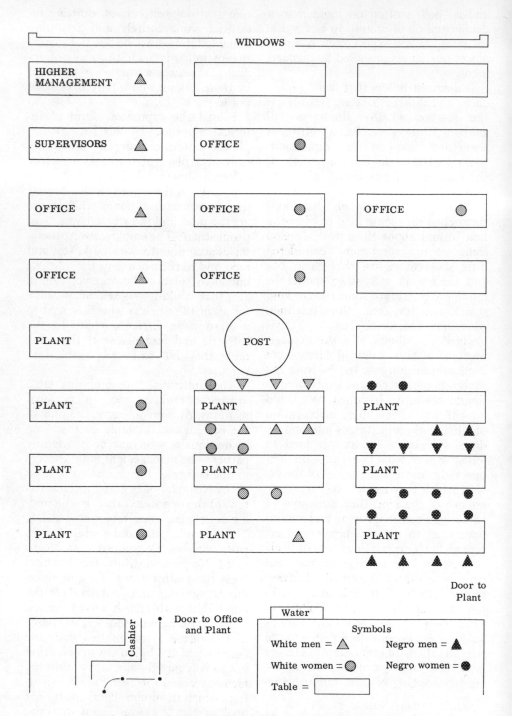

FIG. 1. Seating by Rank, Sex, and Race in a Factory Cafeteria

form a small nucleus based on special function.

I mention these examples first, not because of the inherent significance of seating arrangements in cafeterias and at picnics, but because they illustrate so vividly what I mean by a grid of relationships. Incidentally, in both cases the Negroes—with the exception of the few union committeemen at the picnic —fitted into that space in the pattern whose occupants were most numerous and of the lowest rank. None of them had characteristics which would set up any expectation that they might fit anywhere else.

On the job itself, the patterns of relationship are subject in varying measure to the physical layout of the shop, the distribution of workers of different races among the various kinds of jobs, by the degree of dependence of one worker upon others for successful performance of his work, as well as by the social atmosphere created by management, supervision, the union, and the workers themselves. Furthermore, the informal relations among workers are not always so immediately visible as in the cafeteria and at the picnic. But generally such relations are there, although not all workers are part of any network of groups of people who cooperate in some special way to control what goes on with reference to work or other matters.

The Fixing Room

A department called the fixing room in a certain plant illustrates one kind of grid or grouping at work and its consequences for race relations. The work is done by teams of three men. The members of a team meet and exchange tools and materials without a word and without even a direct look at each other. In fact, there is something of a cult of silence among them. The bonus, which is a large part of their income, is based upon the product of a team. The skills are learned on the job from the other members of the team to which one is assigned. The men are nearly all Poles, past middle age, bound together by kinship and neighborhood. The teams and the whole group together are notoriously and successfully impervious to management's attempts to control their relations, and even the choice of new employees. They pick their own fellows. The labor shortage of the war dried up the sources of new men of their kind, and management tried to get new help—Negroes. Several Negro men were hired, but all left after a few days. Interviews with these Negro men revealed that they were subjected to a not very subtle, but very effective torture by the other members of the teams to which they were assigned. Later, the management tried the device of hiring a whole Negro team, which complicated the matter of learning the job; they stayed for some time, achieved a very creditable rate of production, and . . . quit in a group. We have not yet found out what happened, but I venture to say that it was fundamentally a case of rejection by the older

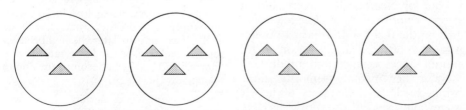

FIG. 2. Fixing Room (Each circle is a closed work team of three men.)

workers. In this shop there is no place for the solitary individual. One must be integrated into a team clique to work at all. The homogeneity and traditional solidarity and autonomy of the whole department conspired to make the men unwilling to accept new kinds of workers and make management impotent to bring about change against their will.

The power of resistance was probably increased by connivance of the foremen. Many of the foremen in this plant are old-timers, who worked for the father of the present manager. They have a sort of proprietary interest in the departments they supervise; their idiosyncrasies are rather affectionately tolerated. The foremen can thus be, in effect, leaders of departmental cliques. A change of policy thus meets a very dense and intricate resisting structure. In their efforts to hire Negroes in the fixing room, management did not succeed in penetrating it.

The Polishing Room

The polishing room in another plant shows another type of both formal and informal organization operating in relation to race. In this room, each girl works independently on a machine like all the others. At intervals, all workers are moved along to the next machine. No one has a vested interest in a machine. By dint of good production and long service workers hope to get on the day shift. Many of the white girls of longer service have gravitated to this shift; it is about two thirds white, in fact. The swing shift has a larger proportion of Negroes; the night shift, a strong majority of them. The few white girls on the night shift appear to prefer it because of some family reason. A girl cannot by especially high production increase her income; seniority alone brings small fixed increases of hourly wage; long service also brings certain benefits and an annual bonus. Some-

thing is made of the principle that only those who have good production records will be kept on when and if layoffs become necessary. There is thus very little in the situation and in the policies of management to induce either a strong individualism or a close grouping of the employees. One would expect it to be a situation into which Negro help could be fairly easily introduced, and so it has been. But there is, nevertheless, an informal organization of workers. To quote from the report of the observers:[3]

An analysis of clique formation and membership provides some clearer insights into such acceptance as the Negro has achieved and into the attitudes and expectation of Negro workers in the plant. There are several recognizable cliques in the polishing room; their functions are well defined by their members. The clique is concerned with production and procedure, and with the status and behavior of the individual workers.

The cliques in this room are not mutually exclusive and sharply defined. There is a central group, the "old girls," made up of young women of from twenty-two to thirty-three years of age and of an average length of service of about five years. The "old girls" eat in the cafeteria; each usually manages to eat with at least one or two of her clique fellows. Another group, also of long service, bring their lunches and eat in the lounge. But there is little association between them and the "old girls'" clique. There are a number of smaller satellite cliques, each attached by at least one common member to the "old girls." It appears likely that a new girl may be sponsored into the organization through the satellite cliques. We observed one girl who was, when first interviewed, unfriendly toward other workers, a "lone wolf." Two months later she had been accepted, had ceased to be a rate-busting "horse," and had even become much more tolerant to the Negro girls.

[3] To preserve the anonymity of the plant, I must leave out the names of the observers. My apologies to them.

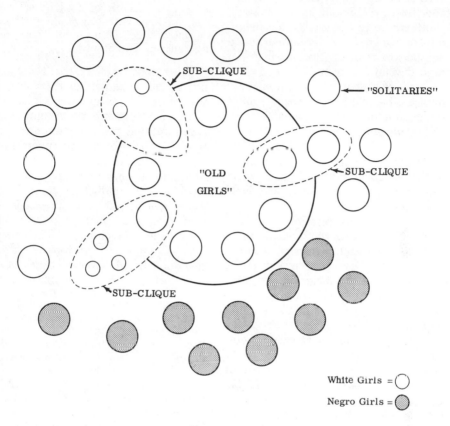

Figure content labels:
SUB-CLIQUE
"SOLITARIES"
"OLD GIRLS"
SUB-CLIQUE
SUB-CLIQUE
White Girls =
Negro Girls =

FIG. 3. Polishing Room

The clique organization of the polishing room may be shown as in Fig 3.

The girls in the central clique and those oriented toward them seem to be of such skill that they are without anxiety about being able to keep up to or even to surpass the usual rate; they maintain good levels of production, but make statements which make it clear that one of the functions of the group is control of the average rate of production.

White workers have defined a "good day's work" as falling within the limits of one hundred and 106. Many say that it would be easy to produce more. The girls who say this claim to be fast workers; they explain their failure to produce more by a well-developed rationale: to do more would be to ruin the job for the diligent, but slower, workers. But "rate breaking" is condoned for a day or so for a worker who has fallen behind and wants to bring her average up to par. Apparently a girl who is socially well established in the group can consistently break the rate a little with only mild teasing as punishment. But outsiders who break the rate are severely punished by ridicule and scorn; if they persist, they remain outsiders and, if associations are important to them, they may be forced off the job. Here is an apparent paradox: Admittance to the group may be secured only by adherence to the established definitions of the group, while unquestioned membership carries the privilege of some deviant behavior.

This is of course not a paradox at all; for it is characteristic of social groups to demand of the newcomer a strict conformity which will show that he accepts the authority of the group; then, as the individual approaches the center of the group and becomes an established member, they allow him a little more leeway.

Outside the organization are some white women and all the Negro women. The white women outsiders are a varied lot. Some are older women who must, or think they must, struggle to produce enough to keep their jobs. Some of them say that they are no longer young enough to be able to play. Others show in one way or another that some outside concern is so important as to make them defy or ignore the opinions of their fellow workers. Some are probably not acceptable for one reason or another—perhaps dress, personal hygiene, or general queerness.

But no Negro girl, no matter what her length of service, her production rate, or her personality, has found a place in the system of cliques of the white girls. The observers report that among the girls in the cliques:

It is generally understood that Negro workers are to be accorded tolerance and a measure of friendliness. There is ample evidence that there was opposition at first to the hiring of Negroes. In the two years that have elapsed a studied, but tentative acceptance has occurred. Negro and white workers meet each other with good will and friendliness on the job. They carry on conversations at their machines. But this friendliness does not extend beyond the work situation, and it varies in degree within the lesser cliques. White and Negro workers do not eat together except occasionally by accident. Not in any case is a Negro a member of a clique of white girls, and apparently conversation between the races seldom touches problems that are mutually important.

This means, in effect, that the Negro girls do not take part in the conversation of social gestures by which the rules and sentiments of the group are communicated to the newcomer, and by which she is offered membership in the clique as a reward for accepting its discipline. Insofar as white girls complain of the conduct of their Negro fellow workers, it is in precisely the terms they use about white girls who are not in the cliques. "The Negro girls," they say, "are all for themselves; they don't try to help each other." One white girl summed up the matter thus:

"Some colored girls . . . don't care what the next person does. They're that way about everything. If one of them makes 110 (a very high production), the rest of them don't care. Now when a white girl makes that much, we make her slow down because we know how hard it is for some of 'em to make the average."
Interviewer: "Why do you think the Negro girls don't try to pull their rates down?"
"Well, they're just like that about everything. They don't even try to help each other."
Interviewer: "What do you mean?"
"They don't get into a group. They just mingle with everybody. I don't think the colored girls have any little groups like we have. . . ."
Interviewer: "How do you account for that?"
"It's 'cause they're all for themselves. Now you take the white girls; the younger ones will mix with the older girls and they find out what they are supposed to do."

The same worker said of a new white girl: "She won't keep no high average. She's mingling more with the other girls now." Thus she implicitly recognized mingling with other girls and sensitivity to their opinions as a desirable, steadying experience. She apparently did not see that the very reason for the Negro girl's undesirable production habits is probably that she is excluded from the rewards of group membership. In effect, she is complaining that the Negro girls do not form their own cliques.

That the Negro girls have not developed an organization in this case is borne out by the observers. We do not know why this is so. But certain considerations concerning the probable reasons bear directly on the points thus far made and on the final one which I have to make.

Some of the white girls are, to use Mayo's expression, "solitaries." Most of the Negro girls are so. The records of production seem to indicate this, as well as their other actions and talk. A few Negro girls have very high rates, and indulge in racing with other workers. Some are erratic in production. Others anxiously struggle to get their rates up to the point where they can feel secure against being the first to be laid off. There is evidence that they think that they are on trial. This is highly individualistic behavior; it is also typically anxious behavior.

We may ask, although we cannot answer with much assurance, why the Negro girls in this room are so unorganized. First, they are not in the white clique organization because they are not given the chance to be in it. Then why do they not form an organization of their own? Perhaps because they are new, relatively speaking. Perhaps because on the day shift, where the main white clique developed, they—the Negro girls—are in the minority and would hesitate to form what would be considered a rival group. Perhaps it is that there are no Negro girls who feel secure enough in their positions to form a

disciplining group which would, as part of its discipline, control production. In this particular plant the management has undoubtedly made a strong attempt to reduce discrimination. Now the way they have done it is to emphasize that the Negro girl will be hired, kept, and promoted strictly according to her individual merits.

This is a point on which we may make some tentative generalizations. This very emphasis on treating the individual on his merits can become a source of overindividualistic anxiety. For the statement "you will be judged on your own merits" repeated too often becomes a dinning into one's ears of the thought "you are on trial. I doubt whether you can make it, but if you do I will give you credit. Most people of your kind can't make it. I shall be astonished if you do. If you do, you will certainly be an exception. You've got to show me." This bit of imagined talk is, in fact, not far from what foremen do say to Negro workers in many plants. It contains an invitation, almost a threatening command, to the Negro worker to be a "solitary."

Now this might not work with Negroes of the least ambitious class or those working at traditional Negro jobs. But in the polishing room the Negro girls show potential or actual middle-class behavior and sentiments, as do also most of the white girls; nor are they employed at "Negro jobs." And this brings us to our general point. The individualistic or "rabble" hypothesis of industrial management—that each worker is an individual who may be induced, and who ought to be able to be induced to work for his own ends without regard to his fellows—is almost unconsciously applied with redoubled force to the Negro worker. The behavior it encourages is, in its essence, the behavior of the ambitious person. The ambitious white worker may dissociate himself from his fellows to some extent, and in spite of being somewhat disliked he may get promotions for it. The Negro worker apparently feels and is made to feel in some situations that he has to dissociate himself from others and be a "solitary" in order merely to keep his job. I do not think the polishing room is a situation in which this is unusually so. But the combination of individually separate work, with the particular pattern of white informal organization from which Negroes are excluded, and a management policy which gives the Negro girls definite hope that they can gain security by individual effort—and in no other way —might be expected to keep them a somewhat anxious series of solitaries rather than a stable, organized group.

The fixing room illustrates the problem which arises in a shop where the informal organization consists of a series of closely related tight teams into which the individual worker—white or Negro—must fit in order to work at all. The polishing room has an open formal structure, easy for the individual to enter, and a moderately open, but nevertheless powerful, informal structure of cliques. But it is not quite open to Negroes, and the results are as have been reported.

These two cases are, however, alike in that no attempt has been made to modify the informal organization so as to relate Negroes to it. In the fixing room, after a first attempt to put Negroes into existing teams failed, management attempted to set up Negro teams, but without trying to define their relations to existing teams. In the polishing room, management tried to create general tolerance. In other cases, a union or management has made a more definite effort in this regard. It seems fairly common for a vigorous union administration successfully to encourage biracial groups of shop leaders. We have observed a few cases in which foremen who are the centers of informal groups of their own workers have developed something of an interracial organization. More often the opposite occurs where the foremen occupies such a position. I cite these additional cases, without the description necessary for you to judge of them, to indicate the variety of situations which may occur, and also to introduce a final point; namely, that the situation may often be changed by some active force, either union or management, which takes the pattern of informal relations into account.

Ethnic Factors in Social Mobility

OSCAR HANDLIN   MARY F. HANDLIN

This paper applies historical techniques to the examination of one aspect of social mobility in the United

Oscar Handlin and Mary F. Handlin, "Ethnic Factors in Social Mobility," *Explorations in Entrepreneurial History*, **9** (October, 1956), 1-7. Copyright 1956 by Oscar and Mary F. Handlin.

States. Unfortunately, significant aspects of the problem have frequently been neglected through inability to view it in the time perspective. Investigation of social mobility has generally focused upon a single point in time and has taken for granted the stability of the social and economic context. Alone, such investigations offer only a limited basis for judgments of differential rates of mobility as among different societies and as among different historical periods. Such important questions as whether some countries and some epochs are more mobile than others cannot fully be answered without some consideration of developments over a considerable length of time.

It has, for instance, been said frequently that American society has been characterized by a high degree of upward mobility. There has been extensive discussion as to whether mobility was relatively greater than in other societies, and whether its rate has been rising or falling. The answers to such questions will necessarily be inconclusive until data from the historic past can be brought to bear upon them. Such studies simply do not yet exist.

That deficiency is partly due to the fact that the kinds of quantitative data available to a contemporary investigator do not exist for earlier periods—at least not in the United States. It is also due to the fact that historians have not formulated for themselves meaningful problems of research.

This paper hopes to deal with the last-named failing. It attempts to set forth a number of hypotheses capable of being tested through research in the materials of the past. More specifically, the focus of inquiry will be upon the elements that have created differences in the rate of upward mobility of diverse ethnic groups in American society. An outline of the influence of ethnic factors on social mobility may offer some useful insights into the nature of the problems of historical research in this whole field.

The ethnic group in the United States is a loose agglomeration of individuals, aware of a common identity and organized to some degree in voluntary associations, which transmits a definable social and cultural heritage from generation to generation. Within it, the family plays an important role, for it is through the family that ethnic influences are extended in time. The group is in some respects less, and in others more, cohesive than the family unit. The family is thus the unit within which property descends from parents to children, while the group as such has no relationship to the tenure of property. On the other hand, the group rather than the family is the meaningful unit within which the marriages that will establish new families are formed.

The ethnic group is not legally defined. Its status has been recognized by law only in a few exceptional instances —notably in the case of the Negro, whose situation was thereby significantly complicated. More generally, the law has not only failed to recognize distinctions based on ethnic affiliations, but in some respects has actually forbidden such recognition. Therefore, again with a few exceptions, ethnic groups have been formed by the voluntary accession of their members. In consequence they have been fluid and susceptible to easy change. In the American past, such groups have usually formed about one, or a combination, of the three following points of differentiation.

Almost from the start, color was a distinguishing feature that drew together significant groups. The history of the Negro and his evolving status as a slave created a heritage that persisted for centuries. The position of the Indians on the frontier, resisting the advance of white settlement, created another. And the situation of the small groups of Orientals on the Pacific coast created still another. These historical circumstances, together with the high degree of visibility and the racial transmissibility of certain physical features, have given the resulting groupings exceptional durability.

The long history in the United States of internal and external migration brought into being other ethnic groups based upon national or sectional origin. The encounters among foreign immigrants in the free and fluid society of the New World evoked and fixed in them a vivid consciousness of group identity. In the rural countryside, such folk as the Pennsylvania Germans have continued to act as a group apart for more than 200 years. To some extent, the persistence of the features of group life varied inversely with the duration of settlement. But in almost all groups some degree of identification remained the fourth generation and beyond. In this respect internal migration was also significant. In the expansion of settlement in the middle of the nineteenth century, for instance, the migrants from New England and from the old South retained an awareness of their ethnic identity for considerable periods; and that affected their cultural and social adjustment.

Finally, religious differences were at the basis of the formation of a third set of ethnic groupings. Despite the individualistic ideals of American courtship, religious affiliations have always influenced the selection of marriage partners and thus the evolving family and ethnic groups. Furthermore, well-defined cultural and social traits associated with the major religious denominations confirmed their group character. The American Quakers thus have held to their identity for more than two centuries.

These groups, therefore, form a complex array; analysis reveals literally hundreds of them based on either color, or national origin, or religion. Furthermore, they are not necessarily mutually exclusive; an individual may not only pass from one to another, but may sometimes find himself simultaneously affiliated with several—as a Puerto Rican, a Catholic, and a colored man, for instance.

It will not be profitable to attempt to describe the experience of one or several of the American ethnic groups in isolation. An assessment of their influence upon social mobility will more readily emerge from an examination of the historic context within which they operated.

In the seventeenth century, ethnic affiliations had a preponderant importance. The New England colonies were restrictive and exclusive in their attitude toward new settlers. Effectively the paths upward, in politics, in land ownership, and in trade were closed off to those who were not church members or not related to established families with command of capital. Strangers were somewhat more capable of gaining status in the South. But there the line between black and white servants became the line between slaves and free men. And everywhere fixed conceptions of status impeded the social advance of outsiders.

These attitudes did not survive the first generation of settlement in the United States. For more than two centuries, from 1680 onward, the influence of the frontier and of changing social and political attitudes operated in the direction of greater looseness in social organization, and that transformed the role of ethnic grouping as a factor in social mobility. Early in the eighteenth century, the legal bases for stratification began to drop away; by the end of the century the process was complete.

In Virginia, Maryland, and South Carolina in the South and along the great river valleys in New York and in New England, the large-scale land-holding families for a time nurtured aristocratic pretensions after the English example. But these families were never capable of closing their ranks against outsiders. Then, and later, the availability of land always permitted newcomers with capital to buy their way in. There is no evidence that ethnic factors, as such, influenced the opportunities of various groups to enjoy the advantages of land holding.

After the first century of settlement, moreover, land holding lost steadily in importance as a differentiating element in American society. The landed gentry, down to the Revolution, retained some privileges and considerable political and social power. But it achieved only a limited stability. The great families of 1775 were not the same as those of 1675. Furthermore, the Revolution destroyed the legal props of the great landed estates when the laws for primogeniture and entail were abolished.

For a time, the persistence of the plantation system in some regions of the South created a group of land holders with aristocratic attributes. But it had not the time to acquire stability or permanence. Made up largely of new men who had acquired status in their own lifetimes, it was destroyed by the Civil War and the abolition of slavery. The inescapable fact was that by then possession of land had ceased to be the primary fulcrum of economic, political, or social power, and the easy availability of land in the United States made this a ready avenue rather than an obstacle to upward social movement.

However, in the last two centuries the more important means of rising in social status were through the acquisition of a fortune in trade or in industry and through access to some desirable profession or occupation. In each of these spheres, although to different degrees, ethnic factors were significant.

Through most of American history, commerce was the road to wealth. The qualifications of the successful merchant were access to some capital with which to start and ability to manage, save, and invest it skillfully, and both were influenced to some extent by ethnic group affiliations. Very little capital in the United States was the product of noncommercial accumulation. Although farming and some other extractive enterprises were frequently profitable, they rarely yielded surpluses sufficient for significant reinvestment. Agriculturists did not often enter commerce, even when it came to dealing in livestock, grains, or other commodities close to their interests. The millers and other rural processors seem to have been a group apart. Generally, the ability to enter trade depended upon access to existing stores of capital sufficient to make a start and to protect the entrepreneur against the inevitable hazards and setbacks of speculation. In the most expansive areas of the American economy, outsiders who enjoyed such access to capital were at an enormous advantage.

Family relationships were directly important, for they decisively extended the capital available to the individual promoter. But wider ethnic connections were fully as significant. In an unstable economic and social order decisions often rested on personal judgments of a man's trustworthiness. Derivation from a known background, membership in a proper church, reputation for virtues defined in accordance with standards accepted by the ethnic group were of inestimable importance in this respect. Innumerable illustrations of the operations of this factor range from the experience of the Jewish immigrant able to embark on a career of peddling and trade with credit from wholesalers, to the facility with which Rockefeller at critical points commanded the respect and confidence of influential fellow Yankees in recruiting capital.

Such connections were also the key

to a wider range of opportunities. In the eighteenth and nineteenth centuries, when trade moved over great distances under conditions of poor communications, it depended often on the ability of merchants to rely upon their correspondents overseas. The Quaker merchants of Philadelphia who dealt with other Friends in London or the Jews in Newport who traded with co-religionists in the West Indies had a reasonable expectation that their interests would be protected across the long distances involved.

Such influences persisted through the nineteenth century, as the ability of the German-born railroad promoter Henry Villard to command the confidence of European investors showed. But perhaps the most striking instance was the network of communications among Yankee firms that reached from New England through New York and out into the Middle West, an informal but potent set of associations that extended into business life from common religious, social, and cultural affiliations. By the end of the century, these associations were embedded in a variety of prestige-bearing forms which no doubt gave the members of this ethnic group decided advantages in upward mobility.

Buttressing the strength of these associations was the fact that certain skills were likely to be more highly developed in some ethnic groups than in others. The Yankee trader was already a familiar figure in American folklore at the end of the eighteenth century. From childhood, the New Englander was taught the importance of method and discipline in every dealing, the value of frugality and thrift, and the necessity of being a "sharp trader." A more extensive educational system than existed elsewhere gave him the ability to write and to reckon, skills extremely helpful in finding and holding a place in the economy. Other

groups with these entrepreneurial skills, the Greeks and Jews, for instance, found themselves similarly at an advantage after their migration to the United States.

These skills did not develop in isolation, but rather within an ideological framework, difficult to evaluate but certainly significant. Members of ethnic groups detached from that ideology were unlikely to rise. Those who came from peasant societies, for instance, were bound by a view of status that prevented them from even conceiving the possibility that they might lift themselves above the position in life into which they had been born and for which they were destined. That attitude was often transmitted across several generations and carried over into the habits of life of the group long after the period of immigration.

Ethnic groups with peasant origins were also unlikely to develop attitudes favorable to the effective use of capital. Their total earnings were generally given over to current consumption, and if surpluses appeared, those were hoarded rather than invested. A traditional fear of debt and inability to comprehend the intangible evidences of wealth deprived them of the means of financial maneuver in a capitalist society. Finally, attachment to the land was often deceptive under American conditions. Many families were tempted to put disproportionate shares of their income into the purchase of homes or farms and were thus prevented from accumulating capital for investment in more profitable ways.

Analogous influences limited the capacity of other groups for entrepreneurial success. Southern society was long dominated by ideals hostile to the habits conducive to entrepreneurial success. The social order dominated by the plantation put a high premium on hospitality, upon expensive homes, and upon a lavish style of life; it encouraged unproductive debts; it exhausted incomes and prevented the utilization of earnings for further investment. Such habits ultimately weakened the capacity to hold wealth under the circumstances of American life. The merchant in Memphis or New Orleans in the 1850's was less inclined to use his gains for investment in railroads or factories than for the purchase of an expensive plantation. Since the aristocracy toward which he aspired never materialized, he was likely, in a short time, to find himself the embarrassed possessor of the empty symbols of status, with no substance. In every part of the country, men nurtured under this tradition labored at a considerable disadvantage in the effort to rise.

By contrast, the merchant of Boston, at the same period, no matter how wealthy, labored under a continual obligation to withhold part of his income from consumption and to use it for reinvestment. A persistent ideology, rooted in his Puritan antecedents, encouraged risk taking and the management of capital toward defined ends. Consumption was not the objective of earning; and the virtues of thrift were celebrated not simply as protection against a hazardous future, but also as the means to further production. Such a complex of attitudes maximized the potentialities for entrepreneurial success and also prevented the dissipation of fortunes. It thus increased the prospects for upward mobility in the group and diminished the hazards of a fall in status.

There were nevertheless elements of considerable unpredictability in the situation. A great deal of wealth in the United States was the product of windfalls. Capitalist thinking tended to obscure this fact in the will to believe that all fortunes were earned by virtue and thrift. The prohibition of lotteries and the disapproval of gambling reflected that faith. Yet it nevertheless remained true that virtue was not always rewarded and that rewards often fell into the hands of those conspicuous for their lack of virtue. Speculation and lucky discoveries of gold or oil were frequently the starting points of great fortunes.

So, too, some individuals found their position as members of disadvantaged groups strategically useful as a base from which to advance. There were closed circles of trade where the special knowledge of tastes, communal affinity, and the ability to command confidence opened unique opportunities to the Negro or Jewish or Chinese merchant or banker. Or again, the power to recruit and control the labor supply was a valuable asset in industries in which labor was a crucial factor in the cost of production. The fact that Jewish workers predominated in the garment trades and Italians in construction work gave to entrepreneurs drawn from these groups an immediate competitive advantage.

Yet in these cases, as with windfalls, there was a significant limiting factor. To keep the initial advantage over a long period called for entrepreneurial aptitudes similar to those discussed above. Otherwise, after the first generation, the fortune or competitive advantage fortuitously gained tended to dissipate itself. Therefore the ability to advance along the social scale, and the ability to keep from slipping back, depended upon endowment with the attributes of successful entrepreneurship; and ethnic factors consistently influenced the distribution of those attributes among individuals.

One alternative mode of upward social mobility stood apart. For a long time, the shortage of skilled or specialized or educated personnel put a high premium on their labor. In this society talent was highly valued and there were few bars to its attainment of status. In the late eighteenth and early nineteenth centuries, some professions, notably medicine and law, attempted to achieve some degree of exclusiveness through licensing, statutory or corporate. These efforts failed; and as the old system of apprenticeship dropped away to be replaced by training in ever-more numerous professional schools, the way into such occupations became more and more accessible. Down to 1900, few elements of ethnic restriction seem to have applied. Since talent was unpredictably distributed throughout every level of society and less conditioned by cultural and social factors, men from every ethnic group had some opportunity to rise through its use. It was true that individuals with greater skill and literacy found more opportunities open to them. But ethnic affiliation as such was neither an asset nor a liability except as it affected literacy and degree of education. Most important of all, so long as professional status could not be handed down from generation to generation, a high degree of fluidity persisted.

In the four decades between 1900 and 1940, that situation changed significantly. The competition for place became more extreme, and a developing pattern of discriminatory practices tended to limit upward social mobility. After 1920, as the rate of population growth slackened, many Americans feared that the United States was approaching a plateau at which the long process of economic and social expansion would come to an end. The cumulative effects of repeated depressions, in 1907, 1913, 1921, and 1929, were discouraging, and there was an inclination to save the best places for favored groups.

Significantly, the lines of restriction were not those of the family, but of the ethnic group. A code of extralegal practices limited access to employment and to professional education. A network of societies and clubs that were the signs of advancing status closed their membership to outsiders, and there was a notable falling off in the rate of upward mobility.

Yet these restrictive measures proved temporary. The economy was still expansive; and the two world wars heightened the fluidity and the mobility of the society. In any case, social disapproval and occasionally the force of law undermined the patterns of social discrimination.

For all but a very short period, therefore, the skilled occupations and the professions remained free and offered a relatively open road to social mobility. It was no more possible in the United States for a group to fix the status of its members through this means than through land holding.

This accounts for the strategic role of entrepreneurship in the history of social mobility in the United States, for it was through the aptitudes involved in successful entrepreneurship that the most valued places in American society were attained. And it was in regard to those aptitudes that ethnic differences had greatest significance.

the polity

four

In at least three areas, economists have stressed the interplay between economic and political variables: in labor-management conflict; in governmental regulation of business; and in imperfect competition, where one or a few agents exercise control over prices and output. Sociological investigators have pushed the study of this political-economic interplay even further. A sample of these interdisciplinary efforts is presented in this section. The first selection, by Dalton—which is in the general "human relations" tradition of economic sociology—illustrates the importance of networks of communication and informal group membership in the relations between labor and management. The article by McMullan explores the phenomena of bribery and corruption—by virtue of which economic sanctions invade political organizations—and tries to place these phenomena in their social-structural setting. The final three selections concern the relations between governments and economic agents. Deyrup explores the ways in which governments in the developing areas have attempted to control the activities of unions; Hoselitz offers a promising typology of the ways in which economic development is coordinated by political authorities; and, in the last selection, Schulze presents a case study of the changing role of business and financial interests in the politics of a local community in the United States.

The articles in this section correspond to pp. 44-57 of *The Sociology of Economic Life*.

Unofficial Union-Management Relations

MELVILLE DALTON

The purpose of this paper is to discuss some phases of informal behavior occurring between union and management at the plant level in some of the

Melville Dalton, "Unofficial Union-Management Relations," *American Sociological Review*, **15** (1950), 611-619.

larger industrial organizations working under national labor agreements. At this level, contrary to expectations of top union and management, there are frequent departures from provisions of the negotiated contract. It is this area of activity that will be examined: the unofficial and often formally unacceptable behavior, evading and manipulating the formal labor agreement, but nevertheless constituting a great part of the actual functioning relations between management and union at the plant level.

Data for this report are drawn from participant experiences in three factories.[1]

Methodologically, there are obvious limitations to the activities of the industrial participant observer. Regardless of the number and variety of positions such an observer may hold, or the number of years he may spend in industry, or the aid given him by participating intimates, he cannot hope to cover all behavior important for his purposes in large organizations. He is further handicapped when, as in the present case, the behavior in which he is interested is carefully guarded. Hence the discussion here does not presume to cover all the informal behavior that occurred in these plants[2] in the category of union-management relations.

But despite such limitations, there were discernible axes along which behavior moved. From a study of these, informal union-managment relations appeared in the main to stem from (1) a tacit agreement by members of both union and management to work outside the contract when "necessary," (2) lack of union consciousness among workers, (3) managerial incohesiveness, and . . . (4) the effects of economic and production pressures. These four conditions will be used as analytical categories.

Tacit Evasion of the Contract

The plants to be discussed were all under contract with national unions, but both labor and management in the local plants winked at the agreement. This attitude was not the result of intentional neglect by top officials, for the national unions and corporation headquarters periodically sent questionnaires to both groups requesting statements of their problems. These requests were treated lightly. There was much cynicism about the ability of top officials to care for local problems. Local groups believed the contracts were too general and inflexible to cover the problems of many widely scattered plants functioning under different conditions.[3]

[1] The writer spent several years in various departments of these factories, both as a worker and a member of management. Some aspects of experiences at the work level were reported earlier as "Wage Incentive and Social Behavior" (unpublished M.A. thesis, Department of Sociology, University of Chicago, 1946); "Worker Response and Social Background," *Journal of Political Economy*, **55** (August, 1947), 323-332; "The Industrial 'Rate-Buster': A Characterization," *Applied Anthropology*, **7** (Winter, 1948), 5-18, an intensive study of the personality characteristics of workers likely to respond most strongly to the appeal of money incentive. Research among managers was reported as "Conflicts Between Staff and Line Managerial Officers," *American Sociological Review*, **15** (June, 1950), 342-351. A report of several areas of managerial behavior in one plant only was given in "A Study of Informal Organization Among the Managers of an Industrial Plant," (unpublished Ph.D. thesis, Department of Sociology, University of Chicago, 1949).

[2] Names and locations are confidential, but these are the same plants—ranging in size from 4500 to 20,000 employees—that were discussed in the earlier paper on staff-line conflict. As noted in that paper, there were at least three additional areas of conflict: (1) the union-management relations of the pres-

ent paper, (2) interdepartmental power struggles to keep operational costs down and win favor with top management, and (3) the disturbing influence of numerous managerial officers seeking to increase their status in the hierarchy. These areas were interrelated and often reciprocally compromising. Because of this a separate discussion of union-management relations will be admittedly somewhat unrealistic. Areas (2) and (3) are probably also characteristic of many other organizations, industrial and otherwise.

[3] It is likely that some element of rationalization existed in these beliefs, for, as will be shown, behavior in the plants was so expedient and variable that probably the most detailed local contract would have been evaded to some degree. Slichter stresses the remoteness

In one of the plants a departmental superintendent declared: "[The plant manager and his assistant] have both said they don't give a damn what kind of arrangements are made with the union as long as things run smoothly and it's kept out of writing."

Grievance committeemen made similar statements. Two of those whom I knew intimately were quite specific. One stated: "The top people [policy makers] lay down too many hard and fast rules to follow. But we get around the contract by doing a lot of things that we can work out and keep off the record." The other said:

Top union and management are always bothering the local plant. We can work out our own arrangements if they'll leave us alone. [The plant superintendent and assistant] told us they don't care what arrangements we make, but if we get in trouble the contract will have to be followed to the letter right down the line.

This was the only case in which a union officer admitted direct informal communication from management approving evasion of the contract, but actual behavior was similar in all the plants, and had a character that could hardly have existed if local managerial and union officers had been opposed to evasion.

Lack of Union Consciousness

Ninety per cent or more of the production workers of the three plants were union members. They responded

to strikes called by the national union. They showed considerable solidarity in holding production to agreed levels. However, there was a general lack of union consciousness among them.

On matters that could be handled secretly, even enthusiastic supporters of the union engaged in private dealing that was advantageous to them in terms of income, a better work position, desirable days off during the work week, preferred weeks of the year for vacation, and so on. This covert bargaining usually involved a grievance committeeman and a departmental superintendent. These officers would trade favors that often led to the development of an exchange structure. For example, there were cases (occurring too often to be exceptional) of workmen being reclassified from lower to higher pay categories without actually proving the skill formally required by tests.[4] For such considerations the grievance committeemen would accept "frozen schedules" (easy to prepare but less flexible than workmen liked), refrain from forcing "tough" or "rotten" grievances on the superintendent, and so on.

The behavior of successful . . . grievance committeemen was revealing with respect to informal union-management relations. They were skilled in manipulating both workers and managers. Some of them confidentially stated that

---

of professional officers of the national union from the rank and file [S. H. Slichter, *The Challenge of Industrial Relations* (Ithaca: Cornell University Press, 1947), p. 15]. This may have been a factor in the complaints and behavior of workmen in the two larger plants discussed here. In a sense they were rebelling against the restrictive effects of this distance on their control of policy. Simultaneously the white collar workers were competing with the production workers for favors from the national union and felt that their numerical inferiority was a handicap "because we can't make as much noise as they can."

[4] For example, a machinist wished to move from "B" to "A" rating. By arrangement between his grievance committeeman and departmental superintendent, he won his reclassification by giving only the appearance of passing the test. Formally the test required setting up and operating the machine for one hour unaided. In this case the candidate found the job already set up. The cutting heads were adjusted, the tool bits were properly ground and inserted to the correct depth and at the proper angle. The feeds and timing were adjusted so that the machine could have run unattended beyond the required hour. The candidate had but to press the starting button, stand by the machine one hour, and press the stopping button.

a measure of political artifice was necessary for success in that office.[5]

Quite often expediency drew grievance officer and superintendent together in alliance against similar cliques. Though leaks of these practices sometimes occurred, the uncertainty among all participants as to what behavior future situations might require of them served to check formal protests. Two brief cases will indicate the strength to which some union-management cliques could grow.

In the largest of the three plants, the superintendent of a division of 3500 workers was demoted to a foremanship which he had earlier held. The committeeman with whom he had dealt as superintendent volunteered to call a wildcat strike (which the foreman opposed) for the purpose of returning him to his former position.

In the plant[6] of 4500 employees such a strike *was* initiated by a grievance committeeman and nearly a hundred workers because their foreman failed to get the vacated office of assistant superintendent. Though the strike lasted but four days and failed of its purpose, its significance is apparent.

Relationships of the successful grievance committeeman with his constituents are instructive. Grievance officers who succeeded in being re-elected were those showing political astuteness rather than fiery opposition to management. For instance, in each shop there were informal leaders whom the area grievance man employed as political whips. They defended his behavior to workmen and campaigned for his re-election. In return he rewarded them with favors growing out of his unofficial dealings with management, as in the case of reclassification noted above which was given to an informal leader. As a rule, the belligerent committeeman served only one term. Instead of such an officer, the rank and file preferred a griever who could win them individual and group gains—even though he might "play ball" with management to some extent. Admittedly the behavior of committeemen and their informal leaders was somewhat oligarchical, but the fact that such officers were re-elected indicated that a majority of the work-

---

[5] Explaining his third re-election, one officer said: "Industrial relations is all based on good relations. You've got to be friends to some extent. You can't have industrial relations without giving and taking on both sides. You'll always win more cases by getting along with supervision than by being tough. You've got to swap for swap and make trades. . . . A griever [committeeman] has the problem of holding the union together and keeping peace in it while he tries to please both the union and management. Some of the big shots don't like me—they want to win all the time. But I figure that some of the best friends I have are big shots here in the plant. Sometimes I have to talk like hell to explain some of the deals I make with them—and sometimes I keep what I'm doing to myself if I see a chance to get something good later on. The thing some grievers never get through their heads is that a lot of the bosses are on the spot theirselves. If you go a little easy on them when they're on the pan, by G— you make friends—they'll stand by you sometime when you're back of the eight ball. Sometimes when I have a rotten grievance, I'll take the case up to the soop [supt.] and let him know I won't push it hard."

[6] In this same plant informal bargaining involved the president of the union local.

Management wished to drop a wage incentive system that had got out of hand, and was prepared in the future to pay workmen "average earnings," i.e., the average of bonus pay (above guaranteed hourly pay) that had been earned over a specific period. The president of the local, whose average earnings were 9.5 cents an hour, opposed management. Shortly thereafter the records of his past performances were "lost," and his average earnings were found to have been "in error." After recalculation his average earnings were 34.5 cents an hour. He agreed to withdrawal of the incentive plan. At the same time he did not oppose reduction from 2.5 cents to 1.5 cents in the average earnings of several aging, unaggressive workmen.

men, consciously or not, accepted this as the best practical working arrangement.

Available data suggest that the successful griever quickly learned to settle grievances informally and to use formal procedure only as a last resort. Data on nine of the seventeen (of a total of forty-six) committeemen who had served more than one term showed that each officer's annual total of formally processed grievances (those in the first three steps[7]) declined with each succeeding year in office. The total in each of these steps also declined annually.[8] Decline in number of grievances among these committeemen did not necessarily mean a decrease in union-management tensions, but rather that friction was more and more being resolved informally.

At least up through the divisional level,[9] grievance officers found managers who, because of the contradictory situations in which they were caught, were quite willing to settle their differences informally. . . .

---

[7] Steps in the formal grievance procedure were as follows: first step, the foreman; second step, the departmental superintendent; third step, the plant manager or assistants; fourth step, between representatives of the national union and management; fifth step, arbitration.

[8] For example, the total first-step grievances during their first year in office for each of the nine committeemen ranged from 149 to 194; total second-step grievances ranged from sixty-five to ninety-one, while those settled in the third step varied from fifteen to thirty-one. By the fourth year, formal grievances in the same steps for the same men varied respectively from thirty to ninety-eight, ten to forty-four, and two to nine.

[9] Strata of the managerial hierarchy from the worker level up were, in order, first-line foremen, general foremen, departmental superintendents, divisional superintendents, and plant manager. In the two larger plants there were usually additional strata consisting of "assistants" at most of the levels indicated.

Managerial Incohesiveness

Industrial organizations are usually regarded as bureaucracies in the technical sense of having hierarchies of officials, with specific authority and status, functioning inside a set of guiding rules. Contrary to the assumption that such structures are integrated and function impersonally, the plants discussed here showed much rule evasion, disorganization, and conflict.

First-line foremen, for instance, often considered themselves as abandoned by higher management to the union. Many of their earlier functions, such as hiring, firing, and influencing the pay of workmen, had been assumed by various staff organizations. Entertaining ambivalent sentiments toward higher management, first-line foremen defended themselves and salvaged what they could from the situation. Having been reversed many times by their superiors because of decisions they had made that led to the filing of grievances, these foremen in most cases refused to process grievances and instead passed them on to the general foremen, thus working contrary to expectations of the managerial organization. On the other hand, first-line foremen sought to control, or at least bargain with, the union in officially unacceptable ways.

One control device was to delay giving reclassification tests to workmen after the latter had received official approval to take the tests. During the interim the foremen derived satisfaction from indicating to the candidate that he had better be a "good guy" or expect to receive a "tough" test.[10]

An extreme case will make clear the process of informal bargaining at the work level. A first-line foreman had an arrangement with the grievance com-

---

[10] Standardization of tests, in terms of skill or knowledge required, was usually next to impossible.

mitteeman of the division which allowed the foreman to give his brother,[11] a workman, higher-paying jobs than other members of that work group (numbering eighteen) received. In return, the foreman was to approve by signature the use of certain bonus-increasing factors (when questioned by management's incentive appliers as to whether use of the factors was warranted by "good shop practice") applicable to the operations of another group of ninety-five workers also under his authority. The larger group was content with the arrangement, but the other eighteen men were not. They made threats, but filed no grievances, for occasionally they did receive "good" jobs. Formal action would have precluded their ever getting such jobs or winning a "legitimate" grievance.

Informal bargaining of this kind occurred also among departmental and divisional heads. The case above of worker reclassification without meeting formal requirements was fairly common and, as earlier mentioned, was usually effected with the aid of the departmental chief.[12] In another case, however, a departmental superintendent refused to cooperate. He gave the tests strictly according to rules to three candidates sponsored by the committeeman. All three failed. The griever then carried the case to the divisional head and claimed that the tests had been "too tough." The division chief himself had two employees, whom he considered to have uncommon ability, that he wished to promote, but they lacked seniority and he knew the union would block their promotion. So he now brought the case of his two protégés to the attention of the committeeman. The latter agreed to their promotion if his three men were given tests they could pass and if he were allowed to witness the testing of the superintendent's two candidates.

In another case bargaining between a division head and a grievance man evolved a method for inducing the less enthusiastic members of the union— under certain conditions—to sign the check-off ticket.[13] In those parts of two of the plants where workmen were reclassified on the basis of proven skill, they petitioned for a test. When the division chief received this request he indicated his approval by signing it and passing it back to the petitioner's foreman. However, in the present case the griever succeeded in having the division chief return such petitions to him rather than the foreman. If the candidate had not signed the check-off, the griever then told him that he could not take the test until he did sign. Once he signed, the grievance man notified the

---

[11] Plant rules forbade individuals related by blood or marriage to a member of management to work directly or indirectly under his supervision.

[12] It was not always possible to conceal these relations, as shown by the sequel to one case. When two workmen learned of a manipulated reclassification, they asked their committeeman for a similar favor. The superintendent (who had aided others in this way before) feared that he was going too far and refused to cooperate. In seeking a way out of his dilemma, the griever and his informal shop leaders utilized the safety rules to win the superintendent's cooperation. They contended that a safety hazard existed when a candidate was placed before a strange machine to prove his skill without benefit of communication with others, and that certain other workmen should be allowed to caution him if and when they saw him about to endanger himself or others. The superintendent agreed, thus allowing, as he knew, manipulation of the safety rule so that a candidate who might not be ready for the test could receive helpful hints from his friends.

[13] . . . The Labor Management Relations Act of 1947 forbids the employer to check off union dues unless the employee authorizes it in writing.

division head that the petition was ready for final approval.[14]

In another case a departmental superintendent made an informal pact with his committeeman which allowed the bonus hours for certain jobs to be increased. However, the bonus system had been developed by the industrial engineering staff which restudied the jobs and cut the time to its original figure. The aggressive committeeman then coerced the superintendent (who was too deeply involved in unacceptable activities to risk exposure) into bargaining with the staff organization for a compromise. This was a case of one managerial group bargaining with another in the same plant for the benefit of the union.

Unofficial behavior of management toward the union as an organization also showed a marked absence of the usually presumed antipathy. For example, many of the managers (1) revealed sentiments of indebtedness toward the union for salary increases, (2) insisted that workmen sign the check-off, and (3) bought raffle tickets from the union knowing that the proceeds would be used to strengthen the union as an organization.

Concerning (1), all members of management in all three plants received unannounced salary increases soon after every general wage increase won by production workers. At least in some cases the percentage of increase was greater than that received by workmen. Numerous managerial officers, from first-line foreman through department heads, confidentially declared that they "might never" get a salary increase "if it wasn't for the union." One high officer regarded by some workmen as "reactionary," said:

After all these years of just existing, now for the first time my wife and me are able to get our noses up for a breath of air. And by G— we owe it all to the union! If the union hadn't come in we'd stayed in the same damn old rut. In the last few years I've put four kids through high school and three of them through college. They're all on their own now, but they'd never have had a chance if my income hadn't shot up. I still believe in the law of supply and demand, but by G— I know which side my bread's buttered on, too.

A case was cited above of a divisional superintendent cooperating covertly with a union officer to force workmen to sign the check-off. But in a number of other cases in that plant and others, general foremen and department heads personally urged reluctant workers to authorize the check-off, and (according to workmen) in some cases threatened them with discharge. Workmen were told that they should sign for their "own good," and because failure to sign "makes the other men sore and causes trouble."

In a similar vein was management's purchase of raffle tickets from the union. Television sets, automobiles, and other articles were raffled off by the union. Especially from 1946 on, presidents of the locals, grievance men, and shop stewards went about the plants freely selling chances to everyone, with the managers buying more per person than the workers. Management was aware that the proceeds were being used for political action, because a receipt of membership in the union's political organization was offered with each minimum purchase of three chances.[15]

---

[14] Top union officials not only were ignorant of this arrangement (according to the committeeman), but had issued specific orders, when the Labor Management Relations Act became law, that unwilling workers were not to be coerced into signing the check-off.

[15] Remarks after these purchases gave an insight into managerial fantasies. Though all the managers smilingly declined receipts of

Possibly the most objective indication of management's lack of antipathy toward the union as such was the fact that individuals were often members of both management and the worker's union. Data are incomplete, but in over thirty cases in these plants first-line foremen were also dues-paying members of the union, and many of them were known to be members at the time they were selected as foremen.[16] And in one of the plants the president of the local was called on each summer to substitute for vacationing foremen.

These cases indicate that management, like the union, was guided in its behavior less by sentiments of group loyalty than by the demands of ex-

membership, some of them later expressed a fear concerning "what might happen" to them if the signatures they had given for the tickets should "turn up in some . . . spy-investigating committee."

[16] These cases of workmen entering management suggest that American workers have not yet resigned themselves to remaining in that category.

Though policy was contradictory on the point of whether individuals could be members of both the workers' union and management, when such aspirants did become managers and were able covertly to strengthen the unofficial exchange structure, union officers usually gave informal approval. For example, one such officer stated: "We don't try to keep our men from entering supervision. We've got a number of men in supervision who are in the union. . . . We're glad to see them get up. It helps us as long as they remember who helps them out and keeps things running smooth for them. We help them by seeing that their seniority runs unbroken. If they go on salary and become officially part of management, they can still pay their dues and keep their seniority. . . . In case they get bumped, we'll stand back of them. When cases like this come up, we argue that we only *lent* the men to the company and that they never ceased being part of the union. So far we've got away with it. It's a good policy for us to follow. You know, the company *could* dislike a man and put him on salary so they could can [discharge] him. But they can't do that the way we work it."

pediency and friendship, and the fear of exposure for rule evasion.

Economic and Production Pressures

Pressures by top management for greater production caught the first-line foreman between the union and his superiors. (Some of his escapes were noted earlier.) Since the union prevented application of any large-scale productive coercion, the foreman discreetly sought to reward those workers who "put out" with such favors as giving them (1) the higher-paying jobs; (2) more desirable jobs in terms of the ease with which they could be done, and/or their freedom from dirt, heat, hazard, unpleasant odors and drafts; and (3) available overtime in his own and other departments in which he knew such time was to be had. The characteristic willingness of workmen to accept confidential favors made such exchanges relatively easy, and sometimes grievance committeemen collaborated by (1) denying to suspicious workmen that such conditions were deliberate, and (2) refusing to process grievances filed on such issues.

Cost to the union of carrying grievances to the fourth step was a compulsion toward settlement at some lower step. The fourth step in disputes was argued in the "area office" of the plants. This office was sufficiently distant that the unions regarded the cost of travel and maintenance of personnel as a strain on their resources. Depending on the number of men involved and the number of conferences required, each grievance taken to the fourth step cost the union from $200 to $400. Hence it carried to the fourth step only those grievances it felt sure of winning. These economic limitations reduced the union's aggressiveness at the third step for fear that management might throw the grievance into the fourth step.

(Union officials confidentially admitted that bluffing was a major element in their tactics at the third step.) This constraint to settle grievances preferably below the third step and certainly below the fourth thus intensified informal bargaining.

According to some of the divisional superintendents, management, too, had its fear of the fourth step because the central offices "preferred" that grievances be settled in the local plant. And in the local plant, from the divisional level down, managerial officers feared the wrath of top local management which, as mentioned earlier, had indicated its approval of any informal arrangements that could be contained, and had implied its dislike of being drawn into grievances by vague threats of strict interpretation of the contract if such involvement occurred. The fear which middle- and lower-level officers had of top officers has already been indicated by their use of nonpecuniary bribes, favors, and exchange devices in connection with union-management relations.

Summary and Implications

Study of three factories showed that despite the existence of labor agreements to guide union-management relations, the formal contracts were often evaded. These unofficial relations were analyzed as due largely to (1) the belief by union and management that the agreements were, paradoxically, both too general and inflexible; (2) the lack of group consciousness among both workers and managers and a willingness among members of each group to bargain privately with members of the other; (3) the intricate conflict system in which other processes, such as staff-line friction and interdepartmental struggles occurred and colored union-management relations, and in which

dynamic situations called for quick, compromise decisions that fully satisfied no one and were hence subject to ceaseless pressures by individuals and groups for further changes to bring conditions more in line with demands; (4) the wish among managerial and union officers to realize personal goals, deal with enemies, reward friends, protect themselves, increase their status, and the readiness to use expedients for these ends; (5) the economic restrictions on the union and production pressures on management, with the expectation by top officials that differences between the two be settled below a certain level of argumentation.

The conditions in these plants probably have importance for union-management relations in most large corporations. Instead of the clear-cut behavioral distinctions in which this phase of industrial life is usually presumed to operate, relations become a shifting, intermixed matter of conflict, cooperation, and accommodation carried on largely through the media of personal relations between members of management and of the union. In the area of these immediate relations there is little of the strict adherence and loyalty of members to the presumed interests respectively of management and the union.

Implications for communication and control of members in giant organizations are important. American managerial theory, in terms of an efficient and impersonally functioning hierarchy, is in most cases similar to that presented by Max Weber as the ideal-type bureaucracy, but the actual relations in industry are seldom covered by such theory. Our changing society, our lack of an administrative tradition, and our emphasis on individual success combine to prevent impersonal relations in this area. Exhortations for union-management cooperation sometimes appear only to aggravate disapproved informal relations. Often union and managerial officers are forced to make decisions when they are not prepared to act and when alternative courses of action cannot be brought into the open because of prior informal commitments and possible damage to their own status and/or the status of individuals who have claims on them and on whom they in turn are dependent for favors. In such cases formal rules and communication channels are likely to be sidestepped.

There was little indication that the workers in these plants were inclined to regard themselves as members of the "lower class," or as permanent members of labor unions. The latter condition would seem to be essential for continued strong union consciousness. The relative absence of such feeling may be in part related to (1) forgetfulness with increasing distance from the critical union-fomenting period of the early thirties, (2) over a decade of high employment and income, and (3) the growing number of workers who never experienced responsibilities during the recent depression.

Some social scientists contend that friction between union and management would disappear if industrial "bureaucracy" could be eliminated and if "inflexible executives" could be "educated to their responsibilities." If bureaucracy as here used refers to impersonal relations and blind adherence to rules as a cause of industrial friction, it is clear that such thinking does not explain what occurred in the plants reported here, where relations were informal and personal, yet not without conflict. Furthermore, in most corporations executives themselves are employees (rather than owners) subject to orders and with little power to initiate formal changes. In such cases it may be extreme to put the onus of blame on management when many of its members, like the worker, are caught in a scheme that limits mobility, causes anxiety and frustration, and stimulates evasion.

There is no wish here to present informal union-management relations as a type of behavior unique in our society. We all know the dynamic and experimental nature of our institutional life, especially in the areas of political and sexual behavior. There is probably much similar conduct in our theoretically rigid and impersonal bureaucracies. Ralph Turner has indicated the need of personal, rule-evasive behavior to survive in at least one area of a military bureaucracy[17] (which, unlike industrial bureaucracies, has the power of life and death to enforce its rules).

The extreme positions, that destructive union-management conflict is unavoidable or that perfect cooperation is possible, may need modification. In practice, the sharing of a common human nature stimulates members of both union and management to work under an appearance of conformity and cooperation while manipulating top-level contractual expectations to ease multiple pressures and win personal aims.

This condition[18] is likely to continue as long as (1) workers (a) hope to rise socioeconomically, (b) crave personal

[17] R. H. Turner, "The Navy Disbursing Officer as a Bureaucrat," *American Sociological Review*, 11 (October, 1946), 501-505.

[18] It is possible that behavior in these plants was exceptional, but according to a lawyer who has been intimate for several years with union-management relations at the plant level in northeastern United States, the conditions depicted in this paper are common. However, this informant insisted during a conversation on the subject that I have "misinterpreted the meaning" of informal relations. He declared with feeling that behavior of the kind described here is not evasion of the contract but "democracy at work," and that a "semantic approach" would clarify the seeming difficulty.

distinctions, (c) elect ambitious union officers on the strength of their political skills, and (d) aspire to enter the ranks of management; and as long as (2) union and managerial officers find that evasion is of more aid than adherence

to rules in protecting themselves against the resentments, aggressions, and expectations of others as all persons involved behave expediently in a social order holding personal success as a major value.

Labor and Government in Underdeveloped Countries

FELICIA J. DEYRUP

Insufficient attention has been paid to those aspects of economic development which make the current position of organized labor in underdeveloped countries so critical and at the same time so different from either the contemporary or historical position of organized labor in industrial countries. It is the purpose of this article to show how the peculiar role of government in developing countries appears to have reshaped the industrial struggle, inevitably resulting in conflict between government and labor as well as between labor and management. While forecasts cannot hold much validity in a field so undefined as that which includes development problems, it nevertheless seems probable that a serious conflict of interest between government and labor will persist in these countries so long as serious efforts toward development are being made, and that therefore organized labor's position in these economies, and hence its tactics and even its goals, will tend to resemble those in advanced countries only after the major aims of development have been achieved.

Felicia J. Deyrup "Organized Labor and Government in Underdeveloped Countries: Sources of Conflict," *Industrial and Labor Relations Review*, **12** (1958-59), 104-112.

The Position of Organized Labor

It should be made clear that the general line of argument to be developed applies with a varying degree of validity to different countries, depending on the degree to which organized labor has emerged in each country. In India and the countries of Latin America, unions date back to the late decades of the nineteenth century, or at least to the early 1900's. In other countries, like Ceylon and Malaya, the First World War or the depression of the 1930's gave the impetus necessary for labor to organize. In still other places, such as Turkey and large sections of Africa and the middle eastern countries, apart from the oil concessions one can hardly say that organized labor as yet exists. Government intervention in the affairs of organized labor ranges in these countries from the relatively benign efforts found in some British possessions to the stringent control and even crippling of independent unions in certain Latin American countries. In general, labor organization in underdeveloped countries has been much stimulated by the Second World War, by postwar nationalism, and in some instances by Communism, so that even in those countries where organization is in its infancy the problems connected with the relation of labor to other elements in society are nevertheless of vital importance.

The structure of labor organization in underdeveloped countries tends to follow rather easily anticipated lines. The strongest and most vocal unions are concentrated among transport, factory, and mining labor and in some cases among white collar workers, particularly government employees. There is only sporadic union activity among farm labor and plantation labor, although unions in certain countries, such as those in Ceylon, Indonesia, and Malaya, show real strength in these fields. The significant form of unionism, for obvious reasons, tends to be industrial rather than craft, although there are many craft unions. The labor movement, where such a generalized phenomenon exists, embraces intellectual as well as political elements. Leadership varies from strictly worker leadership to intellectual leadership. Strikes which are directed initially against one employer or a section of an industry frequently spread through other industries and in some cases become general strikes. At present a major purpose of strikes is to support demands for very large increases in wages to offset inflationary rises in the cost of living. While there is little detailed evidence available concerning membership, it appears that unions do not consider the regular payment of dues as the essential criterion of membership, but claim to speak even for workers who have not been regular members in the past.

The tremendous effort that must be expended to bring wages and working conditions in these countries up to even modest welfare standards and the eagerness of a relatively small body of organized workers to try every possible avenue of improvement explain the marked political character of their labor organizations. This gives these organizations an apparent resemblance to the labor movements of Europe. However, organized labor in underdeveloped countries differs in very essential ways from politically oriented labor as well as from other labor organizations in industrial countries.

Comparisons with Industrialized Countries

Brief consideration of the tactics which organized labor has used in the past in economically advanced countries will help clarify the different position occupied by labor in underdeveloped countries today. As western countries became industrialized, the activity and even the very existence of unions were challenged by employer resistance, by reduction of the bargaining strength of skilled workers as a result of mechanization, and by a host of formidable institutional barriers, such as anticonspiracy laws, paternalistic attitudes on the part of the state, and popular belief in individualism, competition, and freedom of contract. Organized labor's reaction to the frustration of its efforts to attain job control has varied from country to country and from one historical period to another. In some cases craft organization has been succeeded by pressure for more inclusive organizations, either of the "one big union" type, like Robert Owen's Grand National Consolidated Trades Union and the Knights of Labor, or of the modern variety, industrial unionism. In other cases labor has turned to politics, as in the Chartist movement in England, and later on in the widely spread Social Democratic movements. In yet other cases, despairing of receiving justice within the framework of society as it has been modified by industrialization, labor has turned to revolutionary activity, to anarchism or syndicalism, or more recently, to Communism. In some instances labor has adapted to an unfriendly environment by withdrawing its claims to represent most industrial workers and concentrating on the "best bets"—the élite among the skilled workers. This was the reaction of the American Federation of Labor when faced with the furious drive of employers for the open shop in the 1920's.

Organized labor as a member of the economic community accepted by the rest of society, entitled to certain rights and capable of assuming certain responsibilities, has come of age at a relatively late stage in the industrial development of most western countries. The passage in 1935 of the National Labor Relations Act, which established on a permanent basis the right of labor to bargain collectively, may be taken as the date at which labor's majority in the United States was unequivocally accepted. In England and Europe, labor's value as an ally of liberal political groups gave it substantial recognition at an earlier time, but in general one may conclude that organized labor was not accorded full recognition in industrial society until well into the twentieth century.

In this respect the position of organized labor in underdeveloped countries today is decidedly superior to that of labor in advanced western countries at a comparable stage of the industrial process. Just as underdeveloped countries need not recapitulate the early, simpler stages of industrial growth found in the history of advanced countries, so organized labor in underdeveloped countries need not repeat the historic struggles to win acceptance in society. It would be difficult to find in an underdeveloped country a political party or a responsible political leader of any importance who would deny labor a place of dignity in the structure of society. This does not necessarily imply that independent labor organizations are welcome everywhere; totalitarian and authoritarian governments which have crushed trade unions have made much of their devotion to the cause of labor. Also, many legal and traditional barriers to labor organization exist in underdeveloped countries, especially in parts of Latin America, where opposition to organized labor is strongly entrenched, and in the Middle East, where recognition of labor's rights dates only from the end of World War II. But the open admission that labor is a valuable part of society places unionism in these countries far beyond its comparable position in the countries which were becoming industrialized in the nineteenth century, when labor problems were ignored and unions repressed with a relatively good conscience.

This recognition of labor's rights is formalized in the statute and even the constitutional law of underdeveloped countries. Some countries, such as Indonesia, Korea, Mexico, Bolivia, Ecuador, Argentina, Cuba, and Brazil, have established the freedom to form trade unions as a constitutional right. Less specifically, the freedom to form associations—which includes freedom to form employers' as well as workers' associations—is either provided by special legislation or is guaranteed under the constitutions of Burma, India, the Philippines, and Thailand. Many countries which have not elevated to a constitutional right the privilege of belonging to a union have passed special legislation allowing the formation of trade unions. Organized labor in underdeveloped countries owes this strategic advantage of open recognition by society to the labor movements of economically advanced countries and to the whole tradition of liberal western political and social philosophy, for knowledge of the practical achievements of western labor movements and the intellectual influence of the western philosophy have percolated throughout underdeveloped countries.

Nevertheless, though organized labor in underdeveloped countries is strategically bolstered by its general acceptance as a member of the community, its position is not an easy one. Sometimes it is a tool of government, and sometimes it is heavily dependent on government. But most important, if organized labor is to obtain improved conditions and wages for its potentially large membership from economies still in the early phases of industrial growth, it must resort to political as well as economic means, and when labor enters the political field it finds government deeply involved in the various aspects of economic growth. It is this involvement of government with economic development that leads to strained relations between the government and organized labor in underdeveloped countries.

Role of the Government

During the early stages of industrial growth in the economically advanced countries, government in general took a relatively passive role in conflicts between workers and employers, acting as a neutral or, at worst, a temporary ally of employers. For the most part, government was a spectator of the industrial conflict, endeavoring only to protect private property, prevent personal injury, and maintain law and order. It was not within its province to determine the over-all justness of wages or working conditions, the less so since the right of bringing such matters into question could hardly be accorded to labor until unions were thoroughly accepted by society. When organized labor in industrial countries turned to political means to reach its goals, it naturally sought to force government into a truly neutral, if not prolabor, position. On occasion, labor also attempted to involve government directly in production activities, in the belief

that workers would be treated more generously by government than by private employers. The test of this last hypothesis, on a scale large enough to be meaningful and under conditions of political freedom, has only been partially undertaken in England and a few other countries. But it is significant that in all cases where labor has substantially improved its position by political means, it has done so within the framework of a society in an advanced state of industrialization. In such cases the major problems of industrial growth had already been solved.

In striking contrast with this situation, labor in underdeveloped countries need not spend any effort to induce government to take an active interest in industrial life in general or industrial relations specifically. Government is vitally interested in labor problems because of their bearing on economic development. However, government in these countries is interested not merely in labor-management relations, but also in many other things, including the complex issues of capital formation, expansion of entrepreneurial activity, market development and control, and price stabilization. In these circumstances government must divide its attention and its support among conflicting groups and interests, and organized labor may find it unresponsive, even hostile, to justifiable demands. Indeed, even a labor government in a developing country may fall far short of labor's expectations in the attention it pays to organized labor. In a sense the more a government is devoted to development, the less it can afford to pay special attention to organized labor.

The Problem of Inflation

At present, relations between government and organized labor in underdeveloped countries are most frequently strained by the conflict of interests engendered by inflation. Whether or not control of endemic inflation is possible in an underdeveloped country, there is no doubt that such control has been accepted as one of the major goals of government. So far, despite all efforts, inflation persists. Organized labor, one of its chief victims, reacts to continuing inflation by demanding wage increases which seem utterly unrealistic to those familiar with the labor history of advanced countries. Proposals for wage increases of 20, 30, or even 40 per cent are not uncommon and are not motivated solely by labor's desire to receive a larger share of the returns of production. Unions make it clear that such extreme demands must be made so that wages may merely keep pace with other prices as inflation progresses, and the fragmentary data available on consumer prices in underdeveloped countries suggest that indeed organized labor is often seeking only to maintain rather than to better its position.[1]

The consequence of demands for large-scale wage increases appears to be twofold. On the one hand, employers can hardly be expected to take such

---

[1] For example, nearly one-half million industrial workers in São Paulo, Brazil, struck in support of demands for a 45 per cent wage increase in the fall of 1957. This followed a rise in the cost of living during 1956 and 1957 unofficially estimated at forty per cent. A general strike of industrial and transportation workers in Argentina in the fall of 1957, called to enforce demands for wage increases to offset a thirty per cent increase in the cost of living, was broken when the government declared a state of siege. At about the same time, Ceylon was beset by a wave of strikes in support of demands by government workers for improved working conditions and a rise in the minimum basic wage rate of 68 per cent (from twenty-nine cents to forty-nine cents per hour). These demands, too, were made to offset the rising cost of living. *New York Times* (October 15, 1957), 10; (October 23, 1957), 11; (November 21, 1957), 15; (November 28, 1957), 13.

demands seriously, when neither the bargaining strength of the workers nor the sustained productivity of many businesses would warrant doing so. Much more important to this analysis, however, is the reaction of government to these demands. While unions are merely seeking to protect their members from the effects of inflation, to government such action is a serious political challenge. Inflation strikes all workers impartially, not only those initially asking for the wage increase, so that if the demands of this group are met, similar demands from other workers may be expected. If these were also granted, the inflationary spiral would undoubtedly take one more upward turn—and it is at this point that government, determined to check inflation, becomes a major opponent of labor. Probably this is clearly seen by all parties. Labor's principal weapon, the strike, turns easily into a general strike, a protest, or even a threat directed as much against government as against employers. Government frequently responds with suspension of civil rights and imprisonment of labor leaders.

This explains the surprising uniformity of government action in underdeveloped countries when unions make major wage demands, no matter whether the complexion of government is prolabor, neutral, or antilabor. Nor does there appear to be any solution for the problem, so long as government feels that its duty compels it to check inflation and unions feel that their duty compels them, in turn, to protect their members from the undesirable effects of inflation. Only economic development will make possible permanent reduction of these tensions.

The situation becomes more complicated when a bona fide labor government or a government truly sympathetic to labor has been established. Here the basis for conflict remains despite the ties that bind government and labor together. It is true that if government cannot or does not try to check inflation, or if labor exercises great self-control, open warfare can be postponed, if not ultimately avoided. But any serious efforts to combat inflation may drive a wedge between labor and the friendliest government. Such a disaster was . . . [once] avoided in Bolivia in a most remarkable manner. President Hernan Siles, heading what appear[ed] to be a government deeply committed to the cause of labor, instituted in the fall of 1956 a program for controlling inflation. This was challenged by wholesale demands for wage increases backed up by widespread strikes. In other countries, the government would almost certainly have broken with labor and arrested union leaders. But in fact, the president himself, in an ultimate personal appeal to the union membership, began a hunger strike in protest against the strikes. The unions backed down, leaving the government victorious, yet with its ties to organized labor unbroken.[2]

It may be noted that strains between organized labor and government over inflationary wage increases are probably even more conspicuous in industrialized countries than in underdeveloped countries. Such strains have been acute since World War II, especially in those countries faced with reconstruction of war-damaged economies. The importance of resolving this issue is shown by the record of Germany, whose amazing revival is to a great degree attributable to a sustained program of voluntary wage restraint. But while inflationary wage pressures may seriously embarrass the government of any industrialized country, more particularly one faced with economic reconstruction, there is a sig-

nificant difference in the impact of such pressures in industrialized countries and in underdeveloped countries. In industrialized countries, either the extreme sensitivity of the economy generally or manufacturers' ability to exercise a certain amount of market control may make it possible rapidly to pass on increased labor costs to consumers or to absorb them for a time at least without undue damage to production. In underdeveloped countries, consumers may not accept so readily a wholesale price rise due to increased labor costs, and the capacity of producers to absorb costs may be limited. Thus increased wages may seriously check production. Also, any marked increase in the purchasing power of workers, combined with the relative difficulty of expanding production in underdeveloped countries, may cause capitalists to concentrate on commodity speculation rather than on production, while farmers may hoard food rather than bring it to market. In the extreme case, inflationary wage pressures may spread so far through the economy as to cancel out the government's developmental efforts, and even to threaten the very existence of the government.

Domestic Capital Formation

A second basis of conflict between organized labor and government in underdeveloped countries concerns domestic capital formation. At present this problem is obscured by those resulting from inflation, and all its ramifications cannot be anticipated. However, it may well become prominent in the near future, unless outside capital enters underdeveloped economies more rapidly than it is at present inclined to do and unless it also moves into other fields than those it prefers at present. Here again the degree of conflict between government and labor will de-

[2] *New York Times* (October 18, 1956), 16; (October 19, 1956), 26; (December 29, 1956), 3; (December 30, 1956), 13.

pend very much on the extent to which government is committed to economic development; where government is keenly interested in development, whether under its own auspices or under private initiative, the conflict will be more intense.

While it cannot be proved unequivocally, it is probable that in the past in industrial countries a considerable amount of capital formation was made possible by the generally low level of wages. It is true that the practice of paying low wages may be self-limiting, because wages so low as to reduce physical efficiency are uneconomical. However, this limitation is most pronounced in the later stages of industrialization. Provided workers whose efficiency has declined as a result of low wages can be replaced by new workers without undue difficulty, employers will have no incentive for paying higher wages. This was probably the general situation in the early stages of industrial production in advanced countries. Certainly the early English cotton textile industry that used and abused young children; the coal mines that physically exhausted the men, women, and children who worked in them; and the early American steel industry, which operated on the basis of poorly paid and overworked immigrant labor, were all geared to a system of low wages and high rates of labor turnover. All of these industries made profits and contributed substantially to capital formation.

It may be assumed that public opinion as well as the growing political strength of organized labor in underdeveloped countries will check such obviously abusive treatment of labor, but for this very reason the rate of capital formation may be materially reduced below that experienced in the early history of industrial countries. Since labor tends to organize and press for improved working conditions and wages in response to industrial growth, it is probable that at just those points of an underdeveloped economy where rapid capital accumulation is particularly desirable—in the expanding industries—labor may be particularly insistent that its demands be met. Most policy makers today would deplore capital formation which clearly takes place at the expense of workers, yet many hard decisions will have to be made concerning the alternatives of reasonable wages and higher rates of capital accumulation. While the majority of these decisions will probably be made in private bargaining between employers and workers, government will find some of these problems brought to it for solution. Even the question of protective labor legislation, if existing laws are to be fully implemented, must be reviewed in light of the need for capital formation. In dealing with these matters, government will inevitably find itself at times in opposition to organized labor.

Future Course of Government and Labor

What, then, may be expected in the relations between government and organized labor in underdeveloped countries? The basic goals and strategic position of each are obvious enough so that some generalizations may be safely made. In marked contrast with the attitudes of employers and organized labor toward each other, both government and labor will probably stoutly deny the fact that there is a bona fide cause for conflict between them. Each needs the other to achieve its ends, and each sees this clearly. Government will not wish to alienate labor because it is potentially or in fact an important political force. Because political help is vital to meeting its needs in the foreseeable future, labor will not wish to antagonize government. Hence government in a developing country is likely to maintain that it has the welfare of organized labor at heart and that any existing conflict is not with labor as such, but with certain irresponsible individuals or radical groups attached to the labor movement. In the same way, organized labor may be expected to be reluctant to break openly with government, or to place its interests ahead of the developmental interests of the country as a whole. It, too, will single out for attack certain individuals, such as the minister of labor or president, and certain items of public policy, rather than the government's program as a whole.

Each side may also be expected to make use of traditional weapons to support its position. During any widespread demonstration of labor, government will exercise its functions of maintaining law and order and in so doing may arrest or otherwise silence active labor leaders. In Latin American countries, for example, the old device of withdrawing recognition from unions, which has been used in the past by governments distinctly hostile to labor, may in the future be used to curb aggressive unions which, in government's opinion, threaten the country's development program. The historic technique of declaring a stage of siege to break a strike probably will also continue to be used in Latin America, as will the prohibition of strikes in key industries, sympathetic strikes, and general strikes. Thus through the use of familiar devices for the control of labor unrest, a government earnestly interested in economic development, even though neutral or friendly to labor, may appear to have reverted to the traditional antilabor attitude of its predecessors.

Organized labor, for its part, may ap-pear much more radical than it is in fact. Mass demonstrations and demands for wage increases far beyond the capacity of a developing country to satisfy may threaten not merely development efforts, but the very stability of government. Thus unions which may be only eager or overeager, inept or undisciplined, may be branded as radical. The role of Communism in the labor movements of underdeveloped countries should not of course be underestimated. In some countries, such as Chile and Guatemala, Communism has been firmly entrenched in recent years. . . . In most countries, a relatively unimportant Communist group may make every major strike an occasion for fishing in troubled waters. Yet for the most part, organized labor in underdeveloped countries is probably a poor seedbed for Communism—unschooled in its ideology, undisciplined in its tactics, and in the last analysis often unsympathetic with its goals. Nevertheless in a highly sensitive, developing economy, aggressive action by organized labor may frequently be misinterpreted as Communist activity.

It may also be expected that both government and organized labor will try to find ways to avoid open conflict. Even the dictatorial governments of Peron in Argentina and Vargas in Brazil appeased organized labor by giving it a sense of place and social significance in the process of industrial growth. Socialist or labor governments automatically invite labor to participate in public affairs, and thus the latter's attention may for a time be diverted from its own narrower interests. In addition, government can avoid conflict by developing radical nationalism in organized labor, a tactic to which labor may respond with vehemence.

If organized labor can be convinced that government intends to give it its due in the long run when substantial development has occurred, then it may voluntarily restrain itself in the immediate present. It has been suggested that this attitude holds in check the restlessness of labor in India.[3] There, counting on the ultimate development of a Socialist state, some sections of the labor movement accept less than the minimum wage and even endorse compulsory arbitration. In short, the emphasis of certain dramatic aims or the assumption of certain ideological positions by either government or labor in an underdeveloped country may serve to reduce the tensions between them, although the basic causes of these tensions cannot be removed.

Thus it would appear that until the

[3] Oscar Ornati, "Problems of Indian Trade Unions," in J. P. Windmuller, ed., "Current Issues in International Labor Relations," *Annals of the American Academy of Political and Social Science*, **310** (March, 1957), 156, 159.

main goals of economic development have been achieved, and government has the opportunity, if it so desires, to reduce its activities to the exercise of the functions traditionally expected of it, the structure of industrial relations in underdeveloped countries will tend to differ markedly from that commonly found in economically advanced countries. Government will be deeply concerned with economic life, anxious that the conflicts between employers and workers should not interfere with the process of development. Antagonism between organized labor and employers may often indeed be partly obscured by antagonism between organized labor and government. But since government and labor are clearly aware of the value of each to the other, the conflict of interest between them, though persisting, cannot be fought out to a drastic conclusion.

A Theory of Corruption

M. MCMULLAN

There is some corruption in all governments and in the public services of all countries. Some countries, however, suffer from a greater degree of corruption than others. Only very recently and in only a handful of countries has such corruption been so far reduced as to be practically negligible, that is to say so far reduced that it does not normally enter into a citizen's relations with his government. In most countries throughout most of their known history such corruption has been an accepted feature of life. In extreme cases today it can be a major obstacle

M. McMullan, "A Theory of Corruption," *Sociological Review*, **9** (1961), 181-201.

to economic development and a major cause of political instability. It deserves attention for its intrinsic interest as part of the "pathology" of bureaucracy, for its practical importance for the political and economic development of the poorer nations of the world, and for the contribution that an analysis can make to sympathetic understanding of what may otherwise be a repulsive feature of some societies. In this paper I try to relate the corruption observed in the British Colonies and ex-colonies of West Africa to the social conditions and histories of those countries and to make some tentative generalizations from a comparison of conditions there and in other parts of the world.

I am not asserting that these West African territories are peculiarly given to corruption; there are many countries in the world where the governments are more corrupt and many more where they were equally corrupt in the recent past; the choice of these countries is dictated only by the accident of the writer's own experience.

The Effects of Corruption

Understanding is desirable, but it is wrong to underrate the evil consequences of widespread corruption. People sympathetic to African and other nationalist movements are sometimes tempted to brush aside corruption as being a "passing phase" of no real political or social importance. Whether it is a "passing phase" or not in West Africa I do not know, though I shall give reasons for thinking that it is at least not a phase that will pass quickly; but I am certain that it is of real political and social importance. Some of the evils which widespread corruption may be expected to bring are:

1. Injustice. This needs no explanation.

2. Inefficiency. In countries where the general standard of technology is low this is a serious matter. Railway accidents are cause by station masters' corruptly agreeing to load logs that are too heavy for the wagons. Patients in hospitals may be denied treatment they require or bribe nurses to give them treatment they want (in West Africa usually injections), but which may be unsuitable for their condition. Corruption in making appointments may be relatively unimportant in a country where the general standard of competence is high, but in West Africa, where professional and technical competence is still rare, corruption results in the appointment of unsuitable people and the waste and frustration of the right man.

3. Mistrust of the government by the citizen. This is peculiarly serious where the government is anxious to carry out a program of economic development for which the enthusiasm of the population needs to be enlisted. It also increases the difficulties of enforcing criminal, revenue, and other laws.

4. Waste of public resources. Corruption in the government involves the ultimate transfer of public funds to the pockets of politicians or officials. The businessman who has to bribe to get a government contract ultimately charges the bribe to public funds.

5. Discouragement of enterprise, particularly foreign enterprise. Corruption adds an incalculable hazard to the normal thickets of bureaucratic procedure. The final bribe is never paid. Investors and entrepreneurs are dismayed and frustrated, and may find that the unofficial cost of starting an enterprise is too great for it to be profitable.

6. Political instability. In a country where there is a great deal of corruption, political attacks on people in positions of power are easy to mount and easy to get popular support for. Much of the political history of some unfortunate countries could be told as the "ins" being accused, correctly, by the "outs" of corruption; popular indignation at the corruption causing the replacement of the "ins" by the "outs," who in turn become corrupt and are attacked by a new group of "outs," This process could be demonstrated in detail from the history of some local government bodies in West Africa during the past ten years. At the national level it can lead either to political chaos, or

7. Repressive measures. It may be easier to deal with the accusations of corruption than with the corruption itself.

8. Restrictions on government policy. I recall a conversation with an American doctor who was an admirer of the British National Health Service.

"No such service would at the moment be possible in my home state," he said, naming the state. "The civil service is too inefficient and corrupt to be capable of running it." A corrupt civil service and police force restricts the range of policies available to a government.

Evidence

There is one preliminary problem which must be faced but cannot be solved: the problem of evidence. Arguments and statements about corruption cannot be demonstrated by factual or statistical evidence of the type normally acceptable as a basis for political or sociological generalization. There are plenty of reports, histories, and trial records exemplifying corruption in different countries, but corruption is not a subject which can be investigated openly by means of questionnaires and interviews. Even if it were, in principle, possible to quantify the phenomenon, there would be no practical possibility of doing so. The reader is asked to accept as a premise of the argument of this paper that there is more corruption in these West African countries than in, for instance, the United Kingdom. This is a view based on my own observations over a decade, broadly shared by other well-placed observers and supported by public expressions of concern by indigenous political and religious leaders in West Africa. But it cannot, nor can many of the other statements in this paper, be proved in the ways in which statements about less disreputable aspects of society can be proved. Corruption still awaits its Kinsey report. This difficulty must be recognized, but we cannot refuse to discuss important topics simply because the best type of evidence is not available.

Definition

I shall not attempt a comprehensive or legally precise definition of corruption,[1] and will content myself with the common understanding that a public official is corrupt if he accepts money or money's worth for doing something that he is under a duty to do anyway, that he is under a duty not to do, or to exercise a legitimate discretion for improper reasons. Institutions have official aims; the human beings that work them have personal aims. The ideal relation between the individual and the institution is that the individual should be able to satisfy his personal aims in harmony with, and while forwarding, the official aims of the institution. It is nothing to the Home Office that the prison warder has six children to feed, but the prison warder is acting legitimately in working as a prison warder so that he can feed his six children with his salary. Should he find his salary insufficient, however, and take money from the prisoners for doing them favors, he will be described as corrupt. He will be using his position in the prison to forward his personal aims in a way which conflicts with the official aim of the institution. There is a conflict between the attitudes and aims of a corrupt official and those of the service, and an equally important divergence between the attitudes and aims of the member of the public who induces the corruption of the official and the aims and attitudes of the society as

---

[1] In England there are a large number of laws against corruption. The most comprehensive definition is that in Sec. 1(1) of the Prevention of Corruption Act 1906, which includes not only corruption by public officials, but also similar behavior by any agent or employee. Of course the type of behavior which is the subject of this paper is not in West Africa or anywhere else confined to public officials. Similar behavior is common among the employees of private companies, educational institutions, and so forth.

a whole. These divergencies may be defined by reference to the laws and regulations in which the official aims and attitudes are set out.

The Argument

The corruption discussed here is, by definition, illegal. People break laws because they do not accept them, or because they have other interests or desires which they prefer or are impelled to follow. Some laws in a society find almost universal acceptance; other laws are broken by large numbers of people. Head hunting, for instance, is illegal in New Guinea and in France, but the laws against it are more often broken in New Guinea than in France. Obviously the law against head hunting in New Guinea is further from the popular attitude toward that activity in New Guinea than is the similar law in France from the popular attitude there. If there is greater corruption in West Africa than in Denmark, the popular attitude toward corruption in West Africa must be different from that in Denmark.

Thus far is tautology. The problem is to identify the reasons for the popular attitude. The argument of this paper is that a high level of corruption is the result of a wide divergence between the attitudes, aims, and methods of the government of a country and those of the society in which they operate, in particular of the procedures and aims of the government which put particular groups of the population at a special disadvantage: that therefore the different levels of corruption in different countries depend on the extent to which government and society are homogeneous.

Precolonial Society

The question of how far corruption can be said to have existed in precolonial times in West Africa, and how far present corruption is the result of the persistence of attitudes from that time, is an extremely difficult one. To discuss it adequately would require far greater knowledge of those societies than I can pretend to, and a great deal of space if due regard was to be had to the variety of social and political structures which existed. I shall, therefore, make only three points about precolonial society, points which are possibly obvious, but which are too important to be taken for granted.

1. Precolonial West African societies were familiar with conflicts between personal aims and official or social aims, hence their laws and customs and the punishments and other sanctions by which they were enforced, *but* although men wielded political power, judged causes, led armies, and collected taxes, their functions were less precisely defined in relation to those activities than they are in the bureaucratic governments of colonial and postcolonial times. The judicial functions of a chief were not sharply distinguished from his familial function as arbitrator and peace maker, or his political function as a leader concerned with the manipulation of power, so that impropriety in the exercise of his judicial function, such as favoritism, could less easily be attributed to him as corruption than in the case of a modern magistrate whose sole function is to judge. To say this is to come near to saying that, as there was no public service in precolonial West Africa, there could be no corruption of it; but this is not quite accurate. In fact, examples could be given of behavior clearly recognizable as corrupt (and recognized as such in the precolonial society) from the histories and legends of the peoples concerned. Such examples might be expected to be most common among the larger and more articulated political systems, such as those of Northern Nigeria, which had

evolved many bureaucratic features long before the advent of the colonial bureaucracy.

2. A man may of course be bribed with a horse, a woman, or a gun as effectively as with a roll of notes, but the possibilities and utility of bribery obviously increase with the growth of a money economy. In precolonial West Africa, money played a relatively minor part, though its importance varied from place to place. To take an extreme instance: in an area where the people lived at subsistence level and, as would be likely, had a political structure almost without full-time professionals, there would be neither the need for, nor the means of, bribery. Even more important perhaps is the availability of the sort of goods and opportunities on which to spend money that makes money of greater value than any other single commodity. This is relevant to the claim that the Communist government of China has greatly reduced corruption in that country, once notorious for it. Obviously, corruption must lose much of its attraction if there is little on which to spend the proceeds, and the acquisition of wealth is in itself (quite apart from the question of punishment for law breaking) looked on with disfavor. Only in a money economy and a society which allows a good deal of freedom to individuals in disposing of their property will the types of corruption we are dealing with be widespread.

3. In considering the relationship between corruption and traditional society in West Africa, observers often isolate the customary exchanges of gifts as the element in traditional life which has led to the growth of corruption in modern times. While not denying the relevance of customary gift exchange to bribery, the facility with which a bribe may be disguised as a customary gift, and, indeed, the genuine ambiguity of customary gifts in some traditional contexts, it is, in my opinion, wrong to isolate one feature of traditional life in this way. There were and are many features of the traditional way of life which, in the context of colonial and postcolonial society, contribute to the prevalence of corruption. My argument is that it is this clash of old customs, attitudes, and so forth, with the new forms of government that gives rise to corruption. The customary gifts are just one example. Other examples are easily found: the extended family system, which leads to the overburdening of an official with family responsibilities so that his pay is insufficient; his family and tribal loyalties, which obscure his devotion to the national community; the absence of an established class system, which makes it hard for the official to cultivate the aloofness which perhaps must, for most people, be the accompaniment of official integrity.

Corruption in Colonial and Postcolonial Times

In modern times my thesis concerns the disharmony between the government and the traditional society on which it is imposed and which it seeks to change. Specifically of course this modern government was in West Africa the colonial bureaucratic government. It was alien to West Africa in obvious ways: it was controlled from a distant land, and the controllers were subject to pressures and had aims often quite unrelated to the situation in West Africa; its key men were foreigners, often with little understanding of West African society, usually with no understanding of the indigenous languages, while its junior officials recruited from the indigenous peoples struggled to find a balance between their alien masters and the demands of their own people. The disharmonies were innumerable, and I shall consider only two of the most important; the first typical of an economically underdeveloped country, [the] second of a type found universally but which can be seen particularly clearly in West Africa. Before dealing with these, however, there is one important general topic.

The Climate of Corruption

Some years ago, I was escorting [to his car] an African judge from the court in which he had just sentenced a murderer to death. . . . The large crowd which had assembled to hear the case lined the path, cheering and dancing to express their pleasure at the verdict. One phrase was shouted over and over again, and was eventually taken up by the whole crowd and chanted in chorus. The judge asked me if I understood what it meant, and I said that I could catch the first words, "You're a good judge . . ." but could not understand the rest. "What they are shouting," said the judge, "is 'You're a good judge, we thought you had been bribed, but you haven't.'" With that he got into his car and was driven away.

No one there was surprised. A wryness of tone was the judge's only comment on the compliment that he was being offered. No one in the crowd saw any reason to disguise the implication that there would have been nothing surprising if the judge had been bribed. We were all living in a country where corruption was a very normal part of the scene, and the assumption of corruption was part of everyone's equipment for his daily business.

Such a climate of corruption is in itself an important factor. There is a continuous interaction between the willingness of people to pay bribes and the willingness of officials to receive them. People normally behave in the way that the people they live with behave. In a society with a high level of corruption, hardly any citizen can carry out his business, avoid trouble with the government, and generally get through life comfortably, without acquiescing to some extent at least in the prevailing corruption. There are not a few such societies in the world, and persons from more fortunate countries must, when visiting them or doing business with them, conform (or at least acquiesce), unless they prefer empty gestures which will inconvenience themselves to no useful purpose. At the other extreme, in an ideally uncorrupt society, the single corrupt man would offer to give or receive bribes in vain.

Divergencies Between Government and Society

The two examples of divergence between governments and West African society in colonial and postcolonial times which I shall discuss are: (1) that between a literate government and an illiterate society, and (2) that arising from laws in conflict with popular attitudes.

Literate Government in an Illiterate Society

Colonial rule in West Africa was and is the rule of an illiterate society by a literate government. The government operates in accordance with and by means of written rules and regulations. No one who cannot read and write can hope to occupy effectively any position in the public service. Entry into even the lowest grades is only for those who can read and write. Not only [are] reading and writing essential, but reading and writing *in English*, a foreign tongue. The majority of the population is illiterate and has little or no understanding of English. (Literacy and understanding English are in these countries almost synonymous). Friction between the literate public servant and the illiterate population is inevitable, and is of course greatest at the base of the public service pyramid, where functionaries and contacts with the public are most numerous, and it is at this level that the greatest *volume* of corruption occurs (the amount of damage done and money involved may well be greater at higher levels). Between the public and the functionaries with whom they most often deal, there is a constant flow of presents and bribes, given willingly or unwillingly, pressed on the official or extorted from the public.

Many examples of this process could be given (and it should be borne in mind that the public service in economically underdeveloped and colonial territories is of infinitely greater importance as the main channel of social initiative and the main route of personal advancement than it is in countries like Britain), but as an example of literate government operating in an illiterate society and how it differs from the same situation in an almost wholly literate society like our own, consider the confrontation of a police constable and a farmer. The farmer is barefoot, and the policeman is wearing a pair of large, shiny boots, and this difference may stand as a symbol of their relative ability to protect themselves in modern West Africa. The police constable is literate, he has learned (at some pain perhaps) not only to adapt himself to a specific set of rules and regulations, but to wield them against others; he is an authority on the law, at least at his own level; he can arrest the farmer, or report him, and he has, again at his own level, innumerable official and semiofficial contacts with officers of other branches of government service.

The farmer is relatively a child. He is uncertain of the exact contents of the various laws that affect him, and uncertain how he stands in relation to them. He knows he should have a license for his shotgun but cannot be sure that the one he has is still valid, or if the clerk who issued it cheated him with a worthless piece of paper. He knows he should have paid his taxes, but he has lost his receipt, and anyway there is something called a tax year, different from a calendar year, which "they" keep on changing, so perhaps he should have paid some more anyway. Even if he feels sure that he has committed no crime, he cannot defend himself against the policeman. To complain to the constable's superior would not be much good in the face of the *esprit de corps* of the police. He can defend himself only by going to some other member of the literate class, a letter writer perhaps, or if the case is really serious, a lawyer, but has none of the skills necessary to choose a competent practitioner, and he may be so misunderstood that his real case is never put. Even if he has a good case and wins, it may not do him much good. All the policeman's colleagues will know about it, and sooner or later of course he *will* break a law. Much better give the policeman what he is asking for, or if he is not asking for anything, better give him something anyway so that when something does go wrong, he will be more likely to be nice about it. A *man does not*, says the Ashanti proverb, *rub bottoms with a porcupine.*

Consider for a moment a similar scene in, say, the prosperous county of Sussex. In Sussex the farmer would be as well if not better educated than the policeman, and will know those parts of the law which affect him better than does the policeman. The farmer may be himself a magistrate or a local government counselor, or know magistrates and counselors and perhaps the chief constable socially. For *this* policeman to demand money from *this* farmer for doing him a favor or not doing him a disfavor would be a laughable miscalculation.

This contrast may be overdrawn, but serves to make the point. The illiterate man entangled in the toils of a literate government is under a disadvantage for which practically nothing can compensate him, but wealth can help.[2] Sometimes the West African farmer, in addition to his other disabilities, would be poorer than the policeman, though the pay of a police constable in West Africa is not high; but if he were a cocoa farmer, a rubber farmer, a coffee farmer, or not a farmer at all, but one of the large number of persons who, although illiterate, make more money than a police constable, then the temptation for the farmer to compensate himself for his lack of power and knowledge by use of his money becomes clear. Equally clear are the opportunities for an ill-paid policeman to turn his power over wealthy illiterates into a supplement to his pay. This exchange of wealth for power, and power for wealth, is of course the typical pattern of corruption.

The phenomenon of a literate government in an illiterate society arose in West Africa with the imposition of colonial rule, but it does not of course pass with the coming of independence. The independent governments in Nigeria and Ghana are quite as much committed to literate government as was the colonial regime, indeed, since

independence, departments, officials, laws, and regulations have multiplied at a great rate. The removal of this particular disharmony cannot be achieved by the abolition of literate government, but only by the abolition of illiteracy in the society.

The Operation of the Law

My second example of persons and groups put under a disadvantage by official policy and thereby becoming a source of corruption is the operation of certain laws. All laws put certain persons under a disadvantage, i.e., those who do or wish to do what the laws forbid. Such persons are a source of corruption in every country.
But laws differ:

(1) in the extent to which public opinion supports them;
(2) in the case with which their breach can be detected;
(3) in the profits to be made by breaking them.

(2) and (3) of course stem to some extent from (1).

If a man tries to land an airplane in a suburban garden, he will find:

(1) that all the neighbors are anxious to assist the police;
(2) that his transgression has become instantly notorious;
(3) that the financial rewards are not impressive.

If he tries to sell alcoholic drinks after hours he will find:

(1) that many members of the public will be very pleased;
(2) that it can often be done without the police getting to hear of it;
(3) that it is a source of financial profit.

Obviously, it is breaches of the law of the second sort which are most likely to be a source of corruption.

---

[2] It is worth mentioning here that in many countries with a largely illiterate population the defence of the unlettered man against government officials is often an important function of political parties. Here the illiterate is buying protection in exchange for his vote or his general support for the party.

Laws regulating gambling and drinking, for instance, usually have little general support from the population, will be broken by otherwise law-abiding citizens, are difficult to enforce, and frequently broken. They tend to bring all laws into disrepute, and, by the creation of a large class of persons vulnerable to legal action at the hands of the petty officers of the law, they encourage corruption. An extreme example of this type of law was of course prohibition in the United States. Postwar rationing in the United Kingdom had similar consequences, fortunately on a smaller scale, but will remind us that such laws are occasionally necessary whatever the price that must be paid for them.

Let us return for a moment to our Sussex policeman. Is there any group of people with whom his relations are similar to the relations of his West African confrere with the West African farmer? The answer is yes. There are, first of all, the professional criminals, those who habitually break the law. Such people he can harrass, and they find it very hard to strike back at him, however unjustly he may beset them. Criminals are a notorious source of corruption in any police force. Next, and perhaps more important, as they usually have more money than the criminal classes proper, are people who engage in trade and activities where the line between legality and illegality is so fine, and the regulations so complex, that they are always in danger of unwittingly committing an offence, nearly always being tempted to commit one, and can therefore plausibly be accused of an offence at almost any time. Notable examples are public-house keepers, bookmakers, and motorists.[3] Any government must, and

does, put some activities out of bounds; each time it does so, however, it puts some of the population at a disadvantage and anxious to defend themselves by corrupting those whose duty it is to enforce the laws.

For obvious historical reasons, these West African territories have an unusually large number of laws which, by the criteria I have suggested, are likely to give rise to corruption. A colonial regime, especially one like the British, responsible to a representative government in the metropolitan country, is bound, and indeed most people in the metropolitan country regard it as duty bound, to frame its laws with more regard to British than West African standards of desirable behavior. Particularly during the early years of colonial rule, the colonial governments were more responsive to British than to West African pressure groups. For instance, the abolition of slavery was brought about by a popular agitation in Britain, but brought the British government's representatives in West Africa into conflict with powerful and traditionally respectable elements of African society. Another example is the rules which arose from the British government's adherence to the Geneva Convention restricting the sale of spirits to the inhabitants of protectorates. These may have been excellent, but did not spring from West African conditions or West African demands, and were consequently a source of conflict and alienation between rulers and ruled. The enforcement of these laws was of course sporadic and uncertain, so lightly were the territories administered and policed. Many of the diffi-

---

[3] In West Africa, lorry drivers are always complaining about extortion by the police. It is often alleged that the police on road patrol simply collect a toll from all passing lorry drivers. If the driver refuses to pay, it is of course never difficult for the police to accuse [him] of some driving offence or to find some detail of [his] lorry that does not conform to the, inevitably, complex regulations.

culties that might have arisen from the imposition of alien laws were avoided by the sheer impossibility of enforcing them and the wide discretion given to district officers to adjust the intentions of the statute book to the realities of the local situation. But not all conflict could be avoided. The Second World War, for instance, produced a great many laws intended to regulate economic activity. Without adequate means to enforce such regulation, and without any understanding by the population of why such regulation was desirable, laws of this sort served mainly to corrupt the officers charged with their enforcement. An excellent example is the exchange control laws. Introduced during the war, when the imperial government understandably required all sterling territories to have approximately similar laws concerning the import and export of currency, and so forth, they were practically unenforceable against the indigenous merchants who crossed and recrossed the unpatrolled and often undefined land frontiers of West Africa. At the same time, "smuggling" of currency was, and still is, profitable and completely devoid of any "criminal" stigma; after all, the evasion of currency regulations was widely practiced in the United Kingdom, where the population had much more reason to appreciate the need for them. Still, the law was there, and was, through honest zeal, malice, or with intent to extort, spasmodically enforced, so that many who regarded themselves as honest merchants were vulnerable to attacks from officers of the law, and under the necessity of buying them off. Trade across the frontier in West Africa is often extremely profitable, and these laws became a serious focus of corruption for enforcement officers. At some customs stations a pro rata tariff was extracted by the officials from those travelers who wished to import foreign currency, but were too lazy to walk through the bush with it.

Once again, this type of conflict between the government and society first arose with colonialism, but it does not disappear with the coming of independence. President Nkrumah's government, for instance, is more strongly committed to the transformation of Ghanaian society than the colonial regime ever was, and this transformation is bound to involve acute strains between the laws and the behavior of the ordinary Ghanaians. This is particularly true of course of laws controlling economic behavior in one way or another, inevitable when a government is committed to developing the country as rapidly as possible. High taxation, for instance, will enroll many normally honest people into the semi-criminal ranks of the tax evaders. Any form of direct control of rare resources has the same effect.[4] No society can be transformed without laws that go against the interests and accepted behavior of some people in it; these laws will set up the sort of conflicts which give rise to corruption. A wise government might be expected, while recognizing this regrettable fact, to limit such laws to what it regards as absolute essentials. Such attractive possibilities as the prohibition of nudity, polygamy, or football pools might be thought to be unnecessary additions to the strains and frictions which will

---

[4] The allocation of market stalls by local government councils in West Africa is a regular cause of scandals. The trouble is that these exceedingly valuable properties are usually let at rents greatly below what they are worth. The difference inevitably transforms itself into bribes. The simple device of charging as much rent as the traders would be prepared to pay does not, perhaps understandably, commend itself to the counselors and officials.

be imposed by a nationalist government's essential program.

The Subjective Element

As I said earlier, there is a constant interaction between the willingness of officials to receive bribes and the willingness of the public to give them. It is part of the general conflict between the aims and methods of the government and the society which is being governed that the subjective attitude of many officials in these countries should not be in harmony with their objective roles. The official role is not one indigenous to West Africa, but an import from another society, where it has grown up flanked and buttressed by many attitudes and social forces missing in its new environment. Many West African officials have successfully adopted and internalized the qualities required for their role, but it is not surprising that many have not been completely successful. The West African official, subject to pressures of which his British colleague knows nothing, is caught and squeezed precisely at the point of conflict between the colonial (or postcolonial) government and the indigenous society. The British official in West Africa is an overseas projection of a well-established and understood mode of metropolitan behavior, protected by traditions of aloofness and difference, and the approval of those that matter most to him (other British officials) from the alien pressures of West African society. This subjective aspect of the question, the question of the individual morality, is of great importance, and I shall touch on it again when I discuss possible remedies for corruption.

High-Level Corruption

I have so far been dealing mainly with corruption at the lower levels of the government, the level at which hundreds of petty officials enforce the laws on the general public. Corruption at a high level, corrupt behavior by cabinet ministers, judges, ambassadors, presents different, though related, problems. A cabinet minister who accepts bribes is trading his power for money just as surely as is the police constable, but we are here moving out of the realm where sociological generalization is *necessarily* useful. A cabinet minister may be corrupt in any society, but this may have much more to do with his individual circumstances than any generalization that can be made about the society. Yet most informed people would agree that these West African territories are more troubled by corruption among cabinet ministers or their like than is, say, Denmark. This fact can be related to certain features of these societies.

1. A climate of corruption in a society will affect ministers as well as policemen, and, perhaps more important, will lead to public condonation of corruption by cabinet ministers. It is a most disconcerting feature of these societies that ordinary citizens will believe, and recount, the most fantastic stories, some of them palpably untrue, of corruption among their leaders, with no or very little sense of indignation. Even when official inquiries have disclosed instances of undoubted corruption, this has often had no effect on the political careers of the persons involved.

2. Politicians in West Africa do not come from an established patrician class. Most of them are "new men" and have therefore had no opportunity to develop standards different from the rest of society, such as can develop in a particular class or group, and are not personally wealthy (at the beginning of their careers at least). Elevation to cabinet rank therefore presents them at once with new needs for money . . .

and new opportunities for acquiring it by trading their power for the wealth of others.

3. As ministers in a British-type parliamentary regime, they are playing roles not well suited to their own education or to the society in which they are expected to play them. I will give two examples:

(a) The sharp distinction that has grown up in Britain between the purposes for which public funds can and cannot be used creates special difficulties in a West African context. In England in Henry VII's day, the King's money was the King's money, and was used for forwarding the interest of his government in every way. Subsequently there grew up a constitutionally important, but by no means wholly logical, distinction between those functions of the government on which public money could be spent and those functions (e.g., the organization of public support) for which politicians organizing themselves in parties were expected to find finance elsewhere. In England, money for political parties is available from the large funds accumulated by business or trade unions, but in West Africa such sources are not available. As in most other parts of the world, standard subscriptions from ordinary party members are not sufficient to finance this important aspect of government. Governmental corruption, "kickbacks" on profitable contracts, the sale of profitable or prestige-giving appointments are an obvious source of party funds. A great deal of the corruption at ministerial level in West Africa is to be explained along these lines, and in these cases really amounts to a transfer of public funds from one type of political expenditure (i.e., legitimate by British criteria) to the other type (i.e., party political expenditure).

(b) In Britain, the distinction between the official and private capacities of the holders of high office is widely understood and accepted. As a private person, a minister of the Crown is not expected to be particularly hospitable or lavish in his hospitality. In West Africa, if a man holds high office, he is often expected to entertain his relations, tribesmen, political supporters, for such generosity may be a condition of continued political eminence.

4. The desire for wealth, for whatever purpose, is reinforced in many cases by a sense of the impermanence of the new status. It is not easy for a man who has risen from poverty to eminence and riches in a few years, as many African leaders have done, to feel confident that the present affluence will continue. There are rumors of secret bank accounts in Switzerland and other foreign countries; if such accounts exist they are hoards against the possibility of lean years ahead.

The Function of Corruption

What is the social function of corruption in West Africa? Although damaging to official ideals and aims, it is clearly not a subversive or revolutionary phenomenon. It is rather an emollient, softening conflict and reducing friction. At a high level it throws a bridge between those who hold political power and those who control wealth, enabling the two classes, markedly apart during the initial stages of African nationalist governments, to assimilate each other. At the lower level it is not an attack on the government or its instruments by the groups discriminated against, but an attempt by them to reach an accommodation by which they accept their inferior status but avoid some of its consequences. In spite of the damage it does to a government and its policies, it may be of assistance in reducing resentments which might otherwise cause political difficulties. This useful role can be demonstrated by the semiofficial recognition given by the British colonial regime to a practice which in the United Kingdom would be classified as corrupt—the acceptance of gifts from local chiefs by district officers. This well-established, well-known, but never, for obvious reasons, officially recognized practice, grew from the traditional custom of presenting gifts to chiefs when approaching them with requests for favors. It was tolerated by the colonial regime, albeit in a limited form, because of its value for that regime. The colonial district officer was, to most of the chiefs of his district, an unpredictable alien, wielding wide, undefined, powers according to incomprehensible criteria, whose arrival in the local rest house was often a cause of alarm. The courtesies of the offer and acceptance of gifts of eggs and chickens brought this alarming official some way into the chief's familiar world, threw some bridge across the gulf which separated the two men, and created a relationship in which the inevitable frictions were softened by a personal familiarity and a traditional context. This was of course of great value to the district officer in doing his job, and was therefore tolerated by the colonial authorities. A similar softening of what might otherwise be an intolerable relationship between the official and the people he deals with can result from more heinous dealings. Indeed, the greater the corruption, the greater the harmony between corruptor and corruptee.

Application and Development of the Argument

I cannot attempt a detailed application of my tentative thesis to other societies, but on a superficial view it seems to have much to recommend it. Countries such as the Scandinavian states, with a marked homogeneity of society, are, it is generally agreed, fairly free from corruption. The shortcomings in this respect of the United States can be related to its large immigrant populations and its second-class races. The role of immigrants in the corruption of big-city politics is a commonplace of American political science. The corruption in Spain, Portugal and some middle eastern countries might be explicable in terms of the wide divergence between the very wealthy classes, who have a considerable voice in government, and the general poor. Despotic and dictatorial government might be found to be more likely to produce, and indeed to protect, corruption than forms of government more responsible to the views of the ruled. A theoretically interesting limiting case is that of slavery. Slaves are a group under an extreme disability, with an obvious need to protect themselves. Under many forms of slavery, however, they have no money or other means to corrupt their overseers. The extreme degrees of disability therefore may not result in corruption, as they remove the means of protection. The optimum conditions for corruption, according to this theory, surround a group under a harsh disability but still possessed of considerable wealth—a Jewish moneylender in a nineteenth-century Polish ghetto, for instance—a Negro bookmaker in an Arkansas town —a wealthy brothel owner in London. These conclusions do not seem to be contradicted by what we know of the facts.

Remedies for Corruption

Responsible leaders in West Africa often make statements denouncing the prevalence and the dangers of corruption and not infrequently launch campaigns to "root it out." I am unaware of any such campaign which has had any lasting effect, or indeed has even led to many prosecutions. Various remedies from prayer to flogging have been suggested, but none has been seriously tried.

Draconian programs for combating corruption are sometimes elaborated. These involve extremely heavy punishments together with a highly trained, well-paid corps of *agents provocateurs*. The combination of the two is supposed to alarm all potential corruptors or corruptees so much that they are frightened ever to offer or accept a bribe for fear of being denounced. Unfortunately, such violent police pressure unsupported by public opinion would be quite likely to result in an *increase* of corruption and of blackmail. The *agents provocateurs* themselves would have to be members of the society in which they were operating, and it is hard to imagine that such a job would attract persons whose integrity would be beyond doubt. Frequent change of personnel would be required so that large numbers of such agents would be needed, making it even more difficult to ensure a high standard. Their opportunities for blackmail would be immense, and it is easy to see that such a campaign could only lead to unpleasantness far outweighing any possible beneficial result.

Given the continued desire by the governments of the West African countries for rapid economic development and general modernization, conflicts fruitful of corruption will continue and are, indeed, almost certain to increase, so that no immediate improvement is at all likely. It will be a long time before the societies are remolded and homogeneous with the government; even total literacy will take considerably more than a genera-

tion. Does this mean that there is nothing useful that can be done except to wait for the slow evolution of the society?

The answer is, I think, that a great many useful things can be done, but none which will have dramatically rapid results. To achieve anything at all of course, the leadership of the country concerned must regard the problem as really important, and be prepared on occasion to sacrifice political advantage by, for instance, making an example of a corrupt minister even though he has a politically useful following in the country. Given such leadership, and it cannot be taken for granted that it is always available, the following measures suggest themselves:

1. Exemplary proceedings against ministers or other important functionaries to publicize the government's determination.

2. A slight increase of police pressure against corruption at all levels.

3. A fairly low pitched, but steady and continuous, educational effort in schools, colleges, and in the newspapers, and by other means of publicity. Not just a short and violent campaign, but one continuing over years and becoming a normal part of all educational processes.

4. Most important of all, a special effort with the public service. This is the most hopeful line of approach and might produce relatively quick results. If I am right about the effect that development and modernization will have on these societies, there is no hope of removing the public servant's opportunities for corruption. It may, however, be possible to train him not to take advantage of his opportunities. Small groups of people can be trained to have different standards in some respects from those of the generality of people, and in any society this is a normal feature of specialization; each

specialized group has special standards in respect of its own work. By educational pressure and disciplinary measures it should be possible to raise the standard of the public service. Such a policy could only succeed, however, if service conditions and salaries were good and the status of the service high.

5. Careful scrutiny of existing and projected laws to eliminate those that tend to increase the opportunities for corruption unnecessarily.

It will be seen that I have not included in this program any reference to religious or social emotions sweeping through the population. Such events are, however efficacious, not usually to be invoked by statesmen.

Conclusion

In conclusion, I should like to emphasize two points.

1. In the West African countries under consideration, the colonial regime is the obvious historical source of the conflict between the government and the society. It is not suggested that similar conflicts cannot arise without colonialism, or that colonialism is exceptionally potent as a cause of corruption. There are countries which have never been colonies in the sense in which the word is used of West Africa, where corruption is much greater than it is in these countries. Moreover, as I have indicated, the succession regimes there are committed to a far more thoroughgoing program of change than their colonial predecessors, so that the conflicts productive of corruption may be intensified after independence. Moreover, corruption under the colonial regime was limited by the presence of colonial service officials whose standards were those of the British public service. It is not yet certain how far an indigenous civil service can have the same effect.

2. Corruption is an evil, but the avoidance of corruption cannot be more than a subsidiary aim of government policy. If my thesis is correct, colonialism and the modernizing, westernizing policy of succession governments give rise to corruption—but this, in itself, is not a condemnation of colonialism or [of] a modernizing policy. Governments must frequently act in ways which result in conflicts fruitful of corruption. The means of control, forced purchase and rationing necessary to deal with a local famine, for instance, are always productive of corruption, but no one would hesitate to pay this inevitable price when people are threatened with starvation. What one may, however, hope, is that a consciousness among policy makers that corruption is a phenomenon with causes that can be understood will lead to a choice of methods designed to minimize corruption, and to an understanding of the need to strengthen factors working against it—the most important of which is the subjective integrity of the public service.

Patterns of Economic Growth

BERT F. HOSELITZ

Much of the current discussion of theories of economic growth is colored

Bert F. Hoselitz, "Patterns of Economic Growth," *Canadian Journal of Economics and Political Science*, **21** (1955), 416-431.

by one of two factors which repeatedly crop up in the pertinent literature. The theoretical treatment of economic growth is either too strongly policy oriented, or it is stated in an overly general form whose results are applicable only with difficulty, and often with grave reservations, to actual cases of economic growth.

Since the practical needs of policy makers in the United Nations and its specialized agencies and in national governments concerned with developmental policies or colonial development have provided a strong impetus for the recent study of economic growth, it is not surprising that the literature on this subject should have taken on a strong[ly] policy oriented coloration. What the practitioners needed and continue to need are general guidelines for their work. What they ask from the theorist, therefore, is to prescribe for them a series of relatively simple formulae which make up the basic equipment of the toolkits they can take to the four corners of the world and from which they can select, as the situation demands, the appropriate item for application. The result of this situation has been the elaboration of a large amount of knowledge, the parts of which are little integrated. This is especially unfortunate since the concept of technical assistance has tended to embrace knowledge in many fields of social science and has brought together scholars and administrators in various fields and with varied technical competence.

The tendency of overgeneralization in growth theory has a somewhat different effect from the tendency of excessive policy orientation. Its result has been to reduce the number of variables upon which the growth process was said to depend. A general model is easier to construct if the number of variables is small and the relations among them simple. But in such general models, much of the variety of the historical experiences of the countries which underwent economic development is lost. Perhaps an example may make clear what I have in mind. Among the most highly developed countries today are Canada and Switzerland. To what extent can a theory of growth adequately explain the processes of economic development which took place in these two countries? To what extent could such a theory, even if it were sufficiently emaciated to account for the common features in the developmental processes of these two countries, serve as an instrument of predicting trends of development in India?

I do not wish to deny that we may identify the bare bones of a theory which relates such variables as movements of population, accumulation of capital, technological change, and the generation of gross output in a quite general form. But in attempting to predict what changes we may expect in some presently underdeveloped country and what obstacles it is likely to encounter in its process of development, we must have models with more flesh and muscle than can be provided by a theory which relates a few very general variables in a purely abstract manner.

Yet it would be wrong to argue that if general models are inadequate we should turn to the other extreme and regard every case as . . . unique. We cannot pretend to search for a theory of economic growth if the variables in each society are combined uniquely so as to allow us no other generalization but the trite observation that the only thing we can learn from history is that we can learn nothing from history. Such a position would be wrong simply because the purely economic relations which determine the growth process can be stated in a very general way.

The question is reduced then to asking how we can incorporate the role of governments and of social and cultural factors in a theory or theories of growth. Next it is necessary to ask what use can be made of the historical experience of countries which achieved a high level of economic performance and what insights can be gained from this experience. In what follows, I should like to outline at least some significant variables outside the field of economics which might be incorporated into theories of economic growth. The result is not a single, uniform theory of growth, but rather an array of typical situations conducive to growth. This is attained by constructing a series of "boxes," each of which may be obtained by describing contrasting conditions under which economic growth has occurred or may occur. I hope to show that these distinctions are meaningful, at least to the extent of providing us with a number of boxes into which actual cases can be placed rather than with an array of empty boxes.

I

The first problem to which we will address our attention is the ratio between population and the natural resources available to that population in the initial phase of the development process. That this ratio, which has sometimes somewhat inaccurately been called the "man-land ratio," is of overriding importance is a platitude. Yet it is strange that, in spite of its importance, it has achieved very little attention, apart from the obvious observation that some societies, as, for example, India, with a relatively high density of population in agriculture, face formidable difficulties of development on this account alone. If we turn to countries which have achieved a high level of economic performance, we find among them some which exhibited, at the time of their early growth, serious pressure of population upon resources, though perhaps not of the magnitude with which this phenomenon manifests itself in India,

Java, or Egypt. On the other hand, we find countries whose population was confronted with almost unlimited natural resources. Examples of the first type are Holland or Switzerland, and of the second the United States, Canada, or Australia.

Though in all these countries the problem of economic growth was solved by the accumulation of capital and the development of human skills which resulted in higher productivity of labor and capital, the actual processes by which the solution occurred differed substantially. If one were to apply Toynbeean language one would say that the challenge presented to the two kinds of society differed though the over-all final objective to which the challenge pointed was similar.

In the United States and Canada, the problem was to bring vast idle resources under the control of society. In Switzerland and Holland, it consisted in developing the relatively scarce natural resources by combining them in optimal fashion with additional capital and the relatively most abundant resource, labor. Seen from the standpoint of the accumulation of capital, the growth of the new countries was essentially a process of widening capital. In the older countries, it was one of deepening capital. Seen from the standpoint of the development of the human factor, the new countries had to find suitable methods for the extensive employment of labor, the older countries for the development of high skills and the intensive application of labor. I propose to call the first process of economic growth an *expansionist process* and the second an *intrinsic process* of growth.

The distinction between expansionist and intrinsic patterns of economic growth serves not merely to show that in each case different optimum combinations of productive factors are likely to prevail, but to relate each form of economic growth to noneconomic factors and institutions. Expansionist development implies the consecutive incorporation of new territory. This can take place either through colonial settlement or by a process of creating new political units which become politically and economically coordinated on a basis of equality with the older portions of a country. What interests us here, above all, is not so much the question of constitutional or power relations between different provinces or parts of a country or empire, but rather the impact of ideologies which accompanied expansionist patterns of growth. Why did some societies seem to take up the challenge presented by wide open spaces so much more easily than others? Why did the farmers and settlers on the North American continent undertake long journeys into the unknown in search for virgin land or perhaps the pot of gold at the end of the rainbow? Why do we find, on the other hand, societies in which migration occurs rarely and is undertaken on a relatively large scale only in response to overwhelming pressures? Compare the degree of spatial mobility of the early settler in the uplands of Virginia or New England with the Javanese who remains in his overcrowded village even though the neighboring islands offer large stretches of good and fertile land.

I believe that the tendency to expansionist economic growth is a phenomenon which is as unusual in the history of the world as the development of modern western technology and rational economic organization. This trend of development is not identical with empire building as such. History knows many instances of empire building from the time of the ancient Egyptians to the Muslim expansion over Nether Asia and North Africa and the empires of Charles V and Napoleon. An explanation for these historical events has been suggested by Schumpeter in his famous essay on the "Sociology of Imperialism." The carrier of these expansionist ventures is a "machine of warriors created by the wars which required it, which now creates the wars it requires."[1] The object of this class is to maintain its élite position in society, and it can do so only by trying to pull its society behind it in the expansionist ventures which it unleashes. This ideology was foreign to the settlers of the North American continent. The star which led them across mountain and prairie was not the notion of empire building. The need for a continental empire was a rationalization of the politicians, but what inspired the masses who settled the continent was the "myth of the garden," as Henry Nash Smith has called it.[2]

To be sure, once an empire was conquered the spoils of the conquest accrued to the victors. The Muslim khalifs profited from the riches of Syria, Egypt, and the Maghreb, and the Catholic kings from the gold and silver mines of Mexico and Peru. But in all these instances the impetus given to expansion was either short-lived plunder or the force of a religious creed which upheld the *élan* of the conquerors. The goals of American, Canadian, and Australian settlers were different. They went not to conquer but to set up farmsteads and to form communities. The personal motives of migrants doubtless varied a good deal. Some went west because they felt that their domestic economic situation was hope-

---

[1] Joseph Schumpeter, *Imperialism and Social Classes*, Heinz Norton, trans. (New York: Meridian Books, Inc., 1955), p. 25.
[2] H. N. Smith, *Virgin Land* (Cambridge: Harvard University Press, 1950), pp. 123ff., *et passim*.

less. Others tried to solve by escape a family or personal difficulty with which they could not otherwise cope. Some ran away because they had been involved in a crime or other dishonest act; others again were religious fanatics or plain adventurers who were attracted by the romance and freedom of the frontier. But whatever the personal motives, they all became translated into analogous action through the operation of a powerful ideology according to which opportunity and success were to be found in the vast empty area toward which they felt themselves drawn as if by manifest destiny. In the long run this expectation of success was confirmed. The gradual settling of the American and Canadian West contributed not only to the maintenance and even the improvement of the already elevated real incomes of those who remained behind, but also, in the long run, to the prosperity of those who had traveled west themselves. Many did not experience this prosperity, but their children and grandchildren benefited from the endurance of the first settlers and became living proof that their sacrifices, their abstinence, had paid off. By the end of the nineteenth century much of the early romanticism of the westward movement had disappeared, but so had also the worst risks and hardships. In exchange, the grain and meats of the West, its minerals and fruits and its lumber had begun to conquer the markets of the world.

The result of this ideology of success was a society based on a strong sentiment of egalitarianism. To be sure, there exist class distinctions in the countries with autonomous expansionist patterns of development, but they are less harsh and rigid there than elsewhere. Contrast the American or Canadian class structure with the forms of social organization in countries which followed an intrinsic pattern of growth. Even where a society was founded originally on egalitarian principles its development was accompanied by a gradual tightening of the hierarchy of social classes and a tendency toward oligarchic or aristocratic governments and social structures. Take the medieval city state, the classical example of intrinsic economic growth. In the early twelfth century the citizens formed a group of brethren with equal rights and little difference in wealth. By the fifteenth century urban oligarchies controlled the fate of most city states in the economically more advanced portions of Europe, such as northern Italy, the Low Countries, the Hansa towns, and the towns of upper Germany. The new immigrant could find, in the vast number of cases, a place only on the lower margin of the social scale. Even today in Switzerland, a country with far-reaching democratic traditions, the social distance between workers and burghers, peasants and city magistrates, is much greater than in Anglo-Saxon North America, and the barriers against upward movement in the social scale are almost insurmountable.

II

In addition to the dichotomy between expansionist and intrinsic patterns of growth I wish to list two more distinctions which are of significance. The first relates to the degree of dependence upon one or more foreign countries experienced by a society in the course of its economic development. The second relates to the active role played by a country's government in stimulating and directing the process of economic growth.

I wish to propose first the dichotomy between countries with a "dominant" and those with a "satellitic" pattern of economic growth. The ideal case of a dominant pattern would be exhibited by a country with a fully autarchic economy, with no need to resort to foreign borrowing for purposes of capital accumulation, and without exports. At the other extreme we would have a society which draws all its capital for development from abroad and which develops only those branches of production whose output is entirely exported. If we further stipulate that all, or the bulk, of the capital imports come from one source and that all, or the bulk, of the exports go to one destination, we have the ideal-typical case of a country with a satellitic pattern of growth. It is obvious that neither of these two extremes is, or even can be, realized in practice. But we find some actual cases in which the one or the other extreme was or is approached more or less closely. Many countries began their economic growth as satellites to a foreign economy and gradually emancipated themselves, adopting a progressively more dominant pattern of economic growth. If we compare Canada of the 1880's with Canada of today, we see this change clearly. The same change took place in the United States somewhat earlier, and in Australia somewhat later, than in Canada.

But although larger countries endowed with relatively varied resources usually can and will make this change in the course of economic growth, some countries, especially some smaller ones, remain permanently in the position of a satellite. In other words, the distinction between satellitic and dominant patterns of economic growth is not necessarily correlated with low and high levels of economic development. On the contrary, the pure theory of international specialization leads to the conclusion that a country's real income is maximized if it specializes in the production of that commodity or set of commodities in which it has the greatest comparative advantage. Thus we would expect that, *caeteris paribus*, in a world free of absolutely insurmountable barriers to international trade, a country's real income could be increased by its engaging in more specialized production and thereby becoming more dependent upon the outside world. Yet this seems to be an outcome which most countries try to avoid.

I believe that the explanation for this behavior lies in two facts. First, the extraordinarily high risk which dependence on one or a few commodities as export staples is supposed to imply. A study of actual cases would reveal that, apart from serious depressions, these risks are, in general, exaggerated. But the vulnerability of a one-crop economy is increased if it depends for its foreign-exchange earnings not merely upon exporting one or a few staple products, but, in addition, upon marketing its exports in one country. It is this factor which establishes the satellitic character of an economy with respect to another and which is feared and resented because it is thought to facilitate, and even invite, political dependence and the possibility of "imperialistic" intervention and all that nasty word implies. The most typical satellitic economies are, therefore, also colonial countries, where the "act of imperialism" preceded the establishment of a satellitic economy, and those countries which are small and helpless and have, at various times of their existence, been subject to the impact of pound, franc, or dollar diplomacy.

Much more interesting than these countries, which have, with few exceptions, not yet experienced a startling progress toward high levels of productivity and income, are other countries, which have shown considerable capacity for growth even though the pace and magnitude of that growth depended upon events outside their own boundaries and often upon the pace and magnitude of economic growth in one or two other countries. A more or less permanent satellitic pattern of development has been accepted and the best has been made of it. This has shaped general attitudes in such a country and endowed its population with a less rigorously nationalistic outlook than that of countries with dominant patterns of economic growth.

Some evidence for this conclusion can perhaps be adduced by referring to an historical event which may be regarded as having exerted a serious and rather sudden shock upon several countries, and by examining the response to that shock.[3] In the late 1870's the agriculture of most European countries was placed under severe stress through the increasing flood of American grain. What was their response? Some countries hastened to protect their own agriculture, others refrained from doing so and tried to adjust themselves to the new situation by taking advantage of it. The countries which raised their tariff walls were Germany, France, Italy, Spain, Portugal, Sweden, and Austria-Hungary. Those that did not were Britain, Holland, Belgium, Switzerland, and Denmark. With the exception of Britain, which is in a special class, since the decision to admit foreign agricultural products free of duty had already been made some thirty years earlier, all the countries that tried to adjust themselves to the new situation were small countries whose economic growth already, before this large-scale inflow of American grain, had been adapted to fit into the trading patterns of the larger countries surrounding them. The two most notable

[3] The episode reported in the paragraph has been analyzed in greater detail by C. P. Kindleberger in "Group Behavior and International Trade," *Journal of Political Economy*, **50** (February, 1951), 30-46.

instances are Switzerland and Denmark. They both accepted the new cheap grains and altered the general composition of their agricultural output by substituting the production and export of high-grade foodstuffs (bacon, eggs, and dairy products) for the production of domestic grain. In other words, the adjustment to the new situation increased their dependence upon foreign markets. Since Denmark's economic progress depended clearly, under these conditions, upon its finding a market for its products in either Britain or Germany, the satellitic character of its growth was made more definite. Switzerland's dependence upon any one or two foreign countries was less pronounced, but even so almost 56 per cent of its total exports in the 1890's went to the three main trading partners: Germany, France, and Britain. Swiss exports consisted not merely of agricultural products, but chiefly of watches and other forms of complex machinery. An analysis of the commodities making up Swiss export trade yields, however, the unmistakable result that its productive effort was directed largely to the supplying of certain specialized goods which it was particularly fitted to produce. The development of the Swiss economy in the nineteenth century could not have taken place in the form in which it actually did occur but for the capacity of the Swiss to adjust their productive pattern to the needs and opportunities of the countries surrounding them. Hence the Swiss economy, like the Danish, tended to exhibit a satellitic pattern of growth.

The very different response of Germany and France to the inflow of American grain confirms the view that they were engaged in a dominant pattern of growth. On the surface there is no reason why they should not have followed the British example and imported agricultural commodities free. In fact, this course of action was urged in both countries by certain sections of public opinion. I am not overlooking the fact that pressures against imitating the British example were overwhelming both in France and Germany, but why could these pressures be exerted in their full strength? Why was resistance to the protectionists so weak and based essentially on doctrinaire reasoning rather than the claims of a sound economic policy? I believe that the atmosphere prevailing in each of these two countries which were engaged in dominant growth induced representatives of the most varied political and ideological persuasions to favor a pattern of simultaneous, vigorous development of all branches of productive activity as a necessary prerequisite of "balanced" economic progress. In other words, the general orientation prevailing with respect to developing the country's resources tended to favor a high degree of self-sufficiency and self-reliance in economic performance.

III

The distinction between dominant and satellitic patterns of growth takes on particular importance if we consider a further dichotomy, that between autonomous and induced economic development. This dichotomy relates to the role of active governmental intervention in the development process. In characterizing the two types of patterns, here again we could stipulate ideal types which represent extremes not actually realized in practice, but at best approached more or less closely. The ideal autonomous pattern of growth is one in which all decisions affecting economic growth are made by individuals other than those holding political power. In other words, the ideal of an autonomous pattern is real-

ized in the entirely liberal state in which the system of political checks and balances within the government is supplemented by a system of checks and balances in the distribution of social tasks.

Except in very primitive societies, it is wealth, education, and political power that confer the highest status. The ideal form of the liberal state is based upon the assumption that crucial decisions in each of these three fields of social action will be exercised by a different social group or class, and that decisions affecting economic "values" will be made essentially on the basis of self-interest. A system which operates in this way fulfills in practical performance the classical model according to which autonomous economic growth, that is, an increase in output and, with it, material welfare, results from each person's pursuing his self-interest and in this way unconsciously, as it were, contributing to the common good. It will be remembered that an important aspect of the Marxian criticism of "bourgeois capitalism" was based on the assertion that this separation did not exist, or existed only in appearance, and that in Friedrich Engels' words, "the modern state, no matter what its form, is essentially a capitalist machine, the state of the capitalists."[4]

At the other extreme is the social system in which economic decisions are entirely determined by a central planning agency. Ideally such a system would imply distribution not by means of the price mechanism but by a system of rationing or some similar form of direct allocation. All economic growth in such a system would be strictly induced, that is, provided for and planned by a central authority.

[4] Friedrich Engels, *Socialism: Utopian and Scientific*, Edward Aveling, trans. (Chicago: Charles H. Kerr & Company, 1902), p. 123.

No contention is made that these ideal types of distributing decision-making functions among holders of political power and independent private individuals are realized anywhere in practice. Even in a country with so extensive a degree of planning as the U.S.S.R., some autonomy in making economic decisions is maintained. Indeed, it may be argued that a fully planned system would impose such rigidities as to make effective economic growth almost impossible. However, actual cases again come more or less close to the ideal types. Certainly most of the economic growth in the nineteenth century occurred in the form of autonomous development, whereas in the present century increasing reliance is placed upon patterns of induced development. The chief argument in favor of induced development is that it makes for more rapid economic growth. Bronfenbrenner has presented . . . three models exhibiting the relative rates of growth of systems with autonomous and induced growth.[5] He concludes that, on theoretical grounds, growth rates are higher in a system in which all capital is confiscated and investment decisions centrally made than in a system in which investment decisions are made by private individuals. We have, moreover, some empirical evidence which would tend to confirm his conclusion. Kuznets has . . . collected a series of long-term growth rates for various countries, covering the last three decades of the nineteenth, and the first four or five decades of the twentieth, centur[ies].[6] Of the four-teen countries for which Kuznets presents data, only one, Japan, experienced induced growth. Japanese rates of growth are higher than those of other countries, whether computed on an over-all basis or on a per capita basis. If the seventy-year period is broken down into subperiods of approximately two decades each, Japan also leads the field. There are, however, several subperiods in which the rates in some countries with autonomous patterns of growth come close to those of Japan. For example, the two decades in the United States from 1878 to 1898, in Canada from 1880 to 1900, in Sweden from 1890 to 1910, in Germany and Italy from 1870 to 1890, exhibit over-all (though sometimes not per capita) rates close to those of Japan. Unfortunately no reliable information is available on rates in the Soviet Union, but the researches of Gregory Grossman seem to indicate that in the period from 1928 to 1937 over-all rates amounted to between 90 and 100 per cent per decade.[7] Even if these data should prove exaggerated, and we accept the lower estimates of Colin Clark, Jasny, and Wyler, which fluctuate around 5 per cent per annum, the compounded rate of decennial growth would amount to 63 per cent, which is higher than any rate recorded in a country with an autonomous pattern of development. The highest rate ever reached by Japan was 60.7 per cent per decade, by the United States 52.4 per cent, by Canada 45.7 per cent, and by Germany 44.5 per cent. All other countries discussed by Kuznets had rates of less than 40 per cent per decade. It is questionable whether a rate such as that of Soviet Russia can be maintained for long in any country, but if it is true

[5] Martin Bronfenbrenner, "The Appeal of Confiscation in Economic Development," *Economic Development and Cultural Change*, 3 (April, 1955), 204-209.

[6] Simon Kuznets, "Population, Income and Capital" in L. H. Dupriez, ed., *Economic Progress: Papers and Proceedings of a Round Table Held by the International Economic Association* (Louvain, 1955), pp. 43-45.

[7] Gregory Grossman, "National Income" in Abram Bergson, ed., *Soviet Economic Growth* (New York: Harper & Row, Publishers, Inc., 1953), pp. 8-10.

—as is sometimes maintained—that the chief difficulty of countries that are at present underdeveloped is in overcoming an initial hump, then they would be more likely to gather momentum by induced growth than by autonomous growth.

I have already pointed out that pure induced and pure autonomous patterns of growth do not exist in practice. This brings up the delicate question of where to draw the line between them. The types of inducements to growth may vary with the times and the circumstances. A program of tariff protection may, under certain conditions, provide an overwhelmingly powerful inducement for private investment decisions in the direction of a high rate of growth. At other times and under different conditions, such a program may have only negligible effects. The same holds for other policies short of out-and-out planning. For example, many persons make Germany's currency reform of 1948 responsible for initiating a period of rapid growth in that country. Another instance which has sometimes been cited is the liberalization of trade and the diminution of governmental intervention under Napoleon III in France, which were associated with a noticeable speeding up of economic growth in that country.

These instances suggest another difficulty in classifying countries according to this criterion. Governmental practice may not coincide with the norms stipulated for the conduct of the political authorities. In other words, the relations between government and private individuals in the economic sphere may be so conceived as to leave, ideally, all significant decisions to the private individuals, yet government may impose narrow limits within which private initiative may be exercised or may use various forms of subsidies, so that, in practice, the process of growth depends primarily upon the government's "inducements" rather than upon autonomous private decisions. This situation can become even more complex since governmental paternalism may extend to areas other than economic life. It is conceivable that, on the one hand, a government may be quite autocratic in the political sphere and yet leave a relatively high degree of freedom to private economic decisions. On the other hand, it is possible for a government to employ relatively few constraints in the political sphere and engage simultaneously in a program of extensive direct and indirect subsidization in the economic sphere. These differences in governmental behavior in different arenas of social life and this contradiction between theory and practice with respect to governmental intervention in the economic process [have] caused and continue to cause some confusion in distinguishing autonomous from induced patterns of growth.

In view of the autocratic political tendencies of Imperial Germany in the forty years before the First World War, it is often asserted that in that country economic growth was largely induced by the government. Though the German government pursued a vigorous economic policy, its over-all intervention in the free market was not more extensive, and perhaps less so, than that of most western governments at that time. Even the much touted social security legislation of Bismarck, which in radical-liberal circles was regarded as rank Socialism, was much milder than many social security programs which are currently thought to be perfectly reconcilable with a system of capitalistic free enterprise. If, therefore, we draw our line of distinction between induced and autonomous patterns of growth in such a way as to include in the former only those types of governmental action which have the aim of consciously allocating productive factors in a specified direction, the policies of almost all governments in the period before 1914 should be regarded as permitting an autonomous process of growth.

If we go back still further in time than the early nineteenth century and consider policies of European states in the mercantilist period, we are faced with a more complex and difficult situation. The mercantilist policies of different countries have sometimes been distinguished in that in some of them, especially in Britain and Holland, the regulation of commerce was seen as the principal economic goal of mercantilism, whereas in others, notably in France and some of the German states, the stimulation of manufactures was considered to be the chief aim of governmental policy in the economic sphere. Though this distinction is perhaps exaggerated, the emphasis in the policy orientation of the economic literature of the seventeenth and eighteenth centuries in Britain, Holland, France, and Germany tends to lend some validity to this distinction. But although continental governments were eager to foster manufacturing, they were only to a very limited extent engaged in direct industrial "planning." To be sure, the French government and some German principalities established state-owned enterprises, but the main reliance for industrial development was on private decisions. The administrations of Laffemas and Colbert, the two chief protagonists of the pro-industrialist policy of France, were filled with attempts to induce private individuals to engage in, or increase the scale of, manufacturing. The government offered premiums and prizes, exemptions from taxation, and subsidies in cash to stimulate private entrepreneurship in industry. Here we have an instance where ideally the decisions for growth were entrusted to private persons acting presumably in pursuit of self-interest, yet where actually a very active role was taken by government in stimulating and channelling private actions in directions selected by the political élite. This was a case of governmental paternalism in the economic sphere which produced a tradition of dependence upon governmental aid on the part of industrial entrepreneurs and which had the effect of weakening and even stunting private initiative when the hand of government was withdrawn. This appears to be one of the reasons why, with the introduction of more liberal economic policies during the Second Empire, French industrial growth never reached the pace of British and German, and why even then it had to be buttressed by an elaborate system of investment banking in which many of the crucial investment decisions were made by bankers rather than by industrialists.

IV

We now have assembled all the building blocks for our array of boxes. Combining the three sets of dichotomies with one another we obtain eight possible types of cases or ideal types. To each type can be assigned, on a priori grounds at least, some country or countries whose developmental experience or possibilities for growth correspond most closely to that type. A list of these eight types would contain the following cases:

1. Expansionist, dominant, autonomous: the United States, from 1830 to 1890.

2. Expansionist, dominant, induced: the Soviet Union, from 1928 to the present.

3. Expansionist, satellitic, autono-

mous: Australia to 1914 or Canada to 1900.

4. Expansionist, satellitic, induced: Manchuria under Japanese control, and perhaps some areas in Africa now undergoing economic development. . . .

5. Intrinsic, dominant, autonomous: nineteenth-century France or Germany.

6. Intrinsic, dominant, induced: Japan or Turkey since 1922.

7. Intrinsic, satellitic, autonomous: Denmark or Switzerland before 1914.

8. Intrinsic, satellitic, induced: the so-called "people's democracies" in eastern Europe.

Of the countries in Asia we would expect India to try to follow a pattern of intrinsic, dominant, and probably strongly induced development, and countries like Burma and Thailand, and perhaps also the Philippines, all of them having large areas that can be made fit for settlement at relatively low cost, to follow an expansionist, induced pattern. The degree of dominance in the different countries may vary. Many parts of Latin America will probably remain dependent upon the United States and other countries of the West for a long time, in spite of vigorous efforts to attain greater self-sufficiency, whereas in South and East Asia, for cultural and political reasons, tendencies toward dominant—possibly regionally dominant—growth patterns will be attempted.

The first result of our system of classification is thus to distinguish more clearly between different patterns of development which may be prescribed for different underdeveloped countries by their resources, role of government, and interaction with the world economy. But the classification provides us with more than merely a way of distinguishing cases of development more neatly. It has independent value in permitting more accurate insights into the functional relations between economic and noneconomic variables determining the rate and direction of economic growth. Its value may be exemplified by two instances, one drawn from the historical experience of western Europe and the other relating to alternative means of achieving the developmental objectives of a region little developed economically.

First let us examine whether the procedures of this paper permit us to cast more light on a problem which has provoked some dispute among social historians. I refer to the economic decline of northern Italy in the post-Renaissance period, but especially in the late sixteenth and seventeenth centuries. There exist of course several explanations for this phenomenon. Some attribute it primarily to the failure of nerve, the stunting of the spirit of enterprise, and the flaccidity of morals resulting from the corrupting influence of wealth and luxury. Others attribute it mainly to the shift of the geographical centers of world commerce and the impact of the discoveries which moved the key trading routes from the Mediterranean to the Atlantic. Others again attribute it largely to the impact of a religious ethic which prevented the development of industrialism organized on capitalistic lines, though it had not been able to thwart fully the realization of human cupidity in the form of gains derived from commerce and financial speculation. Some writers have assigned more importance to one factor than to the others; but they have all been stressed with different emphasis. The problem has attracted attention because its explanation bears a crucial relation to the explanation of the social and economic conditions of capitalistic development and with it of the economic growth typical of the western world.

There is no question but that the

discoveries and the opening up of new trade routes, markets, and sources of supply profoundly affected the economy of the northern Italian cities. Adjustments of a far-reaching nature were required, and only imaginative, inventive individuals could make them. Why did the north Italian cities fail so miserably to adapt themselves to the changed conditions of the world economy? Why did a people which had produced imaginative and venturesome individuals for centuries all of a sudden cease to produce them, or at least fail to enable them to attain positions in society in which their impact could be felt? Posing the problem in this fashion we may find a clue to a more satisfactory solution.

The Italian city states of the Middle Ages and the Renaissance had small territories with relatively poor natural resources. Under these conditions, virtually the only avenue to the acquisition of wealth and riches open to them was to follow a pattern of partly expansionist, autonomous growth in which they were forced to accept a high degree of dependence upon others. In other words, their concentration upon trade and finance tended to produce a pattern of satellite economic development. The fortunes of these city states, even when, as did Florence, Milan, and Venice, they developed sizable industries—cloth finishing in Florence, shipbuilding in Venice— were dependent upon foreign trade, and hence upon the fortunes of areas beyond their political control. In the case of shipbuilding the dependence is obvious; in the case of Florentine industrial products, the rise of the Calimala guild points to the fact that the real strength of the economy lay in that branch of the cloth industry which was most closely interwoven with foreign trade.

Given the political conditions of the time and the general state of society which made this development of foreign trade possible, the cities built social structures in which the originally autonomous tendencies of growth became more and more controlled by a financial and commercial oligarchy. The satellitic character of the development was therefore made more distinct, since each of the city states became increasingly dependent upon one powerful country or social group outside. Florence tended to become dependent upon the papacy and later upon France, Genoa upon Spain, and Venice, after the fall of Constantinople, upon the Ottoman Empire. At the onset of the sixteenth century we find the top of the social hierarchy occupied by a mercantile and financial aristocracy which is jealous of its monopoly and dependent for its political and economic fortunes upon one or, at best, a limited number of outside powers.

With the geographical shifts produced by the discoveries, and the rise of competitors to Italian commercial hegemony in Portugal and the Netherlands and to Italian financial hegemony in upper Germany and France, the task which Italian communities faced was to further their own development. It would have been important for northern Italy to give up its dependence on outsiders and to enter upon a policy of dominant development, to underplay the tendencies of commercial and financial expansionism and to stress intrinsic industrial development, and finally to reattain the degree of autonomy which it had reached in the early Middle Ages. This course would have required a reallocation of social and political power in the cities. It did not occur, though it was the only effective means of preventing the gradual economic decline of the region. In other words, given the changed conditions in which these city states found themselves and which were produced by developments beyond their immediate control, their further prosperity depended upon a change in the pattern of growth which they had followed successfully in the past. The very success of the past pattern had entrenched in power a social class which resisted change and which was successful in its resistance because it was so powerful.

It would of course be wrong to assert that the financial and commercial élite of the Italian cities did not sense that the economic future of its society lay in a change of the pattern of development. The senate of Venice introduced a textile industry. Similarly in Milan steps were taken to foster industrial development. Grand Duke Ferdinand I of Tuscany undertook a large-scale program of agricultural development, which included the reclamation of the Val di Chiana and the Siennese Maremma. He attracted immigrants—a common mercantilist device—and supported the textile, especially the silk, industry. But all these steps were inadequate. The only practical method would have been to follow a pattern of autonomous, rather than induced, development. It was imperative to attract the medium-sized and small bourgeoisie, to open up for it—as was done in Britain and Holland, and to a lesser extent in France—channels for upward mobility in the social scale and to place a positive valuation on the acquisition of wealth through industrial enterprise. The failure of the Reformation to take hold in Italy was probably a factor which prevented this development. But the control of the financial aristocracy was too complete to permit a loosening of the social order in which greater upward mobility by means other than land holding or financing governments became possi-

ble. Evidence for this contention is supplied best by the role of Ferdinand of Tuscany himself. His energetic measures for intrinsic development have been mentioned. But he also set up a government monopoly in the grain trade, he participated in the industrial and banking enterprises stimulated by him, and he was believed by common rumor, at the end of his reign, to have been the richest man of his age.

The answer to the problem of the reasons for the economic decline of northern Italy takes on a surer and more compelling form when we state it in terms of the variables discussed in this paper. To be sure, the factors which have been commonly stressed are not deprived of their validity, but their interrelation is made plainer and more logical. The role of Protestantism [and] the shift of world commerce to the Atlantic are not seen as independent, unrelated events, but as causes and consequences logically bound up with the changing patterns and needs of the economic growth of Italy. And the failure of nerve is not attributed in a naïve fashion to the degenerating influence of wealth and luxury, but rather to the structure of society, which grew out of one pattern of economic development, but was an impediment to the evolution of another more suited to meet the challenge presented by the changed conditions.

V

I now wish, in conclusion, to show the applicability of our set of variables to a problem of economic development in the contemporary world, in particular the economic problem faced by the five countries of Central America, which together have 8,000,000 inhabitants, the most populous of them 3,-000,000. Up to 1840 these countries formed a political unit, but each has followed an independent course since that time. Their economies are similar. They are all exporters of one or two staple agricultural crops. Coffee and bananas make up approximately 85 per cent of the total exports of the region. These countries, which, in terms of per capita incomes, are among the poorest in Latin America, have plans for economic development which were worked out with the help of the World Bank, United States Technical Aid Missions, or the United Nations Technical Cooperation Administration. The United Nations has strongly supported regional economic integration, and feeble first steps in the implementation of this policy have been taken.

The problem before these countries is to choose between individual plans pursued independently and joint planning for the development of the whole region. Though it is often asserted that this second alternative would require political unification, it might be achieved merely by economic union administered by regional development boards with real power. We may disregard for the time being the constitutional issue, because, in practice, a regional planning board with real powers will be as difficult to achieve as political unification or federation.

The difficulties in the path of effective economic cooperation favor the alternative that each country follow its own development plans. But in view of the smallness of each country and its undifferentiated resources, the only possible path to development is one in which the satellitic character of the relation of each country to the United States is preserved, and possibly even strengthened. This is precisely the outcome which these countries wish to avoid. They wish to embark upon a program of development which will enable them in the near future to follow a path of dominant growth.

Moreover, as long as the countries follow independent plans of development and hence continue to be dependent upon the United States market for bananas and coffee for their foreign exchange receipts, they will continue to pursue an intrinsic developmental policy. Yet in all five countries there are sparsely populated tropical lowlands into which population could be moved. Apart from very limited shifts in population, especially in the course of the opening up of new banana lands, the present and planned developmental policies—notably in the fields of transportation, agriculture, and industrialization—do not foreshadow an expansionist pattern of growth. Nor would, under present conditions, such a policy be of much value. The choice before the countries, therefore, is either to accept induced satellitic intrinsic development and maintain full economic independence from one another, or to follow a path of induced, partially expansionist, and ultimately dominant development and enter into a federation or regional economic block.

In a sense the position of the Central American countries today is analogous to that of Canada before confederation. Even the incentives for common economic action in Central America are similar to those which prevailed in Canada in 1867. The need for railway building, for the development of the western provinces, and for the creation of an internal market for the industries of Ontario, and the grave financial problems faced by all the colonies were among the chief economic factors favoring confederation. The relation of the colonies to Britain and the United States remained satellitic in character to some extent after confederation, but expansionism became economically possible and profitable. This pattern ultimately led to an integration of resources under one government which could, after a period, embark upon a policy of fostering dominant economic growth and in this way attain higher economic integration of the country coupled with higher real incomes.

In Central America, also, economic union will mean the extension of railways and other transportation facilities to the lowlands; this in turn may lead to the production of new commodities to supply growing internal markets and may further produce an impetus for domestic industrialization; finally, an economic union would benefit the countries' finances since it would prevent competitive overinvestment in a few lines of industrial production,

such as textiles and cement. Though the countries would remain satellites to the United States market for some time to come, they would have a real possibility of entering eventually upon dominant economic growth.

The procedures applied in these two cases could be extended also to others. I do not pretend that they will revolutionize our insights about the conditions of economic progress. But they may make possible a more fruitful integration of economic and noneconomic variables which together provide an adequate explanation of the different patterns of economic development that have been ascertained in the historical experience of the advanced countries and that are so warmly discussed in the underdeveloped parts of the world.

Economic Dominants in Community Power Structure

ROBERT O. SCHULZE

That persons occupying positions of economic importance are among the key wielders of local influence and control ·has long been one of the most commonplace assumptions of American sociologists and one of the most consistent findings of research concerned with American communities and community power structures. With very few exceptions, however, most studies relevant to the role of economic dominants in community control structures have focused on current power configurations. Relatively little research attention has yet been devoted to historical shifts in local power structures associated with the metropolitan and

Robert O. Schulze, "The Role of Economic Dominants in Community Power Structure," *American Sociological Review*, **23** (1958), 3-9.

bureaucratic drift of American life. Likewise, while most relevant studies have indicated that a considerable number of persons of significant local influence are men of economic substance, they have not revealed the pattern of community involvement (nor changes in that pattern) of the economically most powerful considered as a category. Thus we have heard a good deal about the activities and influence of the "X" family and its equivalents in American communities, but rather less about the "Y" families, and almost nothing at all about the ratio of "X's" to "Y's" either currently or over time.

This paper reports some findings of an investigation of the power structure of a middle-sized American community —findings concerned primarily with the historical role of the economic dominants in that community's power structure. Although the study has among its numerous limitations those inevitable in any piece of single-community research, it is hoped that it might be theoretically and methodologically suggestive for research in other communities, especially those which—like the subject of this study—have become satellites in a society increasingly dominated by giant metropolitan centers and large national corporations.

The rudimentary theory underlying this research may be briefly summarized. The basic assumption was that as the functional relationship of the community to the larger society changes, so does the nature and form of its control structure, and so, too, does the role of its economic dominants in that structure.

It was hypothesized that in the community *relatively* self-contained and uninvolved in the larger social and economic system, the community with few and scattered commitments beyond its borders, local power would tend to be structured as a pyramid and heavily concentrated at the apex. More specifically, it was surmised that those persons who exercised major control over the community's economic system would tend to be the same persons who exercised preponderant control over its sociopolitical system, and that this latter control would be reflected, at least in part, by their active leadership and participation in the political and civic life of the community.

With increasing urbanization and as the community passed beyond what Lloyd Warner has called "the period of local capitalism,"[1] however, it was suggested that the economic dominants would begin to withdraw their interest and active attention from the

local sociopolitical system. Although the major economic units would have grown in size and potential influence, it was hypothesized that several factors would militate against the effective exercise, the actual "cashing in" of their power in the community. The most significant of these would be the fact that the local community would have become ever less important to the survival and prosperity of its dominant economic units. As the activities of these units became increasingly directed toward—and by—populations and groups other than the local ones, the relevance of local community organizations and the impact of local political influences on the major economic units would accordingly diminish. As this occurred, the local power structure would, in effect, bifurcate—with those who exercised primary direction over its sociopolitical system no longer being essentially the same set of persons who exercised primary control over its economic system.[2]

----

[1] W. L. Warner and J. O. Low, "The Factory in the Community," in W. F. Whyte, ed., *Industry and Society* (New York: McGraw-Hill Book Company, 1946), p. 35.

[2] It is not suggested that the decline in the economic dominants' leadership and participation in community decision-making processes stems wholly from their diminishing concern with local affairs. With their attenuation of local involvement, it is obvious that effective contact and meaningful communication between economic dominants and diverse elements of the community population are likewise reduced, contributing to what has been referred to as the loss of "multiclass leadership" by the top business groups in American communities. In such a situation, economic dominants—when they occasionally may want to influence community decisions—may find that their local leadership base has so shrunken that their effectiveness is impaired. Somewhat illustrative of this was the case of Cal Lamkin, the general manager of a large industrial plant in the community studied. Long inactive in local political and voluntary associational affairs, Lamkin was eventually prevailed upon to stand for election to the board of directors of the local Chamber of Commerce. To the considerable embarrassment of the Chamber's officials, however, Lamkin failed to muster sufficient votes to win a seat on the board.

An effort was made to test this general theory in Cibola, a midwestern industrial community of some 20,000 inhabitants, located approximately thirty miles from Metro City, one of the nation's largest metropolitan centers. Founded in 1823, Cibola grew rather slowly until World War II. Between 1940 and 1950, however, its population increased over 50 per cent, a shift symptomatic of countless other changes to which the community has lately been subject. One of the principal changes has been the gradual absorption of its major industrial plants by large, absentee-owned corporations, a trend sharply accelerated during the World War II period.

In our research, we attempted to reconstruct Cibola's economic dominants from the time of its founding in 1823 until 1955, and to determine the general nature and extent of their overt involvement in the political and civic life of the community.

The economic dominants for the various historical periods were operationally defined as those persons who: (1) occupied the top formal roles in the largest industries and banks in the community; or (2) were members of the boards of directors of two or more of these industries and banks, thus serving formally to "interlock" the dominant economic units; or (3) were the largest property owners in the community.[3]

Insofar as local involvement was re-

See Wilbert E. Moore, *Industrial Relations and the Social Order* (New York: The Macmillan Company, 1951), pp. 547-553. Although presented in causal terms somewhat different from those suggested in this paper, the best-known and perhaps most sanguine statement of the American business élites' loss of multigroup leadership is contained in Kenneth Galbraith, *American Capitalism and the Concept of Countervailing Power* (Boston: Houghton Mifflin Company, 1952).

[3] Specific criteria for classification as an economic dominant in each historical period were based on such measures as number of

flected by occupancy of formal offices in the political and civic organizations in the community, the research tended clearly to support the basic hypothesis. *The historical drift has been characterized by the withdrawal of the economic dominants from active and overt participation in the public life of Cibola.* Tables 1, 3, and 4 are presented to illustrate this withdrawal.

TABLE 1 Number and Percentage of Economic Dominants in Public Office, 1823-1954 Periods

Period	Number of Economic Dominants	Number of Economic Dominants in Public Office	Percentage of Economic Dominants in Public Office
1823-60	12	10	83
1860-1900	21	17	81
1900-40	43	12	28
1940-54	31	7	23

Table 1 indicates that prior to the turn of the century, fully four fifths of Cibola's economic dominants held public office in the community, while since 1900, the proportion has declined to approximately one quarter.[4] Likewise, as shown in Table 3, the propor-

employees (industries), capital worth (banks), and assessed valuation of holdings (property owners). Various source data were utilized in the determination of these measures, including county tax records, city directories and histories, newspapers, records of individual companies and of the Chamber of Commerce, and the State Historical Collections, plus such standard references as *Poor's Register of Directors and Executives* and *Polk's Bank Directory.*

[4] It might be suggested that the declining proportion of economic dominants in public office was a function of the fact that the number of dominants increased at a greater rate than the number of available offices, and therefore that the declining proportions are spurious. This was not the case. Changes in the number of economic dominants throughout the four periods were very closely paralleled by proportionately similar changes in the number of available public offices. (See Table 2.)

TABLE 2   Changes in Number of
Economic Dominants and Number
of Available Offices, 1823-1954
Periods

Period	Percentage Change in Number of Economic Dominants	Percentage Change in Number of Public Offices in City Government
From 1823-60 to 1860-1900 periods	+ 75	+ 80
From 1860-1900 to 1900-40 periods	+ 105	+ 183
From 1900-40 to 1940-54 periods	− 28	− 30

tion of economic dominants who have held the top political office in Cibola has sharply diminished. Not indicated in either of these two tables is the fact that *none* of the most recent type of economic dominant—the managers of the absentee-owned corporations—has held any public office (elective or appointive) in the community.

There was some evidence that in the early decades of this century the arena of active local involvement of Cibola's

TABLE 3   Number and Percentage of Economic Dominants in Office of Village President or Mayor, 1823-1954 Periods

Period	Number of Dominants in Office of Village President or Mayor	Percentage of Dominants in Office of Village President or Mayor	Percentage of "Politically Active" Dominants in Office of Village President or Mayor*
1823-60	5	42	50
1860-1900	7	33	41
1900-40	2	5	17
1940-54	1	3	14

* "Politically Active": All those economic dominants who had held *any* public office.

TABLE 4   Number of Economic
Dominants in Offices of the
Chamber of Commerce,
1920-1955*

Period	Median Number of Memberships per Year on Board of Directors	Number Serving as President
1920-27	6	3
1927-34	3	2
1934-41	3	0
1941-48	2	1
1948-55	1	0

* The Cibola Chamber of Commerce was founded in 1920. From that date until 1953, the number of directors was fifteen; in the latter year, the number was increased to eighteen. Directors serve two-year terms and are eligible for reelection.

economic dominants shifted from politics to the important voluntary associations. Even in this area, however, an appreciable subsequent diminution of active participation has been apparent —perhaps best reflected by the declining number of dominants holding responsible office in the community's most influential association, the local Chamber of Commerce.

It is suggested that the withdrawal of the economic dominants was primarily a consequence of the changing relationship of the community's economic system to that of the larger society. Prior to about 1900, three aspects of Cibola's economic life were especially notable: (1) all of its economic dominants were local residents; (2) all of its dominant economic units were locally owned; and (3) the majority of its dominants were associated in extensive economic networks *within* the community.

Our research established that in the pre-1900 period, almost 70 per cent of the economic dominants had known business or financial ties—as partners, co-officers or codirectors—with other dominants in the community. Thus throughout most of Cibola's history, its "average" economic dominant was not only a local resident, or merely the head of a single major economic unit; he was also directly and indirectly linked with a considerable number of other major economic units and dominants within the community.

Combined, these factors provided most economic dominants with deep, branching roots in Cibola. The business and financial links, in particular, afforded many of them a basis for shared concern in the local community. The economic networks served to weld together blocs of dominants, giving them frequent and specific occasion for interpersonal contact. By the same token, the very diversity of the "average" dominant's local economic commitments meant that there was always a variety of areas and methods in which local political considerations could impinge upon his pecuniary and related interests. The evidence suggests that these considerations were closely associated with the high incidence of involvement by economic dominants in the sociopolitical system of the community.

The period since 1900, and more particularly since 1930, has been marked by the increasing absorption of the local economic system into the larger industrial complex, especially that of Metro City. While several complex social factors were patently involved, the following three seem most closely related to the eventual withdrawal of the economic dominants from active participation in the political-civic life of Cibola: (1) the establishment by a growing number of locally owned industrial units of direct supplier relationships with a small number of large, nonlocal manufacturing plants; (2) the subsequent introduction into the local economic system of an increasing number of branch plants of large, absentee-owned corporations; and (3) the concomitant dissolution of the extensive networks of interlocking direc-

tor- and officerships which had formerly served to link significant numbers of local economic dominants within the community.

Consequently, the overt direction of the political and civic life of Cibola has passed almost wholly into the hands of a group of middle-class business and professional men, almost none of whom occupies a position of economic dominance in the community. That this has in fact been the case was suggested in another aspect of our research by the finding that only two of Cibola's seventeen current economic dominants were perceived by the local voluntary association heads to have been among the eighteen most influential leaders in the community.[5] And both of these two, by the way, were heads of relatively small, locally owned economic units.

Patently, these data reveal changes only in the level of overt and manifest involvement of the economic dominants in the local power structure. It may be suggested of course that covertly—"behind the scenes"—the economic dominants continue to exercise considerable direction and control of community affairs. However, the findings of another part of our research strongly suggest that things may, in fact, be what they seem.

In an effort to view the community power structure "in action," we endeavored to determine the patterns and processes of local decision making in a series of recent community episodes

[5] The heads of 143 voluntary associations in Cibola were asked a series of five questions intended to elicit their perceptions of the most influential leaders in the community. On the basis of their total "nominations," the eighteen most frequently cited persons were designated as the "public leaders" of Cibola. See R. O. Schulze and L. U. Blumberg, "The Determination of Local Power Elites," *American Journal of Sociology*, **63** (November, 1957), 290-296.

(including a successful campaign to change the structure of municipal government from a mayor-aldermen to a city manager form, and an ambitious but unsuccessful annexation effort).[6] Our findings in this aspect of the research forced us to conclude that the recent economic dominants—and especially those representing the growing number of large, absentee-owned corporations—appear indeed to have dissociated themselves from active involvement in Cibola's power structure.

These episodes reflected a growing adherence on the part of the absentee-owned corporations in Cibola to a "hands off" position with regard to local political decision making. And while it cannot be conclusively documented within the limits of the present paper, this evolving policy is graphically suggested by presenting excerpts from interviews with several executives in the larger economic units.

The general manager of the second largest manufacturing plant in the community, commenting on our findings that but two of the top ten officials in his plant actually resided in Cibola, stated:

That's a sore spot with me. I've always felt that if I'm going to work in a town, I ought to live there. But there's no consensus on that by a long ways. It's been discussed at the highest levels in our corporation—I know because I've been on the company's community relations committee ever since it was set up. The company has decided that it won't encourage its executives to live in the communities

where they work if they don't already or if they don't want to. . . . The company doesn't feel its people—at least its executives—have to live in a town in order to have good community relations. Just about the opposite, as a matter of fact. You're always subject to a hell of a lot of local pressures if you're there. If they know where you are, you're always a target. So maybe it's better not to be in a position to be asked to do something than to have to say, "No."

In discussing the paucity of both formal and informal contacts between corporation officials and local leaders, the assistant general manager of the largest industrial plant in Cibola said:

No, I've almost never gone downtown for lunch "with the boys." I sometimes get my hair cut in [Cibola], but outside of that I don't show my face any more than I feel I absolutely have to. . . . The people at the Chamber of Commerce seem to fall all over themselves trying to do anything we want—but the point is, we don't really *want* anything there except for the people to have a good opinion of us. But mostly due to this placating attitude of the town's leaders, I'm afraid to say much or be around much.

The corporations were interested, to be sure (as the title of one company's "kit for divisional executives" indicated) in "Making Friends for [U.S. Motors] in the Local Community," but a growing number of them were coming to regard "making friends" and "getting involved" as inconsonant. The general manager of another large plant summed up his attitude:

One sure way to give [our firm] a black eye would be for me to get myself into things so deeply in town that no matter what I did, I'd end up alienating a lot of people.

And another:

You've got to remember that what I do doesn't affect us just here. The guy who represents our company in this area could

---

[6] In these reconstructions, a variety of source materials was utilized, including intensive interviews with the seventeen current economic dominants, the eighteen persons perceived by the 143 local voluntary association heads as the community's most influential leaders, and a selected number of informants. In addition, relevant newspaper files, Chamber of Commerce records and reports, and city council minutes were reviewed.

affect our reputation a lot of other places as well. . . . Why, if I went out and got myself [involved] in local politics, you'd see a new boy in these shoes so damned fast it'd make your head swim.

Meaningful participation in the decision-making processes of a community such as Cibola was mainly regarded by these corporations as entailing risks to their operations and to their positions in the larger social system—risks which could not be offset by any palpable advantages which might accrue to them through playing significant roles in the local power structure. They were clearly cognizant, for example, of the possibility that involvement by their executives in local affairs might induce conflicting loyalties. Likewise, their executives recognized that decisive involvement in critical community decisions posed the threat of alienating significant superiors and publics at the extracommunity level, thus endangering their larger occupational and public relations objectives. It seems tenable that it was the very sensitivity of the large corporations to sociopolitical determinations at the regional and national levels which militated against their involvement in these matters at the level of the local community.

The central finding of the Cibola study—the bifurcation of the community's power structure, stemming from the withdrawal of the economic dominants from active direction of the political and civic life of the community—appears quite generally to corroborate the investigation of Peter Rossi and his associates of the changing patterns of political participation in a middle-sized industrial community in New England.[7] Likewise, our findings seem to be consistent with C. Wright Mills'

observations regarding the altered position of large economic units in the power structures of local communities.[8] On the other hand, the Cibola findings do not appear consistent with Hunter's research in Regional City, nor, especially, with that of Pellegrin and Coates in Bigtown.[9]

In addition to the obvious and perhaps significant differences in the sizes of the several communities involved, it will be noted that Hunter and Pellegrin and Coates studied the structures and dynamics of community power in southern cities, while Rossi's and the present research concern New England and midwestern communities, respectively. In correspondence with the writer, Pellegrin has suggested that the disparate findings may be largely the function of regional differences: the historical tradition of paternalism being perhaps stronger in the South than in the North. It has also been suggested that economic dominants may become involved in community power structures independent of the desires of their economic units to guide or influence local decision making. Thus, for example, to the extent that economic dominants represent the wealthier interests in the community and are a major source of voluntary donations to local charities and similar activities, they may be coopted into decision structures by those actively "in charge" in order to reinforce the latter's control positions and to guarantee a continued source of contributions. Likewise, to the extent that the economic dominants represent the upper prestige

---

[7] Peter Rossi, "Historical Trends in the Politics of an Industrial Community," paper presented to the American Sociological Society (September, 1956).

[8] C. W. Mills, The Power Elite (New York: Oxford University Press, 1956).

[9] Floyd Hunter, Community Power Structure (Chapel Hill: University of North Carolina Press, 1953), and R. J. Pellegrin and C. H. Coates, "Absentee-Owned Corporations and Community Power Structure," American Journal of Sociology, 61 (March, 1956), 413-419.

levels in a community, they may be drawn into the control structure by the active community leaders in an effort by the latter to legitimize their own prestige positions.

It should be noted, however, that both of the foregoing hypothetical instances cast the economic dominants in the role of rather reluctant participants in local power structures. In such situations, it would be *other* members of the community, not the economic dominants or the dominant economic units themselves, who would have most stake in the latters' local involvement. And this, in turn, would have, perhaps, significant ramifications for the kinds of roles which the economic dominants played in community power structures and for the degree of interest and local concern with which they acted out these roles.

Whatever the reasons for the apparent differences in the nature and extent of economic dominant involvement in local power structures—and the delineation of these reasons should certainly be one objective of future research—the Cibola study appears to document the absence of any neat, constant, and direct relationship between *power as a potential for determinative action* and *power as determinative action itself*. It suggests, likewise, the need to re-examine the role of economic dominance in community power structures in view of the continued drift of American society, on the one hand, toward the concentration of population in suburban and satellite communities, and, on the other, toward the continuing expansion of huge economic bureaucracies.

stratification

five

Space limitations permit the illustration of only two themes from the vast complex of relations between economic activity and social stratification. The first theme—which has especially preoccupied social scientists since Karl Marx—concerns the relations between the structure of an economy and the system of social stratification. The selection by Stinchcombe explores the association between types of agricultural enterprise and types of stratification. The second theme—which has excited much ideological controversy and considerable research in recent decades—concerns the rate of upward social mobility in advanced industrial societies. The selection by Adams presents data relevant to the recruitment into several occupational élites over the past half-century.

The student should read these selections in conjunction with pp. 64-68 of *The Sociology of Economic Life*.

Agricultural Enterprise and Rural Class Relations

ARTHUR L. STINCHCOMBE

Marx's fundamental innovation in stratification theory was to base a theory of formation of classes and political development on a theory of the bourgeois enterprise.[1] Even though some of his conceptualization of the enterprise is faulty, and though some of his propositions about the development of capitalist enterprise were in error, the idea was sound: One of the main determinants of class relations in different parts of the American economy is, indeed, the economic and administrative character of the enterprise.

But Marx's primary focus was on class relations in cities. In order to extend his mode of analysis to rural settings, we need an analysis of rural enterprises. The purpose of this paper is to provide such an analysis and to suggest the typical patterns of rural class relations produced in societies where a type of rural enterprise predominates.

Property and Enterprise in Agriculture

Agriculture everywhere is much more organized around the institutions of property than around those of occupation. Unfortunately, our current theory and research on stratification [are] built to fit an urban environment, being conceptually organized around the idea of

Arthur L. Stinchcombe, "Agricultural Enterprise and Rural Class Relations," *American Journal of Sociology*, 67 (1961-62), 165-176.

[1] This formulation derives from Talcott Parsons's brief treatment in *The Structure of Social Action* (New York: The Free Press of Glencoe, Inc., 1949), pp. 488-495.

occupation. For instance, an important . . . monograph on social mobility classifies all farmers together and regards them as an unstratified source of urban workers.[2]

The theory of property systems is very much underdeveloped. Property may be defined as a legally defensible vested right to affect decisions on the use of economically valuable goods. Different decisions (for instance, technical decisions *vs.* decisions on distributions of benefits) typically are affected by different sets of rights held by different sets of people. These legally defensible rights are of course important determinants of the actual decision-making structure of any social unit which acts with respect to goods.

But a property system must be conceived as the typical interpenetration of legally vested rights to affect decisions and the factual situation which determines who actually makes what decisions on what grounds. For example, any description of the property system of modern business which ignores the fact that it is economically

[2] S. M. Lipset and R. Bendix, *Social Mobility in Industrial Society* (Berkeley: University of California Press, 1959). The exceedingly high rate of property mobility which characterized American rural social structures when the national ideology was being formed apparently escapes their attention. Yet Lipset discusses the kind of mobility characteristic of frontiers and small farm systems very well in his *Agrarian Socialism* (Berkeley: University of California Press, 1950), p. 33. In 1825, occupational mobility concerned only a small part of the population of the United States. The orientation of most nineteenth-century Americans to worldly success was that of Tennyson's "Northern Farmer, New Style": "But proputty, proputty sticks, an' proputty graws."

impossible for a single individual to gain majority stock holdings in a large enterprise, and politically impossible to organize an integrated faction of dispersed stockholders except under unusual conditions, would give a grossly distorted view. A description of a property system, then, has to take into account the internal politics of typical enterprises, the economic forces that typically shape decisions, the political situation in the society at large which is taken into account in economic decisions, the reliability and cost of the judiciary, and so forth. The same property law means different things for economic life if decisions on the distribution of income from agricultural enterprise are strongly affected by urban *rentiers'* interests rather than a smallholding peasantry.

It is obviously impossible to give a complete typology of the legal, economic, and political situations which determine the decision-making structure within agricultural organizations for all societies and for all important decisions. Instead, one must pick certain frequent constellations of economic, technical, legal, and labor recruitment conditions that tend to give rise to a distinct structure of decision making within agricultural enterprises.

By an "enterprise" I mean a social unit which has and exercises the power to commit a given parcel of land to one or another productive purpose, to achieve which it decides the allocation of chattels and labor on the land.[3] The rights to affect decisions on who shall

get the benefit from that production may not be, and quite often are not, confined within the enterprise, as defined here. The relation between the enterprise and power over the distribution of benefit is one of the central variables in the analysis to follow, for instance, distinguishing tenancy systems from smallholding systems.

Besides the relation between productive decisions and decisions on benefits, some of the special economic, political, and technical characteristics which seem most important in factual decision-making structure will be mentioned, such as the value of land, whether the "owner" has police power over or kinship relations with labor, the part of production destined for market, the amount of capital required besides the land, or the degree of technical rationalization. These are of course some of the considerations Marx dealt with when describing the capitalist enterprise, particularly in its factory form. Plantations, manors, family-size tenancies, ranches, or family farms tend to occur only in certain congenial economic, technical, and political environments and to be affected in their internal structure by those environments.

A description and analysis of empirical constellations of decision-making structures cannot, by its untheoretical nature, claim to be complete. Moreover, I have deliberately eliminated from consideration all precommercial agriculture, not producing for markets, because economic forces do not operate in the same ways in precommercial societies and because describing the enterprise would involve providing a typology of extended families and peasant communities, which would lead us far afield. I have also not considered the "community-as-enterprise" systems of the Soviet sphere and of Israel, because these are as much organizational

---

[3] Occasionally, the decisions to commit land to a given crop and to commit labor and chattels to cultivation are made separately, e.g., in cotton plantations in the post-bellum American South. The land is committed to cotton by the land owner, but labor and chattels are committed to cultivation by the sharecropper.

manifestations of a social movement as they are economic institutions.[4]

Systems of commercialized manors, family-size tenancies, family smallholdings, plantations, and ranches cover most of the property system found in commercialized agriculture outside eastern Europe and Israel. And each of these property systems tends to give rise to a distinctive class system, differing in important respects from that which develops with any of the other systems. Presenting argument and evidence for this proposition is the central purpose of this paper.

Variations in Rural Class Relations

Rural class structure in commercialized agriculture varies in two main ways: the criteria which differentiate the upper and lower classes and the quality and quantity of intraclass cultural, political, and organizational life. In turn, the two main criteria which may differentiate classes are legal privileges and style of life. And two main qualities of class culture and organization are the degree of familiarity with technical culture of husbandry and the degree of political activation and organization. This gives four characteristics of rural class structures which vary with the structure of enterprises.

First, rural class systems vary in the extent to which classes are differentiated by legal privileges. Slaves and masters, peons and *hacendados*, serfs and lords, colonial planters and native labor, citizen farmers employing aliens as labor—all are differentiated by legal privileges. In each case the subordinate group is disenfranchised, often bound to the land or to the master, denied the right to organize, denied access to the courts on an equal basis, denied state-supported education, and so on.

Second, rural stratification systems vary in the sharpness of differentiation of style of life among the classes. Chinese gentry used to live in cities, go to school, compete for civil service posts, never work with their hands, and maintain extended families as household units. On each criterion, the peasantry differed radically. In contrast, in the northern United States, rich and poor farmers live in the country, attend public schools, consume the same general kinds of goods, work with their hands, at least during the busy seasons, and live in conjugal family units. There were two radically different ways of life in rural China; in the northern United States the main difference between rich and poor farmers is wealth.

Third, rural class systems vary in the distribution of the technical culture of husbandry. In some systems the upper classes would be completely incapable of making the decisions of the agricultural enterprise: they depend on the technical lore of the peasantry. At the other extreme, the Spanish-speaking labor force of the central valley in California would be bewildered by the marketing, horticultural, engineering, and transportation problems of a large-scale irrigated vegetable farm.

Fourth, rural classes vary in their degree of political activity and organization, in their sensitivity or apathy to political issues, in their degree of intraclass communication and organization, and in their degree of political education and competence.

Our problem, then, is to relate types of agricultural enterprises and property systems to the patterns of class relations in rural social life. We restrict our attention to enterprises producing for

---

[4] However, the origin of the *kolkhoz*, or collective farm, does seem to depend partly on the form of prerevolutionary agriculture. Collectivization seems to occur most rapidly when a revolutionary government deals with an agriculture which was previously organized into large-scale capitalist farms.

markets, and of these we exclude the community-as-enterprise systems of eastern Europe and Israel.

Class Relations in Types of Agricultural Enterprise

The Manorial or Hacienda System

The first type of enterprise to be considered here is actually one form of precommercial agriculture, divided into two parts: cultivation of small plots for subsistence by a peasantry, combined with cultivation by customary labor dues of domain land under the lord's supervision. It fairly often happens that the domain land comes to be used for commercial crops, while the peasant land continues to be used for subsistence agriculture. There is no rural labor market, but rather labor dues or labor rents to the lord, based on customary law or force. There is a very poorly developed market in land; there may be, however, an active market in estates, where the estates include as part of their value the labor due to the lord. But land as such, separate from estates and from manors as going concerns, is very little an article of commerce. Estates also tend to pass as units in inheritance, by various devices of entailment, rather than being divided among heirs.[5]

The manorial system is characterized by the exclusive access of the manor lord (or *hacendado* in Latin America) to legal process in the national courts. A more or less unfree population holding small bits of land in villein or precarious tenure is bound to work on the domain land of the lord by the conditions of tenure or by personal peonage. Unfree tenures or debts tend to be inheritable, so that in case of need, the legal system of the nation will subject villeins or peons to work discipline on the manor.

Some examples of this system are the hacienda system of Mexico up to at least 1920, some areas in the Peruvian highlands at present, medieval England, East Germany before the reconstruction of agriculture into large-scale plantation and ranch agriculture, the Austro-Hungarian Empire, in the main, up to at least 1848, and many other European and South American systems at various times.

The manorial system rests on the assumptions that neither the value of land nor the value of labor is great and that calculation of productive efficiency by the managers of agricultural enterprise is not well developed. When land owners start making cost studies of the efficiency of forced *vs.* wage labor, as they did, for instance, in Austria-Hungary in the first part of the nineteenth century, they find that wage labor is from two to four times as efficient. When land owners' traditional level of income becomes insufficient to compete for prestige with the bourgeoisie, and they set about trying to raise incomes by increasing productivity, as they did in eastern Germany, the developmental tendency is toward capitalistic plantation or ranch agriculture. When the waste and common become important for cattle- or sheep-raising and labor becomes relatively less important in production, enclosure movements drive precarious tenants off the land. When land becomes an article of commerce and the price and productivity of land go up, tenancy by family farmers provides the lord with a com-

---

[5] In some cases, as in what was perhaps the world's most highly developed manorial system, in Chile, an estate often remains undivided as an enterprise but is held "together in the family as an undivided inheritance for some years, and not infrequently for a generation. This multiplies the number of actual owners [but not of haciendas], of rural properties in particular" [G. M. McBride, *Chile: Land and Society* (New York: American Geographical Society, 1936), p. 139].

fortable income that can be spent in the capital city, without much worry about the management of crops. The further the market penetrates agriculture, first creating a market for commodities, then for labor and land, the more economically unstable does the manorial economy become, and the more likely is the manor to go over to one of the other types of agricultural enterprise.

In summary, the manorial system combines in the lord and his agents authority over the enterprise and rulership, or *Herrschaft*, over dependent tenants. Classes are distinct in legal status. In style of life the manor lord moves on the national scene, often little concerned with detailed administration of his estate. He often keeps city residence and generally monopolizes education. Fairly often he even speaks a different language, for example, Latin among Magyar nobility, French in the Russian aristocracy, Spanish, instead of Indian dialects, in parts of Latin America.

The pattern of life of the subject population is very little dependent on market prices of goods. Consequently, they have little interest in political issues. Even less does the peasantry have the tools of political organization, such as education, experienced leadership, freedom of association, or voting power. Quite often, as, for example, in the Magyar areas of the Hapsburg monarchy or among the Indian tribes of Latin America, intraclass communication is hindered by language barriers. A politically active and competent upper class confronts a politically apathetic, backward, and disenfranchised peasantry.

Family-Size Tenancy

In family-size tenancy the operative unit of agriculture is the family enterprise, but property rights in the enter-

prise rest with *rentier* capitalists. The return from the enterprise is divided according to some rental scheme, either in money or in kind. The rent may be fixed, fixed with modification in years of bad harvest, or share.[6] The formal title to the land may not be held by the noncultivator—it is quite common for the "rent" on the land to be, in a legal sense, the interest on a loan secured by the land.

This type of arrangement seems to occur most frequently when the following five conditions are met; (1) land has very high productivity and high market price, (2) the crop is highly labor-intensive, and mechanization of agriculture is little developed, (3) labor is cheap, (4) there are no appreciable economies of scale in factors other than labor, and (5) the period of production of the crop is one year or less. These conditions are perhaps most fully met with the crops of rice and cotton, especially on irrigated land; yet such a system of tenancy is quite often found where the crops are potatoes or wheat and maize, even though the conditions are not fulfilled. An historical, rather than an economic, explanation is appropriate to these cases.

The correlation of tenancy arrangements with high valuation of land is established by a number of pieces of evidence. In Japan in 1944, most paddy (rice) land was in tenancy, and most upland fields were owner-operated. The same was true in Korea in 1937. South China, where land values were higher and irrigated culture more practiced, had considerably higher rates of tenancy than did North China. In Thai-

[6] But share rents in commercialized agriculture are often indicators of the splitting of the enterprise, as discussed above. It most frequently reflects a situation in which land is committed to certain crops by the landlord and the landlord markets the crops, while the scheduling of work is done by the tenant and part of the risks are borne by him.

land, tenancy is concentrated in the commercialized farming of the river valleys in central Siam. In Japan, up to World War II, except for the last period (1935-40), every time the price of land went up, the proportion of land held in tenancy went up.

The pattern of family-size tenancy was apparently found in the potato culture of Ireland before the revolution, in the wheat culture of pre-World War I Rumania and also that of Bosnia-Herzegovina (now part of Yugoslavia) at the same period. The sugar cane regions of central Luzon are also farmed in family-size tenancies, though this is so uneconomical that, without privileged access to the American market, cane culture would disappear. It also characterizes the cotton culture of the highly productive Nile Valley in Egypt and the cotton culture of the Peruvian coast. This pattern of small peasant farms with rents to landlords was also characteristic of prerevolutionary France and southwest England during the Middle Ages. In lowland Burma, a large share of the rice land is owned by the Indian banking house of Chettyar, and much of the rest of it is in tenancy to other landlords. The land-tenure system of Taiwan before the recent land reform was typical family-size tenancy.

Perhaps the most remarkable aspect of this list is the degree to which this system has been ended by reform or revolution, becoming transformed, except in a few Communist states, into a system of smallholding farms. And even in Communist states the first transformation after the revolution is ordinarily to give the land to the tiller: only afterward are the peasants gathered into collective farms, generally in the face of vigorous resistance.

The system of *rentier* capitalists owning land let out in family farms (or *rentier* capitalists owning debts whose service requires a large part of farm income) seems extremely politically unstable. The French revolution, according to de Tocqueville, was most enthusiastically received in areas in which there were small farms paying feudal dues (commuted to rent in money or in kind). The eastern European systems of Rumania and parts of Yugoslavia were swept away after World War I in land reforms. Land reforms were also carried through in northern Greece, the Baltic states, and many of the succession states of the Hapsburg monarchy (the reform was specious in Hungary). A vigorous and long-lasting civil war raged in Ireland up to the time of independence, and its social base was heavily rural. The high-tenancy areas in central Luzon were the social base of the revolutionary Hukbalahaps during and after World War II. The Communist revolution in China had its first successes in the high-tenancy areas of the south. The number of peasant riots in Japan during the interwar period was closely correlated with the proportion of land held in tenancy. Peasant rebellions were concentrated in Kent and southeast England during the Middle Ages. In short, such systems rarely last through a war or other major political disturbance and constantly produce political tensions.

There are several causes of the political instability of such systems. In the first place, the issue in the conflict is relatively clear: the lower the rent of the *rentier* capitalists, the higher the income of the peasantry. The division of the product at harvest time or at the time of sale is a clear measure of the relative prerogatives of the farmer and the *rentier*.

Second, there is a severe conflict over the distribution of the risks of the enterprise. Agriculture is always the kind of enterprise with which God has a lot to do. With the commercialization of agriculture, the enterprise is further subject to great fluctuation in the gross income from its produce. *Rentiers*, especially if they are capitalists investing in land rather than aristocrats receiving incomes from feudal patrimony, shift as much of the risk of failure as possible to the tenant. Whether the rent is share or cash, the variability of income of the peasantry is almost never less, and is often more, than the variability of *rentiers'* income. This makes the income of the peasantry highly variable, contributing to their political sensitization.

Third, there tends to be little social contact between the *rentier* capitalists living in the cities and the rural population. The *rentiers* and the farmers develop distinct styles of life, out of touch with each other. The *rentier* is not brought into contact with the rural population by having to take care of administrative duties on the farm; nor is he drawn into local government as a leading member of the community or as a generous sharer in the charitable enterprises of the village. The urban *rentier*, with his educated and often foreign speech, his cosmopolitan interests, his arrogant rejection of rustic life, is a logical target of the rural community, whose only contact with him is through sending him money or goods.

Fourth, the leaders of the rural community, the rich peasants, are not vulnerable to expulsion by the land owners, as they would be were the land owners also the local government. The rich peasant shares at least some of the hardships and is opposed in his class interests to many of the same people as are the tenants. In fact, in some areas where the population pressure on the land is very great, the rich peasants themselves hold additional land in tenancy, beyond their basic holdings. In this case the leadership of the local community is not only not opposed to the interests of the tenants, but has largely identical interests with the poor peasants.

Finally, the land owners do not have the protection of the peasants' ignorance about the enterprise to defend their positions, as do large-scale capitalist farmers. It is perfectly clear to the tenant farmer that he could raise and sell his crops just as well with the landlord gone as with him there. There is no complicated cooperative tillage that seems beyond the view of all but the landlord and his managers, as there may be in manorial, and generally is in large-scale capitalist, agriculture. The farmer knows as well [as] or better than the landlord where seed and fertilizer is to be bought and where the crop can be sold. He can often see strategic investments unknown to his landlord that would alleviate his work or increase his yield.

At least in its extreme development, then, the land-owning class in systems of family-size tenancy appears as alien, superfluous, grasping, and exploitative. Their rights in agricultural enterprise appear as an unjustifiable burden on the rustic classes, both to the peasantry and to urban intellectuals. No marked decrease in agricultural productivity is to be expected when they are dispossessed, because they are not the class that carries the most advanced technical culture of agriculture. Quite often, upon land reform the productivity of agriculture increases.

So family-size tenancy tends to yield a class system with an enfranchised, formally free lower class which has a monopoly of technical culture. The style of life of the upper class is radically different from that of the lower class. The lower class tends to develop a relatively skilled and relatively invulnerable leadership in the richer peasantry and a relatively high degree of political sensitivity in the poorer peasantry. It is of such stuff that many radical populist and nationalist movements are made.

Family Smallholding

Family smallholding has the same sort of enterprises as does family tenancy, but rights to the returns from the enterprise are more heavily concentrated in the class of farmers. The "normal" property holding is about the size requiring the work of two adults or less. Probably the most frequent historical source of such systems is out of family-tenancy systems by way of land reform or revolution. However, they also arise through colonization of farmlands carried out under governments in which large landlords do not have predominant political power, for instance, in the United States and Norway. Finally, it seems that such systems tend to be produced by market forces at an advanced stage of industrialization. There is some evidence that farms either larger or smaller than those requiring about two adult laborers tend to disappear in the industrial states of western Europe.[7]

Examples of such systems having a relatively long history are the United States outside the "Black Belt" in the South, the ranch areas of the West, and the central valleys of California; Serbia after some time in the early nineteenth century; France after the great revolution; most of Scandinavia; much of Canada; Bulgaria since 1878; and southern Greece since sometime in the nineteenth century. Other such systems which have lasted long enough to give some idea of their long-term de-

velopment are those created in eastern Europe after World War I; good studies of at least Rumania[8] and Yugoslavia[9] exist. Finally, the system of family smallholding created in Japan by the American-induced land reform of 1946 has been carefully studied.[10]

Perhaps the best way to begin analysis of this type of agricultural enterprise is to note that virtually all the costs of production are fixed. Labor in the family holding is, in some sense, "free": family members have to be supported whether they work or not, so they might as well work. Likewise, the land does not cost rent, and there is no advantage to the enterprise in leaving it out of cultivation. This predominance of fixed costs means that production does not fall with a decrease in prices, as it does in most urban enterprises where labor is a variable cost. Consequently, the income of smallholders varies directly with the market price of the commodities they produce and with variability in production produced by natural catastrophe. Thus the political movements of smallholders tend to be directed primarily at maintenance of the price of agricultural commodities rather than at unemployment compensation or other "social security" measures.

Second, the variability of return from agricultural enterprise tends to make credit expensive and, at any rate, makes debts highly burdensome in bad years. Smallholders' political movements, therefore, tend to be opposed to creditors, to identify finance capital as a class enemy: Jews, the traditional symbol of finance capital, often come in

---

[7] Folke Dovring, *Land and Labor in Europe, 1900-1950* (The Hague: Martinus Nijhoff, 1956), pp. 115-118. The median size of the farm unit, taking into consideration the type of crops grown on different sized farms, ranges from that requiring one man year in Norway to two man years in France, among the nations on the continent.

[8] H. L. Roberts, *Rumania: The Political Problems of an Agrarian State* (New Haven: Yale University Press, 1951).

[9] Jozo Tomasevich, *Peasants, Politics and Economic Change in Yugoslavia* (Stanford: Stanford University Press, 1955).

[10] R. P. Dore, *Land Reform in Japan* (London: Oxford University Press, 1959).

for an ideological beating. Populist movements are often directed against "the bankers." Further, since cheap money generally aids debtors, and since small farmers are generally debtors, agrarian movements tend to support various kinds of inflationary schemes. Small farmers do not want to be crucified on a cross of gold.

Third, agrarian movements, except in highly advanced societies, tend to enjoy limited intraclass communication, to be poor in politically talented leaders, relatively unable to put together a coherent, disciplined class movement controlled from below.[11] Contributions to the party treasury tend to be small and irregular, like the incomes of the small farmers. Peasant movements are, therefore, especially prone to penetration by relatively disciplined political interests, sometimes Communist and sometimes industrial capital. Further, such movements tend to be especially liable to corruption, since they are relatively unable to provide satisfactory careers for political leaders out of their own resources.

Moreover, at an early stage of industrial and commercial development in a country without large land owners, the only sources of large amounts of money available to politicians are a few urban industrial and commercial enterprises. Making a policy on the marketing and production of iron and steel is quite often making a policy on the marketing and production of a single firm. Naturally, it pays that firm to try to get legislation and administration tailored to its needs.

Fourth, small-farmer and peasant movements tend to be nationalistic and

xenophobic. The explanation of this phenomenon is not clear.

Finally, small-farmer and peasant movements tend to be opposed to middlemen and retailers, who are likely to use their monopolistic or monopsonistic position to milk the farm population. The cooperative movement is of course directed at eliminating middlemen as well as at provision of credit without usury.

Under normal conditions (i.e., in the absence of totalitarian government, major racial cleavage, and major war), this complex of political forces tends to produce a rural community with a proliferation of associations and with the voting power and political interest to institute and defend certain elements of democracy, especially universal suffrage and universal education. This tends to produce a political regime loose enough to allow business and labor interest groups to form freely without allowing them to dominate the government completely. Such a system of land holding is a common precursor and support of modern liberal democratic government.

In smallholding systems, then, the upper classes of the rural community are not distinct in legal status and relatively not in style of life. Social mobility in such a system entails mainly a change in the amount of property held, or in the profitability of the farm, but not a change in legal status or a radical change in style of life.

A politically enfranchised rural community is characterized by a high degree of political affect and organization, generally in opposition to urban interests rather than against rural upper classes. But compared with the complexity of their political goals and the level of political involvement, their competence tends to be low until the "urbanization of the countryside" is virtually complete.

---

[11] That is, as compared with political movements of the urban proletariat or bourgeoisie. They are more coherent and disciplined than are the lower-class movements in other agricultural systems.

Plantation Agriculture

Labor-intensive crops requiring several years for maturation, such as rubber, tree fruit, or coffee, tend to be grown on large-scale capitalistic farms employing either wage labor, or, occasionally, slave labor. Particularly when capital investment is also required for processing equipment to turn the crop into a form in which it can be shipped, as, for example, in the culture of sugar cane and, at least in earlier times, sugar beets, large-scale capitalist agriculture predominates.

The key economic factor that seems to produce large-scale capitalist culture is the requirement of long-term capital investment in the crop or in machinery, combined with relatively low cost of land. When the crop is also labor-intensive, particularly when labor is highly seasonal, a rather typical plantation system tends to emerge. In some cases it also emerges in the culture of cotton (as in the ante bellum American South and some places in Egypt), wheat (as in Hungary, eastern Germany, and Poland), or rice (as on the Carolina and Georgia coasts in the ante bellum American South).

The enterprise typically combines a small, highly skilled and privileged group which administers the capital investment, the labor force, and the marketing of the crops with a large group of unskilled, poorly paid, and legally unprivileged workers. Quite generally, the workers are ethnically distinct from the skilled core of administrators, often being imported from economically more backward areas or recruited from an economically backward native population in colonial and semicolonial areas. This means that ordinarily they are ineligible for the urban labor market of the nation in which they work, if it has an urban labor market.

Examples of plantation systems are most of the sugar areas in the Caribbean and on the coast of Peru; the rubber culture of the former Federated Malay States in Malaya and on Java; the fruit-growing areas of Central America; the central valleys of California, where the labor force is heavily Latin American; eastern Germany during the early part of this century, where Poles formed an increasing part of the labor force; Hungary up to World War II; the pineapple growing of the Hawaiian Islands; and of course the ante bellum American South. The system tends to induce in the agricultural labor force a poverty of associational life, low participation in local government, lack of education for the labor force, and high vulnerability of labor union and political leadership to oppression by landlords and landlord-dominated governments. The domination of the government by landlords tends to prevent the colonization of new land by smallholders, and even to wipe out the holdings of such small peasantry as do exist.

In short, the system tends to maintain the culture, legal, and political position, and life chances of the agricultural labor force distinct both from the urban labor force and from the planter aristocracy. The bearers of the technical and commercial knowledge are not the agricultural laborers, and, consequently, redistribution of land tends to introduce inefficiency into agriculture. The plantation system, as Edgar T. Thompson has put it, is a "race-making situation,"[12] which produces a highly privileged aristocracy, technically and culturally educated, and a legally, culturally, and economically underprivileged labor force. If the latter is politically mobilized, as it may be oc-

---

[12] E. T. Thompson, "The Plantation as a Race-Making Situation," in Leonard Broom and Philip Selznick, *Sociology* (New York: Harper & Row, Publishers, Inc.), pp. 506-507.

casionally by revolutionary governments, it tends to be extremist.

Capitalist Extensive Agriculture With Wage Labor: The Ranch

An extensive culture of wool and beef, employing wage labor, grew up in the American West, Australia, England, and Scotland during and after the industrial revolution, Patagonia and some other parts of South America, and northern Mexico. In these cases the relative proportion of labor in the cost of production is smaller than it is in plantation agriculture. Such a structure is also characteristic of the wheat culture in northern Syria. In no case was there pressure to recruit and keep down an oppressed labor force. In England, a surplus labor force was pushed off the land. A fairly reliable economic indicator of the difference between ranch and plantation systems is that in ranch systems the least valuable land is owned by the largest enterprises. In plantation systems the most valuable land is owned by the largest enterprises, with less valuable land generally used by marginal smallholders. The explanation of this is not clear.

The characteristic social feature of these enterprises is a free-floating, mobile labor force, often with few family ties, living in barracks, and fed in some sort of "company mess hall." They tend to make up a socially undisciplined element, hard-drinking and brawling. Sometimes their alienation from society takes on the form of political radicalism, but rarely of an indigenous, disciplined radical movement.

The types of agricultural enterprise outlined here are hardly exhaustive, but perhaps they include most of the agricultural systems which help determine the political dynamics of those countries which act on the world scene today. Nor does this typology pretend to outline all the important differences in the dynamics of agricultural systems. Obviously, the system of family-size farms run by smallholders in Serbia in the 1840's is very different from the institutionally similar Danish and American systems of the 1950's.[13] And capitalistic sheep raisers supported and made up the House of Lords in England but supported populistic currents in the United States.

However, some of the differences among systems outlined here seem to hold in widely varying historical circumstances. The production and maintenance of ethnic differences by plantations, the political fragility of family-size tenancy, the richer associational life, populist ideology, corrupt politics of smallholders, and the political apathy and technical traditionalism of the manor or the old hacienda—these seem to be fairly reliable. Characteristics of rural enterprises and the class relations they typically produce are summarized in Table 1.

This, if it is true, shows the typology to be useful. The question that remains is: Is it capable of being used? Is it possible to find indices which will reliably differentiate a plantation from a manor or a manor from a large holding farmed by family tenancy?

The answer is that most of these systems have been accurately identified in particular cases. The most elusive is the manor, or traditional hacienda; governments based on this sort of agricultural enterprise rarely take accurate censuses, partly because they rarely have an agricultural policy worthy of

[13] For example, in the average size of agricultural villages, in the proportion of the crop marketed, in the level of living, in education, in birth rate, in the size of the household unit, in the intensity of ethnic antagonism, in degree of political organization and participation, in exposure to damage by military action—these are only some of the gross differences.

Type of Enterprise	Characteristics of Enterprise	Characteristics of Class Structure
Manorial	Division of land into domain land and labor subsistence land, with domain land devoted to production for market. Lord has police power over labor. Technically traditional; low cost of land and little market in land	Classes differ greatly in legal privileges and style of life. Technical culture borne largely by the peasantry. Low political activation and competence of peasantry; high politicalization of the upper classes
Family-size tenancy	Small parcels of highly valuable land worked by families who do not own the land, with a large share of the production for market. Highly labor- and land-intensive culture, ot yearly or more frequent crops	Classes differ little in legal privileges but greatly in style of life. Technical culture generally borne by the lower classes. High political affect and political organization of the lower classes, often producing revolutionary populist movements
Family smallholding	Same as family tenancy, except benefits remain within the enterprise. Not distinctive of areas with high valuation of land; may become capital-intensive at a late stage of industrialization	Classes differ neither in legal privileges nor in style of life. Technical culture borne by both rich and poor. Generally unified and highly organized political opposition to urban interests, often corrupt and undisciplined
Plantation	Large-scale enterprises with either slavery or wage labor, producing labor-intensive crops requiring capital investment on relatively cheap land (though generally the best land within the plantation area). No or little subsistence production	Classes differ in both style of life and legal privileges. Technical culture monopolized by upper classes. Politically apathetic and incompetent lower classes, mobilized only in time of revolution by urban radicals
Ranch	Large-scale production of labor-extensive crops, on land of low value (lowest in large units within ranch areas), with wage labor partly paid in kind in company barracks and mess	Classes may not differ in legal status, as there is no need to recruit and keep down a large labor force. Style of life differentiation unknown. Technical culture generally relatively evenly distributed. Dispersed and unorganized radicalism of lower classes

the name. Often even the boundaries of land holdings are not officially recorded. Further, the internal economy of the manor or hacienda provides few natural statistical indices—there is little bookkeeping use of labor, of land, of payment in kind or in customary rights. The statistical description of manorial economies is a largely unsolved problem.

Except for this, systematic comparative studies of the structure and dynamics of land tenure systems are technically feasible. But it has been all too often the case that descriptions of agricultural systems do not permit them to be classified by the type of enterprise.[14] Perhaps calling attention

14 For example, the most common measure used for comparative study is the concentration of land holdings. A highly unequal distribution of land may indicate family-tenancy, manorial, plantation, or ranch systems. Similarly, data on size of farm units confuse family smallholding with family tenancy, and lumps together all three kinds of large-scale enterprise. A high ratio of landless peasantry may be involved in family-tenancy, plantation, or manorial systems. Ambiguous references

to widespread typical patterns of institutionalizing agricultural production will encourage those who write monographs to provide the information necessary for comparative study.

---

to "tenancy" may mean the labor rents of a hacienda system, or the cash or share rents of family-size tenancy, or even tenancy of sons before fathers' death in smallholding systems. "Capitalistic agriculture" sometimes refers to ranches, sometimes to plantations, and sometimes to smallholdings. "Feudalism," though most often applied to manorial systems, is also used to describe family-size tenancy and plantation economies. "Absentee landlordism" describes both certain manorial and family-size tenancy systems.

American Occupational Elites

STUART ADAMS

One striking characteristic of recent studies in vertical occupational mobility is that they reflect current economic conditions. The field studies of the 1930's, for example, produced a literature heavy with emphasis on crystallizing social structures and narrowing channels of upward mobility; but in the following years of prosperity, sociologists have tended to discover that the American class system is still open and that opportunity at the apex is as great as ever.

Both findings appear to be reasonable, since capacity to change position in the social structure has important economic correlates. It also seems reasonable, however, to believe that mobility rates may be showing some effects of "irreversible" processes in the social system. Several such processes have been noted in recent decades: the passing of the frontier, the increasing differentiation of social structures, the virtual cessation of immigration, the decline of old motivational patterns, and the emergence of a "new" American character. These are all relatively massive processes, each capable of producing effects which might not be

Stuart Adams, "Origins of American Occupational Elites, 1900-1955," *American Journal of Sociology*, **62** (1956-57), 360-368.

wholly obscured by fluctuations in the gross national product.

The apparent absence of such effects in mobility rates may conceivably be attributed to counterinfluences, such as rising levels of education, equalization of economic opportunity, and a growing need for élite skills. The alternative possibility is that the negative findings are largely a consequence of insensitive techniques of investigation. The exploratory character of current research in mobility makes the latter an especially plausible hypothesis.

In the attempt at the precise measurement of vertical occupational mobility reported here, two relatively commonplace procedures were used. Attention was first focused on high-status, or "élite," occupations—in which, presumably, signs of changing mobility should first become evident. Then an occupational prestige scale—the North-Hatt scale[1]—was adopted as the basic

[1] C. C. North and P. K. Hatt, "Jobs and Occupations: A Popular Evaluation," *Opinion News* (1947), 3-13. This scale consists of prestige scores for common occupations, with values ranging from 33 to 96. Assignment of a prestige score to the occupation of an informant's father provides a numerical value for the "occupational origin" of the informant. These North-Hatt origin scores may then be manipulated statistically to obtain mean origin values for groups of informants or to ascertain trends in mean origins among several groups of informants.

measuring instrument. These procedures appeared to offer several advantages in the derivation of sensitive and meaningful indices of occupational origin. Such indices, in turn, could easily be reinterpreted as rates of verticle occupational mobility.

The subjects of the study were approximately 2500 members of five occupations: (1) business leaders—defined as owners or principal executives employing one hundred or more persons, (2) physicians, (3) attorneys, (4) salaried and independent engineers, and (5) high school and college teachers. Not all these occupations are customarily designated as "élite," but each is well above the mean status of the average United States male worker as measured on the North-Hatt scale.[2]

Data on the social histories of the informants were collected between 1947 and 1955 in four regions. In three —the Northeast, the Midwest, and the West Coast—systematic samples of members of the occupations were reached first by mailed questionnaire, then by follow-up interviews with random samples of nonrespondents in the mail canvass. In the fourth region—the Great Plains area—only the occupation of attorney was sampled. In this area, as in the two regions to the east, the sample of attorneys was reached by personal interview exclusively. On the West Coast, attorneys were sampled by the typical mail-and-interview procedure.

Sampling was restricted to two middle-sized cities in each region with the exception of the West Coast, where the sample site of all but one occupa-

tional subgroup was a large metropolitan area. This was a sample of college teachers, which was drawn from each of the several units in a state university system. The sample cities were chosen for representativeness of the occupational distribution of the urban male labor force in the states where the cities were located. The metropolitan area, located centrally on the West Coast, was chosen primarily for its accessibility.

The final group of informants numbered approximately 60 per cent of the original sample lists. Mail returns amounted to about 45 per cent, and interview returns roughly 15 per cent of the lists. The 45 per cent returns were relatively uniform across the regions sampled by mail, with a slight tendency for percentage of returns to increase in a westward direction. There were, on the other hand, conspicuous differences in returns by occupation. Lowest returns were by business leaders, ranging from 35 to 40 per cent, while the highest were by college teachers, with a return of about 60 per cent.

Significant differences between mail and interview returns were found only in the eastern regions, and there primarily in medicine and business. Differences between the two types of returns diminished progressively in regions to the west, and on the West Coast discrepancies on key variables were negligible in law, medicine, and business. No interviews were undertaken in engineering and teaching on the West Coast, since mail returns in these occupations had shown relatively little bias in the eastern areas. In the Midwest, no business leaders were interviewed because of pressure of time. However, interview returns from business leaders in regions to the east and west made it possible to obtain certain adjusted values for the Midwest by interpolation.

---

[2] The average American male worker in 1950 had a mean score of approximately sixty points on the North-Hatt scale. This may be compared with 93 for physicians, 86 for attorneys, 84 for civil engineers, 79 for instructors in public schools, and from 82 to 88 for various categories of "business leaders."

For all regional subsamples where both mail and interview returns were obtained, working samples were constructed by weighting the interview component before combining interview and mail returns. The weighting factor was the reciprocal of the fraction of nonrespondents interviewed in the follow-up—roughly one fourth to one third. Subsamples consisting exclusively of interview returns and the mail returns from engineers and teachers on the West Coast were taken as adequate representations of the populations from which they were drawn.

In the analysis of the data, interest centered mainly on two relationships: (1) the trend in occupational origins of each group in the time covered by informant age differences, and (2) regional differences in those trends within each group. The first relationship provided an index of mobility rates over time; the second, an index of mobility rates by geographical regions.

To facilitate analysis, the origin of each informant was expressed as a numerical value, derived by referring the father's principal occupation to the North-Hatt scale. Occupations not listed specifically were scored by analogy. As has been shown elsewhere, the North-Hatt scale appears to have good intergenerational stability;[3] hence its use in scoring occupations over a fifty-year span is warranted empirically. No serious error seems to arise from use of the instrument as an interval scale. This feature of the scale has the advantage that it provides automatic adjustment for minor changes in the composition of the labor force.

As a correction for major changes in the composition of the labor force, i.e., those which alter the mean origin

of those in the labor force significantly over time, it was considered necessary to adjust for secular trend in origins of males in the labor force in the four sample regions. However, the absence of suitable data by region led to substitution of the national trend in origins of males in the labor force as the base for all regions. This basic trend was obtained by scoring each of the Bureau of the Census occupational groupings by the mean North-Hatt score for occupations in that group, computing the mean score for the male labor force in each ten-year period, and using these means to construct a linear trend line for the period from 1910 to 1950. This is, properly speaking, the trend in occupational *status* of the male labor force, but occupational *origin* may be assumed to be a parallel trend for a population of such magnitude. With the regression coefficient of this trend, .05, as a correction factor, it was possible to adjust the raw North-Hatt origin trends of the sample groups so as to measure movement in relation to the mean origin of males in the labor force.

The first point of interest in the analysis was the variation in occupational origins of the several élites in time. Variations were ascertained both as regression coefficients and as graphic representations of trends in cohort origin means. In each case the summary statistics were computed so as to show the trend in relation to the mean origin of males in the labor force. Table 1 shows the pattern of regression coefficients for the several occupations over the four sample regions.

Since a negative coefficient signifies a decline in origin scores with time, the values in the table indicate a general trend toward lower origins among members of the occupations studied. This is equivalent to stating that in the last fifty years there has been a broad movement toward increased vertical

    [3] Stuart Adams, "Trends in Occupational Origins of Business Leaders," *American Sociological Review*, 19 (1954), 542-548, for an elaboration of this point.

TABLE 1 Regression of North-Hatt Origin Scores on Time, by Occupation and Region*

Occupation	West Coast	Great Plains	Midwest	Northeast
Physician	+ .003		− .293†	− .144†
Business leader	− .063		− .095	− .059
Attorney	− .082†	− .091	− .032	+ .043
Engineer, salaried	− .154†		− .037	− .179†
Teacher, high school	− .032		− .274†	− .244†
Engineer, independent	− .020			
Teacher, college	− .146†			

* Average N by occupation and region (interviews weighted), 173.
† Coefficient of regression significantly lower than zero, at .01 level.

mobility into them. The data may also be interpreted as showing that the origins of the élites are tending to converge on the mean origins of males in the labor force.

For some of the occupations under consideration, the values in Table 1 are not satisfactory representations of the actual trend in mean origins. A more realistic picture is available in the curves of mean origin shown in Fig. 1, which are based on means derived from five-year groups of informants classed by date of birth. To reduce fluctuations arising from sampling error, the plotted values are either ten-year or fifteen-year moving averages. The mean number of informants per trend line in the figure is 139 with interviews unweighted and 173 with interviews weighted.

Fig. 1 conveys some impression of a general decline in origins over time, although perhaps not so consistently as might be inferred from Table 1. A number of other patterns are also evident in the origin curves. One noteworthy trend is shown by the independent professionals—attorneys, physicians, and consulting engineers. In the last two decades some movement toward higher origins has occurred in each of these professions in all the regions sampled. The magnitude of the movement varies with region, being maximal in the East and falling off more or less regularly toward the West.

A second notable tendency is apparent mainly in medicine, in law, and among salaried engineers. The tendency is that of phase displacement in the origin curves. In each region recruitment into these occupations appears to have gone through distinct cycles which occurred at different times and in predictable sequence in the several regions. The origin curves for physicians, for example, indicate that this profession was recruited from the highest origins in the Northeast in the late 1880's, in the Midwest in the middle 1890's, and on the West Coast in the early 1900's. In law a similar tendency may be observed with respect to time of lowest origins; a minimum is reached in the West Coast area some thirty years after the Northeast. Among salaried engineers, the peak in origins in the Northeast lies outside the limits of the smoothed curve, but the peaks in the Midwest and West Coast curves come in the early and late 1890's, respectively.

A third point of interest is the suggestion in the curves of origin of the engineers and business leaders in the two eastward regions of a reaction to the depression of the 1930's. In both groups of curves there is a cresting of origins in the cohorts which were most likely to have been entering their occupations in the depression years. The crest for business leaders occurs several years earlier than for engineers,

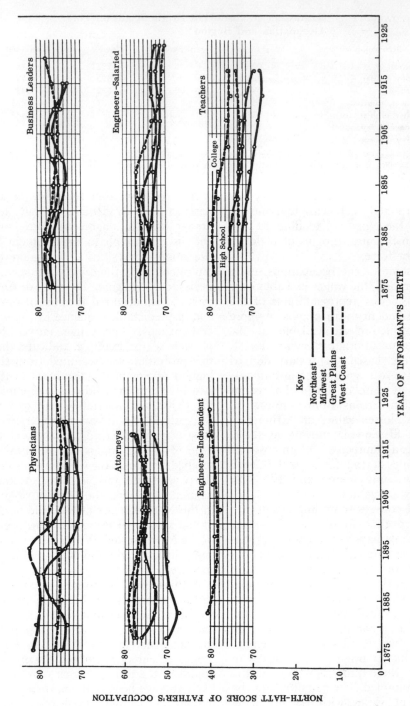

FIG. 1. Trends in North-Hatt Origins of Selected Occupational Elites, 1900-1955.

implying that the critical ages for gaining a foothold are several years apart for the recruits in these two fields. The absence of phase displacement in these crests indicates that the cause operated simultaneously in the several regions and hence is of a different character from that responsible for the crests and troughs in the curves for physicians and attorneys.

A final point of interest in Fig. 1 is the idiosyncratic features of the curves of origin for the West Coast, primarily in the data on business leaders, salaried engineers, and high school teachers. The curve for business leaders shows an absence of cresting for the 1900-09 cohort; it also shows rising origins at a time when the two other regions experienced decline, i.e., during the last fifteen or twenty years. The curve for engineers is of interest primarily for its failure to crest markedly during the depression, and the curve for high school teachers for its reversal of the pattern for teachers in the two regions to the east. In two of these occupations, at least, it appears that trends in West Coast mobility are qualitatively different from those in regions to the east.

One aspect of the origin curves which merits special consideration is the relationship between the regional curves within each occupation. Invariably the curve for the Northeast lies in the lowest mean position in Fig. 1. The curve for the West Coast, on the other hand,

appears to lie in the highest position. This pattern suggests that mean occupational origins tend to rise in an east-to-west direction.

To throw further light on this possibility, origin means for the several occupations were computed by region, as shown in Table 2. Values for the four occupations which were not sampled in the Plains were obtained by extrapolation from values to the eastward, the attorney means serving as a system of reference.

The regional means show a general trend toward higher values in a westerly direction until the Plains area is reached, followed by a decline on the West Coast. The assumption that the four other occupations, like law, reach their highest origins in the Plains may at first appear gratuitous. This assumption seems more reasonable upon examination, however, even apart from the analogy in the trend of attorney means. The two factors most clearly associated with low origins—high density of educational institutions and high proportion of foreign born—are less characteristic of the Plains than of the other regions studied. Furthermore, high-status fathers of attorneys in the Plains sample had appreciably more male offspring than equivalent fathers in the samples of attorneys of the Northeast and Midwest. Hence birth-rate differentials, as well as accessibility of education and proportions of second-generation immigrants, op-

TABLE 2   Origin Means and Standard Deviations by Occupation and Region

Occupation	West Coast		Great Plains		Midwest		Northeast	
	M	σ	M	σ	M	σ	M	σ
Physician	77.4	8.2	78.7*		77.7	10.4	74.3	9.9
Business leader	76.7	7.7	77.5*		77.3	7.0	76.5	7.9
Attorney	77.0	7.6	77.8	7.4	76.4	8.3	71.8	10.9
Engineer, salaried	74.4	8.3	74.4*		74.3	7.9	73.9	6.1
Teacher, high school	74.2	9.0	74.2*		73.6	8.6	71.7	8.9
Engineer, independent	80.2	6.0						
Teacher, college	77.3	7.4						

° Extrapolated from values in regions to the east.

erate in favor of the highest occupational origins in this region.

The engineering and business means, which showed some common characteristics in the temporal curves, show further similarities in the regional data. The origins of the two occupations exhibit less variation between regions than do those of the three other occupations and, in particular, less of a tendency to decline sharply in the eastern region.

There are no readily apparent clues as to the probable trend in origins of college teacher and consulting or independent engineer which might be found if these groups were to be sampled in regions to the east. The most plausible assumption is that the independent engineers would parallel the business leaders in origin, while the college teachers would follow a trend like that among physicians and attorneys.

The foregoing analysis has shown that mobility into the upper occupational strata of this society is a fairly complex phenomenon. Within the five occupations studied, at least three patterns of mobility have been distinguished. The first is a simple movement toward lower origins—i.e., gradually increasing vertical mobility. This is the most general trend evident in these occupations. The second is a transient cresting phenomenon—an abrupt rise, followed by an equally abrupt decline to former levels of origin. This may occur simultaneously throughout an occupation or, more typically in the present case, be displaced chronologically across geographical regions. In the latter case, the displacement is invariably in an east-to-west direction. The third pattern is that exhibited by the independent professions—a period of decline followed by a gradual movement toward higher origins in recent decades.

The present report is not intended as a definitive explanation of the phenomena observed here. However, provisional interpretations are offered of some of the tendencies.

The most general process observed —the broad movement toward lower origins—probably has a fairly ready explanation: the demand for high social and technical skills is outrunning reproduction in families in the higher social strata, and the growing deficiency is being met by recruitment of abler individuals from lower strata. Downward recruitment is being facilitated in the present era by the growing accessibility of education, standardization of cultures across strata, equalization of incomes, and similar tendencies.

There are undoubtedly several reasons for the variations in trends as between the salaried and independent professions. One is variability in criteria of admission to the occupation—a factor probably reflected both in mean level of origin and in fluctuations in origin as the criteria of admission are modified. A second reason is the differential in effective need for the types of skill involved. Engineering and teaching are professions whose growth is more rapid than the rise in general population; law and medicine are not. The disparity in rate of growth found among the professions appears to be mirrored in the divergent patterns of their trends in origin in recent decades.

Shifting values and declining motivation to enter the independent professions also appear to be involved in the diverging trends. This may be one aspect of the growing desire for the "secure" job—the salaried professional job or managerial position—which is allegedly becoming characteristic of college graduates, particularly in eastern communities.[4] There may also be

---

[4] As an example, "Class of '49," *Fortune* (1949), 92ff., reports a survey in which only 2 per cent of "U.S. college seniors" state that they are "going into business for themselves,"

a growing disinclination on the part of American youth to commit itself to the long pull of medical or legal training in view of the expanding number of attractive alternative careers.[5]

As in the case of the occupational differences in trends of origin, there are probably several reasons for some of the striking regional differences, the two principal explanations being, probably, again differences in the availability of education and in proportion of foreign-born persons in the population. The latter seems especially important in the northeast sample, and there particularly in the independent professions. The children of foreign-born parents exhibit relatively high motivation toward these professions and achieve professional status in numbers significantly higher than the social status of the family would appear to warrant.

Within the Northeast, also, discrimination in employment appears to enter into the significant differences between mean occupational origins. The failure of origins of engineers and business leaders to show an appreciable falling off there may be attributed to the inability of members of minority groups to enter these fields as readily as law, medicine, or teaching.

The phenomenon of cresting in the temporal curves of origins appears to

in contrast to 75 per cent or more of the seniors in two universities in the Southwest.

[5] In "Not Enough Medical Students," New York Times (May 29, 1955), E9, an investigation into reasons for the "steady decrease in number of applicants to medical schools throughout the nation over the past five years" is discussed. The principal findings: "unwillingness to undertake the long training, adverse publicity given the profession by advocates of government control, lack of sufficient financial support, fear of excessive requirements of military service, desire to marry early and rear a family, attractive industrial jobs and increasing opportunities for earning a good living earlier in life in other scientific fields."

have two principal causes: depression and rising requirements for entrance. Depression apparently shifts some candidates for a profession who have low status into other careers, leaving a permanent hump in the curve at the location of the cohort most directly affected. Rising entrance requirements apparently operate in much the same manner, with rising standards of living and increasing accessibility of education acting to reduce origins to the previous level once more. Among the occupations studied, business and engineering are evidently most susceptible to cresting because of depression. The remaining occupations, on the other hand, show no evidence of a similar cresting but appear to be quite sensitive to rising professional standards. Engineering is the only one of the occupations which shows what may be interpreted as definite reactions to both influences.

The most conspicuous reaction to altered training requirements appears in the medical profession, which experienced a drastic lifting of standards at the turn of the century. A less conspicuous example is the West Coast high school teacher: the requirement of five years of training apparently produced a moderate rise in their origins in the last two decades. The effect of the requirement has probably been augmented by good salaries and aggressive recruiting. The rise, interestingly enough, has brought the origins of high school and college teachers in this area into relatively close juxtaposition.

Phase displacement or staggered cresting of origin curves suggests a link between mobility rates and the order in which a given social form emerges in the several regions. This phenomenon is clearly evident only among physicians, attorneys, and salaried engineers, but there are suggestions of it among teachers and business leaders. It may be explained by the formal or informal requirements for entering these occupations. New requirements usually involve some rise in occupational origins. Insofar as the requirements are likely to originate in older communities, then diffuse gradually into the newer, a systematic displacement from east to west should result.

The rise in origins of business leaders on the West Coast during the last two decades is perhaps the least explicable of all the trends in origin in Fig. 1. Prior to a detailed analysis of parental histories, place of birth, education, migration, job histories, types of firms managed, and other personal data, it is possible only to infer that selective factors analogous to those acting on the West Coast high school teachers have given a unique character to the recruitment of the business leaders there.

In conclusion, it appears to be possible, by use of the procedures employed in this study, to derive highly sensitive and meaningful indices of occupational origins of specific working groups. Examination of such indices for the subject groups discloses significant differences in occupational origins and in vertical mobilities rates between geographical regions, occupational groups, and chronological periods. The indices also reveal several patterns of vertical occupational mobility probably relevant to occupations other than those here considered.

Perhaps the most general of these patterns is the trend toward lower occupational origins—higher rates of vertical mobility—during the past half-century in most of the occupations studied. Within this general trend there are two subsidiary patterns: transient fluctuations in trend in origin, occurring either simultaneously in all regions or displaced chronologically,

east to west, and emerging countertrends, consisting of sustained movement toward higher origins in some occupations in recent decades.

Many of the transient fluctuations in origin may be nonrecurrent, particularly if programs of professional training have become stabilized and also if there are no more serious economic depressions. The probable duration of the countertrends, which have emerged primarily in the independent professions, is difficult to predict. Since these upturns appear to be largely the result of shifts in personal motivation rather than increased restrictions on entrance into the independent professions, they might be expected to continue until popular values change or until there is some provision of additional incentives to enter training or to seek a career in the affected professions.

The continued decline in origins in the salaried professions, which comprise the great bulk of professional workers, suggests that vertical mobility rates are continuing to rise in this society. At the same time, the behavior of the independent professions seemingly indicates that the rate of increase is diminishing, although perhaps only temporarily, in the current decade.

During the period under observation in this study, origins of individuals in high-status occupations have tended to converge on the mean origin of males in the labor force. The rate of convergence has possibly declined in the last two decades, but, as a summary judgment, the process is continuing. Two major effects seem to be implied in this convergence: access to high-status or élite occupations appears to be growing easier in this society; and there may be a concomitant reduction, if not in the vertical dimension of the American class structure, at least in variability in status within that structure.

Part 2

sociological
analysis
of economic
processes

production processes

one

For the economist, a business firm constitutes the nexus into which the factors of production flow, combine, and emerge as some sort of marketable commodity. For the sociologist, the firm has a number of different meanings; it is a complex network of communication, an interrelated system of roles, an authority system, and a prestige system. Sometimes these sociological features create adjustment problems in the firm that influence the productivity of workers and the efficiency of the enterprise. In this section are included several analyses of the relations between the economic and sociological aspects of productive organizations—two articles on role and status conflict (by Homans and Dalton), one of the effects of turnover of personnel at the managerial level (by Guest), and one on the ramifying social consequences of a change in product (by Cottrell).

These selections parallel the issues discussed on pp. 70-86 of *The Sociology of Economic Life*.

Status Among Clerical Workers

GEORGE C. HOMANS

Students of industrial organization have long been interested in the con-

George C. Homans, "Status Among Clerical Workers," *Human Organization*, **12** (Spring, 1953), 5-10.

nection between the relative status of workers on different jobs and the characteristics of these jobs, especially differences in pay. But surprisingly few studies of this connection have been reported in any detail. In this paper, I shall describe how a group of workers complained because the high status conferred on them by some features of their job was not reflected in other features. By the *status* of a job I shall mean the rank assigned to the job by the workers, insofar as it is better or worse than other jobs and according to the degree they feel it realizes certain values or norms.

I encountered this "status problem" in the course of a series of studies I made of clerical workers in a certain company. All the reader needs to know about the company is that it had a large number of customers to whom it sent out monthly bills. From December, 1949, through April, 1950, I made a study of one division of this company, consisting of sixty workers and supervisors, men and women, who carried out various operations in accounting for the payment of these bills.

Method of Study

The study went through several phases. I obtained the approval of the management and the union executive committee for making the study. The union was then an independent one which, while not a "company union," was limited in membership to the workers of the company in question. The workers have since voted to join a[n AFL-]CIO union, whose officers have approved various later studies in the company. I explained the purposes and methods of the study to the supervisors of every echelon who were responsible for the division in which I planned to work. Then I made the same explanation to the supervisors and workers of the division itself, assuring them that I would make no private report of my findings either to the management or to the union, and that if I published any report—as I am doing here—I should not quote anything any person said to me in such

a way that it could be traced back to him to his detriment.

Immediately after this explanation, I moved to a small table at the back of the large room in which the division worked, so placed that it commanded a substantially clear view of the whole room. With this as a base of operation, I spent about a month introducing myself to each of the workers individually, learning the various clerical procedures, some of them quite complicated, that the division carried on, and getting a general impression of behavior in the room. The period of social constraint due to the presence of a stranger seemed to end after I attended the workers' Christmas office party. From then on, I could get no evidence from the supervisors, the union representative, or the office boy in the room that the workers' behavior was any different than it had been before I came in; but output, in those operations whose output was measured, showed a tendency to go up, and the industrial relations department was inclined to give me undeserved credit for an improvement in morale.

The second phase of the study, which took two weeks, was systematic observation of interaction in the room, specifically of which persons talked to which other persons, and how often.

With sixty persons in the room, I could obviously not keep a continuous interaction record, so I adopted a sampling procedure. Every fifteen minutes I scanned the room and made a note of which persons were talking together at that time.[1] In theory, talking except on business was discouraged. In practice, it was tolerated, and there was a great deal of strictly social chit-chat,

[1] This method, plus the distances at which observations were made, precluded accurate recording of *originations* and *receipts* of interaction. I could only see *which persons* were interacting.

especially among the younger girls. Naturally I was not interested in checking up on the workers, but in getting a quantitative record of interpersonal contacts. Yet I must report, incidentally, that contrary to official ideas, but not to the unofficial ideas of some of the supervisors, there turned out to be no inverse relation between talking and output. In fact, some of the girls who talked most also produced most.

The third and longest phase of the study consisted of individual interviews with the supervisors and workers, conducted on company time in a private room away from the office floor. Before the interview, I asked each worker individually whether she was willing to talk to me; they all agreed, except one whom I did not press further. The interviews, which lasted from one to two hours, were nondirective except in two respects. After explaining again the purpose of the study, I always began the main body of the interview with the question: "How do you like your job?" That is, the focus of the interview, at least in the beginning, was on attitudes toward the job. Then at some appropriate time in the course of the interview, I asked the sociometric question: "Who are your close friends in here?" I wanted to get further evidence on informal social organization. Though it has no bearings on the main theme of this paper, I must report that there turned out to be a significant correlation between the rank order of workers in terms of the number of times they were chosen as friends and their rank order in terms of frequency of interaction. Those often chosen, often talked or were often talked to. I recorded each interview as I remembered it as soon as possible after it finished.

During the interviewing period I kept in touch with the division office every day to make arrangements for the next interviews, and so on. When the interviews were over, I returned to my table in the office for two weeks to check my first impressions and to make further interaction records. The whole study took four and one half months. Let me say here that I enjoyed very much my association with a fine body of American men and women. In fact I had a wonderful time.

The Jobs

The "status problem" was not my only focus in the study of the division, and to describe it I need consider, besides the supervision, only the two largest of the job groups within the division—the cash posters and the ledger clerks. The workers of the division were mostly women, all of whom were at least high school graduates. The cash posters were ten young women from about seventeen to about twenty-five years of age who had from less than one to about four years' service in the company; the ledger clerks were twenty women, from about twenty-one to over sixty years of age, with from three to thirty years' service. Thus the two groups differed greatly in average age and length of service. . . .

The usual channel of advancement in the division started with a job of pay grade I, then went to cash poster (grade II) and then to ledger clerk (grade II). Overturn was high among the younger girls who were much interested in getting married, and a company rule stated that when a girl married she had to leave its employ. The result was that promotion to cash poster might come after three or four months' service in the division, and promotion to ledger clerk hardly more than two years later, but promotion from ledger clerk to a grade III job might take decades. Promotion was largely by seniority; overturn among the older ledger clerks was slow, as those who were going to marry and leave had already done so, and the others stuck to their jobs because of the company's well-deserved reputation for providing job security. ("Nobody ever gets fired around here.") Thus many of the ledger clerks were older women with high seniority in the division and in the company.

The management had tried to make amends for the very slow advancement in the ledger clerk's job by giving grade III pay to four of the most senior of the ledger clerks, as well as the title of "group leader." These were not in fact supervisory jobs. The group leader continued to do her regular job as ledger clerk, but held herself ready to answer the questions of less experienced clerks.

Though the transfer from cash poster to ledger clerk was officially considered a promotion, the two jobs were in the same pay grade with equal pay for a forty-hour week of five eight-hour days. It was common knowledge that three of the girls in the division had refused a "promotion" to ledger clerk when it was offered to them. The reasons the two jobs paid equally were at least in part historical. In the not-too-distant past, cash posting had been done at night by men and, therefore, had commanded relatively high wages which were not changed when it was transferred to the daytime and to women.

The titles "cash posters" and "ledger clerks" came from the processes of old-fashioned double-entry bookkeeping, though more modern methods had long ago replaced the ledger book and the written entry. The "ledgers" now consisted of ten blocks of files, each holding the accounts of one main section of the company's customers. In these files were trays of cards representing the sums of money each customer had been billed during the month, that is, the "arrears." All the customers were not billed on the first of the month; instead, to avoid enormous peak loads, a certain number of customers were billed on each working day of the month.

The cash-posting job was essentially as follows: Bundles of bill stubs, representing paid bills, came from the cashier's office to the desk of the posters' supervisor. A cash poster took one of these bundles, went to the right "ledger," and pulled out the cards whose numbers corresponded to those on the stubs. Hence cash posting was popularly known as "pulling cash." The removal of a card from the ledger meant that the customer was not billed for this amount in the following month, and thus in effect his bill was recorded as paid. When a cash poster had finished one bundle she started on the next one, while the "pulled" cards and their stubs were sent to another room to be tabulated against one another. At this point, the number of cards in the bundle was counted and credited to the girl who had pulled them. If cards and stubs did not balance due to some mistake the poster had made, such as pulling the wrong card, this fact also was recorded. Thus output, in terms of cards per hour, and accuracy, in terms of mistakes per day, were recorded for every cash poster and appeared on the supervisor's desk daily for the girls to see. Cash posting was the only job in the room for which output records were or could easily be kept. The bundles varied somewhat, thus influencing the speed with which a poster could finish them, but each poster was bound in the long run to get equal numbers of "good" or "bad" bundles. The supervisors expected each poster to "pull" an average of at least 300 cards per hour, and each one did. This was the "quota." But aside from this there was no group norm of output and no incentive pay, and individual posters varied from just over 300 to almost 500 cards per hour.

This was the main job of the cash posters. They had other, minor ones, which I do not need to describe. Each poster had a small table to which she could bring trays of cards if she wished, but for the most part the posters worked standing up at the ledger files. Since they had to move from file to file according to the kind of stubs they received, they had plenty of chance to meet each other and the ledger clerks. Many of them were able to work fast and talk at the same time.

Two ledger clerks were assigned as partners to each of the ten ledgers, dividing the work between them as they saw fit. They sat at desks between the ledger files and within easy talking distance of one another. Their supervisor changed the assignment to partner and to ledger in the last hour of the last working day of every year, to the accompaniment of a good deal of excitement. Of the ledger clerks' job, it is enough to say that they did everything necessary to keep customers' accounts up to date, except cash posting, transfers of address, breakdowns of over- and underpayments, and so forth. One of the two desks at each ledger was equipped with a phone, and the clerks answered questions regarding the state of the accounts from customers themselves and from other employees of the company. Whereas the cash posters had, in the main, to do one single repetitive job on a production basis, requiring little thought but plenty of physical mobility, the ledger clerks had to do a number of nonrepetitive clerical jobs on a nonproduction basis, requiring some thought but little physical mobility.

I must mention one other vital fact. The supervisors thought of the ledger clerks, the largest group in the room, as the chief reservoir from which womanpower could be drawn when other jobs in the room were short-handed. They also regarded cash posting not as the most important job of the division, but as the one they could least afford to get behindhand with: it had to be cleaned up every day. It was therefore standard daily procedure for their supervisor to take some of the ledger clerks (but not the group leaders) off their stations in rotation and send them to fill in on other jobs, usually cash posting. This happened far less often to other groups in the room. Since many of the ledger clerks had been "promoted" from cash posting, they were thoroughly familiar with the work.

Informal Organization

I do not need to describe in detail the informal social organization of the division, except for some points in the relation between cash posters and ledger clerks. In spite of the fact that both groups worked at the same ledgers, only one of the ledger clerks (Clary) interacted more with posters than with other ledger clerks. She was also the only ledger clerk chosen as friend by more cash posters than ledger clerks. She had, in fact, only recently been "promoted" to ledger work. Only one of the cash posters (Burke) interacted more with ledger clerks than with cash posters. She also was the only cash poster chosen as friend by more ledger clerks and others than by cash posters. She was the oldest of the cash posters. Burke and Clary were themselves mutual friends. In short, cash posters and ledger clerks, in relation to one another, tended to form distinct social as well as job groups. So far as any informal leadership was exercised in the room, Clary and Allen, two of the younger ledger clerks, tended to exercise it. Of all the ledger clerks, Allen was first in sociometric choices given to her, and tied for first with Clary in number of persons contacted, that is, in range rather than frequency of interaction. Clary talked more often than any other ledger clerk and more than all but one of the cash posters. (All names are changed from the originals.)

Attitudes Toward Jobs

The above information about the two jobs is objective in the sense that I could have gotten most of it without talking to the women themselves. The "status problem" was not discovered in the same way: it led to no outbreak in overt action that I observed, but emerged instead from the attitudes expressed in interviews. Since it was a "problem" chiefly for the ledger clerks, I shall concentrate on their attitudes. In my experience in holding nondirective interviews with persons who interact frequently with one another, I have found that many of them express the same opinions in almost the same words, often without realizing that they are doing so, and giving instead every impression that they think their views are original. I do not know why I once found this surprising, but I did. The workers of the division were no exception to this rule. Although the accidents of an interview may prevent any one person from expressing all the opinions he holds, I assume that, given enough interviews and the freedom of the nondirective situation, the frequency with which particular attitudes are expressed is an index of their relative importance in the group as a whole.

I interviewed nineteen of the twenty ledger clerks—one refused. Each interview began with the question: "How do you like your job?" and thirteen out of the nineteen said they liked it, none that they positively disliked it. (Of course a person is always under pressure to say she likes her job, for to say she does not is to confess herself a fool for not trying to get out of it. In the case of the ledger clerks, the very low rate of leaving the job except for promotion and marriage is some evidence that they *did* like it.) More important are the reasons given for liking the job. In this connection, ten of the ledger clerks spoke of the general friendliness of the division, and six said they liked their bosses; these of course were not conditions specific to the ledger job itself. Of the more specific conditions, eleven women mentioned the pay, and six the job security as being good. Ten said that what they liked about the job was its responsibility, eight its variety, eight the chances for contact with customers by telephone, and four the pleasure of "straightening things out." In the minds of the ledger clerks, as in those of most of us, a job is "responsible" to the degree you can do harm if you make an error. The pleasure the clerks found in contact with the customers (which I myself found somewhat surprising) seemed to derive both in the wider social contacts so made, and in contacting the persons to whose needs it was the ultimate purpose of the company to minister. The clerks felt an admirable responsibility to the consumer. "Straightening things out" meant bringing order out of chaos in a customer's account. Clearly the women were appraising their jobs favorably in terms of the values of pleasant social atmosphere, good bosses, pay, security, responsibility, variety, outside contact, and what we may call "problem solving."

Though attitudes toward the ledger job were generally favorable, the women held that the job had two specific drawbacks. The first, mentioned by eleven of the nineteen, was that it offered little or no chance for advancement and that seniority and ability received little recognition when promotions were made. This opinion was fully justified by the facts. The second drawback, related to the first, was the "status problem" on which this paper is focused. But here I had better begin by quoting directly from an interview with one not untypical clerk:

I like the work. There's only one thing I don't like about it. Everybody talks around here as if cash posting was the only job that counted. They take us off stations [ledgers] to work on cash, and they think that the stations can just take care of themselves. The work piles up and you get behind. Of course we've got to get the cash out, but I think the station work is just as important. And it's much more responsible. Cash posting, most of it, is just mechanical, but station work is a responsible job. You have to deal with the customers, and with the stores, and if you don't do something right, someone is going to suffer. Of course that's true of cash posting, too, but there are a lot more things that a station clerk has to do. It's a more responsible job, and yet the station clerks get just the same pay as the cash posters. It seems that they ought to get just a few dollars more to show that the job is more important.

This states the chief recurring theme of the "status problem," and with this background let me return to crude statistics. Fourteen of the nineteen ledger clerks interviewed said that the ledger clerks ought to get more pay than the cash posters, usually adding, like the clerk I have quoted, that they ought to get "just a couple of dollars a week more, to show that our job is more important." (The only ledger clerk who specifically disagreed with this view was Clary, whose peculiar social position has been described above.) Note that they were pretty well satisfied with their general pay level, at least in the sense that they felt they could not do better in another company. What they wanted was a pay differential between themselves and the cash posters.

Thirteen ledger clerks complained that they were "taken off their own jobs" to fill in on cash posting and other jobs, and thirteen further complained that when this happened they got "behind in their own work." This calls for further comment. The ledger clerks did indeed get taken away from the ledgers. I could not determine independently whether their own work suffered, but I am quite ready to believe them when they say it did. Eight of the ledger clerks said they liked cash posting when they did it: it was not the cash posting itself that hurt, but being taken away from their "own" job. What is more, the bosses made no objection when they fell behind on the ledger work as a result of filling in on other jobs: they suffered not through criticism from the bosses but through damage to their own sense of closure— of "straightening things out." In fact, when they complained, the bosses seem to have taken the line: "You get paid to stay in here for eight hours a day. What odds does it make to you what kind of work you do? We don't bawl you out if you get behind"—a good example of the conflict between the "logic of management" and the "logic of the worker," especially identification with one's "own job." The ledger clerks summed the situation up by saying they got "pushed around."

Ten of the ledger clerks also claimed that "our boss won't stand up for us." Let us see what this means. When the supervisor or one of the other work groups in the division felt he needed extra help, he would go to the supervisor of the ledger clerks and ask for a certain number of women. The ledger boss seems always to have acceded to such requests and to have picked out the women whose turn it was to go off their own jobs. When they said their boss did not stand up for them, the clerks meant that he should not automatically have agreed but, rather, should have refused to release them if their own work might thereby suffer, especially as the women felt it was wrong for them to be taken off their own jobs at all. He allowed others, theoretically his equals, to originate action for him. It is hard to see how the ledger supervisor could have done otherwise, as it was standing policy in the division that the ledger clerks should serve as the main pool of floating labor. The members of a job group have an almost pathetic expectation that their boss should represent their interests and help them behave according to their own norms as against everybody else's norms, including management's. When he cannot or will not, the workers will try to find some other agent who can and will. This need for someone to exercise the "representative function," and not in matters of pay alone, is one of the strongest reasons for the formation and behavior of unions. Some of the ledger clerks had in fact complained to their union representative, but, as they said, "nothing happened." All the union had done was to help get the group leader job set up. The feeling that in this, as in other cases, the union had been inactive was probably one of the reasons why the workers voted to abandon the independent union for the [AFL-]CIO.

The fact that the ledger clerks were taken off their own jobs to fill in on others, especially on cash posting, while the cash posters did not fill in on the ledgers, led to the further comment, made by seven of the clerks, that "we can do what the others do, but they can't do what we do," which carried the inference that it was therefore wrong that both should get paid the same amount. Finally, eight of the ledger clerks mentioned the fact that

some of the cash posters had refused "promotion" to the ledgers, the inference here being that if ledger clerking were given the recognition it deserved, this would not have happened.

To round out the picture, let me give a few of the attitudes of the cash posters bearing on the "status problem." Nine out of the ten cash posters said they liked their job, and six mentioned the friendly atmosphere. Of the specific job characteristics, four mentioned the pay as good, but only three thought the job was varied or interesting, and none talked about its responsibility. Four simply made the comment, "it's a job," that is, better than no job at all. As for their attitudes toward the ledger-clerk job, four said they did not like it or would not blame a girl for not taking it, and four (two of them the same as the first four) mentioned the fact that the pay was the same. Burke's comment was characteristic:

I wouldn't mind going on stations. . . . I probably will go on stations pretty soon. Cal is engaged and I probably will take her place. Jessie is senior, but she will probably be married pretty soon, so unless they bring someone in from outside, I will probably get the job. I wouldn't turn it down. It's got more variety than cash posting. Some of them have turned it down. . . . I don't blame them for not taking station clerk. After all you don't get paid any more. But I wouldn't turn it down.

As a matter of fact, she did turn it down a little later. I asked her why, and she said, "it's too much trouble."

So far as I can speak of a general opinion among the cash posters, it was that the ledger-clerk job offered more variety and responsibility than cash posting—though less chance for moving around, which appealed greatly to some of the younger girls. But, as usual, the better job was the more demanding job, and unless the rewards, in this case the pay, were appropriate, no girl was to be blamed for not taking it.

The Status Problem

The problem described in this case was not an acute one. The ledger clerks felt aggrieved; some of them had complained to the supervisors and the union; nothing had been changed, but there was no further revolt. My impression was that the general morale in the division remained good. Nevertheless, I think the case illustrates some of the features that will be found in more serious cases of status conflict.

Why do I call this a status problem at all? I do so because the ledger clerks felt—and the cash posters somewhat grudgingly conceded—that they had the *better* job, that is, the higher rank or status. They felt their job had more variety—and on any definition of "variety," it certainly had. They felt it had more responsibility—and according to their definition of "responsibility," which is much like yours or mine, it certainly had. They felt it demanded more skill—they could do their own job and the cash posters' too. The transfer from cash poster to ledger clerk was held to be a promotion, and certainly in service to the company the ledger clerks were senior, sometimes by decades, to the cash posters. By all these standards the ledger clerk's job was a higher status job than the cash poster's. The problem arose because by some other standards the ledger clerk's job was no better and even worse than the cash poster's. In particular, it brought no higher pay—and by emotional logic, if one job is better than another, it ought to get better pay, although not necessarily a great deal higher. And in some ways it had even less autonomy—for the ledger clerks were taken off their own jobs and put on others far more often than the cash posters, and with-

out their having any say in the matter. As they said, they felt "pushed around." To add insult to injury, when they were taken off their own jobs, they were often put "down" on the cash posting job. The better job was not being recognized as such by the management or by some of the workers themselves, for a few of the cash posters had refused promotion to ledger clerk.

Let us now put the matter in somewhat more general terms. The status, or rank, of a job, in comparison with that of other jobs, is determined by the degree to which it realizes certain values. (More generally, the rank of a member or subgroup within a group is determined by the degree to which the member's or the subgroup's activities realize certain values.) Values, I hardly need to say, are *ideas*, ideas of what is *desirable*, even if not always what is in fact *desired*—what you ought to want, even if at heart you do not really want them. And values are many. There are probably few cases where rank is measured by a single value. In this particular division, these values were such things as pay, security, seniority, responsibility, knowledge and skill, opportunity for outside contact, and autonomy (not being "pushed around"). The values were not always called by these names, but they were present nonetheless. A basis for an established *ranking* of jobs (or of the activities of persons or subgroups)—that is, agreement that job A is better than job B and worse than job C—exists to the extent that the facts about the jobs are admitted and the values are shared by the persons concerned. This sharing depends on the interaction between the persons and on the background of ideas (culture) they bring to the company from society at large. The interviews in the division showed that the facts about the different jobs were certainly common knowledge and that the values were very largely shared, that is, the members of each job group, in evaluating their own job or other jobs, mentioned the same values. It is true that a minority of the values were *not* shared. For one thing the younger girls, for obvious reasons, set more store by the chance to move around on the job than did the older women, whose feet got tired. Certainly there was very general agreement on the ranking of the different jobs. Even the cash posters were inclined to admit that the ledger job was, or should be, better than their own.

The fact that the values by which jobs are ranked are many has an important consequence. To the extent that one job is better than another job by *all* the important values of a group, to that extent its rank in relation to the other job is *established*. The job may present human problems, but they will not be status problems. This condition was realized by some of the highest-status jobs of the division—jobs I have not described. No complaints were made involving comparison of these jobs with others. This condition was also realized by the lowest-status job, that of filing clerk. It was highly repetitive, physically tiring, low paid, closely supervised (little autonomy), and allowed little social contact or mobility. But since it was held by the girls newest to the division, all the status factors were "in line," and there was no status problem. While the filing clerks did not like their job, they felt, in effect, it was just and right they should have it.

But if one job is better than another by many of the values of a group but not by all, then there are apt to be status complaints and efforts to bring all the status factors "in line," that is, an effort on the part of the generally higher-ranking group to make their job better than the next lower on all counts. This was the situation of the ledger clerks in relation to the cash posters. Their demand that they should get paid a little more than the cash posters, and that they should not get "pushed around," can be interpreted as an effort to bring all the status factors in line in their favor.

I can now raise some hypothetical questions. Suppose there are two work groups, each of whom ranks higher than the other on about half the important values. Will the situation be stable, such that they rank as equals? Or will there be some form of jockeying for position? Not enough research has been done to answer this problem. (I sometimes feel that the laws of sociology are the laws of snobbery.)

And what if the ledger clerks had gotten a little more pay than the cash posters, but were still taken off their own jobs and put on posting? Would they be more satisfied or even madder? That is, what are the conditions of greatest status dissatisfaction? Again we do not know.

Let me mention one other obvious point. Some of the characteristics of a job are apt to be only dubiously rewarding. Take "responsibility." To the extent that a responsible job is a high-status job, it is rewarding, but we all know that responsibility can also be a burden. One of the ledger clerks said:

I have done both cash posting and ledger work. There's a lot to cash posting, but when you've done your posting you're all through. At the end of the day there's not one thing you have to think of. But on the ledger you go home at the end of the day and you wonder whether you have done everything right. . . . And you think of what you have to do when you come in the next morning. It's really a more responsible job.

Other characteristics of a job are much less ambiguously rewarding: pay is an example, hence in part its great importance. When many of the characteristics of a job are ambiguous from the reward point of view, its unambiguous rewards may be increased if people are to be motivated to take it.

Some Implications for Administration

A case like this always has implications for administrative practice. I shall mention only two. It suggests, first, that in setting up wage differentials through job evaluation, a company and a union will minimize dissatisfaction if the relative pay assigned to different jobs reflects the relative evaluation of these jobs by the workers themselves. I believe that this is what successful job evaluation always accomplishes, though often under a smoke screen of "scientific" procedures. In practice of course this rule is hard to follow in detail. It might lead to the multiplication of small wage differentials and thus to the creation of a wage structure difficult to administer, especially when company and union must consider not one small division, but a

multitude of jobs in the company as a whole, and when the workers in one division know pretty well what is going on in the rest of the company. A certain amount of jockeying for position is probably unavoidable.

The case suggests, second, that when arrangements must be made, as they often must, for workers to fill in on jobs other than their "own," there will be less dissatisfaction where holders of lower-status jobs fill in on higher-status ones than where, as in the division I have described, the opposite takes place. This rule of course comes into conflict with the strong union feeling that if a worker can do a certain job, even if only temporarily, he should have the pay of the job and seniority on the job; and it is true that the rule could easily be abused by management. Nevertheless I feel that these rules represent the human ideal and that wise administrators will seek to approach them as closely as circumstances will allow.

Conflicts Between Staff and Line

MELVILLE DALTON

In its concentration on union-management relations, industrial sociology has tended to neglect the study of processes inside the ranks of industrial management. Obviously the doors to this research area are more closely guarded than the entry to industrial processes through the avenue of production workers, but an industrial sociology worthy of the name must sooner or later extend its inquiries to include the activities of all industrial personnel.

Melville Dalton, "Conflicts Between Staff and Line Managerial Officers," *American Sociological Review*, **15** (1950), 342-351.

The present paper is the result of an attempt to study processes among industrial managers. It is specifically a report on the functioning interaction between the two major vertical groupings of industrial management: (1) the *staff* organization, the functions of which are research and advisory, and (2) the *line* organization, which has exclusive authority over production processes.

Industrial staff organizations are relatively new. Their appearance is a response to many complex, interrelated forces, such as economic competition, scientific advance, industrial expansion, growth of the labor movement, and so on. During the last four or five decades these rapid changes and resulting unstable conditions have caused top industrial officials more and more to call in "specialists" to aid them toward the goal of greater production and efficiency. These specialists are of many kinds, including chemists, statisticians, public and industrial relations officers, personnel officers, accountants, and a great variety of engineers, such as mechanical, drafting, electrical, chemical, fuel, lubricating, and industrial engineers. In industry these individuals are usually known as "staff people." Their functions, again, for the most part are to increase and apply their specialized knowledge in problem areas, and to advise those officers who make up the "line" organization and have authority[1] over production processes.

This theoretically satisfying industrial structure of specialized experts advising busy administrators has in a number of significant cases failed to function as expected. The assumptions that (1) the staff specialists would be reasonably content to function without a measure of formal authority[2] over production, and that (2) their suggestions regarding improvement of processes and techniques for control over personnel and production would be welcomed by line officers and be applied require closer examination. In practice, there is often much conflict between industrial staff and line organizations, and in varying degrees the members of these organizations oppose each other.[3]

The aim of this paper is, therefore, to present and analyze data dealing with staff-line tensions.

Data were drawn from three industrial plants[4] in which the writer had been either a participating member of one or both of the groups or was intimate with reliable informants among the officers who were.

Approached sociologically, relations among members of management in the plants could be viewed as a general conflict system caused and perpetuated chiefly by (1) power struggles in the organization, stemming in the main from competition among departments to maintain low operating costs, (2) drives by numerous members to increase their status in the hierarchy, (3) conflict between union and management, and (4) the staff-line friction

---

[1] Inside their particular staff organization, staff officers also may have authority over their subordinates, but not over production personnel.

[2] To the extent that staff officers influence line policy, they do of course have a certain informal authority.

[3] Some social scientists have noted the possibility of staff-line friction, and industrial executives themselves have expressed strong feelings on the matter. See B. B. Gardner, Hu-

man Relations in Industry (Homewood, Ill.: Richard D. Irwin, Inc., 1945) and H. E. Dimock, The Executive in Action (New York: Harper & Row, Publishers, Inc., 1945). Dimock believes that we are too "staff minded" and that we should become more "executive minded" (p. 241). A high line officer in a large corporation denounced staff organizations to the writer on the ground of their "costing more than they're worth," and that "they stir up too much trouble and are too theoretical." He felt that their function (excepting that of accountants, chemists, and "a few mechanical engineers") could be better carried out by replacing them with "highly select front-line foremen [the lowest-placed line officers] who are really the backbone of management, and pay them $10,000 or $12,000 a year."

[4] These plants were in related industries and ranged in size from 4500 to 20,000 employees, with the managerial groups numbering from 200 to nearly 1000. Details concerning the plants and their location are confidential. Methodological details concerning an intensive study embracing staff-line relations and several other areas of behavior in one of the plants are given in the writer's unpublished doctoral thesis, "A Study of Informal Organization Among the Managers of an Industrial Plant" (Department of Sociology, University of Chicago, 1949).

which is the subject of this paper.[5] This milieu of tensions was not only unaccounted for by the blueprint organizations of the plants, but was often contradictory to, and even destructive of, the organizations' formal aims. All members of management, especially in the middle and lower ranks,[6] were caught up in this conflict system. Even though they might wish to escape, the obligation of at least appearing to carry out formal functions compelled individuals to take sides in order to protect themselves against the aggressions of others. And the intensity of the conflict was aggravated by the fact that it was formally unacceptable and had to be hidden.

For analytical convenience, staff-line friction may be examined apart from the reciprocal effects of the general conflict system. Regarded in this way, the data indicated that three conditions were basic to staff-line struggles: (1) the conspicuous ambition and "individualistic" behavior among staff officers; (2) the complication arising from staff efforts to justify its existence and get acceptance of its contributions; and, related to point two, (3) the fact that incumbency of the higher staff offices was dependent on line approval. The significance of these conditions will be discussed in order.

Mobile Behavior of Staff Personnel

As a group, staff personnel in the three plants were markedly ambitious, restless, and individualistic. There was much concern to win rapid promotion, to make the "right impressions," and to receive individual recognition. Data showed that the desire among staff members for personal distinctions often overrode their sentiments of group consciousness and caused intrastaff tensions.[7]

The relatively high turnover of staff

---

[5] Because these conflict areas were interrelated and continually shifting and reorganizing, discussion of any one of them separately —as in the case of staff-line relations—will of course be unrealistic to some extent.

[6] From bottom to top, the line hierarchy consisted of the following strata of officers: (1) first-line foremen, who were directly in charge of production workmen; (2) general foremen; (3) departmental superintendents; (4) divisional superintendents; (5) assistant plant manager; (6) plant manager. In the preceding strata there were often "assistants," such as "assistant general foreman," "assistant superintendent," and so on, in which case the total strata of the line hierarchy could be almost double that indicated here.

In the staff organizations the order from bottom to top was: (1) supervisor (equivalent to the first-line foreman); (2) general supervisor (equivalent to the general foreman); (3) staff head—sometimes "superintendent" (equivalent to departmental superintendent in the line organization). Occasionally there were strata of assistant supervisors and assistant staff heads.

The term "upper line" will refer to all strata above the departmental superintendent. "Middle line" will include the departmental superintendent and assistants. "Lower line" will refer to general and first-line foremen and their assistants.

"Lower," "middle," and "upper" staff will refer, respectively, to the supervisor, general supervisor, and staff head.

"Top management" will refer to the upper line and the few staff heads with whom upper-line officers were especially intimate on matters of policy.

[7] In a typical case in one of the plants, a young staff officer developed a plan for increasing the life of certain equipment in the plant. He carried the plan directly to the superintendent of the department in which he hoped to introduce it, but was rebuffed by the superintendent, who privately acknowledged the merit of the scheme but resented the staff officer's "trying to lord it over" him. The staff organization condemned the behavior of its member and felt that he should have allowed the plan to appear as a contribution of the staff group rather than as one of its members. The officer himself declared that "By G—, it's my idea and I want credit. There's not a damn one of you guys [the staff group] that wouldn't make the same squawk if you were in my place!"

personnel[8] quite possibly reflected the dissatisfactions and frustrations of members over inability to achieve the distinction and status they hoped for. Several factors appeared to be of importance in this restlessness of staff personnel. Among these were age and social differences between line and staff officers, structural differences in the hierarchy of the two groups, and the staff group's lack of authority over production.

With respect to age, the staff officers were significantly younger than line officers.[9] This would account to some extent for their restlessness. Being presumably less well established in life in terms of material accumulations, occupational status, and security, while having greater expectations (see below) and more energy, as well as more life ahead in which to make new starts elsewhere if necessary, the staff groups

were understandably more dynamic and driving.[10]

Age conflict[11] was also significant in staff-line antagonisms. The incident just noted of the young staff officer seeking to get direct acceptance by the line of his contribution failed in part—judging from the strong sentiments later expressed by the line superintendent—because of an age antipathy. The older line officers disliked receiving what they regarded as instruction from men so much younger than themselves, and staff personnel clearly were conscious of this attitude among line officers.[12] In staff-line meetings staff officers frequently had their ideas slighted

---

[8] During the period between 1944 and 1950, turnover of staff personnel in these plants was between two and four times as great as that of line personnel. This grouping included all the nonmanagerial members of staff and line and all the hourly paid (nonsalaried) members of management (about sixty assistant first-line foremen). Turnover was determined by dividing the average number of employees for a given year (in line or staff) into the accessions or separations, whichever was the smaller.

[9] Complete age data were available in one of the larger plants. Here the thirty-six staff heads, staff specialists, and assistants had a mean age of 42.9 years. This value would have been less than forty years, except for the inclusion of several older, former line officers, but even a mean of 42.9 years was significantly less (C.R. 2.8) than that of the thirty-five line superintendents in the plant who had a mean age of 48.7 years. The age difference was even more significant when the staff heads were compared with the sixty-one general foremen who had a mean age of fifty years. And between the ninety-three salaried, first-line foremen (mean age of 48.5 years) and the 270 salaried, nonsupervisory staff personnel (mean age of thirty-one years), the difference was still greater.

[10] One might also hypothesize that the drive of staff officers was reflected in the fact that the staff heads and specialists gained their positions (those held when the data were collected) in less time than did members of the line groups. For example, the thirty-six staff officers discussed above had spent a median of ten years attaining their positions, as against a median of eleven years for the first-line foreman, seventeen years for the general foremen, and nineteen years for the superintendents. But one must consider that some of the staff groups were relatively new (thirteen-fifteen years old) and had grown rapidly, which probably accelerated their rate of promotions as compared with that of the older line organization.

[11] E. A. Ross in *Principles of Sociology* (New York: Appleton-Century Crofts, Inc., 1938), pp. 238-248, has some pertinent comments on age conflict.

[12] Explaining the relatively few cases in which his staff had succeeded in "selling ideas" to the line, an assistant staff head remarked: "We're always in hot water with these old guys on the line. You can't tell them a damn thing. They're bullheaded as hell! Most of the time we offer a suggestion it's either laughed at or not considered at all. The same idea in the mouth of some old codger on the line'd get a round of applause. They treat us like kids."

Line officers in these plants often referred to staff personnel (especially members of the auditing, production planning, industrial engineering, and industrial relations staffs) as "college punks," "sliderules," "crackpots," "pretty boys," and "chairwarmers."

or even treated with amusement by line incumbents. Whether such treatment was warranted or not, the effects were disillusioning to the younger, less experienced staff officers. Often selected by the organization because of their outstanding academic records, they had entered industry with the belief that they had much to contribute and that their efforts would win early recognition and rapid advancement. Certainly they had no thought that their contributions would be in any degree unwelcome. This naïveté was apparently due to lack of earlier, first-hand experience in industry (or acquaintance with those who had such experience) and to omission of realistic instruction in the social sciences from their academic training. The unsophisticated staff officer's initial contacts with the shifting, covert, expedient arrangements between members of staff and line usually gave him a severe shock. He had entered industry prepared to engage in logical, well-formulated relations with members of the managerial hierarchy, and to carry out precise, methodical functions for which his training had equipped him. Now he learned that (1) his freedom to function was snared in a web of informal commitments, (2) his academic specialty (on which he leaned for support in his new position) was often not relevant[13] for carrying out his formal assignments, and that (3) the important thing to do was to learn who the informally powerful line officers were and what ideas they would welcome which at the same time would be acceptable to his superiors.

Usually the staff officer's reaction to these conditions is to look elsewhere for a job or make an accommodation in the direction of protecting himself and finding a niche where he can make his existence in the plant tolerable and safe. If he chooses the latter course, he is likely to be less concerned with creative effort for his employer than with attempts to develop reliable social relations that will aid his personal advancement. The staff officer's recourse to this behavior and his use of other status-increasing devices will be discussed below in another connection.

The formal structure, or hierarchy of statuses, of the two larger plants from which data were drawn, offered a frustration to the ambitious staff officer. That is, in these plants the strata, or levels of authority, in the staff organizations ranged from three to five as against from five to ten in the line organization. Consequently there were fewer possible positions for exercise of authority into which staff personnel could move. This condition may have been an irritant to expansion among the staff groups. Unable to move vertically to the degree possible in the line organization, the ambitious staff officer could enlarge his area of authority in a given position only by lateral expansion —by increasing his personnel. Whether or not aspiring staff incumbents revolted against the relatively low hierarchy through which they could move, the fact remains that (1) they appeared eager to increase the number of

[13] Among the staff heads and assistants referred to earlier, only 50 per cent of those with college training (thirty-two of the thirty-six officers) were occupied with duties related to their specialized training. For example, the head of the industrial relations staff had a B.S. degree in aeronautical engineering; his assistant had a similar degree in chemical engineering. Considering that staff officers are assumed to be specialists trained to aid and advise management in a particular function, the condition presented here raises a question as to what the criteria of selection were. (. . . The answer appeared to be that personal—as well as impersonal—criteria were used.) Among the college-trained of 190 line officers in the same plant, the gap between training and function was still greater, with 61 per cent in positions not related to the specialized part of their college work.

personnel under their authority,[14] (2) the personnel of staff groups *did* increase disproportionately to those of the line,[15] and (3) there was a trend of

personnel movement from staff to line,[16] rather than the reverse, presumably (reflecting the drive and ambition of staff members) because there were more positions of authority, as well as more authority to be exercised, more prestige, and usually more income in the line.

Behavior in the plants indicated that line and staff personnel belonged to different social status groups and that line and staff antipathies were at least in part related to these social distinctions. For example, with respect to the item of formal education, the staff group stood on a higher level than members of the line. In the plant from which the age data were taken, the thirty-six staff officers had a mean of 14.6 years of schooling as compared with 13.1 years for thirty-five line superintendents, 11.2 years for sixty general foremen, and 10.5 years for ninety-three first-line foremen. The difference between the mean education of the staff group and that of the highest line group (14.6-13.1) was statistically significant at better than the 1 per cent level. The 270 nonsupervisory staff personnel had a mean of 13.1 years—the same as that of the line superintendents. Consciousness of this difference probably contributed to a feeling of superiority among staff members, while

[14] This was suggested by unnecessary references among some staff officers to "the number of men under me," and by their somewhat fanciful excuses for increase of personnel. These excuses included statements of needing more personnel to (1) carry on research, (2) control new processes, (3) keep records and reports up to date. These statements often did not square with (1) the excessive concern among staff people about their "privileges" (such as arriving on the job late, leaving early, leaving the plant for long periods during working hours, having a radio in the office during the World Series, and so on), (2) the great amount of time (relative to that of line officers) spent by lower staff personnel in social activities on the job, and (3) the constantly recurring (but not always provoked) claims among staff personnel of their functional importance for production. The duties of middle- and lower-staff personnel allowed them sufficient time to argue a great deal over their respective functions (as well as many irrelevant topics) and to challenge the relative merit of one another's contributions or "ideas." In some of the staffs these discussions could go on intermittently for hours and develop into highly theoretical jousts and wit battles. Where staff people regarded such behavior as a privilege of their status, line officers considered it as a threat to themselves. This lax control (in terms of line discipline) was in part a tacit reward from staff heads to their subordinates. The reward was expected because staff superiors (especially in the industrial relations, industrial engineering, and planning staffs) often overlooked and/or perverted the work of subordinates (which was resented) in response to pressures from the line. This behavior will be noted later.

[15] In one of the larger plants, where exact data were available, the total staff personnel had by 1945 exceeded that of the line. At that time the staff included 400 members as against 317 line personnel composed of managerial officers and their clerical workers, but not production workers. By 1948 the staff had increased to 517 as compared with 387 for the line (during this period *total* plant personnel declined over 400). The staff had grown from 20.8 per cent larger than the line in 1945 to 33.6 per cent larger in 1948, and had itself increased by 29.3 per cent during the three years as against a growth in the line

of 22.1 per cent. Assuming the conditions essential for use of probability theory, the increase in staff personnel could have resulted from chance about 1.5 times in a hundred. Possibly postwar and other factors of social change were also at work but, if so, their force was not readily assessable.

[16] This movement from staff to line can disorganize the formal managerial structure, especially when (1) the transfering staff personnel have had little or no supervisory experience in the staff but have an academic background which causes them to regard human beings as mechanisms that will respond as expected; (2) older, experienced line officers have hoped—for years in some cases—to occupy the newly vacated (or created) positions.

the sentiment of line officers toward staff personnel was reflected in the name calling noted earlier.

Staff members were also much concerned about their dress, a daily shave, and a weekly haircut. On the other hand, line officers, especially below the level of departmental superintendent, were relatively indifferent to such matters. Usually they were in such intimate contact with production processes that dirt and grime prevented the concern with meticulous dress shown by staff members. The latter also used better English in speaking and in writing reports, and were more suave and poised in social intercourse. These factors, and the recreational preference of staff officers for night clubs and "hot parties," assisted in raising a barrier between them and most line officers.

The social antipathies of the two groups and the status concern of staff officers were indicated by the behavior of each toward the established practice of dining together in the cafeterias reserved for management in the two larger plants. Theoretically, all managerial officers upward from the level of general foremen in the line, and general supervisors in the staff, were eligible to eat in these cafeterias. However, in practice the mere taking of one of these offices did not automatically assure the incumbent the privilege of eating in the cafeteria. One had first to be invited to "join the association." Staff officers were very eager to "get in" and did considerable fantasying on the impressions, with respect to dress and behavior, that were believed essential for an invitation. One such staff officer, a cost supervisor, dropped the following remarks:

There seems to be a committee that passes on you. I've had my application in for three years, but no soap. Harry [his superior] had his in for over three years before he made it. You have to have

something, because if a man who's in moves up to another position, the man who replaces him doesn't get it because of the position—and he might not get it at all. I think I'm about due.

Many line officers who were officially members of the association avoided the cafeteria, however, and had to be *ordered* by the assistant plant manager to attend. One of these officers made the following statement, which expressed more pointedly the many similar spontaneous utterances of resentment and dislike made by other line officers:

There's a lot of good discussion in the cafeteria. I'd like to get in on more of it, but I don't like to go there—sometimes I have to go. Most of the white collar people [staff officers] that eat there are stuck up. I've been introduced three times to Svendsen [engineer], yet when I meet him he pretends to not even know me. When he meets me on the street he always manages to be looking some place else. G—d—such people as that! They don't go in the cafeteria to eat and relax while they talk over their problems. They go in there to look around and see how somebody is dressed or to talk over the hot party they had last night. Well, that kind of damn stuff don't go with me. I haven't any time to put on airs and make out I'm something that I'm not.

Complications of Staff Need to Prove Its Worth

To the thinking of many line officers, the staff functioned as an agent on trial rather than as a managerial division that might be of equal importance with the line organization in achieving production goals. Staff members were very conscious of this sentiment toward them and of their need to prove themselves. They strained to develop new techniques and to get them accepted by the line. But in doing this they frequently became impatient, and gave already suspicious line officers the impression of reaching for authority over production.

Since the line officer regards his authority over production as something sacred, and resents the implication that after many years in the line he needs the guidance of a newcomer who lacks such experience, an obstacle to staff-line cooperation develops the moment this sore spot is touched. On the other hand, the staff officer's ideology of his function leads him to precipitate a power struggle with the line organization. By and large he considers himself as an agent of top management. He feels bound to contribute something significant in the form of research or ideas helpful to management. By virtue of his greater education and intimacy with the latest theories of production, he regards himself as a managerial consultant and an expert, and feels that he must be, or appear to be, almost infallible once he has committed himself to top management on some point. With this orientation, he is usually disposed to approach middle and lower line with an attitude of condescension that often reveals itself in the heat of discussion. Consequently, many staff officers involve themselves in trouble and report their failures as due to "ignorance" and "bullheadedness" among these line officers.

On this point, relations between staff and line in all three of the plants were further irritated by a rift inside the line organization. First-line foremen were inclined to feel that top management had brought in the production planning, industrial relations, and industrial engineering staffs as clubs with which to control the lower line. Hence they frequently regarded the projects of staff personnel as manipulative devices, and reacted by cooperating with production workers and/or general foremen (whichever course was the more expedient) in order to defeat in-sistent and uncompromising members of the staff. Also, on occasion (see below), the lower line could cooperate evasively with lower staff personnel who were in trouble with staff superiors.

Effect of Line Authority over Staff Promotion

The fact that entry to the higher staff offices in the three plants was dependent on approval of top line officers had a profound effect on the behavior of staff personnel. Every member of the staff knew that if he aspired to higher office he must make a record for himself, a good part of which would be a reputation among upper line officers of ability to "understand" their informal problems without being told. This knowledge worked in varying degrees to pervert the theory of staff-line relations. Ideally the two organizations cooperate to improve existing methods of output, to introduce new methods, to plan the work, and to solve problems of production and the scheduling of orders that might arise. But when the line offers resistance to the findings and recommendations of the staff, the latter is reduced to evasive practices of getting some degree of acceptance of its programs, and at the same time of convincing top management that "good relations" exist with officers down the line. This necessity becomes even more acute when the staff officer aspires (for some of the reasons given above) to move over to the line organization, for then he must convince powerful line officers that he is worthy. In building a convincing record, however, he may compromise with line demands and bring charges from his staff colleagues that he is "selling out," so that after moving into the line organization he will then have to live with enemies he made in the staff. In any case, the need among staff incumbents of pleasing line officers in order to perfect their careers called for accommodation in three major areas:[17] (1) the observance of staff rules, (2) the introduction of new techniques, and (3) the use of appropriations for staff research and experiment.

With respect to point one, staff personnel, particularly in the middle and lower levels, carried on expedient relations with the line that daily evaded formal rules. Even those officers most devoted to rules found that, in order not to arouse enmity in the line on a scale sufficient to be communicated *up* the line, compromising devices were frequently helpful and sometimes almost unavoidable both for organizational and career aims. The usual practice was to tolerate minor breaking of staff rules by line personnel, or even to cooperate with the line in evading rules,[18] and in exchange lay a claim on

the line for cooperation on critical issues. In some cases line aid was enlisted to conceal lower staff blunders from the upper staff and the upper line.[19]

Concerning point two, while the staff organizations gave much time to developing new techniques, they were simultaneously thinking about how their plans would be received by the line. They knew from experience that middle- and lower-line officers could always give a "black eye" to staff contributions by deliberate malpractices. Repeatedly top management had approved, and incorporated, staff proposals that had been verbally accepted down the line. Often the latter officers had privately opposed the changes, but had feared that saying so would incur the resentment of powerful superiors who could informally hurt them. Later they would seek to discredit the change by deliberate malpractice and hope to bring a return to the former arrangement. For this reason there was a tendency for staff members to withhold improved production schemes or other plans when they knew that an

---

[17] The relative importance of one or more of these areas would vary with the function of a given staff.

[18] In a processing department in one of the plants, the chemical solution in a series of vats was supposed to have a specific strength and temperature, and a fixed rate of inflow and outflow. Chemists (members of the chemical staff) twice daily checked these properties of the solution and submitted reports showing that all points met the laboratory ideal. Actually, the solution was usually nearly triple the standard strength, the temperature was about 10° C. higher than standard, and the rate of flow was in excess of double the standard. There are of course varying discrepancies between laboratory theory and plant practice, but the condition described here resulted from production pressures that forced line foremen into behavior upsetting the conditions expected by chemical theory. The chemists were sympathetic with the hard-pressed foremen, who compensated by (1) notifying the chemists (rather than their superior, the chief chemist) if anything "went wrong" for which the laboratory was responsible and thus sparing them criticism, and by (2) cooperating with the chemists to reduce the number of analyses which the chemists would ordinarily have to make.

[19] Failure of middle- and lower-staff personnel to "cooperate" with line officers might cause the latter to "stand pat" in observance of line rules at a time when the pressures of a dynamic situation would make the former eager to welcome line cooperation in rule breaking. For example, a staff officer was confronted with the combined effect of (1) a delay in production on the line that was due to an indefensible staff error, (2) pressure on the line superintendent—with whom he was working—to hurry a special order, and (3) the presence in his force of new inexperienced staff personnel who (a) were irritating to line officers and (b) by their inexperience constituted an invitation to line aggression. Without aid from the line superintendent (which could have been withheld by observance of formal rules) in covering up the staff error in controlling line personnel, the staff officer might have put himself in permanent disfavor with all his superiors.

attempt to introduce them might fail or even bring personal disrepute.

Line officers fear staff innovations for a number of reasons. In view of their longer experience, presumably intimate knowledge of the work, and their greater remuneration, they fear[20] being "shown up" before their line superiors for not having thought of the processual refinements themselves. They fear that changes in methods may bring personnel changes which will threaten the breakup of cliques and existing informal arrangements and quite possibly reduce their area of authority. Finally, changes in techniques may expose forbidden practices and departmental inefficiency. In some cases these fears have stimulated line officers to compromise staff men to the point where the latter will agree to postpone the initiation of new practices for specific periods.

In one such case an assistant staff head agreed with a line superintendent to delay the application of a bonus plan for nearly three months so that the superintendent could live up to the expedient agreement he had made earlier with his grievance committeeman to avoid a wildcat strike by a group of production workmen.[21] The lower engineers who had devised the plan were suspicious of the formal reasons given to them for withholding it, so the assistant staff head prevented them (by means of "busy work") from attending staff-line meetings lest they inadvertently reveal to top management that the plan was ready.

The third area of staff-line accommodations growing out of authority relations revolved around staff use of funds granted it by top management. Middle and lower line charged that staff research and experimentation was little more than "money wasted on blunders," and that various departments of the line could have "accomplished much more with less money." According to staff officers, those of their plans that failed usually did so because line personnel "sabotaged" them and refused to "cooperate." Specific costs of "crackpot experimentation" in certain staff groups were pointed to by line officers. Whatever the truth of the charges and countercharges, evidence indicated (confidants in both groups supported this) that pressures from the line organization (below the top level) forced some of the staff groups to "kick over" parts of the funds appropriated for staff use[22] by top management. These compromises were of course hidden from top management, but the relations described were carried on to such an extent that by means of them—and line pressures for manipulation of accounts in the presumably impersonal auditing departments—certain line officers were able to show impressively low operating costs and thus win favor[23] with top management that would relieve pressures and be useful in personal advancement. In their turn the staff officers involved would receive more "cooperation" from the line and/or recommendation for transfer to the line. The data indicated that in a few

[20] Though there was little evidence that top management expected line officers to refine production techniques, the fear of such an expectation existed nevertheless. As noted earlier, however, some of the top executives *were* thinking that development of a "higher type" of first-line foreman might enable most of the staff groups to be eliminated.

[21] This case indicates the overlapping of conflict areas referred to earlier. . . .

[22] In two of the plants a somewhat similar relation, rising from different causes, existed *inside* the line organization with the *operating* branch of the line successfully applying pressures for a share in funds assigned to the *maintenance* division of the line.

[23] The reader must appreciate the fact that constant demands are made by top management to maintain low operating costs.

such cases men from accounting and auditing staffs were given general foremanships (without previous line experience) as a reward for their understanding behavior.

Summary

Research in three industrial plants showed conflict between the managerial staff and line groups that hindered the attainment of organizational goals. Privately expressed attitudes among some of the higher line executives revealed their hope that greater control of staff groups could be achieved, or that the groups might be eliminated and their functions taken over in great part by carefully selected and highly remunerated lower-line officers. On their side, staff members wanted more recognition and a greater voice in control of the plants.

All of the various functioning groups of the plants were caught up in a general conflict system; but apart from the effects of involvement in this complex, the struggles between line and staff organizations were attributable mainly to (1) functional differences between the two groups, (2) differentials in the ages, formal education, potential occupational ceilings, and status group affiliations of members of the two groups (the staff officers being younger, having more education but lower occupational potential, and forming a prestige-oriented group with distinctive dress and recreational tastes), (3) need of the staff groups to justify their existence, (4) fear in the line that staff bodies by their expansion, and well-financed research activities, would undermine line authority, and (5) the fact that aspirants to higher staff offices could gain promotion only through approval of influential line executives.

If further research should prove that staff-line behavior of the character presented here is widespread in industry, and if top management should realize how such behavior affects its cost and production goals—and be concerned to improve the condition—then remedial measures could be considered. For example, a corrective approach might move in the direction of (1) creating a separate body[24] whose sole function would be the coordination of staff and line efforts, (2) increasing the gradations of awards and promotions in staff organizations (without increase of staff personnel), (3) granting of more nearly equal pay to staff officers, but with increased responsibility (without authority over line processes or personnel) for the practical working of their projects, (4) requiring that staff personnel have a minimum supervisory experience and have shared repeatedly in successful collaborative staff-line projects before transferring to the line, (5) steps by top management to remove the fear of veiled personal reprisal felt by officers in most levels of both staff and line hierarchies (this fear—rising from a disbelief in the possibility of bureaucratic impersonality—is probably the greatest obstacle to communication inside the ranks of management), (6) more emphasis in colleges and universities on realistic instruction in the social sciences for students preparing for industrial careers.

---

[24] This body, or "Board of Coordination," would be empowered to enforce its decisions. Membership would consist of staff and line men who had had wide experience in the plant over a period of years. The Board would (a) serve as an arbiter between staff and line; (b) review, screen, and approve individual recommendations submitted; and (c) evaluate contributions after a trial period. Such a body would incidentally be another high status goal for seasoned, capable, and ambitious officers, who too often are trapped by the converging walls of the pyramidal hierarchy.

Managerial Succession in Complex Organizations

ROBERT H. GUEST

This paper compares two studies of managerial succession in complex industrial organizations: (1) Alvin W. Gouldner's study of a gypsum plant reported in *Patterns of Industrial Bureaucracy*,[1] and (2) a study recently completed by this observer in a large American automobile plant.[2]

Both studies examine the process by which organizational tensions are exacerbated or reduced following the succession of a new leader at the top of the hierarchy. Succession in Gouldner's case resulted in a sharp increase in tension and stress and, by inference, a lowering of over-all performance. The succession of a new manager had opposite results in the present case. Plant Y, as we chose to call it, was one of six identical plants of a large corporation. At one period in time the plant was poorest in virtually all indices of performance—direct and indirect labor costs, quality of output, absenteeism and turnover, ability to meet schedule changes, labor grievances, and in several other measures. Interpersonal relationships were marked by sharp antagonisms within and between all levels.

Three years later, following the succession of a new manager, and with no

Robert H. Guest, "Managerial Succession in Complex Organizations," *American Journal of Sociology*, **68** (1962-63), 47-54.

[1] A. W. Gouldner, *Patterns of Industrial Bureaucracy* (New York: The Free Press of Glencoe, Inc., 1954).

[2] R. H. Guest, *Organizational Change: The Effect of Successful Leadership* (Homewood, Ill.: Richard D. Irwin, Inc., 1962).

changes in the formal organizational structure, in the product, in the personnel, or in its basic technology, not only was there a substantial reduction of interpersonal conflict, but Plant Y became the outstanding performer among all of the plants.

The differences between what happended in Gouldner's study and this observer's study is explained by the kinds of administrative actions which each manager initiated: These actions were shaped in large measure by the social system which each inherited upon succession to office.

The analytical framework used by Gouldner was derived from his modification of Weber's concept of authority based on "discipline" as distinguished from authority based on "expertise." The former mode of administration he calls "punishment centered," the latter, "representative."[3] The Plant Y study made use of the Homans' thesis, which held that effective authority as measured by performance is related to reciprocal interactions and favorable sentiments.

[3] Gouldner separated two broader strands of Weber's theory which Weber himself had not clearly distinguished. The first was Weber's observation that modern bureaucratic organization was effective and maintained itself because the organization was administered by "experts." Members willingly obeyed the directions of superiors, reasoning that such obedience was the best way of realizing the acknowledged goals of the organization (Gouldner, *op. cit.*, p. 32).

Weber's second emphasis, Gouldner observed, was that bureaucracy was a mode of organization in which "obedience was an end in itself. The individual obeys the order, setting aside judgments either of its rationality or morality, primarily because of the position occupied by the person commanding" (*ibid.*, p. 32).

In spite of differences in the way the empirical material was handled, the two central hypotheses in each study are quite similar.

Gouldner says: "Internal tensions are more likely to be associated with the punishment-centered bureaucracy than with representative bureaucracy."[4] In the Plant Y study, the hypothesis was phrased in these terms: "To the extent that interactions between people at various levels of a hierarchy are originated primarily by superiors, sentiments of hostility will increase and performance will be lowered." Gouldner's association of "close" supervision and rule enforcement with the punishment-centered mode of administration is empirically similar to the notion that sentiments of hostility to superiors can be associated with an administrative pattern in which interactions are originated primarily by superiors.

What follows is a comparison of the conditions in the two organizational systems before and after succession which in large measure influenced the way authority was exercised by the respective managers.

The successor at the gypsum plant (Peele) and the successor at Plant Y (Cooley) had similar mandates from the parent organization. Both men were told that their respective plants had been "slipping" and that production had to improve. In assigning them to their new jobs, both men were told that the primary criterion on which they would be judged would be results —increased production to meet competitive market conditions.

"Peele, therefore, came to the plant sensitized to the rational and impersonal yardsticks which his superiors would use to judge his performance."[5] Cooley came to Plant Y "sensitized"

to the same yardstick. Like Peele, he knew he was "on trial" with his superiors and that to hold his job or to expect future promotion he had to "make good." The promotion of both in itself symbolized the power which higher management held over both men, and they knew it. Both were expected to take action in keeping with the rational value system of higher management.

As Gouldner observed, Peele, by the sheer fact of succession, "had heightened awareness that he could disregard top management's rational values only at his peril."[6] Cooley was aware of these same risks but, according to what he said and did at the time of his succession, one can see the beginnings of a fundamental difference in his perception of his role vis-à-vis his superiors. Cooley accepted his role as top management's agent charged with achieving the goals of greater production, but he did not necessarily accept his superiors' value system when it came to the *method* of fulfilling their expectations. His superiors (at least some of those in the main office) made it quite plain what methods he was expected to use. He was expected, and they said so, to utilize to the fullest extent the power formally vested in the office of manager, the power of discipline. He was told to "clean house" and to get rid of those in supervision who were failing to perform properly. Like Peele, he was told he could make what Gouldner called "strategic replacements," and that top management would wholly support him in such action.

Although Gouldner never said it explicitly, he inferred that Peele took the same instructions of "tightening up" and of "cleaning house" as an order. Cooley, on the other hand, did not accept his instructions as orders.

4 *Ibid.*, p 243.
5 *Ibid.*, p. 72.
6 *Ibid.*, p. 72.

Indeed, pressures were brought to bear on his immediate divisional superior to "allow Cooley to run his own show" without close supervision from his superior.

That Peele was deeply concerned about top management's expectations is revealed in Gouldner's observation that his behavior in the early period of succession was marked by considerable anxiety. "Comments about Peele's anxiety were made by many main office personnel, as well as by people in the plant who spoke repeatedly of his 'nervousness.'"[7] If Cooley had deep anxieties, he never displayed any signs of "nervousness" either to his superiors, to members of the plant organization, or to this observer. A point to make here is not to deny basic differences in personality traits, but to suggest that there was also some difference, at least, in the *strength* of the organizational pressures from above that were brought to bear on each man. Putting it another way, Peele was under some of the same kinds of pressures that Cooley's predecessor, Stewart, had been under.

Stewart's feelings and perceptions are revealed in one comment he made during a crisis:

The central office keeps saying to me, "Why can't you [keep to the schedule]? So and so in another plant can." When I get this kind of pressure on me I get butterflies in my stomach. We have a labor turnover hitting close to sixty men a day (in a plant of 5000). Just yesterday I jumped a man who was not on his job. It's impossible for me alone to keep everybody in line, but I do the best I can.

Thus Stewart, like Peele in Gouldner's study, found it expedient and even necessary to initiate punishment-centered methods of administration. The two successors, Peele and Cooley, shared one thing in common upon succeeding to office. Both were "outsiders" to their respective plant organizations. Neither had had any previous involvement in the social system of the plant. This allowed both men, as Gouldner stated it with respect to Peele, "to view the plant situation in a comparative, dispassionate light."[8] They were unhampered by previous personal commitments to the in-group. They did not have to be concerned about breaking any long-standing friendship ties. The only "commitments" were to their superiors.

Peele, however, faced two problems that Cooley did not have to face. First, it had been a tradition at the gypsum plant that the "legitimate heir" to the manager's job had always been someone promoted from within the local organization. Also, the previous manager, who had held the job for several years, was well known and highly thought of in the close-knit community surrounding the plant. Thus the condition which allowed Peele to view the organization with impersonal detachment was the same condition which, in the eyes of his subordinates, denied from the start the legitimacy of his succession.

Peele faced a second, related problem. His predecessor had left behind a core of supervisors who had been intensely loyal to him. And because of the "indulgency pattern," which had characterized the previous administration, authority had been derived from a *personal* loyalty and not an impersonal respect for the office of manager. Peele could not count on an automatic transfer of respect for the office such as one might find in a military or other highly bureaucratized organization.

At Plant Y, managers changed frequently, a new manager taking over

---

[7] *Ibid.*, p. 72.

[8] *Ibid.*, p. 72.

once every three to five years. New managers almost always came from other plants in the division. Being in a large metropolitan area, there had developed no close association between a manager and the local community. Thus Cooley was not, by the act of succession, breaking any precedent that otherwise might have generated resistance from the start. More important, Cooley's predecessor had not left behind a core of "lieutenants" who were personally loyal to him. Just about everyone was glad to see his predecessor, Stewart, "retired."

The fact that Peele's succession in itself generated some intense "institutional" hostilities and Cooley's did not must be given considerable weight in explaining what Gouldner would call the "type of bureaucratic method" which each man, following his succession, found legitimate and expedient.

Not long after Peele took over he became aware of the resistance that he could expect from the subordinate organization. Gouldner points out that Peele never carefully analyzed the causes of resistance or the implications of the causes to the methods he would use to institute changes. It was simply resistance, and it had to be overcome.

According to Gouldner, Peele had "two major avenues of solution available to him: (1) He could act upon and through an informal system of relations; (2) He could utilize the formal system of organization in the plant. Stated differently, Peele could attempt to solve his problems and ease his tensions either by drawing upon his resources as a 'person,' or by bringing into operation the authority invested in his status as plant manager."[9]

Peele chose the latter course. Given the situation he faced, he found it was difficult to do otherwise. As he per-

ceived the situation, he could not use the "personal touch" because his aim—and his mandate from above—was to uproot precisely this kind of informal, "indulgent" pattern of relationships which had existed earlier at all levels from manager on down. Nor were his subordinates too concerned with cutting costs and raising productivity. This lack of interest was all part of the general indulgency pattern. Peele's aims and those of his subordinates were different from the start. As Gouldner points out: "It is difficult to maintain, and *especially to create*, informal solidarity in pursuit of ends which are so differently valued by group members."[10]

In many respects Cooley had available to him the same two general alternatives of action when he became manager. He could establish informal personal ties with his subordinates as preliminary action leading ultimately to action that would cut costs and increase productivity. On the other hand, he could use the raw power of his office to force changes and bring about improvements. He could immediately issue new orders, institute new rules; he could insist on stricter enforcement of old rules. He could let it be known that any deviations would be punished. He could insist that all information flow through the formally established vertical channels and that various control, reporting, and service functions live up to the letter of the operating manual. In short, he, too, had the alternative of bringing about further bureaucratization of Plant Y.

Such measures had been undertaken by his predecessor—and had failed. Cooley, therefore, found it more legitimate and expedient to take the path which Peele could not, or at least did not, take. He decided to ignore the

[9] *Ibid.*, p. 84.

[10] *Ibid.*, p. 84.

legal powers vested in the office of manager and find out through informal contacts with his subordinates what they thought was needed to raise the plant's operating efficiency.

Here again it is necessary to underscore the historical conditioning factors explaining why Peele took one course of action and Cooley another. Putting it simply, Peele's subordinates wanted no change either in interpersonal relationships or in production results. Cooley's entire group was anxious to change both. It is perhaps more accurate to say that Cooley's subordinates wanted to eliminate both the "fear-pressure complex" which had pervaded the organization and the technical and administrative bottlenecks which prevented the assembly line from operating smoothly and which, in turn, intensified interpersonal hostilities.

In the process of trying to bridge the communications gap between manager and subordinates, both men took different steps. Peele, not trusting his subordinates' willingness to give him the necessary information on which to base decisions, personally went out into the plant at unexpected times and places to "check up" on supervisors and hourly workers to see to it that they were working properly and obeying the rules and regulations. Cooley also spent considerable time "out in the shop," also showing up at unexpected times and places. In Peele's case, his object, which he acknowledged and which others perceived, was to personally "straighten out the shirkers." Cooley's acknowledged intention was to observe the technical problems and to encourage subordinates to suggest improvements.

Peele's actions, part of many to follow, signaled the beginning of the punishment-centered mode of administration based on *discipline*. Cooley's ac-

tions were the manifest start of the representative mode based on Gouldner's elaboration of Weber's term "expertise." In the language of Homans, Cooley was, by his own behavior, encouraging subordinates to initiate interactions *to* superiors.

Peele, finding it difficult to maintain direct and "close supervision" over all of his subordinates simultaneously, looked for some other alternative. He decided to bring in some "trusted lieutenants" from the outside. Gouldner labels these as "strategic replacements." They enabled "the new manager to form a new informal social circle, which revolves about himself and strengthens his status. It provides him with a new two-way communication network: on the one hand, carrying up news and information that the formal channels excluded; on the other hand, carrying down the meaning or 'spirit' of the successor's policies and orders."[11] Gouldner goes on to make the important observation that a successor under these circumstances is relying not on the existing bureaucratic structure, but is in fact establishing an additional structure based upon "extraformal" ties.[12]

Cooley brought in no trusted lieutenants to serve as the communication link between himself and the 300 members of supervision and 5000 workers below him. For most routine communications he used normal channels. No alterations were made in the structure. He did, however, introduce one communication mechanism which his predecessor did not adopt and which Peele in the Gouldner study could not adopt —group meetings at all levels within and between departments. In his early period in office Cooley met regularly with his immediate staff. The purpose of these meetings was not to relay pres-

---

11 *Ibid.*, p. 92.
12 *Ibid.*, p. 92.

sures down from the corporate organization, but rather to encourage ideas from below which had been withheld previously. In time, and without the manager's directing the action, similar meetings "sprang up" at all levels and departments. The manifest purpose of the group meetings was to solve "business" problems, yet the experience had unanticipated consequences. Each member gained a feeling of reinforcement and support not provided for in the formal "scalar" relationships. Those at higher levels were able to return to their separate departments knowing that they had the support of peers and superiors. This reinforcement process carried down through each level. There was a reverse process as well. Subordinates, having the opportunity to interact frequently and without restraint in a group situation, felt they had more "organized" support in bringing suggestions and complaints to those at higher levels. The reinforcement effect was especially important to the manager himself in his dealings with corporate officials. He had full support from below, a condition which neither his predecessor nor Peele in Gouldner's study ever enjoyed.

The sharpest contrasts between Peele's and Cooley's methods of administration can be seen with respect to the way each made use of the formal rules. One of Peele's first acts, one which generated considerable hostility within the organization, was to fire an employee for violating a rule that had rarely been enforced by his predecessor. In time, as Gouldner points out, many formal rules "that had been ignored were being revived, while new ones were established to supplement and implement the old."[13] New directives and daily reports on production, accidents, and breakdowns were required. Restric-

tions were imposed for loitering. Rest periods were banned. A system of warning notices was installed on a series of "offenses," including smoking, absenteeism, safety, and others. Rules were set up regulating the times for punching in and out. A "cold impersonal 'atmosphere,'" Gouldner noted, "was slowly settling on the plant."[14]

After he took over as manager of Plant Y, Cooley showed little indication that he was concerned about rule enforcement as the primary legitimate means for motivating his group of 300 supervisors. This is not to say that rules were not being enforced. There were elaborate "legal" mandates and restrictions superimposed on the plant in keeping with standard requirements of the division and corporation. The actions of the manager and his staff were highly circumscribed by the labor agreement, budgetary restrictions, work standards, and a system of paperwork required by higher authorities. The point is that Cooley, unlike Peele, relegated rule enforcement to a second level of importance. Again, unlike Peele and unlike his own predecessor, Stewart, he rarely found it necessary to use the extreme penalty of discharge against his supervisory staff. This was his announced policy, and he abided by it throughout his term of office.

At this point it would be more useful to compare Peele not with Cooley, but with Cooley's predecessor, Stewart. Just as Peele "was seen as bringing the plant into line with established company rules,"[15] so Stewart was seen turning more and more to the impersonal mechanism of rule enforcement as greater pressures were brought to bear on him from higher management. Stewart to an increasing extent was demanding rigid enforcement of the rules

---

13 *Ibid.*, p. 69.

14 *Ibid.*, p. 69.
15 *Ibid.*, p. 95.

relating to absenteeism. Wash-up time was eliminated as supervisors were ordered to work the men from "whistle to whistle" as required by the rules. With more intense rule enforcement the union was filing more grievances, arguing not that the rules were not "in the books," but that according to past practice many rules had not been enforced previously. When disputes arose between production and nonproduction departments, Stewart stressed the separate responsibility of each as prescribed by the formal rules rather than subordinating the rules themselves to the practical solution of problems.

Stewart's use of punishment-centered actions and their consequent effects is revealed typically in the following comment by an inspection foreman:

I remember one time getting called on the carpet by the plant manager, and he told me, "If you're afraid of the production people, then you're not a good inspection foreman. If you don't like the way it's going, then you just stop the line. If you can't do that, then you're not an inspector. Never be afraid of the production people." The manager ordered me to have the maintenance department install a series of buttons throughout the shop, and he told me that any time I didn't like something to just go over and push the button and stop the line. Well, I had the buttons installed all right, but I never used them. I thought it would do more harm than good. After all, I have to live with those production people every day.

This comment illustrates the dilemma in which members of Plant Y often found themselves—that of carrying out orders and enforcing rules which they did not feel were legitimized by subordinates.

Just as Peele was anxious to justify his punishment-centered actions "should the main office ever examine or challenge them,"[16] so Stewart took steps to

16 *Ibid.*, p. 94.

assure the legitimacy of his actions. On at least two occasions Stewart recorded his staff meetings and played them back to his corporate superior to demonstrate that he was issuing the proper orders and carrying out the rules as prescribed by superiors. "He did it just to put us on the spot" was the typical reaction of his staff members.

Thus the actions of Peele, the *successor* at the gypsum plant, and those of Stewart, the *predecessor* at Plant Y, show remarkable parallels: the methods used clearly followed the punishment-centered pattern.[17]

We can now briefly sum up the "institutionally derived pressures" which, apart from possible differences in individual personalities, shaped the actions of the two "successors," Peele and Cooley.

1. Peele was under constant pressure, or so he perceived it, by his superiors to institute bureaucratic routines and to use disciplinary measures to gain efficiencies.

Cooley, after his initial instructions, was not under these pressures from superiors. They wanted results but left the methods up to him.

2. Peele had to overcome a deeply embedded tradition that only "insiders" should succeed to the office of man-

17 P. M. Blau in personal correspondence made the enlightening observation that "the person who comes in after an indulgent leader has a very difficult time trying to establish bureaucratic procedures, while the person who comes in after a disciplinarian leader can maintain bureaucratic disciplines and still not appear as a disciplinarian. He can be perceived as a 'good guy' because he can relax a few of the authoritarian measures the former administrator had instituted. This suggests that bureaucratic institutions help a manager to achieve a position of genuine leadership, help him to be perceived by subordinates as carrying out legitimate ends, simply by his not enforcing all the bureaucratic procedures available to him."

ager. There was no such tradition at Cooley's plant.

3. Managerial authority at the gypsum plant had been based on *personal* loyalty. Authority in the much larger and more complex Plant Y organization had been based on respect for the office of manager.

4. Lack of community acceptance was a source of resistance for Peele. The plant-community relationship in the Plant Y metropolitan area was no problem for Cooley.

5. Peele faced the pressures of subordinates who wanted to hold on to the old "indulgency" pattern based upon close informal ties. The pressure from above was to destroy this pattern through the impersonal mechanism of rule enforcement.

The pressure from Cooley's subordinate group was to do away with the former authoritarian mode of administration and to adopt not necessarily an "indulgency" pattern, but one that would allow greater participation in decision making.

6. Peele was under pressure from above to increase productivity, but there were no complementary pressures on him from below to run the plant more efficiently. Cooley's subordinate group was anxious to eliminate the technical difficulties which had kept productivity low and which had generated interpersonal hostility.

7. Peele brought in strategic replacements as his communications link. Cooley used the personnel at hand without superimposing an extraformal link. He also encouraged the establishment of groups which served as communication and decision-making centers.

In a general qualitative sense the two studies confirm Gouldner's hypothesis that internal organizational tensions are more likely to be associated with a punishment-centered bureaucracy than with a representative bureaucracy. The need the present writer saw was not only to confirm or reject the hypothesis. In the Plant Y study an attempt was made to add a quantitative dimension to the vague terms "punishment-centered" and "representative." This was done by extrapolating from the eighty interviews conducted before and after the succession of the manager certain *interaction* data. In most interviews it was possible to determine (1) how frequently subordinates, superiors, and peers interacted with one another under both administrations, and (2) who tended to originate action for whom.

It was found that total interaction frequencies had not changed quantitatively. Closer examination, however, revealed that the character and content had changed considerably. During the Stewart administration the plant operated under chronic emergency conditions. As one foreman put it, "This place is just one damned emergency after another." Members of the organization were forced to interact frequently in order to take care of immediate emergencies. Under the new administration the rate of "emergency interaction" was sharply reduced. The organization as a technical system functioned more smoothly. But new kinds of interactions could be observed. Members were engaged much more frequently in long-range planning sessions in pairs and in groups.

The more significant change was in *direction* of interaction. In Period I there were approximately five superior-originated interactions for every one subordinate-originated interaction. After three years under the new manager the ratio was approximately two to one. Standing alone such data take on meaning only when coupled with the pattern of sentiment change under the administration of the successor. Whereas formerly all forty-eight of those members of supervision interviewed expressed a high degree of hostility toward top plant management, almost no one expressed any hostility toward top managment in Period II.

The modest suggestion implied here is that the use of quantitative interaction data plus information on sentiments may help to give a more sophisticated operational meaning to general terms Gouldner uses, such as "punishment-centered" *vs.* "representative" modes of administrative behavior in complex organizations.

Finally, quantification of *performance results* is crucial if any significance is to be attached to one form of administrative behavior as contrasted with another. In the present study such evidence was clear-cut. By every measure of performance Plant Y improved following the succession of the new manager, and in most performance indices it went from bottom to top position among six plants which were almost identical in size, technology, and organizational structure.

As a conclusion one is tempted to go beyond the limited substantive and methodological comparisons of the present study and that of the gypsum plant. On a level of practical and theoretical interest there emerges from both studies encouraging evidence suggesting that it is possible for democratic processes to function in an otherwise authoritarian bureaucratic social system. The successful efforts of the mining group in Gouldner's gypsum plant to resist increased bureaucratization was due to what he calls a "proto-*democratic* process of legitimation" of the supervisor's authority. If one goes to the heart of what caused Plant Y to become an outstanding success, it was that the leader's authority was derived in large part from the "consent of the governed." In an era when social scientists are "under the gun" from business for suggesting that greater democracy in business enterprises is not only possible but desirable, these findings, limited as they are, are encouraging.

Death by Dieselization

W. F. COTTRELL

In the following instance it is proposed that we examine a community confronted with radical change in its basic economic institution and to trace the effects of this change throughout the social structure. From these facts it may be possible in some degree to anticipate the resultant changing attitudes and values of the people in the community, particularly as they reveal

W. F. Cottrell, "Death by Dieselization: A Case Study in the Reaction to Technological Change," *American Sociological Review*, **16** (1951), 358-365.

whether or not there is a demand for modification of the social structure or a shift in function from one institution to another. Some of the implications of the facts discovered may be valuable in anticipating future social change.

The community chosen for examination has been disrupted by the dieselization of the railroads. Since the railroad is among the oldest of those industries organized around steam, and since therefore the social structure of railroad communities is a product of long-continued processes of adaptation to the technology of steam, the sharp contrast between the technological requirements of the steam engine and those of the diesel should clearly reveal the changes in social structure required. Any one of a great many railroad towns might have been chosen for examination. However, many railroad towns are only partly dependent upon the railroad for their existence. In them many of the effects which take place are blurred and not easily distinguishable by the observer. Thus the "normal" railroad town may not be the best place to see the consequences if dieselization For this reason a one-industry town was chosen for examination.

In a sense it is an "ideal type" railroad town, and hence not complicated by other extraneous economic factors. It lies in the desert and is here given the name "Caliente" which is the Spanish adjective for "hot." Caliente was built in a break in an eighty-mile canyon traversing the desert. Its reason for existence was to service the steam locomotive. There are few resources in the area to support it on any other basis, and such as they are they would contribute more to the growth and maintenance of other little settlements in the vicinity than to that of Caliente. So long as the steam locomotive was in use, Caliente was a necessity. With the adoption of the diesel it became obsolescent.

This stark fact was not, however, part of the expectations of the residents of Caliente. Based upon the "certainty" of the railroad's need for Caliente, men built their homes there, frequently of concrete and brick, at the cost, in many cases, of their life savings. The water system was laid in cast iron, which will last for centuries. Businessmen erected substantial buildings, which could be paid for only by profits gained through many years of business. Four churches evidence the faith of Caliente people in the future of their community. A twenty-seven-bed hospital serves the town. Those who built it thought that their investment was as well warranted as the fact of birth, sickness, accident, and death. They believed in education. Their school buildings represent the investment of savings guaranteed by bonds and future taxes. There is a combined park and play field which, together with a recently modernized theatre, has been serving recreational needs. All these physical structures are material evidence of the expectations, morally and legally sanctioned and financially funded, of the people of Caliente. This is a normal and rational aspect of the culture of all "solid" and "sound" communities.

Similarly normal are the social organizations. These include Rotary, Chamber of Commerce, Masons, Odd Fellows, American Legion, and the Veterans of Foreign Wars. There are the usual unions, churches, the myriad little clubs to which the women belong. In short, here is the average American community with normal social life, subscribing to normal American codes. Nothing its members had been taught would indicate that the whole pattern of this normal existence depended completely upon a few elements of technology which were themselves in flux. For them the continued use of the steam engine was as "natural" a phenomenon as any other element in their physical environment. Yet suddenly their life pattern was destroyed by the announcement that the railroad was moving its division point, and with it destroying the economic basis of Caliente's existence.

Turning from this specific community for a moment, let us examine the technical changes which took place and the reasons for the change. Division points on a railroad are established by the frequency with which the rolling stock must be serviced and the operating crews changed. At the turn of the century, when this particular road was built, the engines produced wet steam at low temperatures. The steel in the boilers was of comparatively low tensile strength and could not withstand the high temperatures and pressures required for the efficient use of coal and water. At intervals of roughly a hundred miles, the engine had to be disconnected from the train for service. At these points the cars also were inspected, and if they were found to be defective, they were either removed from the train or repaired while it was standing and the new engine being coupled on. Thus the location of Caliente, as far as the railroad was concerned, was a function of boiler temperature and pressure and the resultant service requirements of the locomotive.

Following World War II, the high tensile steels developed to create superior artillery and armor were used for locomotives. As a consequence, it was possible to utilize steam at higher temperatures and pressure. Speed, power, and efficiency were increased, and the distance between service intervals was increased.

The "ideal distance" between freight divisions became approximately 150 to 200 miles, whereas it had formerly been one hundred to 150. Wherever possible, freight divisions were increased in length to that formerly used by passenger trains, and passenger divisions were lengthened from two old freight divisions to three. Thus towns located at one hundred miles from a terminal become obsolescent, those at 200 became freight points only, and those at 300 miles became passenger division points.

The increase in speed permitted the train crews to make the greater distance in the time previously required for the lesser trip, and roughly a third of the train and engine crews, car inspectors, boilermakers, and machinists and other servicemen were dropped.

The towns thus abandoned were crossed off the social record of the nation in the adjustment to these technological changes in the use of the steam locomotive. Caliente, located midway between terminals about 600 miles apart, survived. In fact it gained, since the less frequent stops caused an increase in the service required of the maintenance crews at those points where it took place. However, the introduction of the change to diesel engines projected a very different future.

In its demands for service, the diesel engine differs almost completely from a steam locomotive. It requires infrequent, highly skilled service, carried on within very close limits, in contrast to the frequent, crude adjustments required by the steam locomotive. Diesels operate at about 35 per cent efficiency, in contrast to the approximately 4 per cent efficiency of the steam locomotives in use after World War II in the United States. Hence diesels require much less frequent stops for fuel and water. These facts reduce their operating costs sufficiently to compensate for their much higher initial cost.

In spite of these reductions in operating costs, the introduction of diesels ordinarily would have taken a good deal of time. The changeover would have been slowed by the high capital costs of retooling the locomotive works, the long period required to recapture the costs of existing steam locomotives, and the effective resistance of the workers. World War II altered each of these factors. The locomotive works were required to make the change in order to provide marine engines, and the costs of the change were assumed by the government. Steam engines were used up by the tremendous demand placed upon the railroads by war traffic. The costs were recaptured by shipping charges. Labor shortages were such that labor resistance was less formidable and much less acceptable to the public than it would have been in peacetime. Hence the shift to diesels was greatly facilitated by the war. In consequence, every third and sometimes every second division point suddenly became technologically obsolescent.

Caliente, like all other towns in similar plight, is supposed to accept its fate in the name of "progress." The general public, as shippers and consumers of shipped goods, reaps the harvest in better, faster service and eventually perhaps in lower charges. A few of the workers in Caliente will also share the gains, as they move to other division points, through higher wages. They will share in the higher pay, though whether this will be adequate to compensate for the costs of moving no one can say. Certain it is that their pay will not be adjusted to compensate for their specific losses. They will gain only as their seniority gives them the opportunity to work. These are those who gain. What are the losses, and who bears them?

The railroad company can figure its losses at Caliente fairly accurately. It owns thirty-nine private dwellings, a modern clubhouse with 116 single rooms, and a twelve-room hotel with dining room and lunch counter facilities. These now become useless, as does much of the fixed physical equipment used for servicing trains. Some of the machinery can be used elsewhere. Some part of the roundhouse can be used to store unused locomotives and standby equipment. The rest will be torn down to save taxes. All of these costs can be entered as capital losses on the statement which the company draws up for its stockholders and for the government. Presumably they will be recovered by the use of the more efficient engines.

What are the losses that may not be entered on the company books? The total tax assessment in Caliente was $9946.80 for the year 1948, of which $6103.39 represented taxes assessed on the railroad. Thus the railroad valuation was about three fifths that of the town. This does not take into account tax-free property belonging to the churches, the schools, the hospital, or the municipality itself, which included all the public utilities. Some ideas of the losses sustained by the railroad in comparison with the losses of others can be surmised by reflecting on these figures for real estate alone. The story is an old one and often repeated in the economic history of America. It represents the "loss" side of a profit-and-loss system of adjusting to technological change. Perhaps for sociological purposes we need an answer to the question "just who pays?"

Probably the greatest losses are suffered by the older, "nonoperating" employees. Seniority among these men extends only within the local shop and craft. A man with twenty-five years' seniority at Caliente has no claim on the job of a similar craftsman at another point who has only twenty-five days' seniority. Moreover, some of the skills formerly valuable are no longer needed. The boilermaker, for example, knows that jobs for his kind are disappearing and he must enter the ranks of the unskilled. The protection and status offered by the union while he was employed have become meaningless now that he is no longer needed. The cost of this is high both in loss of income and in personal demoralization.

Operating employees also pay. Their seniority extends over a division, which in this case includes three division points. The older members can move from Caliente and claim another job at another point, but in many cases they move leaving a good portion of their life savings behind. The younger men must abandon their stake in railroad employment. The loss may mean a new apprenticeship in another occupation, at a time in life when apprenticeship wages are not adequate to meet the obligations of mature men with families. A steam engine hauled 2000 tons up the hill out of Caliente with the aid of two helpers. The four-unit diesel in command of one crew handles a train of 5000 tons alone. Thus to handle the same amount of tonnage required only about a fourth the manpower it formerly took. Three out of four men must start out anew at something else.

The local merchants pay. The boarded windows, half-empty shelves, and abandoned store buildings bear mute evidence of these costs. The older merchants stay, and pay; the younger ones, and those with no stake in the community, will move; but the value of their property will in both cases largely be gone.

The bondholders will pay. They can't foreclose on a dead town. If the town were wiped out altogether, that which would remain for salvage would be too little to satisfy their claims. Should the town continue, there is little hope that taxes adequate to carry the overhead of bonds and day-to-day expenses could be secured by taxing the diminished number of property owners or employed persons.

The church will pay. The smaller congregations cannot support services as in the past. As the churchmen leave, the buildings will be abandoned.

Home owners will pay. A hundred and thirty-five men owned homes in Caliente. They must accept the available means of support or rent to those who do. In either case, the income available will be far less than that on which the houses were built. The least desirable homes will stand unoccupied, their value completely lost. The others must be revalued at a figure far below that at which they were formerly held.

In a word, those pay who are, by traditional American standards, *most moral*. Those who have raised children see friendships broken and neighborhoods disintegrated. The childless more freely shake the dust of Caliente from their feet. Those who built their personalities into the structure of the community watch their work destroyed. Those too wise or too selfish to have entangled themselves in community affairs suffer no such qualms. The chain store can pull down its sign, move its equipment, and charge the costs off against more profitable and better located units, and against taxes. The local owner has no such alternatives. In short, "good citizens" who assumed family and community responsibility are the greatest losers. Nomads suffer least.

The people of Caliente are asked to accent as "normal" this strange inversion of their expectations. It is assumed that they will, without protest or change in sentiment, accept the dictum of the "law of supply and demand." Certainly they must comply in part with this dictum. While their behavior in part reflects this compliance, there are also other changes perhaps equally important in their attitudes and values.

The first reaction took the form of an effort at community self-preservation. Caliente became visible to its inhabitants as a real entity, as meaningful as the individual personalities which they had hitherto been taught to see as atomistic or nomadic elements. Community survival was seen as prerequisite to many of the individual values that had been given precedence in the past. The organized community made a search for new industry, citing elements of community organization themselves as reasons why industry should move to Caliente. But the conditions that led the railroad to abandon the point made the place even less attractive to new industry than it had hitherto been. Yet the effort to keep the community a going concern persisted.

There was also a change in sentiment. In the past the glib assertion that progress spelled sacrifice could be offered when some distant group was a victim of technological change. There was no such reaction when the event struck home. The change can probably be as well revealed as in any other way by quoting from the Caliente *Herald:*

. . . [Over the] years . . . [this] . . . railroad and its affiliates . . . became to this writer his ideal of a railroad empire. The [company] . . . appeared to take much more than the ordinary interest of big railroads in the development of areas adjacent to its lines, all the while doing a great deal for the communities large and small through which the lines passed.

Those were the days creative of [its] enviable reputation as one of the finest, most progressive—and most human—of American railroads, enjoying the confidence and respect of employees, investors, and communities alike!

One of the factors bringing about this confidence and respect was the consideration shown communities which otherwise would have suffered serious blows when division and other changes were effected. A notable example was . . . [a town] . . . where the shock of division change was made almost unnoticed by installation of a rolling stock reclamation point, which gave [that town] an opportunity to hold its community intact until tourist traffic and other industries could get better established—with the result that . . . [it] . . . is now on a firm foundation. And through this display of consideration for a community, the railroad gained friends—not only among the people of . . . [that town] . . . who were perhaps more vocal than others, but also among thousands of others throughout the country on whom this action made an indelible impression.

But things seem to have changed materially during the last few years, the . . . [company] . . . seems to this writer to have gone all out for glamor and the dollars which glamorous people have to spend, sadly neglecting one of the principal factors which helped to make . . . [it] . . . great: that fine consideration of communities and individuals, as well as employees, who have been happy in cooperating steadfastly with the railroad in times of stress as well as prosperity. The loyalty of these people and communities seems to count for little with the . . . [company] . . . of this day, though other "Big Business" corporations do not hesitate to expend huge sums to encourage the loyalty of community and people which old friends of . . . [the company] . . . have been happy to give voluntarily.

Ever since the . . . railroad was constructed . . . Caliente has been a key town on the railroad. It is true, the town owed its inception to the railroad, but it has paid this back in becoming one of the most attractive communities on the system. With nice homes, streets, and parks, good school . . . good city government . . . Caliente offers advantages that most big corporations would be gratified to have for their employees—a homey spot where they could live their lives of contentment, happiness, and security.

Caliente's strategic location, midway of some of the toughest road on the entire system, has been a lifesaver for the road several times when floods have wrecked havoc on the roadbed in the canyon above and below Caliente. This has been possible through storage in Caliente of large stocks of repair material and equipment— and not overlooking manpower—which has thus become available on short notice.

. . . But [the railroad] or at least one of its big officials, appearing to be almost completely divorced from policies which made this railroad great, has ordered changes which are about as inconsiderate as anything of which "Big Business" has ever been accused! Employees who have given the best years of their lives to this railroad are cut off without anything to which they can turn, many of them with homes in which they have taken much pride; while others, similarly with nice homes, are told to move elsewhere and are given runs that only a few will be able to endure from a physical standpoint, according to common opinion.

Smart big corporations the country over encourage their employees to own their own homes—and loud are their boasts when the percentage of such employees is favorable! But in contrast, a high [company] official is reported to have said only recently that "a railroad man has no business owning a home!" Quite a departure from what has appeared to be [company] tradition.

It is difficult for the *Herald* to believe that this official, however "big" he is, speaks for the . . . [company] . . . when he enunciates a policy that, carried to the latter, would make tramps of [company] employees and their families!

No thinking person wants to stand in the way of progress, but true progress is not made when it is overshadowed by cold-blooded disregard for the loyalty of employees, their families, and the communities which have developed in the good American way through the decades of loyal service and good citizenship.

This editorial, written by a member of all the service clubs, approved by Caliente businessmen, and quoted with approbation by the most conservative members of the community, is significant of changing sentiment.

The people of Caliente continually profess their belief in "the American Way," but like the editor of the *Herald* they criticize decisions made solely in pursuit of profit, even though these decisions grow out of a clear-cut case of technological "progress." They feel that the company should have based its decision upon consideration for loyalty, citizenship, and community morale. They assume that the company should regard the seniority rights of workers as important considerations, and that it should consider significant the effect of permanent unemployment upon old and faithful employees. They look upon community integrity as an important community asset. Caught between the support of a "rational" system of "economic" forces and laws, and sentiments which they accept as significant values, they seek a solution to their dilemma which will at once permit them to retain their expected rewards for continued adherence to past norms and to defend the social system which they have been taught to revere, but which now offers them a stone instead of bread.

Implications

We have shown that those in Caliente whose behavior most nearly approached the ideal taught are hardest hit by change. On the other hand, those seemingly farthest removed in conduct from that ideal are either rewarded or pay less of the costs of change than do those who follow the ideal more closely. Absentee owners, completely anonymous, and consumers who are not expected to cooperate to make the gains possible are rewarded most highly, while the local people, who must cooperate to raise productivity, pay dearly for having contributed.

In a society run through sacred mysteries whose rationale it is not man's privilege to criticize, such incongruities may be explained away. Such a society may even provide some "explanation" which makes them seem rational. In a secular society, supposedly defended rationally upon scientific facts, in which the pragmatic test "does it work?" is continually applied, such discrepancy between expectation and realization is difficult to reconcile.

Defense of our traditional system of assessing the costs of technological change is made on the theory that the costs of such change are more than off-set by the benefits to "society as a whole." However, it is difficult to show the people of Caliente just why *they* should pay for advances made to benefit others whom they have never known and who, in their judgment, have done nothing to justify such rewards. Any action that will permit the people of Caliente to levy the costs of change upon those who will benefit from them will be morally justifiable to the people of Caliente. Appeals to the general welfare leave them cold, and the compulsions of the price system are not felt to be self-justifying "natural laws," but are regarded as being the specific consequence of specific bookkeeping decisions as to what should be included in the costs of change. They seek to change these decisions through social action. They do not consider that the "American Way" consists primarily of acceptance of the market as the final arbiter of their destiny. Rather they conceive that the system as a whole exists to render "justice," and if the consequences of the price system are such as to produce what they consider to be "injustice," they proceed to use some other institution as a means to reverse or offset the effects of the price system. Like other groups faced with the same situation, those in Caliente seize upon the means available to them. The operating employees had in their unions a device to secure what they consider to be their rights. Union practices developed over the years make it possible for the organized workers to avoid some of the costs of change which they would otherwise have had to bear. Featherbed rules, makework practices, restricted work weeks, train length legislation, and other similar devices were designed to permit union members to continue work even when "efficiency" dictated that they be disemployed. Members of the "Big Four" in Caliente

joined with their fellows in demanding not only the retention of previously existing rules, but the imposition of new ones, such as that requiring the presence of a third man in the diesel cab. For other groups there was available only the appeal to the company that it establish some other facility at Caliente, or alternatively a demand that "government" do something. One such demand took the form of a request to the Interstate Commerce Commission that it require inspection of rolling stock at Caliente. This request was denied.

It rapidly became apparent to the people of Caliente that they could not gain their objectives by organized community action or individual endeavor but there was hope that by adding their voices to those of others similarly injured there might be hope of solution. They began to look to the activities of the whole labor movement for succor. Union strategy, which forced the transfer of control from the market to government mediation or to legislation and operation, was widely approved on all sides. This was not confined to those only who were currently seeking rule changes, but was equally approved by the great bulk of those in the community who had been hit by the change. Cries of public outrage at their demands for makework rules were looked upon as coming from those at best ignorant, ill-informed, or stupid, and at worst as being the hypocritical efforts of others to gain at the workers' expense. When the union threat of a national strike for rule changes was met by government seizure, Caliente workers, like most of their compatriots across the country, welcomed this shift in control, secure in their belief that if "justice" were done, they could only be gainers by government intervention. These attitudes are not "class" phenomena purely, nor are they merely occupational sentiments. They result from the fact that modern life, with the interdependence that it creates, particularly in one-industry communities, imposes penalties far beyond the membership of the groups presumably involved in industry. When makework rules contributed to the livelihood of the community, the support of the churches, and the taxes which maintain the schools; when featherbed practices determine the standard of living, the profits of the businessman, and the circulation of the press; when they contribute to the salary of the teacher and the preacher; they can no longer be treated as accidental, immoral, deviant, or temporary. Rather they are elevated into the position of emergent morality and law. Such practices generate a morality which serves them just as the practices in turn nourish those who participate in and preserve them. They are as firmly a part of what one "has a right to expect" from industry as are parity payments to the farmer, bonuses and pensions to the veterans, assistance to the aged, tariffs to the industrialist, or the sanctity of property to those who inherit. On the other hand, all these practices conceivably help create a structure that is particularly vulnerable to changes such as that described here.

Practices which force the company to spend in Caliente part of what has been saved through technological change, or failing that, to reward those who are forced to move by increased income for the same service, are not, by the people of Caliente, considered to be unjustifiable. Confronted by a choice between the old means and resultant "injustice" which their use entails, and the acceptance of new means which they believe will secure them the "justice" they hold to be their right, they are willing to abandon (insofar as this particular area is concerned) the liberal state and the omnicompetent market in favor of something that works to provide "justice."

The study of the politics of pressure groups will show how widely the reactions of Caliente people are paralleled by those of other groups. Amongst them it is in politics that the decisions as to who will pay and who will profit are made. Through organized political force, railroaders maintain the continuance of rules which operate to their benefit rather than for "the public good" or "the general welfare." Their defense of these practices is found in the argument that only so can their rights be protected against the power of other groups who hope to gain at their expense by functioning through the corporation and the market.

We should expect that where there are other groups similarly affected by technological change, there will be similar efforts to change the operation of our institutions. The case cited is not unique. Not only is it duplicated in hundreds of railroad division points, but also in other towns abandoned by management for similar reasons. Changes in the location of markets or in the method of calculating transportation costs, changes in technology making necessary the use of new materials, changes due to the exhaustion of old sources of materials, changes to avoid labor costs such as the shift of the textile industry from New England to the South, changes to expedite decentralization to avoid the consequences of bombing, or those of congested living, all give rise to the question, "who benefits, and at whose expense?"

The accounting practices of the corporation permit the entry only of those costs which have become "legitimate" claims upon the company. But the tremendous risks borne by the workers and frequently all the members of the community in an era of technological change are real phenomena. Rapid shifts in technology which destroy the "legitimate" expectations derived from past experience force the recognition of new obligations. Such recognition may be made voluntarily as management foresees the necessity, or it may be thrust upon it by political or other action. Rigidity of property concepts, the legal structure controlling directors in what they may admit to be costs, and the stereotyped nature of the "economics" used by management make rapid change within the corporation itself difficult even in a "free democratic society." Hence while management is likely to be permitted or required to initiate technological change in the interest of profits, it may and probably will be barred from compensating for the social consequences certain to arise from those changes. Management thus shuts out the rising flood of demands in its cost accounting only to have them reappear in its tax accounts, in legal regulations or in new insistent union demands. If economics fails to provide an answer to social demands, then politics will be tried.

It is clear that while traditional morality provides a means of protecting some groups from the consequences of technological change, or some method of meliorating the effects of change upon them, other large segments of the population are left unprotected. It should be equally clear that rather than a quiet acquiescence in the finality and justice of such arrangements, there is an active effort to force new devices into being which will extend protection to those hitherto expected to bear the brunt of these costs. A good proportion of these inventions increasingly call for the intervention of the state. To call such arrangements immoral, unpatriotic, socialistic, or to hurl other epithets at them is not to deal effectively with them. They are as "natural" as are the "normal" reactions for which we have "rational" explanations based upon some prescientific generalization about human nature, such as "the law of supply and demand" or "the inevitability of progress." To be dealt with effectively, they will have to be understood and treated as such.

exchange processes

two

The market lies at the heart of economic activity. It is through the market that the factors of production—labor and capital, for example—are shuttled through the economy; and it is through the market that the processes of production and consumption are linked. Markets—or, more broadly, exchange systems —display a great range of structural variation within the same society and among different societies. Only part of this variation can be traced to economic determinants, such as the nature of the product or the number of buyers or sellers.

Another part must be traced to social factors. The first selection in this section (by Strodtbeck and Sussman) analyzes the market structure of a unique service, watch repairing; the second selection (by Firth) deals with changes in market structure as money is introduced into a simple society; the third (by Hoselitz) analyzes the cultural and social determinants of the supply of white collar workers in the developing areas.

The student should read these selections in connection with pp. 86-93 of *The Sociology of Economic Life*.

Relations Between Watch Owners and Repairers

FRED L. STRODTBECK   MARVIN B. SUSSMAN

The amount a watch owner pays for the repair of a watch is not closely related to the repairer's costs. In classical economic theory, discriminative pricing is believed to be a short-run instance of imperfect competition, and it is therefore predicted that a service priced to reflect more closely the cost to the repairer will eventually be brought about. In this paper the writers present the basis for the prediction that a generalized and, in an economic sense, discriminatory price will continue to be charged for watch-repair services.

In each of the three sections which follow, a primary consideration is given the technology of the watch. The groundwork of the argument rests upon the obsolescence of certain previously prestigeful skills and the limited risk to a repairer who guarantees a repair. The repairer's work situation is developed in terms of the historical position of the craft, the requirements of daily operations, and the repairer's ultimate occupational aspirations. Finally, the typical watch owner's perspective of watch mechanisms is presented, to complete

Fred L. Strodtbeck and Marvin B. Sussman, "Of Time, the City, and the 'One-Year Guarantee': The Relations Between Watch Owners and Repairers," *American Journal of Sociology*, **61** (1955-56), 602-609.

the matrix of factors used in the interpretation of current price practices.

The Watch Mechanism and Repair Technology

The evolution from the clock operated by weights to the modern watch involved essentially three inventions: the mainspring, the spiral balance spring, and jewel bearings. The mainspring is believed to have been invented by Henlein, between 1500 and 1510. The principle of motive power involved in this invention, i.e., the use of a coiled steel spring for the source of power, has not been altered since 1700, although improvements in the size, tension, and quality of mainsprings have been made.

The accuracy of the modern watch is dependent upon the invention of the spiral balance spring by Huygens and Hooke in the seventeenth century and upon the promotion of its widespread use by the watchmaker Julien LeRoy a century later. This spring, popularly known as the "hairspring," is a delicate, coiled steel spring "set" on the balance wheel to control the circular motion of the balance. Without the constant harmonic motion of the balance wheel (to and fro, back and forth), accurate timekeeping would be impossible.

Other improvements in the watch mechanism which came after the mainspring and hairspring include the perfection of wheels, gears, pinion teeth, and pivots. The most notable of these was the use of jewels (pierced rubies or synthetic corundum) as pivot holes by Nicholas Fatio, the Swiss geometer, in 1704. Jewel bearings reduced friction between moving parts so that watch pieces could be made smaller, their size being determined by the strength of the steel pivots set in jeweled pivot holes.

By the beginning of the eighteenth century, Henlein, Huygens, and others had discovered the basic principles of watch construction. Watches made for Queen Elizabeth I had been in operation for more than 200 years. The watchmaker, associated with royalty and with the prestige of the sciences of geometry and mechanics, was a skilled craftsman working at the most advanced technology of his time. Although from that time forward development of the theoretical science of watchmaking virtually stopped, the rapid and continuous advance of general machine technology made it possible by 1860 to drill plate holes and manufacture jewels with precision sufficient to allow the setting of jewels by pressure alone.

Up to the turn of the twentieth century the watchmaker, with some salvage parts and bits of metal, could duplicate the wheels, pinions, or any other part needed for repair. The skill required for this task was almost equal to that of earlier times, when the watchmaker started the manufacture of a handmade watch by scratching out pivot locations on a blank metal base plate. Experience and ability to operate complex handtools were essential. But by 1900, machine tools adequate for producing the 125 standardized interchangeable parts which go into the average watch were perfected by Swiss technologists.

In America, after World War I, supply parts catalogues and channels for the distribution of interchangeable watch parts manufactured in Switzerland were rapidly developed. Today a judiciously organized portable cabinet can contain most of the tools and watch parts required to repair a large variety of standard watch models. The other parts a repairman needs in his work can be obtained through material supply houses. If he needs a hairspring vibrated (a skilled operation of coiling the spring and curving of the brequet loop according to the weight of the balance) or a radium-figured dial repainted or if he has a watch that he has failed to repair after several tries, a "sticker," he can obtain the services of more experienced workmen. If a smashed or rusted watch movement, the present of a loved one, must for sentimental reasons be replaced, the repairer can obtain another movement.

There have been no contrasting developments in recent years to complicate watch repair and offset the very great reduction in mechanical skill which this availability of spare parts has involved. This holds despite the increased distribution of very small ladies' watches. The smaller watches demand only slightly more careful handling to insure that parts will not be damaged in the process of repair. The one major innovation in repair technology during the last twenty years is the electronic timer. By replacing a watch in this machine and adjusting it to various positions, the repairer can, in about one minute, extrapolate the accuracy of time performance of the mechanism over a twenty-four hour period. Differential performance in three positions provides a diagnostic test for a number of causes of watch stoppage, e.g., binding gears, oily or bent hairspring, balance out of true and poise, and so forth. Yet while the electronic timer is a recent and helpful innovation, the very great simplification of watch repairing may be attributed almost entirely to the availability of spare parts. The extent of this simplification is illustrated by the ordnance training program utilized during the Second World War: in fifteen weeks, inexperienced men with mechanical aptitude could be taught to use spare parts in the maintenance and repair of army timepieces.[1]

The use of whatever machine skills the repairer may possess to make wheels, pinions, or other watch parts is now "obsolete." Parts are available at very low cost: winding stems for standard-model watches, for example, cost as little as seventy-five cents a dozen. The price is far less than the value of the time required to make a stem from steel stock. If parts are not available, a substitute movement of equal quality can usually be obtained for less than $10.00. If none of these courses is practical, a new watch can be had at low cost, e.g., a new seventeen-jewel, waterproof watch with shock-resistant movement, compactly designed, timed to a probable tolerance of ten to fifteen seconds a day, is available for less than $20.00. Thus during the last thirty years the watch repairer has ceased to be a craftsman and is virtually an assembler and adjuster—a person with primary knowledge of spare parts supply channels, plus experience and a degree of kinesthetic coordination.[2]

The Repairer's Work Situation

In the trade literature two recurrent themes are used to justify watch repairing as an occupation: freedom of action as a self-employable and security. Typical expressions from two interviews in a pilot set of fifteen are given here:

There is nothing like being your own boss. When I come down to the shop in the morning, if I feel like working hard or if I have to, I can run them off the griddle like hotcakes. If I don't feel like working, I can take in a ball game and even close down the shop. As long as you get the work done when you promise it, you can do it on your own time. Nobody knows what you put into it.

As long as you have the skill, you can always do enough repairs to pay the rent, light, and get enough to live on. The rest is gravy. If you sell a watch now and then, you make a 100 per cent profit—it's a gift. Why should I work for someone else?

Virtually all repairers have sales sidelines. Secondhand watches, standard watches, bracelets, and cigarette lighters are the first items stocked. If the repairer is successful, he will increase his sales, rent larger space, and may eventually hope to own a jewelry store.

The repairer at the bench is virtually certain of being able to "make his time" at straightforward repair work. During the spring and summer of 1953 at current rates in New England, a good worker turned out forty repairs and twenty to thirty adjustments per week, which grossed between $150 and

---

[1] War Department Technical Manual TM 9-1575: Ordnance Maintenance, Wrist Watches, Pocket Watches, Stop Watches, and Clocks (Washington, D.C.: U.S. Government Printing Office, 1945).

[2] Lay conceptions of watch repairing emphasize the visual activity, but actually "touch" becomes extremely important in many operations. P. H. H. King has previously described the disposition to overestimate the visual component of a precision job in hosiery manufacture [see "Task Perception and Interpersonal Relations in Industrial Training," Human Relations, 1 (1947), 121-130. 373-412].

$200. If the repairer hires another worker, he may make an additional $75-$100 per week. This income compares favorably with skilled machinist jobs in industry. There are seasonal slumps when work is not available, which reduce this income, but this threat is more than counterbalanced by the possibility of a retail sale.

The nature of the "best practice" to be taught watchmaker trainees is continually under debate in the technical journals of the British and American horological societies. One of the most interesting controversies has dealt with the use of watch-cleaning machines. The conventional way of cleaning disassembled watch parts was to string them on a fine wire, then dip them successively into a cleaning solution and two rinses, then dry them with a hand blower. The cleaning machine utilizes a small wire basket into which the disassembled parts can be dumped, then successively whirled in the three solutions, and dried. The machine is semiautomatic, so the repairer can be working at another job while the cleaning takes place, the parts get a uniform finish, and the repairman is spared the inconvenience of getting his fingers in the various solutions. Watch manufacturers and horological societies generally oppose the use of these machines.

Carpenters' opposition to power saws and painters' opposition to wider brushes are understandable as resistance to the contractor's effort to reduce labor costs, but it is not clear why the horological societies would resist an innovation which would save time for the self-employed watch repairer. The watch repairer, not a contractor, would profit from the economy of time. As we explored this problem with representatives from both sides of the argument, we discovered an interesting variance in the use of the term "cleaned." To clean a watch implies complete disassembly, including the removal of all capped jewels and covered parts. However, it is apparently not unknown for watch repairers to compromise by only partially disassembling the watch. Experts all agree in informal conversation that *if the watch is completely disassembled,* there is no objection to the cleaning machine if the repairer continues to hand clean with peg wood the pivot holes, jewels, and other crevice parts. Thus it appears that the rejection of the cleaning machine because of its possible misuse is a primitive control mechanism which would not be invoked if there was, in fact, an effectively operating system of internal regulation.[3]

Watch Owner's Reactions to Watches and Repairers

In 1941, *Reader's Digest* sent a male and female investigator to 462 watch repairmen in forty-eight states. To each repairman they presented a well-known American watch in first-class running condition except for an obvious defect. Just before entering the shop they would loosen the crown wheel screw, disengaging the gears so that the watch would no longer wind. In the watches used, the screw is conspicuous and accessible. If the repairer failed to replace the crown screw immediately, he was defined as cheating the customer. Of

---

[3] The watch manufacturers have attempted to raise levels of competence and integrity by lending their support to the United Horological Association of America, Inc., which works for licensing laws and related occupational controls. The growth in the number of watchmakers from a prewar total of about 25,000 to 40,000 in 1949 has hampered efforts to maintain high repair standards. This increase is an oversupply, since replacement needs are estimated to be only 1000 per year [*Occupational Outlook Handbook,* U.S. Department of Labor and the Veterans' Administration Bulletin No. 998 (Washington, D.C.: U.S. Government Printing Office,)].

the 462 watchmakers, 236 made the repair immediately. However, 226, or 49 per cent, "lied, overcharged, gave phony diagnoses, or suggested extensive and unnecessary repairs." On the basis of this evidence, Roger William Riis, the *Reader's Digest* editor, chose to title his report, "The Watch Repair Man Will Gyp You if You Don't Look Out." A criterion of value which results in classifying half of the shops contacted as "gyp shops" must be more stringent than the criterion of value which the patrons use. This article undoubtedly did not improve the public's attitude toward watch repair shops. Indeed, the instituting of the study and the tenor of the report may be taken as evidence of generally unfavorable public relations.

A man known to the writers to have a broad command of general technology commented: "Watch repairers are all crooks. They substitute poor parts or works for good. I knew a little old man in Boston. He could be trusted, but he is dead. Now I don't know where to go." It is hard to believe that if he had known the low value of watch parts he would have feared the substitution of parts. The mechanism in a $75 and $200 watch by the same manufacturer is approximately the same, the differences being confined to the case and the trimmings.

The association of the number of jewels with the price of a watch has given rise to the belief that the jewels themselves have intrinsic value. To determine the extent of this belief, the writers administered a questionnaire to 140 adult students in an evening college and found that only 22 per cent knew that watch jewels were synthetic stones or hard glass of little intrinsic value. The remainder believed watch jewels were semiprecious or precious stones. Replacement jewels are obtained by the repairer at costs varying from five to twenty-five cents each. Since watch jewels are easily damaged in removal and the replacement of a jewel takes about a half-hour, it would appear that concern about watch jewels while a watch is in the repairer's custody is unfounded.

The opportunity for exercise of a salesman's guile arises in the conversation in which the watch is accepted for repair. During this conversation, the repairer searches for cues to the motivation of the watch owner. If there is a complaint about previous unsuccessful repair attempts, after checking the marks inside the case to insure that he has not worked on the watch before, the repairer suggests that the previous repairers were "butchers." If the watch owner brings in the watch as a challenge to the repairer's skill, the watch can be taken in with the suggestion that the repair may be expensive; and if a great compulsion by the watch owner to have the "correct" time is revealed, then the idea of buying a new watch will be introduced.

Of the eighty persons in our sample of 140 who had had experience with watch repairers, approximately two thirds received and believed what appears to be poor counsel. For example, one respondent who had been troubled by a series of broken mainsprings, on advice of his repairer, retired his expensive American watch to a bank vault because it was so "sensitive" that changes in temperature broke it. Even though poor technique in installation is a more probable explanation, this respondent described his repairer as "an excellent craftsman." A girl informant had been convinced by her repairer that it was the magnetism of her body that caused her watch to stop. Another informant, who still believed his repairer was "very honest," reported that for a time he had to have his watch "cleaned" every month. When the repairer finally told the owner that "his skin was rough on a watch," the owner complained only that he should have been told sooner that he couldn't wear wristwatches. In the watch industry it is well known that body magnetism and skin condition can have no effects on watch operation.[4]

To obtain a more representative set of the discussion between the watch owner and the repairer when watches are brought in for repairs, the writers arranged to have a concealed microphone placed in a moderate-sized repair shop for a two-week period. While interviewing repairers concerning the time required for common repair operations, additional field observations were made in six other shops. A model discussion is well exemplified by the following:

A customer approached the repairer and told him that her watch would not wind and that she thought the mainspring was broken. The repairer, while seated at his bench, removed the movement from its case and examined it carefully, peering through his eye loop. After a minute or so he turned to the customer and said: "The mainspring is not broken. It is the clickspring that is gone."

"Oh! I thought it was the mainspring because I couldn't wind it," replied the customer.

"No," said the repairer, "it is the little clickspring which holds the click in place —this is broken." He continued: "When did you have this watch cleaned? It is dirty and dry, and probably the clickspring broke because the old oil dried up."

"Well, I don't remember when I had it cleaned, but it was running fine before it broke." The repairer: "I won't want to take it in for just a clickspring and then guarantee it. If I replace the click, it may break again in a week, or some other part

[4] Watches can be made inoperative by magnetism, but such changes cannot be effected by magnetic potentials of the human body. These misconceptions are frequently discussed in the horological literature.

may go at any time. The oil is dried out and the watch should be taken apart, thoroughly cleaned and oiled, and then timed. If we overhaul it, we will replace worn parts and then guarantee it for one year. This is a fine watch and will give you many more years of good service."

"How much will that cost?"

"The complete job, the watch will be overhauled, is $8.50."

"Well, all right, you will guarantee it then?"

"Yes, for one year, if you have any trouble with it, we will take care of it."

"When can I have it?"

"A week from today."

"Oh! Can't I have it for Saturday?"

"Well, I will try. If you are downtown, why don't you drop by?"

Here the owner volunteered a diagnosis involving the mainspring: mainspring breakage is often suggested by people with little mechanical sophistication. Then the repairer corrected the owner's diagnosis before accepting the work, and he assumed certain obligations by promising to overhaul the watch for $8.50. From the owner's standpoint, confirmation was received that repair was possible and that her financial obligation would not exceed $8.50. The "guaranty for one year" was mentioned just before she relinquished her watch.

The clickspring in question is a standard part usually purchased in gross lots. Replacement of a clickspring takes less than ten minutes; careful disassembly, cleaning, and reassembling of the watch takes less than ninety minutes. Why did the watch repairer in this instance insist on the excessive delay? Do such delays impress the watch owner that the repairer is a busy man, or does the watch owner believe that the repairer is going to check the performance of the watch at different times? One might guess that the delay has the partial justification of enabling the repairer to work when he chooses and at his own rate of speed. Delay may also enable him to obtain the spare parts he requires, but our experience strongly suggests that the delay is often utilized as a technique to conceal the simplicity of many repair operations. Such delays are the regular procedure even when spare parts are available and there is no backlog of work on hand.

The owner often questions whether his watch is worth repairing. The common practice is to tell him what it would cost to buy an equivalent new watch. When the watch owner has been negligent, e.g., permitting his watch to become rusty, he is chided by the repairer, "Why didn't you bring this in right away? This is certainly a mess now." If the owner responds as if he does feel guilty for dropping or neglecting the watch, the watch repairer does not work hard to establish the legitimacy of the charge he proposes. He proceeds to sell his service as if he enjoyed the full confidence of the owner, and the owner may reciprocate by expressing his relief to learn that the negligence can be rectified.

When the watch owner questions the repairer's diagnosis, the repairer has his defense. He may introduce technical descriptions with which the layman cannot argue. A spokesman for the industry has recently illustrated this use of technical jargon in remarking:

George Bennett's contention in taking in a watch was . . . no use in telling a customer his watch needs cleaning, give him a good story, mostly something like "your watch can be repaired all right, fusee chain is causing friction on the barrel, making the third wheel bind on the center wheel" or "the hairspring is rubbing on the third wheel, causing friction on the roller jewel." Don't think he ever took in a watch for a mainspring without saying that the center wheel of the third pinion was broken. . . . Surprisingly enough, he never seemed to lose a customer.[5]

Actually, the use of technical terms with the client is not increasing. In the more modern shops the trend is to suggest simply that the watch be cleaned and adjusted (e.g., overhauled) and to guarantee the repair for one year. A price of from $6.00 to $10.00 is quoted for the job, depending upon the location of the shop and the status of the clientele. With a ceiling on the possible cost and mention of a guaranty, the owner turns the watch over to be repaired without further conditions.

Discussion

Most simply stated, watches are mechanisms for slowly releasing tension on springs. They tend to work for long periods without repair of any kind. This essentially technological characteristic enters into the social matrix of owner-repairer relations, insofar as it prevents the owner in most cases from developing the personalized relationship with the repairer that he would with service agents who are visited more often.

The technology of the watch—once the claim of the watchmaker to the highest status in the craftsman hierarchy—is now the point of entry for threats to the watch repairer's status. Interchangeable parts have so reduced the value of metalworking skills that it is fair to say that the bench lathe is more frequently used as a showpiece than as a tool. The continued mechani-

[5] K. C. Saalmans, "General Repairs and the Public," *Horological Institute of America Journal* (December, 1950). The humor of Bennett's story depends on knowledge of timepiece nomenclature: fusee chains were once used in watches, but in modern times their only equivalent is the chain used to wind weight-operated cuckoo clocks.

zation of watch manufacture by the Swiss has held the price of serviceable timepieces very low. A further ceiling upon the value of the watch repairer's service is the elasticity of the supply, for if the rewards for watch repairing were to rise sharply, technical school graduates, who could enter repairing after a year's training, would be quickly attracted to the field.

Since the sale of watches and jewelry is at present widely dispersed, and since at each point of retail distribution the services of a repairer are required, there is little prospect that there will be in the near future an integration of watch repairing into a centralized bureaucratic enterprise. This interdependence of the repairer and the jewelry store has social consequences. A repairer can observe that the jeweler doesn't sell all items for the same markup; and, by analogy, he can ask: Why should I charge in direct relation to bench time?

The outright shift from being a watch repairer to operating a jewelry store is not usually possible, because the repairer lacks the $20,000 capital normally required for the original investment in equipment and stock in a modern jewelry store. Jewelry has a high markup and a slow turnover. As much as fifteen years may be required to develop a firmly established business. The repairer starts with watchbands and lighters, and, if this is successful, more jewelry may be added. This mode of expanding into a jewelry business is now threatened by the very successful expansion of department stores into the jewelry field. Though it is difficult for the repairer to achieve the goal of operating a jewelry store, the importance of the possibility of making profit "like a jeweler" cannot be overemphasized. The sideline sales, the chance of personally profiting from a transaction which involves no bench time—this is what the watch repairer really alludes

to when he says, "you're your own boss."

Whenever an owner appears before a repairman's counter, a conflict of interest is potentially present. The position of confidence attributed to the repairman in such negotiations is strengthened each time he successfully repairs a watch for a particular customer; but it is almost equally true that each time a watch stops, the owner's confidence in the repairer is threatened. The repairer may have worked on component A, and the watch may stop because of a failure of component B; the owner does not recognize these distinctions. The training of the owner into more informed expectations is unlikely, because in many cases he is little interested in detail. His position is pragmatic: he wants his watch in running order. The repairer, on the other hand, avoids discussions which involve possible exposure of the simple exchange of parts which is the base of most repairs.

The horological societies, which have the charter function of improving the watch repairer's "hazy, undefined and rather unfavorable" relationship to the public, do little to discipline repairers.[6] They attempt to create favorable public opinion by stressing the continuation in modern watch repairing of the old craftsman traditions. If the repairer has lost the pride in workmanship of the craftsman, he nonetheless clings to the philosophy of individualism which Veblen and others have associated with handicraft social organization.[7] He does not recognize that his personal profit is related to the public relations objec-

[6] *United We Stand* (New York: United Horological Association of America, Inc., 1952).

[7] Thorstein Veblen, *The Instinct of Workmanship* (New York: The Macmillan Company, 1914), esp. Chap. 6.

tives which may be sought as supraindividual organizational goals. Collateral organizations have not grown to regulate standards and reduce invidious comparisons. Licensing in seventeen states is the closest approach to internal control which has evolved. In the main, the repairer faces the "self-other" dilemmas of his operations outside the framework of a protective or regulative institutional context.

It is almost axiomatic, in the face of the possible exploitation of the watch owner by the repairer, that a means for controlling and regularizing their relations would arise. The point of interest is the form this means will take. The solution now being adopted throughout America emerges quite clearly. Without discussion of the details of the repair, the repairer offers to clean and adjust the watch for a fixed sum. The owner is reassured by a social contract, the continued operation of his watch for one year is guaranteed. The guaranty, quickly given and confirmed by a stub, is an impersonal matter at the time of its issue, but it is at the same time a bona fide promise of performance directed at the very core of the owner's concerns.

At first glance, a repair guaranty appears to have some relation to law and legal authority, but the question of whether or not a particular guaranty is enforcible in the courts is strictly academic. The demonstrable loss that a watch owner might suffer from a failure of the repairer to work further on a watch would not exceed $10.00. In practice, the only loss which threatens the repairer, if he fails to recognize the guaranty, is the loss of a customer and some increment of business good will. On the other hand, if the repairer chooses to recognize the guaranty, as most of them do, the owner is relieved, and the repairer creates a favorable impression as a responsible workman.

Even in the absence of the present-day combination of watch repairing and various sales lines, the repairer has little to lose by taking the time to do an "N.C.," a no-charge job. Now, with the increasing emphasis upon sales on the side, the honoring of a guaranty becomes an asset insofar as it predisposes the watch owner, both by his presence in the store and by his closer and now "tested" relationship with the repairer, to make other purchases.

In summary, Riis's finding that 50 per cent of the repairers wanted to accept the test watch on some grounds unrelated to the immediate difficulty emerges in a new light. What Riis in his popular treatment considered unmitigated chicanery may be alternately viewed as an attempt to use a "clean-and-adjust" job, guaranty included, as a basis for regularizing the business relationship between the watch owner and the repairer.

The emergent business pattern is an amalgam of matters of *time* and the *city*. The old craftsman tradition, the new spare-parts technology, the owner's naïveté, the limited risk of the guaranty, and the similarity in causes of different watch failures are all intertwined in the technology of timekeeping. The threat of exploitative relations and the anonymity arising from mobility and infrequent experience with specialized crafts are a part of the social complex of the city. The "one-year guaranty," serving as it does to meet different, but complementary, needs of the owner and repairer, causes standard costs to be charged for very different services. Noting the increasing use of the "clean-and-adjust, one-year guaranty" practice, and noting also the cost to a customer of collecting sufficient watch information to permit him to defend his claim to a particularized price, one doubts that this trend will be arrested. Despite the contrary predictions of competitive economic theory, it is believed that the present case constitutes a valid instance in which a matrix of social and technological factors now support, and will in the foreseeable future continue to support, a discriminatory pricing system.

Indo-Pacific Economic Systems

RAYMOND FIRTH

My main object in this paper is to examine the social effects of the introduction or expansion of monetary exchange in a peasant economic system. An alteration of this kind in the technical media of exchange, need not, *a priori*, have of itself any social concomitants. It is theoretically possible for the appearance of a novel type of exchange medium, such as money, or for an enlargement of the amounts of money available and of its uses to have effect in economic terms alone, facilitating the circulation of goods and their production without making any substantial changes in the social position of the people involved. In fact, however, this is very unlikely—social values usually tend to be attached to the new income or consumption effects. And even if income and consumption effects are not large, the new experiences acquired in the production and exchange processes, in gaining and using the money units concerned, become matters of social evaluation, and tend to emerge in diferences of social status.

Three points must be made at the outset.

First, the aim of this paper is analytical, not ethnographic. I am taking my examples from the Indo-Pacific region because that is the one I know best. But I am not trying to cover the whole

Raymond Firth, "Money, Work, and Social Change in Indo-Pacific Economic Systems," *International Social Science Bulletin*, 6 (1954), 400-410.

range of phenomena presented by these diverse societies. What I hope to do is to set out some of the main considerations involved when money is introduced to an economy in which it has formerly not been known, or when there is a sudden expansion of the uses to which it can be put. This may indicate a framework of propositions for argument and research. The presentation is helped by the great variations found in the region. On the one hand, there are relatively simple economic systems, such as those of Tikopia or of the central highlands of New Guinea, to which money [has] just [been] introduced; on the other, there is the relatively sophisticated economy of peasant Malays or Indonesians, in which money of various types has been known and used for centuries in some transactions.

Second, at this stage it would be imprudent to pretend to have achieved a clear isolation of factors. In talking of social change it is necessary also to talk of economic change, since the social elements are so often mediated through the economic. It would be superficial to argue, as is sometimes done, that the peasant producer has no interest in a new production technology as such, but only in the income effects to be derived from it. Just as conservatism in retention of traditional tools may be in part a compound of aesthetic and psychophysical elements involved in rhythmic use and quality of results, and of status interest in skill of manipulation, so the welcome given to a new tool or to a machine may be partly a recognition of its better technical quality, the novel skills which can be developed with it, and the social esteem which its control may bring. But on the whole, though these elements may influence the adoption of a new technical device, they are marginal to its permanent establishment. In the long run, it is the effects upon incomes and consumption levels, both experienced and anticipated, that seem to be of major importance. In a peasant economy, technological progress is not conceived as a normal desirable end toward which special sectors of economic effort should be regularly directed. So it is with the use of money. Since social changes associated with a new or expanded technology emerge through economic changes and the social evaluation of them, it is difficult if not impossible at this stage of analysis to disentangle the changes due to the introduction or wider adoption of money in an economy from those due to other aspects of a development process. When young men go out from the village to work for wages, the important social changes that come about may be due as much to the patterns and results of their new type of work as to the fact that they get money for it.

Third, the primary purpose of this paper is social theory, not social application. Already, in some cases, the accumulation and interpretation of data may have been ample and acute enough to allow a counseling program or advisory service to be of use. But on the whole we are still working out the implications of data which are much too inadequate for solid generalization. Our main task is first of all to call attention to the nature of the problems and the means required for studying them.

Characteristics and Exchange Variants in Peasant Economy

Before discussing the social changes associated with the intervention of a money economy in the wide sense, the major characteristics of an Indo-Pacific peasant economy may be outlined. There is a simple equipment and technology, with little use of machinery and no ideology of mechanization. There is no high differentiation of technical training. Market relations are of a limited character, with a relatively small range of goods and services involved. In prices, conventional estimations are apt to play a large part, and a "price" is often not given monetary expression. Control of the means of production is noncapitalistic, i.e., capital exists but the owner of it does not control the productive process; there is no clear separation of capitalist-rentier from worker-management in the persons contributing to production, or sometimes even in function when the person is the same. This merging of factor control is seen also in the merging of rewards of production—the lack of separation of interest, wages and management rewards, for example. The scale of producing units and the volume of product for any single unit are comparatively small. The scheme of economic relations thus tends naturally to be of a more personalized order than in a western economy. This kind of economic system is closely geared to a type of society in which the social units over much of the field of operation are small, with a local community emphasis; in which leadership and authority are largely produced from within the local group, and are often kinship-based or kinship-linked; and in which local religious cults tend to strengthen the community in many of its operations. Despite the great variation in scale and in sophistication, such characteristics are common throughout the region.

Such a system is conservative in the sense that there is rarely a wish to reject radically any of its major institutional elements and substitute others.

But there may be no stubborn refusal to adopt new items. There may be indeed an enthusiastic acceptance of them, with the implication that they are additions to the economic and cultural stock of a system which retains its basic familiar character. So subtly have new crops entered the economy of Indo-Pacific communities that it is almost impossible to reconstruct any "indigenous" production scheme for agriculture. The adoption in recent times of the drought-resisting manioc in Tikopia, for instance, has made significant changes in the crop cycle and is likely to alter correspondingly the system of land use and tenure. The substitution of steel axe for stone axe in the interior of New Guinea—a process now almost complete—seems to have led to greatly increased felling of primary forest, with alteration of the balance in the provision of natural soil cover, and increase in danger of soil erosion and loss of fertility. Thus while the impetus to social change may be said to be given by a technological change, this in itself has been possible only by an acceptance or "committal"—to use a fashionable term —which has welcomed the possibility of increased income in at least some limited spheres. To put the point another way, the real impetus lies not in technology as such, but in seeing the possibility of alternative uses for labor and other resources which will yield the increased income. But apart from realizing the efficiency of the new instruments or processes, one must be willing to subject oneself (or others, if one has command over their labor) to a new discipline. In order to obtain the benefits, one must forgo some types of satisfaction hitherto enjoyed. Change is the implication of human choices. When we speak of the social implications of technological change, we do not mean that the total process is inevitable; we mean only that an initial

acceptance or committal in the technological field is likely to be followed by certain results. Some of these may be foreseen, but others may not. Yet it is these unforeseen results which are often of greatest importance, because they are often undesired. Being unexpected, no provision has been made against them, and being often long-term rather than short-term, they may eventuate long after there is any ordinary possibility of reversing the trend.

Now turn to the monetary aspects of Indo-Pacific peasant economic systems. Several kinds of system may be crudely distinguished here according to the degree to which money of western type is current. There are those few systems where money is not used, and purchasing power is provided by bark-cloth, mats, and shell goods. There are those systems, still common in the Pacific, where western money is used for a limited range of transactions, but where other articles of more traditional type also still have purchasing power. Here again there is variation. Some systems, as on the south coast of New Guinea, using money for most exchanges of goods and services, reserve shell armlets, necklets, and other treasures for certain particularly important transactions, especially those affecting the status of human beings, in which they may play a symbolic as well as an economic role. Others, as on the Gazelle peninsula, may add the complication of dual or multiple exchange media. So in the Rabaul market one may see fruit and vegetables sold indifferently for tobacco, for cowrie shells, or for cash. Again, there are the systems common in Indonesia, the Philippines, Malay[sia], where money is the general medium for a range of transactions comparable with those of a western rural economy. The points of significance in these distinctions are the types of services and goods for the purchase of which money can be employed; and the level or range of purchase which can be undertaken. Every society has its conventions about which kinds of goods and services are proper for calculation and exchange in monetary terms, and which are not. One of the important implications of the introduction or enlargement of a money system in an economy is the re-estimation of goods, and particularly of services, which is likely to follow. This may mean in effect a reorientation of the moral values of the society. One of the most meaningful aspects of the coming of a money economy may be said to be the introduction of a medium of exchange with external as well as internal purchasing power. Reference to an external standard is likely to tend at once to a revision of internal estimations, and, by offering hitherto unknown or unrealizable alternatives, to alter conventional placings of resources. Similar results are likely to follow from a rapid expansion of the monetary medium, as by the opening up of new markets for labor or commodities.

Effects of Introduction to a Wage Economy

Let us now examine in more detail what the economic and social results are likely to be in a community where money with an external purchasing power has not previously operated, or has operated at only a very low volume of transactions. For simplicity, take first situations of money acquisition through wage payments, as in a plantation economy. . . .

[Here money] may introduce an element of uncertainty into the socioeconomic operations of some people, and reduce the relative level of skill and knowledge of those not regularly handling it. In Tikopia in 1929, the use of money was not understood, and the relative values of British coins were unknown. In 1952 there was a spread of knowledge, but unevenly. Some men who had been outside the community to work owned and handled money with reasonable fluency and aptitude. Others, usually older men, might own some money, but handled it with caution and an admittedly imperfect knowledge of its relations and the price levels of commodities within their economic universe. They had to rely on others to undertake transactions for them. By a few old men, and many women, there was still no real understanding of the nature of money and its operations. This situation can be paralleled by the observations of Kunio Odaka and his colleagues on the Li of Hainan during the war. These people had to supply labor for the Shih-Lu iron mines, according to quotas set by the authorities. They were paid in military currency, which was new to them, whatever their acquaintance had been with other money before. They were allowed to buy some ordinary consumption goods with it from stores, and they used it in trading among themselves, though the sums involved were small and their interest in it limited. But they were not able to figure out the values with ease; many women, and even some of the elders, could not distinguish five sen from ten sen, and they confused sen and yen. All this obviously gives an economic advantage, and probably a status advantage, too, to those who take on an interpretative or middleman's role.[1]

The introduction of money from wage labor may result in a temporary inflation or pseudoinflation, in that the amounts of goods and services for which it is regarded as suitable equivalent may be relatively small, and knowl-

[1] K. Odaka, *Economic Organization of the Li Tribes of Hainan Island*, Yale Southeast Asian Studies (1950).

edge of the market imperfect. Hence prices may be uneven as regards alternatives, rise erratically, and give "windfall" profits to some people in positions of temporary advantage.

Money wages may reduce margins of skill, ability, and responsibility between workers in respect of traditional types of tasks. For example, on a plantation, or in similar types of work where there is little differentiation made, the common payment of flat rates per month means that all workers of the same classification get the same income, irrespective of skill. (Steadiness and energy may lead to retention in employment, however.) In the traditional economy, principles of equal sharing in teamwork often operate; but there respect for the work and traditional sanctions often tend to keep up the level of production. Differential treatment, by giving wages for individual or team piecework, or by payment of bonuses for higher output, or by having a graded scheme of jobs, can all tend to give expression to elements of skill and ability. But in all such work there is a general tendency to reduce the level of economic responsibility, of interest in the relation between ends and means, as compared, say, with traditional agriculture. There the worker is always faced by problems of decision about timing and quantity in planting, culling, harvesting, and this gives variety to the occupation.

On the other hand, the creation of new working roles, especially those associated with mechanical operations, may give some workers margins of income greatly in excess of any they might get in the traditional economy, and greatly in excess also of incomes obtained by their fellows in the new working scheme. A Papuan carpenter or electrician in New Guinea, for instance, may get four or five times as much in real wages as his fellow villager working on a plantation or the roads.

Yet the introduction of a money economy may also tend to remove from the labor market some marginal categories of labor which were absorbed and active, as far as their limited capacity went, in the traditional economy. The physically weak, the deformed, and many young persons who are not regarded as worth the flat rate of pay tend to be excluded from wage employment.

The advent of money in wage labor form tends also to alter the economic contribution of women. If a plantation system which handles migrant labor is in operation, the women may be left behind, in which case they may have to put in extra agricultural work. If the women are taken with their menfolk in families, then the reverse may be the case—there may be no place for them in the economic structure. Alternatively, women may find other paid work outside the men's economic scheme.

The income effects of these operations have repercussions in the wider economic and social spheres.

The wage labor pattern tends to provide income in relatively large sums, as against the small increments of local marketing in the more unsophisticated systems, and this may affect consumption patterns. With the advent of a monetary economy, there is also usually an enlargement of consumption patterns by taking in goods not purchasable by the traditional circulating media. This involves the possibility of greater differentiation in property holding, diversification of cultural interests owing to differences in taste and to a wider range of personal incomes.

On the other hand, while the substitution of money for the traditional means of remuneration may enlarge the economic field, it will not necessarily do so, or do so to the extent expected. In the scheme of preferences, the attractions of traditional, nonwage employment may still be high, either subsistence agriculture . . . or cash cropping. The Li of Hainan worked in the iron mines because they were drafted, not for the money. To the question as to which type of work they preferred, they all answered farming. And when asked if their mine pay were increased greatly, to two or three or even twelve times what they were receiving, in addition to their food, they still stated a preference for farm work. Again, while the conventional notion about earning money is that one gets as much of it as one can, the backward-sloping supply curve of labor is often found with the advent of a monetary reward for work. The worker is used to having a certain level of consumption goods as his target, and so long as he can reach this, he is satisfied. So an increase in the rates of wages may result not in an increase of the amount of work done, but in a decrease, since the target is reached sooner. For the Melanau of Sarawak, for instance, the only permanent form of investment is in land, and they are used to preparing sago, their main work, to procure a certain level of income, to meet family obligations, to build a house, to arrange a marriage. Otherwise, they do not produce sago. If the price of sago is high, and cash is therefore easy to obtain, the women tend to reduce the time they spend in trampling the sago pith. If a young man has earned enough money for clothes, and customary presents to girls, he stops felling and rasping sago palms. The hardest workers are married men with young families, or landless orphans approaching marriageable age. For them the marginal value of the product is higher.

The cumulative effects may also mean a modification in the general income structure of the community. In particular, they make available to young, ablebodied men a source of wealth inaccessible to their elders, in quantities far greater than the traditional economic organization can usually afford. But the effects must not be overestimated. Hogbin and C. S. Belshaw have pointed out how for the Solomons, in the traditional agricultural scheme, the accumulation of wealth likewise depended upon the energy of young men, who thereby obtained wives and authority. Today, when the young man works for money, this only provides the initial impetus in dynamic situations. Moreover, as Hogbin points out, proximity to a market may make a great difference to the situation. In Busama, which is near the small market town of Lae, older men can earn small sums themselves, and this mitigates the challenge of the young men.[2]

This alteration in income structure again may not necessarily involve a corresponding alteration in the wealth structure of the community. This depends on how far three elements operate:

1. Traditional arrangements for control of income may still be recognized which secure to the senior members of the community the major handling of what income is obtained. In many Pacific societies, returning plantation laborers hand over to their father or other senior kinsman a considerable portion of their wages. Hogbin notes that among Busama men, on the north coast of New Guinea, it was the usual practice to give to the guardian (father or uncle) about half the wages brought

[2] H. I. Hogbin, *Experiments in Civilization* (London: Routledge & Kegan Paul, Ltd., 1939), pp. 166-172; C. S. Belshaw, "Trends in Motives and Organization in Solomon Islands Agriculture," *Proceedings of the Seventh Pacific Science Congress* (1953), 171-189.

back, about one quarter to another uncle, and to divide about one eighth among other members of the community, thus leaving only about one eighth to the man himself.[3] In 1952 Tikopia laborers abroad followed a conventional practice of making up a "box" for each of their chiefs, with lengths of calico, tools, fish-hooks, and so on. Every man of the group contributed to each of these—to the boxes of other chiefs as well as that of his own clan chief—and they amounted to a substantial tribute.

2. New forms of arrangement may still retain the general control by the senior members of the community, or the community interest in the use of the new wealth. A case of this is the collection of funds by Toaripi people (of southern New Guinea) working for wages in Port Moresby, to help finance the purchase and transport of a trading schooner to carry their copra.

3. Competing attractions for the use of income may tend to drain off some of the accumulated income. In some societies the pressure of the demands of young women results in large-scale spending on female consumption goods, which reduce[s] the amounts of money taken back home. Or again, if savings banks or savings societies have managed to be established, the accumulation of capital there may mean that the alteration of the wealth structure takes a long time to become visible, or to have its effect on production or consumption.

Other effects of a wage labor system may include a reduction in the independence of women, whose incomes now may be comparatively reduced, or who may have to rely more directly on their menfolk for cash to buy what they want. It may mean also the creation of more vulnerable categories of persons—invalids, old folk, deformed, and so forth. Since they cannot be enlisted for labor, they are thrown more on the resources of others, especially if there is a reduction in the traditional forms of employment, or if monetary standards tend also to be applied to employment within the society.

Commodity Production and Trade

Wage labor by itself, especially at the rates generally prevailing in Indo-Pacific conditions, does not offer much prospect of building up capital resources on any scale, and of making major developmental changes in the economic and social structure. Commodity production and marketing, on the other hand, offer more scope. If we consider commodity marketing for cash, such as occurs in many parts of the region, we are at once confronted with a different range of magnitudes than for wage labor. The vegetable marketing of the Malay or Bornean peasant woman may bring in only a few cents per day—an income which, however, does allow of independent subsistence by many members of vulnerable social categories, such as widows or divorcees. At the other end of the scale, a Malay or Chinese master fisherman or vegetable grower or rubber producer, or a New Guinea or Gazella peninsula copra producer may reckon his annual earnings in thousands of dollars or hundreds of pounds. In such areas in the Pacific, at least, a marked change in the size of income has been the concomitant of the transition of many of the people from wage labor to commodity production and marketing.[4]

[3] H. I. Hogbin, *Transformation Scene* (London: Routledge & Kegan Paul, Ltd., 1951). . . .

[4] An interesting description of the processes involved in Indonesia has been given by J. H. Boeke [*The Structure of Netherlands Indian Economy* (New York: Institute of Pacific Relations, Inc., 1942), pp. 104-110].

The same general effects on the income and wealth structure, with similar social repercussions, are observable as with wage earnings. But there are certain significant differences.

There is a different kind of risk that has to be taken. Among the economic attractions of plantation labor, for instance, is the regularity of the income. With commodity production the more incalculable elements of drought, flood, and pests enter more directly. Again, while fluctuations of raw material prices affect both, they are likely to be more sudden and more severe with the commodity producer than for the laborer, since wages tend to have a distinct lag in response to changes in raw material prices. This tends, then, to involve a different type of selectivity in the economic process. The entrepreneur in commodity production or marketing tends to emerge as an individual with more distinct economic responsibilities, sharper in perception of economic advantage, often impatient of claims of his communal obligations. On the other hand, his need for initial capital may make him continue in close relation with others of the community on whom he may draw. And the need for equitable relations with labor may lead him to continue in working association with kinsfolk and others in traditional patterns. There is also the tendency for the general social values of his community to weigh heavily with him, especially if there be added to them additional elements resulting

from interracial competition or conflict.

Hence there is the common tendency for the entrepreneur in such conditions to operate within a local social milieu. The complex interchange of goods and services involved in the production or marketing scheme until the time when the goods reach the alien buyer takes place in ways which are neither according to the traditional forms nor according to ordinary western practice. In the blending of individual and community interest, it may be hard to identify the shares which go to economic functions rather than to persons. As has been often discovered, bookkeeping in such circumstances may be a difficult task. Too literal adherence to the rules of accountancy may rob the operations of much of their spontaneity. Yet a good index of the extent to which the advent of a monetary economy has brought with it western economic notions is the effective accounting system practiced, for example, by some of the cooperative societies in New Guinea and elsewhere. One of the useful functions of the new entrepreneur, however, is to act as stimulus and example to his fellows.

One of the great problems in this whole field is that of capital formation. While commodity production and marketing offer possibilities of building up considerable wealth, they may also lead to great difficulties. The operation of a monetary system, with access to external consumer's markets, can lead to high rates of expenditure, and to the contraction of debts at a level virtually impossible in a traditional, nonmonetary system. If there is a depression in the commodity market, then the situation becomes parlous for many producers. In Malaya, in 1934, an inquiry among coconut smallholders showed that they were practically all in debt, at levels of from $100 to $1500 per holding of ten acres or less in the larg-

---

C. S. Belshaw has drawn attention to the differences in the proportion between plantation labor and peasant agriculture as a function of the type of market organization available. In the Solomons, where no good price was available for village products, natives preferred to sell their labor to Europeans rather than produce themselves, in contrast to the New Hebrides, where the balance was about equal, and to New Caledonia, where few natives worked away from the village (op. cit., p. 181).

est coconut area. The debts were mainly to Chinese and Chettiar money lenders, contracted in times of high prices, and there was little prospect of their ever being repaid. Indebtedness is of course a great bane of the peasant everywhere, and its effects are if anything increased the more the economy is related to external markets. And since so much of the indebtedness is contracted not for the financing or production, but to meet consumption requirements, there is little opportunity of building up capital thereby in any general fashion. When individuals enrich themselves by lending, there is little of the "multiplier" effect produced, in that the loans have a very small income-generating influence. Moreover, the social implications of this type of indebtedness are commonly those of friction and strain in the community.

On the other hand, organizations which both meet the need for capital greater than that which any individual entrepreneur can provide and yet peg the enterprise to some kind of community interest have been devised in a number of areas. Among the Maori of New Zealand, cooperative organizations are of many years' standing. Some establish the communal title holders of land as incorporated owners of land, and give them the legal right of borrowing funds with which to develop the land in the interest of them all. Under the leadership of the late Sir Apirana Ngata, a former Minister for Maori Affairs, state aid was obtained for these organizations in various ways, and pastoral and agricultural undertakings of some magnitude have been the result. To meet the needs of these and other tribal enterprises, a new set of men has emerged, the business managers, who can lay down policy and administer affairs like a western businessman.

Reference to land holding raises another aspect of this problem. In many of the unsophisticated economic systems, there is no free market in land. As the systems become transmuted by the advent of a money economy, a market in land may develop, with relative freedom of transfer, often only with deference to community or kin group approval. In some systems, for instance Tonga, the state early took over all final titles to land, allowing to individuals only very restricted titles, with very limited rights of transfer and transmission. In others, the final titles still lay with specific social groups, but some limitations were placed on transfer, while rights of transmission were regulated by the courts. In such conditions, where the growth of a commodity market gives a fillip to the use of land, changes in the social structure may be stimulated. In the attempt to gain an income from land, either by personal production or by sale or lease, there have been among the Maori of New Zealand and the Cook Islands, for example, an intensified interest in kin ties as giving title to lands; disputes over land, with much litigation in the courts; and a tendency in some cases for departure from traditional customs of land inheritance in favor of testamentary disposition. Apart from this there has in New Zealand been fragmentation of land, and much subsequent consolidation. There are also many landless Maori and some Maori landlords—with European tenants in a number of cases. In less than a century and a half the transition from a simple, nonmonetary peasant economy to an economy of practically western type, with commodity markets and markets for labor, greatly increased the differentiation in the status of people and has affected the Maori social system deeply in other ways.

As another example of how a change in market conditions, with expansion of a price economy, can affect social conditions, consider the results of rubber production in Negri Sembilan, in Malaya. Here is a society of relatively small-scale producers, with a strongly matrilineal system of lineage groups and lineage leadership, and with a traditional interest in the cultivation of valley rice. The advent of rubber has made for substantial changes. In summary, they are these. There was of old a distinction between the ancestral lands, the rice plots in the valleys, worked generation after generation, largely by women, and the new lands, cleared from the jungle by men, and retained by them as the product of their labor. The latter they could transmit to their sons, the former were transmitted through their sisters in their own lineage, and through their wives. No man could pass ancestral lands on to his son. In the clearings were grown fruit and vegetables, essentially secondary in economic importance to the staple, rice. Then, less than half a century ago, came the cultivation of rubber. Soon the economic balance of production tended to be upset. It was far more profitable to produce rubber than rice, and some people even turned their rice lands into rubber land. Some of the upland areas were sold or leased to aliens. The lineages, seeing valuable assets tending to pass out of their grasp, often debated the issue whether the rule of control and inheritance of these cleared rubber lands was through females, as in the case of the ancestral lands, or should be through males, especially from father to son. On the whole the tendency has been for the interest of the men to be strengthened in the control of such lands.

Moreover, the more general tendency has been to promote a change in the inheritance system, from matrilineal to patrilineal. This has not been so in the lands classed definitely as ancestral (*tonah pesaka*), but the pressure has tended to become manifested in land of other types, and also other property. In this struggle—for the issue was often keenly, even bitterly, fought —powerful support was given to the patrilineal interests by the leaders of Islamic orthodoxy, who were in conflict on other grounds as well with the local *adat* (customary rules). Furthermore, these forces together were in support of, and to some degree assisted by, the interest of the ruler and his kinsfolk, a group of patrilineal descent rules, and opposed in some respect to the matrilineal descent leaders by whom they were surrounded and on whom they had to rely in the body politic as a whole. Though opposition between them was not overt, it was clearly to the interest of the ruler that the power of leaders deriving their status from a customary base alien to his own should be diminished. Thus a simple technological change, represented by the different processes involved in the production of rubber, meant also important changes in the social structure.

Finally, one may characterize the subject in more general terms again. As the influence of a monetary economy grows, there is a tendency for the scale of social relations to widen, as new contacts are formed. On the other hand, there is fragmentation and realignment of some social units. Lineage and other kin groups often cease to be effective land-holding units; joint family and allied units tend to break up economically and disperse residentially into simple families. Even the simple, elementary family organization is seen to be vulnerable—changes occur in relations of husband and wife through labor or differential production; there is exaggeration or reversal of the economic differences between generations, and different frames of reference for social experience appear; the authority structure may alter. As the processes continue, new structural arrangements may be formed, with new class alignments and new patterns of leadership. The requirements of new legal norms and the new ethics of business involve different behavioral sequences. There may be a shift of symbols not only of wealth, but also of social status and political authority. As the same time, consciousness of the changes in so many spheres may lead, as in Polynesian societies, to a renewed emphasis on traditional or modified (pseudo-) traditional forms, which are, as it were, obtruded as evidence of a social solidarity which may in fact be threatened or lost in other fields.

The resultant of all these forces is likely to be an economy and a society not in equilibrium but with conflicts of ends, and conflict about means to secure agreed ends. These processes of social and economic change are not novel. But the diversification of technical skills is growing; technical processes are for the most part apparently irreversible; and the pace of technical advance is increasing. The widening of the gap between the skilled and unskilled, and the growing differences in experience, would seem to suggest that it is not in the realm of shared empirical knowledge and skill that common factors of unity are likely to be found. But to think that the future coordinating elements may lie in non-empirical systems of ideas suggests also reliance on fairly short-term solutions.

White Collar Workers in Underdeveloped Countries

BERT F. HOSELITZ

In the discussion of the human problems arising in underdeveloped countries undergoing a process of technological change, the question of the formation and training of an industrial labor force stands in the foreground. It is, indeed, a most important problem, especially if a process of relatively rapid industrialization is envisaged, and if not merely the acquisition of new manual and technical skills, but the entire alteration of the way of life of large masses of the population takes place. Most of the past discussions of the development of an industrial labor force have concentrated on two groups within the new industries: the industrial laborers at the bottom of the scale,

Bert F. Hoselitz, "The Recruitment of White Collar Workers in Underdeveloped Countries," *International Social Science Bulletin*, 6 (1954), 433-442.

and the technical élite, the engineers. Some attention has also been given to the problem of how managers concerned with the organizational and "business" problems of the new industries can be trained and, in some underdeveloped countries, what steps could be taken to induce the development of a class of private entrepreneurs in industry.

The problems which arise in all these areas are complex and differ from one another considerably. The transformation of "peasants and primitives" into industrial laborers is a task involving masses of people, and which affects not merely the place and manner of their daily activity, but their entire social existence. The training of engineers and top managers involves fewer individuals, but because of the strategic positions which these obtain in an industrializing economy, their selection and their most appropriate employment also involve, from the viewpoint of the economy as a whole, various difficult problems.

With all the attention which has been given to the incentives and motivations which may exist for industrial workers, on the one hand, and managers, entrepreneurs, technical leaders, and engineers, on the other, one group has received little attention, though in the last resort their successful recruitment and effective cooperation is indispensable for a process of industrialization. This group is that of the white collar workers. In the subsequent paragraphs I propose to suggest a few thoughts on the role which this group may play in a process of industrialization and on some problems which arise.

Before entering into a discussion of the problem itself, I wish to express two *caveats*:

1. The countries which are commonly designated as "underdeveloped" exhibit great differences in culture, relative level of economic advancement, political structure, and internal social relations. Since my remarks will be couched in general terms, some of them may be inapplicable to individual countries. In fact, it would be impossible to present significant propositions on this (as on almost any other) topic, if one were to make sure that they were really applicable to *all* underdeveloped countries. Some assertions made in this paper must, therefore, be interpreted as describing tendencies in some countries, a real situation in others, and to be of subordinate or no importance for certain others.

2. For reasons of space, some of the situations described will be schematized to a certain extent. I readily admit that such a procedure constitutes a simplification of the real situations, but I hope that oversimplifications can be avoided, and that in spite of some schematization the analysis of at least

the core problems will not lose its validity.

When we speak of white collar workers we deal with a group of people who, in terms of economic position and social ranking, exhibit great heterogeneity. In most of the theoretical treatments, white collar workers, as a group, are counted among the middle class, and I will follow this practice by making use of the classification of the middle class presented by Professor F. Marbach.[1] Marbach distinguishes between the "old" and the "new" middle class, and further between the "self-employed" and the "non-self-employed" members of the middle class. Although, on the whole, there is some overlapping between the "old" and the "self-employed," on the one hand, and the "new" and the "non-self-employed," on the other, the two principles of classification yield four easily distinguishable categories. In this paper we are concerned only with white collar workers, i.e., with members of the non-self-employed sector of the middle class. And here we may distinguish two groups again, one of which corresponds, on the whole, with Marbach's old, and the other with his new, middle class.

The new non-self-employed middle class is made up of white collar workers who perform relatively unskilled labor. Although they do not work with their hands, their real income, in the advanced countries, is normally not above, and frequently even below, that of semiskilled and skilled manual workers. In this group belong the typists, bookkeepers, shipping clerks, filing clerks, and other persons engaged in commercial and industrial establishments and in public service. This group will be designated in this paper as "employees."

The old non-self-supporting middle

---

[1] Fritz Marbach, *Theorie des Mittelstandes* (Berne, 1942), esp. pp. 188ff.

class is made of almost entirely of public officials, normally in the higher ranks of the public service. To this group should be added persons engaged in occupations of similar complexity in the service of private firms or individuals. We will designate this group hereinafter as "officials."

The "employees" are distinguished from the manual laborers in that they work in an office rather than a workshop or a factory, and that their work requires, in general, a higher degree of literacy than most manual jobs. A typist must know how to spell, and a bookkeeper must have, on the whole, a greater ability for arithmetic than most manual workers. The "employees" are distinguished, on the other hand, from the "officials" in that their jobs usually do not involve, nor permit them to make, decisions of any significance. The work of employees is mostly routine work; it requires, apart from certain relatively noncomplex skills, chiefly the ability to be attentive, patient, and careful. Moreover, as a rule, the incomes and also the social position of officials is considerably higher than that of employees, as also of skilled manual workers.

The most characteristic aspect of the economic role of officials is their intermediary position in a bureaucratic hierarchy.[2] This means that they are normally in a position in which they tion, they are usually called upon to make decisions within a rigorously prereceive general directives from the persons in élite positions within their bureaucratic hierarchy, and it is their task to translate these general direc-

[2] I shall not distinguish in what follows always between public, i.e., governmental, and private, i.e., business bureaucracies. Although I shall be concerned mostly with public bureaucracies, most of what applies to them also applies, mutatis mutandis, to business bureaucracies.

tives for their subordinates. In addiscribed field, to iron out differences between their subordinates, and to maintain channels of communication with coordinated portions of their bureaucratic hierarchy. The most significant difference between officials and the members of the "élite" is that only the latter make policy decisions, and occupy, in governmental hierarchies or in business organizations, the positions of ultimate responsibility. As a rule, there is also some difference in the level of income and general social ranking between members of the élite and even the highest-placed officials.

From the distinctions made, it is clear that there exist important differences in the incentives and motivations of employees, on the one hand, and officials, on the other. I shall first briefly consider the former group.

The employees are, in the advanced countries, the "proletarianized" portion of the middle class. Their income often remains below that of manual workers, and this appears to be a correct reflection of the over-all social value of their economic contribution. The particular jobs which they perform require few specialized skills, apart from those acquired by almost all children in school. Whatever skills are needed in addition can usually be learned by a very short training or by some process of on-the-job training. Moreover, since many of the jobs performed by employees are on a low level of technical complexity, the human factor can be replaced relatively easily by machines. In other words, machines plus high-grade engineers can often be substituted for employees—the various types of office equipment from the simple typewriter to the most complex Hollerith machine are examples of this. Whether or not, and under what conditions, such substitutions will take place is a question of relative prices.

But the ease with which such substitution can be accomplished is another factor pressing the incomes of employees to a low level.

Compared with this situation in the advanced countries, a different situation is likely to persist in many underdeveloped countries, at least during the early period of the industrialization process. The differences are due mainly to two factors: the much greater illiteracy rates in underdeveloped countries and the very low prestige that in many of these societies is attributed to manual work which "dirties one's hands." (This last factor plays a certain role, too, in advanced countries.) Some employees endure their economically unenviable position, because being a white collar worker gives the illusion to the outside world—and sometimes even to oneself—that one is above the ordinary crowd of common laborers. This has the consequence, as Marbach has shown, that employees in advanced countries are recruited, on the whole, from a higher social layer than manual laborers, even though the amount and quality of education required for the two types of position are not very different.

In many underdeveloped countries the relative social prestige which attaches to white collar jobs is even greater, and that is in close correlation with the relatively greater scarcity of literate persons. For this reason, white collar jobs which require few or no advanced skills are in great demand, often by people who do not even possess these skills—although they only know how to read and write. This makes the problem of selection difficult, and here another characteristic of many developing countries comes in: the partial absence of impersonal market relations and the much greater weight of family and other primary group relationships in these countries.

In practice these factors have the following consequence: lower-rank employee positions become available to persons with a minimum degree of literacy. In view of the social prestige of white collar positions as compared with manual labor, and because of the relatively greater scarcity of individuals even with a minimum degree of literacy, such positions will normally pay higher wages than those of manual workers and most occupations in agriculture. Hence with an increase of the rudiments of literacy there will be a race for these jobs, and selection for them will depend, to a large extent, on personal connections and friendships between applicants and persons in the higher echelons of an administrative organization. It is no secret that, in many underdeveloped countries, the staffs of certain government offices are composed of relatives or covillagers and other personal friends of one or several heads of a department or division. It is not necessary to point out that this method of recruitment of even the lowest ranks of a public bureaucracy has many undesirable aspects. It tends to keep out many qualified persons; it places professional relationships within the bureaucratic hierarchy on a nonrational basis; it produces vested, almost clannish, interests within the public service; and it endangers the principle of promotion within the bureaucracy from the ranks, since not effective performance, but personal friendship is the decisive criterion. At the same time, this system bears the seeds of producing corrupt administrations, since every applicant for a position will find it desirable to "become a friend" of persons with the power of appointment—if necessary by means of gifts or bribes.

It is of course not suggested that this must be the rule in all public administrations in underdeveloped countries. But we must consider that even its sporadic occurrence may have serious adverse consequences, and we must, moreover, bear in mind that with progressive industrialization the expansion of public and semipublic bureaucracies of various kinds is inevitable. Industrialization leads to great population shifts. New cities arise, villages become towns. New administrative functions become necessary, called forth by the increased need for speedy and accurate communication and transportation and by the new functions which national, provincial, and local governments are forced to adopt.

Moreover, the drafting into industry of peasants and other persons without urban background requires the increase of various welfare, educational, and other administrative agencies which normally only central or local governments can provide. All these trends make necessary a large increase of bureaucracy and thus pose a problem in the recruitment of employees, as well as officials. In view of the pressures which are likely to arise, it is most desirable to found effective "community-oriented" administrations, and the ambiguity in the social and economic position of lower-rank employees may operate against this objective.

An alternative would be the attempt to substitute, wherever possible, machines for employees. But this would lead to the contradictory result that in countries in which labor is cheap, labor-saving machinery would be employed in occupations where a number of new career opportunities could be created which, in the long run, would have an important beneficial effect on the economic growth potential of the country. It would have the other unfavorable result that the scarce foreign exchange would have to be used for the purchase of expensive equipment and that the middle and upper ranks of the bureaucracy would be even more heavily overburdened with work and responsibility. And these persons, who are in crucial positions, are already in short supply. Whatever dangers and inadequacies may lie in the recruitment of employees, the chief bottleneck in the building up of administrative bureaucracies in underdeveloped countries is in fact in the lack of trained officials.

Many of the problems which we observe in the recruitment of employees are also encountered in the building up of a staff of officials, and vice versa. Some of the points which will be discussed below apply also to the expansion of the lower ranks of an administrative organization. The constitution of a bureaucracy is fraught, on all levels, with analogous problems. But the important difference between inducting employees and officials is that because of the differences in the nature of their respective roles different factors are of chief importance in the case of each of the two groups.

As has been pointed out, the peculiarity of the role of officials [is] that they make decisions. They cannot, therefore, be replaced by machines. But in a well-functioning bureaucracy their decisions are not arbitrary, however independently they may be made. I do not refer to the fact that the decisions made by any official are limited by the competence of his department, division, or section, but rather that however free he may be, and may need to be, in some respects, he is merely an instrument implementing policies which were not designed by him, but imposed upon him. To fill the position of an official properly, it is, therefore, necessary that the holder of such an office be ready to place himself fully at the service of the bureaucratic hierarchy he serves and that he ask himself at every juncture whether his activity is in pursuit of the general policy directives under which he functions. In addition he is charged with doing his work in the most efficient manner possible. Efficiency in this context means something very similar to what economists have in mind when they speak of "economizing": the attainment of a given goal with a minimum of means.

These limitations ideally impose upon an official a perfectly "rational" method of action. There is a close analogy between an ideal-typical official and an ideal-typical entrepreneur. The latter "economizes" means in order to maximize profit, the former in order to maximize the implementation of whatever policy he is charged to execute. It is no wonder, therefore, that really efficient bureaucracies exist only in a social framework in which rationality (in Max Weber's sense) has become a widely generalized principle of social action. Weber sums up thus his penetrating discussion of the bureaucracy.

Bureaucratic structure is everywhere a late product of development. The farther we go back in historical development, the more typical become forms of government which lack a bureaucracy and officialdom altogether. Bureaucracy has a "rational" character: it is dominated by rules, purposiveness, means, "objective" impersonality. Its origin and growth ha[ve] had everywhere a "revolutionary" effect, in a special sense; an effect which the advance of rationalism usually produces wherever it occurs. In this process structural forms of government became annihilated which did not have a rational character, in this special sense.[3]

The specific conditions which are associated with this kind of rational action, and without which it cannot function properly as a generalized principle of social action, include at least the following: tasks in a society must be distributed on the basis of achievement, rather than on the basis of a person's

status. That is, in order to implement his job effectively, an official must select those persons and other means which, on the basis of known scientific and technological relations, are most efficient. This demands, moreover, that the exercise of the functions of an official must be "democratic," in that he disregards, in a formal sense, special claims of individuals which are not based on objective criteria of achievement or on clearly established legal claims. Moreover, this rationality of an official's actions will normally lead to his making use of whatever specialized skills exist, in order to achieve an end. Hence rational bureaucratic activity tends to support and sometimes even to initiate division of labor and specialization. Finally, the impersonal quality of the official's purpose requires that he be "community oriented," i.e., that he regard his office as a trust which he administers in the interest of the community as a whole, rather than as a benefice which leads to his own enrichment or the accumulation of power.

Many of these principles of social action are foreign to the value systems dominant in some underdeveloped countries. Moreover, in some countries the social structure and its maintenance work against the introduction of these principles. Hence the development of effective bureaucracies encounters great obstacles. Indeed, really efficient administrative organizations have been created only in economically advanced countries; the governmental and administrative apparatuses of most underdeveloped countries were, until recently, either manned in their higher positions by nonnatives, or experienced periodic breakdowns.[4] In other words,

---

[3] Max Weber, *Wirtschaft und Gesellschaft* (Tübingen, 1947), II, 677-678.

[4] On some of the bureaucracies in antiquity and the middle ages and their differences with the modern type of governmental and business bureaucracies, see *ibid.*, pp. 655ff. One of the outstanding examples of a bureaucracy in a

the administrations of native governments or enterprises in many countries of, say, Latin America or the Middle East, exhibited a degree of inefficiency and instability which was one of the factors accountable for the relative economic backwardness of these countries. The administrations of colonies and foreign-owned enterprises in underdeveloped countries were manned, at least in their higher positions, by citizens of the metropolitan country, who transplanted their own organizational and administrative procedures. With the attainment of independence by many former colonies, and the increasing trend to place foreign investments in all underdeveloped countries under the supervision of the national government, the growth and extension of native bureaucracies is necessary. These must take over the functions exercised until recently by nonnatives. In other instances they must modernize themselves and replace their often inefficient and nonrational methods of operation by the introduction of the principle of rational action on an impersonal, formally egalitarian basis. This process of innovation makes great demands on a new type of manpower, and it is not surprising that the recruitment of officials equal to the tasks demanded of them forms a serious bottleneck in the economic development of underdeveloped countries.

In the subsequent paragraphs I shall try to analyze some of the factors which exert an influence on the number and types of persons who become officials in the bureacracies of underdeveloped countries. This may explain why the

country which did not belong to the group of economically advanced areas was imperial China. But whatever may be said about the merits of the Chinese imperial bureaucracy, one of its main features was its instability, which made it incapable of functioning in a period of social and economic transition imposing increased stresses. . . .

shortages exist and how they might be overcome. One important factor is the absence, in most underdeveloped countries, of well-ordered administrative procedures. Existing bureaucratic procedures are outdated and often derived from the practice of some more advanced country with entirely different conditions. The previous colonial status of some countries and the fact that others, though politically independent, were culturally dependent on an advanced country have caused the adoption of certain European systems of administration which sometimes were altered a little to suit local conditions better, but which in general need considerable overhauling. These very procedures often make public, as well as business, bureaucracies in underdeveloped countries topheavy, cumbersome, and ill-adapted to the needs of the country. Examples of this can be found in the tax and fiscal administrations of many underdeveloped countries, but they exist also in other fields. The most appropriate method to deal with this situation is the substitution of existing administrative procedures by more suitable ones, a task in which the United Nations and its specialized agencies may provide considerable assistance.

In addition to the external cumbersomeness of administrative structures which could be relatively easily removed, if it were not for a multitude of vested interests of office holders or other beneficiaries of the system, there are factors in the social structure of some countries which make the formation of rationally operating bureaucracies difficult. I refer to the excessive inequalities in social position and, resulting from it, the quasifeudal character of some underdeveloped societies. At the top of the social pyramid is a small group which has a virtual monopoly of wealth, political power, and education—the three main status-confering variables. The officials who are appointed under such a system usually stand in a relation to the political power holders which resembles that of the medieval *ministeriales* to their clerical or secular overlords. In other words, the officials do not serve the community as a whole, but the special interests of a politically powerful group. This has the consequence that not only excessive emphasis is placed on the preservation of the status quo, at least as far as the distribution of political power and social prestige is concerned, but it also tends to keep out of the administration persons who have undoubted objective qualifications, but who do not stand in a quasiretainer position to the members of the community's élite. Quite apart from the fact that such bureaucracies are in any case unsatisfactory because recruitment is based not on the principle of achievement, but on that of personal status, a class of discontented intellectuals is created, who often turn to various radical movements in order to attain positions in which their capacity for political leadership can find some expression. But in the shadow of the division of the world into two great camps, the formation of political opposition groups often leads to a repetition of the world conflict between Communism and democracy within the underdeveloped country. Although the radical groups are sometimes illegal and may exist only underground, they are present nevertheless, and impose serious difficulties on the smooth economic progress of the country. Furthermore, this very situation makes the introduction of more rational community-oriented bureaucracies even more difficult. For, as Weber has pointed out, this process of rationalization is "revolutionary" in a certain sense. It has the tendency of reshaping social relations and introducing a principle of formal egalitarianism which the political élite may regard as dangerous to its interests

and whose introduction it will therefore attempt to resist. In such countries —and some of the middle eastern and Latin American nations belong to this group—the introduction of modern bureaucracies may encounter great difficulties. This will, at the same time, affect the speed and ease with which an over-all process of economic development can be accomplished.

Fortunately, the majority of the larger and more important underdeveloped countries do not have quite such rigid social structures. Some rigidities exist there also, and they impede the extension of rational, impersonally operating administrations. For example, Daniel Thorner . . . surveyed the prospects of reshaping the village administrations in India through the establishment of village *panchayats*. He found that in most parts of India the *panchayats* have no power whatever and are not likely to obtain it, and that in those parts where they are effective they have been built into old-established power and social structures reinforcing the caste system where it still exists, and a class system based on differential landownership and wealth, where the caste system is weaker. Thorner sums up his observations with the remark that to rebuild village life would require far greater vision, authority, and popular support than is commanded by the *panchayats* anywhere in India. To approach the goal of rural economic development through the agency of the exisiting village *panchayats* would appear to "be an exercise in frustration."[5]

But although such impediments to the formation of modern rational bureaucracies exist probably in all underdeveloped countries, they have become relatively subordinated in some, especially in the formation of governmental

[5] Daniel Thorner, "The Village *Panchayat* as a Vehicle of Change," *Economic Development and Cultural Change*, **2** (October, 1953), 215.

bureaucracies in the larger administrative units and, above all, also in the business bureaucracies. Yet even there some obstacles still exist, which are due partly to the lack of adequate training facilities for officials, and partly to the absence of traditions of officialdom which prescribe a strong ethic for the profession and produce the sentiment of responsibility and loyalty to one's task so characteristic of bureaucracies in advanced countries.

Although the systems of professional and higher education are being re-examined in almost all underdeveloped countries, there is still too great an emphasis on literary-historical and narrowly legal training. This is also the case with requirements for positions in the higher ranks of the bureaucracy. The notion that an official is often, even predominantly, not a "generalist," but a specialist in a particular field of knowledge, has not yet fully penetrated the public administrations of advanced countries and lags badly behind in underdeveloped countries. One consequence of this fact is that in advanced countries, as well as in underdeveloped countries, private bureaucracies are often staffed with better qualified and sometimes better educated men than public bureaucracies. In underdeveloped countries where specialized technical and professional skills are relatively scarce, the loss of many qualified individuals who might have performed valuable public service to private enterprises is a serious blow to government administration. Again, many officials who go abroad on government fellowships in order to acquire special skills soon after their return drift into better paid or more honorific positions in private business administration.

A sufficiently large supply of adequately trained persons for higher positions in public bureaucracies will be forthcoming only when educational facilities are increased and improved. But here, as in so many other instances, the intermediate schools are in the greatest need of improvement. In some underdeveloped countries there exist excellent universities, and a small number of persons may even receive a university education abroad. The extension and improvement of elementary education [are] also given high priority in all development plans, and this is quite appropriate in view of the still high illiteracy rates. But it is of almost equal importance to modernize and improve secondary education and technical training. Here is a great field of development in which UNESCO can be of inestimable service.

Even the provision of more adequate educational facilities on the secondary level and in special technical fields will have only limited results if traditions of loyalty in service and responsibility are not developed. There are many factors which operate against the rapid and easy introduction of these values. As already stated, in some underdeveloped countries, public officials—and within a somewhat different context, officials in business enterprises—often occupy positions similar to those of personal retainers of their superiors. Although this may be acceptable in business bureaucracies, in the long run it defeats the effective operation of a public administration. But the replacement of this personal tie of service to one's superior by the integration of an official into an impersonal hierarchy is a most difficult process, requiring a total readaptation in thinking and values. It is clear that in order to achieve such a transformation powerful incentives must be present. I can think of only two developments in the societies of underdeveloped countries which may support it. One is the elevation of the prestige and power of officials and the other is the persistence of nationalist sentiments. Neither of these alternatives appears attractive to a person educated in and adhering to the values of western society. The first tendency seems to increase greatly the danger of creating a managerial class, possibly with totalitarian predilections, and the second to contribute to a growth of ethnocentrism and rejection of cultural and other influences from abroad which may ultimately endanger the peaceful development of international relations.

But the dilemma may appear greater than it really is. The growth of managerial tendencies in public administrations may be tempered with an enhanced emphasis on popular democratic processes, and nationalism may perform a positive function in destroying primary loyalties to a family, tribe, or local village group, and replacing them by loyalties to the nation as a whole. We should not forget that also in Europe nationalism passed through this positive constructive phase, and is responsible, in part, for the consolidation of the great nations of contemporary Europe. If the underdeveloped countries can achieve the creation of smoothly functioning bureaucracies without giving way to the excesses of managerialism or nationalism—both of which contain the seeds of political and social totalitarianism—they will have made a contribution to sociopolitical practice in this matter equivalent to any achievement of the already advanced countries.

consumption processes

three

For a long time economists have been interested in explaining various aspects of consumer behavior—how much of consumers' income will be saved and how much spent, how their money will be allocated among different products, and so on. In constructing these explanations, economists have almost always assumed consumers' tastes to be a "given" starting point for analysis; they have not inquired deeply into the social and psychological determinants of tastes themselves. It is evident, however, that consumers' preferences are determined in part by their social milieu. Men and women have different spending needs for clothes, for instance, because they symbolize their sex roles differently in dress; and people who are socially ambitious try to imitate the spending patterns of higher-status groups. Sociologists, then, should have something to say about the determination of consumer behavior. This section includes a theoretical article on the social determinants of consumption (by Roseborough), a broad empirical survey of changes in consumption associated with the rise of a money economy (by Hoyt), and a study of the different uses of leisure among several status levels in the United States (by Clarke).

These selections correspond to pp. 93-98 of *The Sociology of Economic Life*.

Some Sociological Dimensions of Consumer Spending

HOWARD ROSEBOROUGH

In the study of consumer spending a wide variety of factors, ranging from age, sex, and family size, through occupation, religion, and class background, to future expectations, advertising and personal influence, and compulsiveness have been shown to have some influence on consumer taste and demand. Yet the precise influence these factors have and the value which they should be assigned are still largely unknown. This paper offers a theoretical framework as one possible way of treating factors involved in consumer spending in a systematic manner. The approach is still in the process of formulation so that only the general structure of the theory can be presented.

Two assumptions are made about factors which influence consumer spending. First, it is assumed that factors may be treated as aspects of social systems, or subsystems. They may be viewed as contributing to one or other of the problems which all social systems must solve, to what have been called the adaptive, the goal attainment, the integrative, and the pattern-maintenance-tension-management problems. Thus factors are related to one another, in the first instance, by means of their functioning for the solution of system problems. Second, it is assumed that all factors do not have the same order of influence on consumer spending. Rather, factors are related to one another in a

Howard Roseborough, "Some Sociological Dimension of Consumer Spending," *Canadian Journal of Economics and Political Science,* **26** (1960), 452-464.

hierarchical way so that some can be treated as more general in their influence than others, and as unifying the more specific factors in some way. This view is derived from the more general assumption that social systems are composed of a number of distinct levels of structural organization. These levels differ from one another in that the higher ones are more unified in structure and more general in influence, whereas the lower levels are more differentiated in structure and more specific in influence. They are related to one another in that the lower levels are more differentiated and more segmented versions of the levels above them. The factors which influence consumer spending enter into each of these levels of structural organization, and, as aspects of social systems, they contribute to the solution of system problems at each level.

Consumer spending has to do primarily with decisions to obtain and use facilities. Both terms, "facilities" and "decisions," require some explanation. The term "decision" is used very broadly. Consciousness is not a necessary attribute of decisions; it is likely that many of the actions described here as decisions are unconsciously made. By this two considerations are meant. If a person acts, it is assumed that he has made some decision about that action. He need not be conscious that he has made a decision, that he has chosen between alternative modes of acting; he may not be aware that alternative modes of acting are possible. Second, even where decisions are consciously made, it does not necessarily follow that the person is aware of the basis on which his decision rests: he may feel that it is a "natural" way of acting, or an obligatory way, the consequence of some commitment, a right, and so on. For many purposes these various distinctions must be made. For the purposes of this discussion they need not be.

By the term "facilities" is meant not only concrete goods which are adapted to particular purposes, but also more general objects, such as money funds, and, most general of all, purchasing power or legitimate claims on the productive effort of others. Facilities, whether they be specific goods or generalized purchasing power, have two kinds of functions. They are required as means in the performance of acts; these (in Merton's terminology)[1] are their manifest functions. They also have latent functions in that their possessions symbolizes the fact that the possessor has the right to perform such acts, and an obligation to do so. The decision to obtain facilities involves, therefore, both a conviction on the part of the decider, and of other people, that he has the right to obtain the facilities, and the acceptance on his part, and an expectation on the part of other people, that he is obliged to use them.

II

Viewing facilities in this way means that consumer spending involves more than a direct relation between the possession of purchasing power and expenditure on particular kinds of goods. These are the most general and the most specific points in a series of levels at each of which people are expected to make choices. It is assumed that there are at least seven levels involved in this process of choice. At the most general

level, the person must decide whether or not to accept generalized purchasing power. Having made that decision he must, at the next level, make a slightly more specific decision, whether or not to accept the style of life of the society of which he is a member; he may, as witness Canadians who live elsewhere than Canada on income obtained from Canadian investments, decide to reject the Canadian style of life. At the third level, he must make an even more specific decision, whether or not to accept the standard of living[2] which is connected with that style of life. These are the three most general levels, and they involve aspects of the earliest periods in the socialization process, periods in which "taste" is created in the first place. These three levels will not be developed more fully here.

Attention is focused on the four lower levels at which decisions become increasingly more specific and more differentiated; these are the four which can be related most directly to the levels of structural organization of social systems. These will be described briefly, and then will be dealt with in more detail. The most general of these four levels is called the level of consumption standards. Once the person has decided to accept the standard of living of the society of which he is a member, he must, at this level, decide whether or not to accept, as the basis upon which to judge the quality and performance of facilities, the consumption standards which the majority of the members of the society consider as the proper standards by which facilities should be judged. Consumption stand-

---

[1] R. K. Merton, *Social Theory and Social Structure*, rev. ed. (New York: The Free Press of Glencoe, Inc., 1957).

[2] This concept and the following three— consumption standards, plane of living, and consumption level—have been adopted from J. S. Davis, "Standards and Content of Living," *American Economic Review*, 35 (March, 1945), 1-15. My use of the terms differs from their use in that article.

ards are derived from the general value system of a society. The decision to use them as standards of judgment depends upon the degree to which the person has internalized the society's value system and has committed himself to attempting to implement that system in action. The consumption standards in any society will, therefore, depend on the values to which that society gives emphasis. In American society, for example, there is a presumption that facilities should be judged in terms of standards which emphasize effectiveness in solving environmental problems. Thus one judges foods primarily in terms of the degree to which they meet the tests of nutritive standards and hygienic standards and not ordinarily in terms of whether they were eaten by one's ancestors or on the basis of whether they simply taste good. Similarly, the high value placed on "functional design" for furniture, clothing, housing, and transportation means that these facilities are judged primarily in terms of consumption standards relating to the use of time and space, maintenance and care, protection and comfort, and not, or only secondarily, in terms of standards of aesthetics, of religious feeling, or of filial or national piety.

The next and slightly more specific level is called the level of planes of living. Once the person has decided to accept the consumption standards, he must next decide to accept a plane of living which is in accord with those standards. He will be influenced in this decision by the nature of the groups to which he belongs, or technically, the collectivities in which he performs roles. Consumption standards, therefore, set limits upon the possible planes of living which will be present in a society; the particular plane of living chosen will depend upon the nature of collectivity participations.

At the following level the person must make a more specific decision. He must decide whether or not to choose a particular consumption level. The plane of living he has chosen will place limits on the possible consumption levels that he can choose between. Which one he chooses will be influenced by the components of the roles he performs, by the rights and responsibilities he is expected to assume. Finally, at the most specific level, the person must choose particular evaluations of goods and services which are in accord with his consumption level. He will be influenced in this decision by the nature of the activities in which he participates.

These are the levels of considerations, of budgetary decisions, which intrude between control over purchasing power and its expenditure on goods and services. Each level is a more differentiated and segmented version of the level next above it; the elements at each level are part of the situation of the elements at the levels below them, and act as controls and limiters on the possible combinations of elements at the lower order levels. Thus the evaluations of goods and services are a consequence, on the one hand, of the nature of activities in which goods are used and, on the other, of the decisions made with respect to consumption level, plane of living, and consumption standards. A consumption level is a consequence of, on the one hand, the nature of roles, and, on the other, the decisions about a plane of living and consumption standards, and so on, to higher levels of value institutionalization. The features of each of these four lower levels may now be described more fully beginning with the most differentiated and most specific, and proceeding upward to the level of consumption standards.

Each of these levels may be treated as a social system in itself. As such it is possible to analyze the properties of each level in terms of the four major functional problems which any social system must solve. At the most specific level we are concerned with the nature of activities. It is at this level that Alfred Marshall's statement that activities give rise to wants rather than wants to activities is most meaningful.[3]

Activities may be defined as complexes of unit acts which are organized into systems. As a system, an activity may be said to involve four types of unit acts: acts which cope with the situational conditions in which the activity occurs, acts which are directly concerned with the purpose of the activity, interaction of the participants in the activity, and, finally, acts which are concerned most directly with maintaining the motivational commitment of the actors to the norms which guide the other sets of acts: laughing and joking would be two kinds of acts which could be placed in this category. These four component parts of an activity will be called the situational element, the goal element, the interactional element, and the sentiment element, respectively.[4]

Every activity involving two or more persons may be analyzed in these terms. Activities differ from one another in the degree to which one of these elements is emphasized over the others. So, for example, much ceremonial activity, such as Christmas dinner and church communion ceremonies, are activities in which emphasis is placed on the sentiment element. They function primarily to activate and maintain norms which the participants value highly. On the other hand, the situational element is emphasized in such activities as housecleaning and the preparation of meals where coping with conditions of the environment have extra importance. Activities in which the goal element is emphasized would include much economic production as well as many kinds of political and associational activity. Finally, the interactional element is emphasized in activities such as those we call sociability, in much informal activity in industry, in the eating of many meals, especially dinner.

Goods and services are means of accomplishing particular unit acts. As such they enter into activities, and they are evaluated in terms of the activities of which they are a part. The value they are assigned is derived from one or the other of the four elements of which activities are composed. We may speak of goods and services having attached to them symbolic meanings, by which we mean their assigned value. We argue that there is a congruence between the symbolic meaning of the good, or goods, used in a particular activity and the element of the activity which is emphasized. Essentially, advertisers are constantly trying to attach permanently to goods particular meanings which will make their use inevitable in particular activities.

This can be seen most clearly in activities which emphasize the sentiment element in, say, a church communion ceremony where the use of bread and wine and not other foods rests on the fact that these and these alone have symbolic meaning for that activity. But the same principle is at work in all kinds of activities, and ceremonial ac-

---

[3] For a discussion of Marshall's position, see Talcott Parsons, *The Structure of Social Action* (New York: The Free Press of Glencoe, Inc., 1949), Chap. 4.

[4] The terms "interaction" and "sentiment" are from G. C. Homans, *The Human Group* (New York: Harcourt, Brace & World, Inc., 1950), and their meanings are close to those developed by him.

tivities are not simply exceptions. In activities in which the situational element is emphasized, goods which are viewed as coping with environmental conditions will be evaluated more highly than ones which are not so viewed. In industrial societies, and especially in American society, mechanical equipment which can control environmental conditions with the least interference by human beings is evaluated more highly than is equipment in which human beings must participate more fully; such goods symbolize effective control, sometimes over time, as in the sense of timesavers, sometimes over nature in general, sometimes over narrowly defined sectors of the environment. Where the interactional element is emphasized, goods which symbolize good faith between the interacting persons will be evaluated highly. Frequently candy and flowers have this symbolic meaning, and many advertising campaigns with respect to soaps, toothpastes, and mouthwashes, some kinds of clothing, perfume, and grooming supplies, revolve around the attempt to make these goods symbolize the fact that people will like and trust you if you use them.

It does not follow that goods can have only one symbolic meaning. It is probable that all or most goods possess a series of symbolic meanings, although one meaning may have primacy over the others in particular activities. An automobile, for example, is, in many areas, the most effective means of getting from one place to another. No doubt even in areas such as Manhattan, where alternative forms of transportation are more effective, people still respond to the effectiveness symbolism attached to automobiles. But it is likely that they are also responding to the meaning an automobile has as a symbol of other aspects of activities, such as those Veblen subsumed under the concept of conspicuous consumption: evidence of wealth, of rank, and of power in relation to others. A complete analysis of the symbolic meanings of goods, therefore, requires more than an investigation of the elements of single activities. It requires as well an investigation of the way activities themselves are organized into systems, and the ways those systems are in turn organized into higher orders of systems. The next level of organization may now be considered.

IV

Activities are undertaken by persons performing roles. Activities are therefore organized, in the first instance, through being assigned to specific role types. Just as activities are organized into systems through being assigned to role types, so goods and services are organized into complexes and become symbolically attached to particular roles. These complexes are called consumption levels. It is at this level that [John] Hicks's assumption about the interdependence of the demands for goods is most relevant. It is possible, at present, to state one general proposition about consumption levels in their relation to the components of roles: the more a role embodies responsibility for the maintenance and welfare of the system (collectivity) of which it in turn is a part, the higher will be the consumption level of the person or persons filling that role. Conversely, the more a role embodies responsibility for narrowly delimited spheres of activities within the collectivity, the lower will be the consumption level of the person or persons filling that role.

The precise nature of a role will depend upon its components. Using the system problem approach once more, we may say that there are four types of role components which are functionally distinct from one another.[5] First there are executive role components which function for the solution of the goal attainment problem. These components include the definition of goals, decisions about general policy, the allocation of responsibility for carrying out such decisions, and the allocation of rights to insure that the facilities necessary for carrying out policy are available. Second, there are coordinative role components which include obligations to define areas of authority and responsibility, and to set up procedures by which loyalty is maintained and conflicts are reduced to a minimum. Third, there are supervisory role components which involve the supervision of technical services and the management of procedures. Finally, there are technical role components, such as the carrying out of particular technical duties. As examples, two general roles—that of the leader and that of the follower—and the roles involved in one kind of collectivity—the household—will be considered.

The role of leader, in any kind of collectivity, will have among its components the executive ones. The person performing the role will be entrusted with a set of duties which are of central importance in achieving the purposes of the collectivity and of maintaining it as a functioning unit within its environment. He will, for example, be expected to make policy decisions and to allocate responsibility. Not only has the leader the most consequential duties for the internal functioning of the collectivity, but also duties regarding

its functioning in relation to other collectivities. To perform his duties successfully, the leader must have access to more claims on the effort of others than do the incumbents of less influential roles. Such claims include not only purchasing power, but also power in general, loyalty of others, honor, and security.

The leader's consumption level will be higher than that of other role incumbents because he has "need" of more purchasing power (more control over facilities in general) than they if he is to perform his duties, and if he is to remain motivated for doing so. His consumption level is a consequence of his duties. He must budget the purchasing power he controls so that other role incumbents have access to the facilities necessary for achieving the purposes of the collectivity, and so that their contributions are recognized and rewarded. He must also insure (possibly by budgeting for investment expenditures) that sufficient facilities continue to be available to maintain the collectivity as a viable unit. Since these are his responsibilities, he must make greater consumption expenditures than any other member. His consumption level will, therefore, inevitably be higher than that of anyone else.

On the other hand, extensive consumption expenditures are not so necessary for incumbents of roles the main components of which are technical in nature. Decisions regarding general policy, and the ways in which policy is implemented, are not ordinarily components of such roles. Nor, therefore, need incumbents of primarily technical roles budget purchasing power to provide facilities for these kinds of problems. Their consumption level can be lower than that of the leader.

This model is of course a business firm, where the executive has rights of control and use over large amounts of

[5] The present analysis of roles and the subsequent analysis of collectivities are based on theoretical considerations developed by Talcott Parsons. See, for example, *Structure and Process in Modern Societies* (New York: The Free Press of Glencoe, Inc., 1960), Chaps. 1-2.

purchasing power than the laborer has. But the model may also be applied to other types of collectivities.

In the household, these role components are compressed into three kinds of role categories: husband, wife, and child. While households vary with respect to the way the executive, coordinative, and supervisory components are divided between husband and wife, the child role is ordinarily composed of technical components and a few coordinative components—the child is expected to have "confidence" in his parents. But for the most part the child is expected to perform such technical duties as learning to eat properly; to wash and dress himself; to be obedient and respectful; to read, write, and spell; to "get along" with adults and other children; and so on. Children are not usually expected to assume responsibility for making decisions about how they will eat or dress, how they will read or write, and there is even less expectation that they will participate actively in making decisions which affect the welfare and purposes of the household. These responsibilities are ordinarily defined as the prerogatives of adults.

A child's consumption level is certainly different from that of his parents, and, it is argued, it is lower than theirs. Children are expected to eat different quantities of food than adults, and, as infants, possibly different kinds of foods. They are expected to wear different kinds of clothing, so that, for example, a young boy does not "need" the number of suits that his father does or the number of shirts or shoes or topcoats or hats. Children do not have equal access with adults to all the household possessions: legally, for example, they are denied, in American society, the right to use the automobile until late adolescence. In fact their rights to facilities are not only restricted, but also are primarily lend-lease ones, and outright control is granted to them with respect to a relatively small number of facilities.

The components of the roles of husband and wife can differ widely from each other. Among some immigrant families in American society there seems to be a clear-cut difference between them—the executive and supervisory components being concentrated in the husband role, the coordinative components being left to the wife role. Where this occurs, the consumption levels of husband and wife may differ widely. Such a wife may be expected to see that her husband is provided with choicer foods than she and the children eat, that his clothing is kept cleaner and better mended, and that he is allowed access to the more comfortable furnishings of the household. Nor can such a wife legitimately object to her husband's spending more on entertainment in, say, the local tavern than is permitted her.

In other words, consumption levels differ—between children and adults and between men and women—not because the factors of age and sex are important *per se*, but because these factors are frequently used as a basis for organizing role components. The way role components are assigned is one major determinant of consumption levels. Facilities will derive symbolic meaning from the fact that they are assigned to particular role types, as well as, as was said before, from the components of the activities in which they are used.

V

Consumption levels of the incumbents of roles that are part of the organization of the same collectivity must ordinarily differ from one another only within narrowly definite limits. A man, for example, cannot live in sumptuous splendor, and, with impunity, keep his wife and children in rags and at a starvation level. Thus just as roles are organized into types of collectivities, so consumption levels are organized into what have been called planes of living.

A plane of living is a complex of facilities which, on the one hand, is required for the performance of the duties of some particular set of collectivities, and which, on the other, symbolizes the role incumbent's right to perform those duties. Planes of living will, therefore, differ from one another in terms of the ways in which collectivities differ from one another. And collectivities differ in two major ways. They differ with respect to the functions which they have in relation to the larger social system. They also differ with respect to their ranking in relation to one another.

By the use of the functional problem approach once more, collectivities may be divided into four major functional categories. Some collectivities have as their primary function the adaptation of human beings to situational conditions. The activities which have major importance in their organization function for the solution of environmental problems, for maintaining the ecological location of human beings. The term "community" is the general term used for such collectivities, and concrete examples would include kinship groupings, neighborhoods, villages, towns, and cities. A second set of collectivities function primarily for the maintenance of human beings in time. The activities organized in them function for the maintenance and persistence of value patterns from one generation to the next through socialization procedures, and through techniques by which motivational commitment to values is managed. Concrete examples would be households, ethnic groupings, social classes, and na-

tional groupings. Both these types of collectivities have relatively diffuse purposes. The third type of collectivities function for the attainment of particular goals, and the activities organized in them deal primarily with goal achievement. The fourth type have as their primary function integrative considerations. The activities organized in them deal primarily with harmonizing the diverse interests involved in the pursuit of goals. A business firm [and] a university are concrete examples of the third type. A trade union, a professional association, a political party are examples of the fourth.

Roles are organized in terms of these four types of collectivities, and if a person is to perform roles within them, he must be willing to act in a manner appropriate to the purposes for which collectivities exist. This involves committing his effort to the value-approved goals and procedures which form the structure of collectivities. A person has an obligation to use those facilities which are approved for achieving the purposes of the collectivities in which he performs roles if he wishes to remain a member in good standing of the collectivities. He also has a right to use such facilities by virtue of his role incumbency in the collectivities. The right to "claim" facilities is simply the obverse of the obligation to use those facilities.

Collectivities differ from one another with respect to functioning. They also differ in their ranking in relation to one another—by the way they are regarded as contributing to the purposes upon which the members of a society place value. This is most clearly documented for social-class collectivities where the terms "upper," "middle," and "lower" point explicitly to a ranking system. But it is also present, sometimes only implicitly, in, for example, the zonal distinctions made in urban communities, in neighborhood group studies of slums as opposed to Gold Coasts, and Cornervilles *vs.* Lake Forests and Crestwood Heights. It is present as well in studies of various kinds of medical and quasimedical practice—specialists and general practitioners, chiropractors and pharmacists—in the distinction between office and shop in industry; in the pecking order among churches, denominations, and sects; and among ethnic groupings. Ranking connotes an ordering of units into some system of superiority and inferiority in relation to one another. The relative ranks are determined by judgments of the degree to which the units approach an agreed upon set of standards. Those units which approach the standards most closely are ranked as superior to those which do not. We submit that these general considerations are relevant in the ranking of collectivities as well as of persons. Those collectivities which embody, in their purposes, the values which the majority of the members of a society consider most important, rank higher than those which do not, just as those members of a group who, in their behavior, come closest to the norms of the group are ranked, by the members of the group, higher than those who do not.

One way in which ranking is recognized is through the differential administration of sanctions. Sanctions are greater for behavior which is highly valued than for behavior which is not. Both the rewards for proper behavior and the punishments for improper behavior are greater. Among the rewards are rights to make claims on others, among which claims to facilities are only one type. Claims in general accrue in greater proportion to those persons who assume responsibility for implementing in action the most highly valued purposes of a society. Therefore incumbents of roles in collectivities whose purposes are most highly valued, and which, as a result, rank high in relation to other collectivities, will, by virtue of their incumbency, have rights to more claims than will members of lower-ranked collectivities.

They will of course have more duties as well. And both the claims to which persons have rights and the duties which are their responsibility are circumscribed by the same system of values from which are derived the standards by which rights and duties are judged. Claims to facilities must, as a result, be used in such a way that the facilities are, on the one hand, considered the proper ones with which to perform duties in particular collectivities, and, on the other, are ones which meet consumption standards of quality and performance to a degree commensurate with the rank of the collectivities. For example, if the president of an important business corporation who belonged to important clubs, a high-ranking ethnic group, a high ranking church, and had an upper-class background, were to choose to live in a poor neighborhood in a modest house furnished with usable but second-hand furniture and bargain basement objects, he would probably be regarded by other people as eccentric at least, and as having an improper sense of the importance of his various positions.

VI

The final level of factors is the level of consumption standards of quality and performance by which facilities are judged. If we treat them as an institutionalized system of standards which derive from a more general system of values, we may once again make use of the functional problem approach. In these terms, consumption standards may be viewed as involving not one monolithic set of standards, but four sets, each with different system functions to perform. These four sets are named standards of life, standards of status evaluation, standards of taste and morality, and standards of protection.

The standards of life are those consumption standards which are of central importance to the persistence of a society. They are standards which are held in common by all or the majority of the members of a society, and which all or the majority must live up to if they wish to remain members in good standing in the society. Choosing facilities which meet these consumption standards is therefore the act of a good citizen, an act which symbolizes to other people that the person is willing to live up to the expectations of the various roles he performs. Such consumption standards include, at the least, a minimum standard of nutrition, some standard of shelter, of clothing, of cleanliness, of movement, of leisure, and so on. Facilities which meet these standards are necessary for "cultural survival." The term "people who live like animals" recognizes the fact that there are certain central consumption standards in a society which people must live up to if their behavior and their sense of responsibility are not to be suspect. In this sense, standards of life contribute to the solution of the problem of goal attainment.

The second set of consumption standards, standards of status evaluation, are necessary if recognition is to be given to the fact that some persons devote their effort to more highly valued spheres of activity than do others. Claims to facilities which meet these standards are rights which the majority of the members of a society recognize as desirable and as just rewards for, in a sense, "action above and beyond the call of duty." The persons who make claim to these rewards are expected, reciprocally, to assume responsibilities, greater than normal, in the spheres of activity which the members of the society value highly. In this sense, the standards of status evaluation contribute to the solution of the integrative problem. Concretely, the standards of status evaluation are recognized by the presence of facilities which are different in kind and/or quality from those which meet standards of life. A palace as opposed to a log cabin, a servant vs. a broom, a private doctor vs. a doctor in a "free" clinic, custom vs. ready-made clothing are differences in kind and quality of facilities which are recognized by the majority of a society's members as legitimate differences to which some, but not all, people ought to have access.

The third set of standards, standards of taste and morality, are necessary if the potentialities for the rejection of duties and obligations are to be kept within bounds. These standards contribute to the managing of tensions and to the maintaining of motivational commitment to the value system. Accepting the standards of taste and morality provides the person with modes of gratification for impulses which, if not controlled within limits, might disrupt the society. Concretely, these standards are recognized by the presence of styles and fads in goods and services, by modes of entertainment and of leisure activities in general. For example, the North American woman who collects hats which she does not really need but which make her feel better is managing her tensions in a way which is acceptable to North American standards of taste and morality. On the other hand, if she were to collect men, she would be going beyond the limits that these standards set as ones in which tension ought to be managed.

The final set of standards, the standards of protection, are necessary if the society is to persist in its environment. These standards set the manner in which situational conditions ought to be dealt with. Making claims to facilities which meet them provides the person with insurance that his standard of living cannot be destroyed by unexpected or unanticipated changes in external events. These standards therefore function as insurance against possible threats to the person's standard of living and to that of the society as a whole. Standards of protection therefore contribute to the solution of the adaptive problem.

Facilities which meet standards of protection vary, as do the standards themselves, from society to society. In American society there are three major kinds of facilities which meet the standards of protection: the hoarding of liquid funds, capital investment, and insurance of various kinds—fire, theft, accident, collision, and life insurance, medical and pension plans, social security, and workmen's compensation and annuities. In a society such as Dobu, on the other hand, garden magic and magical spells cast on objects of possession are concrete modes of insuring protection of the standard of living.

We may conclude that the decision to select facilities which meet standards of quality and performance involves four sets of standards, not just one. For the society as a whole, purchasing power must be allocated to meet all four sets if the society is to persist. But it does not follow that each member must allocate his purchasing power to meet all four sets in the same way. If he wishes to be considered by himself and his fellows as an acceptable member of his society, he must insure that he budgets enough of his purchasing power to meet the standards of life. If he wants to be considered an important citizen as well, he must also insure

that he budgets enough of his purchasing power so that he meets the standards of status evaluation. If he wants more than this, if he also wants to be considered a model citizen, he cannot appear to be too prodigal. He must insure that he budgets enough of his purchasing power so that he meets the standards of protection. Finally, if he feels that he cannot jeopardize these various aspects of his position, he must insure that enough of his purchasing power is budgeted to control his tensions in ways which meet the standards of taste and morality. The combination of ways in which the person allocates his total purchasing power will produce a plane of living for him. The factors which influence him in his various decisions will, as we have said, depend upon his collectivity participations, the roles he plays, and the activities he performs.

VII

This is as far as it has been possible to carry the theory about consumer spending at the present time. The general structure is relatively clear. What is required is a more detailed analysis of its various components so that more than the most general kinds of propositions can be deduced.

Despite the generality of the theory, it is possible to use it in certain kinds of empirical research. We can demonstrate this in two ways: first by deriving an elementary hypothesis, and secondly by presenting some cautionary remarks about tracing the effects of income change in a society such as our own.

It is possible to combine these dimensions of consumer spending in various ways. It can be argued, for example, that there are, in a society, a number of types of collectivities in which all or the majority of the members of that society participate. A household, a kinship group, a neighborhood, a nation, some kind of economic group would be examples. If we take the household as our point of reference, it is possible to infer that some activities which will be carried on by the members of one household will be similar to those carried on by the members of all other households. It follows from this, assuming a common cultural tradition, that there will be a complex of goods and services, a certain minimum of facilities, which each household will possess or at least will have use of, and which will signify to others that the members of that household are acceptable members of the society. This complex, in American society, has been called a standard package.[6] It is ordinarily what anthropologists mean when they speak of subsistence in the sense of goods necessary for cultural, not biological, survival.

From this kind of argument it is possible to derive one hypothesis: expenditure on the complex of goods and services which compose the standard package of a society will be relatively invariant with moderate changes in income. We may derive two corollary hypotheses from this one. First, persons whose incomes are somewhat below that necessary to buy the standard package will tend to spend beyond their current incomes. Second, those with incomes above that necessary for the standard package will tend to divert their excess income into other channels, into prestige goods, "impulse" spending, and saving. These kinds of hypotheses suggest that in Keynesian theory there is a stickiness of demand on the consumption side

which parallels the stickiness of wage rates on the production side. Thus behind Keynes's assumption of the rigidity of money wages downward are a set of ideas in the minds of men about a standard package of goods and services to which all citizens who are fulfilling their role expectations ought to have access. Wage cutting below a certain level (the level needed to buy the standard package) will therefore run into resistance not only on the part of the workers and their representatives, but also on the part of the employers who offer the wages. The result will be that lowered production will be taken out in the laying off of workers rather than in the cutting of wages, in the removal of workers from one kind of collectivity participation and one system of role expectations which make legitimate their claims for possession of the standard package. To cut wages below the level needed to buy the standard package would be to render illegitimate an expectation that workers fulfill their normal role expectations.

Second, with respect to the effects of income changes, it is possible to make a few remarks. If the effects of a change in income level are to be specified accurately, more than a knowledge of the aggregate shifts in income is necessary. It is also necessary to specify the particular segments of the society which are affected by the income change. It is necessary as well to specify whether the income change is accompanied by shifts in group memberships, in role expectations, and in the activities of the income recipients. Unless these factors change simultaneously and in the same direction as the change in income, a consumption function such as that which Keynes derived cannot predict accurately the effect of an income shift. According to the Keynesian model, a rise in income of per-

_____
[6] David Riesman and Howard Roseborough, "Careers and Consumer Behavior," in L. H. Clark, ed., *Consumer Behavior*, Vol. II (New York: New York University Press, 1956), pp. 1-18.

sons in the middle-income range, sufficient to put them into the top income bracket, should lead to a large increase in saving. But such a prediction may prove very wrong unless it can be shown that the income shift is accompanied by a shift in memberships to more highly valued groups and the assumption of, perhaps, positions of community leadership. If these do not occur, then there may just as likely, if not more likely, be a rapid increase in expenditures on prestige goods and on goods which aid in the management of tensions—what the economists call impulse spending—and a relatively small increase in saving. One can speak, in other words, of propensities to consume or propensities to save as having effects on spending only after the structure of activities, of role expectations, and of collectivities, within which these psychological mechanisms work, have been analyzed and made specific.

Money Economy and Consumption Patterns

ELIZABETH E. HOYT

In this paper I am interpreting my subject as the effect on consumption patterns of situations in which new money income results from new opportunities to make or earn money under conditions of technological change. It is implied in my subject that new opportunities for choice are offered. The most important source of these would ordinarily be the market. There is, however, another source, namely, goods and especially services which may be offered free or at low cost by government, religious, or social agencies; these may directly affect consumption choices and indirectly influence market choices as well.

No situation of economic change in underdeveloped societies is a simple one, and many noneconomic as well as economic influences affect the spending and use of income. These influences vary greatly from time to time and from place to place. Further, we have no complete picture of the im-

Elizabeth E. Hoyt, "The Impact of a Money Economy and Consumption Patterns," *Annals of the American Academy of Political and Social Science*, 305 (May, 1956), 12-22.

pact of economic change on consumption patterns in even one underdeveloped society. Economic change has been studied much more frequently from an interest in production or an interest in distribution than from an interest in consumption. For consumption we have some studies of family expenditures, usually made with primary concern for whether or not people have enough (in no case known to the writer do we have studies relating to the same people at different periods made with the same classifications and interpretations of spending); evidence of change from the production and sale of new goods and services in the economy; some studies relating to particular areas of consumer expenditure, as food and housing; and a variety of more or less organized observations of change, some of them made by careful observers. It would be premature, in fact, to look for accurate measurement in a field in which basic theory needs development and for which we first need to agree on what it is most important to measure.

The subject of consumption change under impact of a money economy might be approached from the point of view of effects of buying on production, effects on trade, effects on stability, and of several other interests to which the actions of consumers contribute. The point of view of this paper is that of consumers as such, their attitudes and behavior, and their welfare insofar as the latter is a matter of objective proof or objective agreement.

Resistance to a New Money Economy

It is safe to say that among underdeveloped peoples there is likely to be some resistance to a new money economy. The attractions of new goods and services do not completely outweigh the objections to regimented production, loss of leisure, closer contact with outsiders as officials or taskmasters. Even freedom from want itself, unless the want is dire, may at first seem less attractive than freedom to carry on in the old way.

The easiest transitions to a new money economy occur when change is slow and people are able to set their own pace.[1] Such an opportunity is found in the agricultural production of peasant proprietors, who can adjust their work and income as their wants expand. In some parts of Africa it is customary for the owners or adminis-

---

[1] Actually the test of successful change is equilibrium among the changes, which is most likely to be achieved when change is slow and the people affected have an opportunity to make their own selections and adjustments. An outside group, say an employer or a colonial government, introducing change is almost certain to interpret success in terms of its own cultural values. When a day of reckoning and confusion comes, the outside group is likely to ascribe the confusion to agitators, failing to recognize that they themselves did not understand the cultural situation with which they were interfering. The people affected need to have adequate opportunity to select among new alternatives which conform to their own sense of equilibrium; this requires not only a variety of alternatives, but time to become acquainted with their significance.

trators of large plantations to offer their workers the opportunity of doing only half-time work for wages, since they find the people more willing to be employed if they can have less money and more leisure, or more time to provide their own food. A similar desire to work shorter hours and provide their own food, or part of it, is found among the Indian employees of the plantations of Guatemala, and employers furnish their workers with *milpas*, small plots of ground for agricultural production. Thus the problem of transition to a money economy is simpler in rural regions than it is in cities, where employees have no opportunity to produce their own food and the employer or some other agency must furnish housing for each employee in a crowded area. In South Africa, East Africa, and Central America, the regions with which I am best acquainted, full-time wage earners in cities or mines very often keep their wives and children in the country; they themselves can escape there when some particular object of spending is obtained or when the pressures of full-time employment become too great. One result of this kind of employment of course is that wages tend to be set at the cost of sustenance for a single man, rather than at a family level; and a major problem of support arises for such wage earners as to bring their families to cities.

Another and curious example of compromise transition is found in the Gezira in the Sudan, where a large-scale social and economic planning project has set up hundreds of peasant proprietors who are under a certain mild compulsion to produce cotton and other economic crops. By means of this, peasant incomes have greatly increased. Many of these "peasants," who have no particular use for all the new consumer goods such incomes could bring, now employ others to do a part of their work for them, while they themselves spend a good portion of their prosperity in leisure or in supervising the work of their employees.

Where people are plunged all at once into a situation away from home in which they have no choice but full-time earning for money, they have lost their familiar anchorages and are without experience to guide them in the new set of conditions and the new opportunities for spending which the money economy brings. Such situations do not automatically take care of themselves. The use of money and opportunity has to be learned, and the price can be a high one.

First New Choices

The first uses of new income are likely to be for more of what has customarily been enjoyed or for new choices which do not much disturb old consumption patterns. They tend to be either easily incorporated additions (like a taste for new sweets within the food pattern) or something which can function outside the existing pattern without much immediate effect upon it (like a bus trip).

The first new choices in general fall into four categories, of which the fourth to some extent crosscuts the other three. The first of these categories is goods making an immediate appeal to sensory tastes which are universal or nearly universal among all peoples, such as sweets of all kinds, including cakes and sweet drinks, tobacco and drugs which give temporary emotional satisfaction, and intoxicants. Most of these have the advantage of being relatively cheap, and traders can readily put them on the market. The introduction of new spirituous liquors to American Indians and of great supplies of opium in Asia are well-known exam-ples. Almost everywhere the per capita consumption of sugar notably increases as a new money economy comes in.

The second category, in some cases related to the first, is proprietary medicines and devices to which magical or semimagical qualities are attributed. The category is smaller than the others, but it may be the most harmful in its effects. It was noted that after various proprietary medicines, or claims for them, were made illegal under the United States Pure Food and Drug Act of 1906, a great increase in their sale took place in Central and South America. A considerable part of the advertising in vernacular papers published among underdeveloped peoples is of proprietary drugs and devices, and even where people cannot read they can be attracted by colored posters, as one I saw in an isolated region of Honduras —Christ holding out to a sufferer a familiar box of pills.

Prestige and Emulation

The third category is of goods and services associated with prestige, either something already in use and approved among the native people (as metal ornaments) or something approved by outsiders whom the native people desire to emulate. Among foods, white flour and white flour products generally have more prestige than the old familiar staples. Very often the most prestige-carrying goods are something to wear, both because what is worn is conspicuous and because such goods, though not necessarily inexpensive, are relatively so compared with housing, house equipment, and vehicles. That beads, metal decorations, and bright cloth should be a part of the equipment of traders going to farflung tropical shores is taken for granted. At the present time, parts of tropical Africa offer an immense market for the second-hand clothing of Europe. Recently there has been a great run in British East Africa for dark spectacles, so much so that an African character wearing dark spectacles is used to typify a vain simpleton, the reason being that dark spectacles are desired for dress wear at social events after the sun has set.

A great deal could be written about the social conditions which most favor emphasis on conspicuous and emulative consumption, and how they favor it. Where caste is rigid or differences between native people and the outsiders introducing change are felt to be very great, emulation favors more expensive or fashionable forms of what is already in the caste or native culture. Where there are social classes but mobility among them is readily possible, people naturally tend to copy the class above, and if the outsiders are admired, the highest native class copies outsiders. A good example is found among the Baganda of Uganda, a stratified but not rigidly stratified society, where each stratum copies the one above, and the top group, represented by the king and his associates, copies the conspicuous culture of British royalty and aristocracy, so far as this culture is known in Uganda. Not only British dress, but the elaborate complex of fashionable social events is taken over by this group. On the other hand, in two more democratic tribal societies with which I am somewhat familiar, that of the Kikuyu in Kenya and the Chagga in Tanganyika, emulative consumption tends to take over some conspicuous traits believed to belong to a world society, and the customs of the British aristocracy as such have no particular appeal.

Targets

The fourth category, to some extent crosscutting the first three, has been described as "targets," a target purchase usually being something relatively important or substantial which stands by itself and is not necessarily bound in with other culture changes. When a person has once hit his target he can sit back and rest for a while—perhaps for the remainder of his life. Regular food and drink would hardly be included in this category, but the giving of a feast might be a target. More expensive clothing purchases are very often targets—shoes, for instance. A target may be almost anything which commends itself to people because of its obvious usefulness or its associations with prestige, but the choice of particular targets depends in part on aggressive salesmanship. The wide introduction of the sewing machine is a case in point. An intelligent African I knew had worked several years to save enough money for a bicycle (a target desired for both its usefulness and its prestige), and the bicycle had become the limit of his horizon; he could not conceive of anything that cost more than a bicycle, even the coronation.

It is true that most target goods serve some "useful" purpose, but it is not true that ability to serve a utilitarian purpose is necessary for their introduction. Immediate sensory and emulative appeal is likely to bring them in; but once introduced, they may remain and more of them be desired because their utilitarian superiorities have become obvious. In respect to targets, Major Orde-Browne says:

. . . Astonishing differences will be found to exist between tribes. Cooking-pots, hurricane lamps, shoes, umbrellas, hoes, and numerous other items will each be found to be the particular favourite of a certain community. . . .

The primitive tribe will as a rule be attracted at first by trifles of little value; a knife, axe, or other useful article may be purchased, but it is often accompanied by a number of quite unnecessary adjuncts, such as shoddy but showy clothing, brightly coloured hats, or toys such as mirrors and mouth-organs. Later, the first novelty of the contents of the store will have worn off, and more sensible things will be favoured; metal cooking-pots have been found superior to easily fractured earthenware, blankets are appreciated, or the attractions of lamps may be discovered.[2]

A special case of target—which also of course may bring about a major modification of culture pattern—is the desire for education, most commonly the education of children, though adult education as a target is not absent. In British East Africa, education is not free, and again and again I was told there that the reason a father or brother had left home to earn was so that the children, or the younger ones, could be educated. In one place, the Kikuyu region of Kenya, where not enough schools were available even if people could pay to go, the building of schools had become a target; and the people were erecting them on every hilltop, contributing their labor. It was said that some families gave to such a target as much as half their money income.

Major Modifications of Consumption Patterns

"Modification of consumption patterns" may apply to the separate patterns of family expenditures—food, housing, clothing, and so on—and it may apply to consumers' use of resources as a whole.

Food

To begin with the separate patterns, and with food, the weight of evidence indicates that in areas that have come under the influence of a modern money economy, diets are poorer than they are in more primitive areas.

[2] G. St. J. Orde-Browne, *The African Labourer* (London: Oxford University Press, 1933), p. 35.

In general, the effect of a cash crop or wage economy on nutrition has been one of lowering the level by disturbing the balance achieved under subsistence economy, introducing processed foods as prestige foods, limiting the amount and quality of subsistence crops in favor of cash crops, or the amount of time spent in preparation and preservation of food for home consumption.[3]

A study of the American Geographical Society supported by the United States Office of Naval Research concluded, on the basis of incomplete evidence it is true, that of 209 tribes selected as "primitive," only twelve had diets defective in both energy and protective foods, seven had diets defective in energy only, and the remaining 190 had diets that were adequate, at any rate for the life the people were leading. On the other hand, most of Asia, about half of Africa, and about half of South America, areas which had come to a greater extent under the impact of a money economy, had diets defective both in energy and in protective foods. The best nourished areas of the world were, in general, those that we regard as the most civilized and those that we regard as the least civilized.[4]

Some deterioration of diets would, on a priori grounds, be expected. The quick expansion of tastes for sweets, mentioned in the preceding section, almost always means less rather than more protective elements in the diet. White sugar contains no protective elements, and a considerable increase in the consumption of sweets usually means a smaller consumption of foods

[3] Margaret Mead, ed., *Cultural Patterns and Technical Change*, a manual prepared by the World Federation for Mental Health (Paris: UNESCO, 1953), p. 260. See also pp. 211-220. . . .

[4] "Study in Human Starvation," Sheet 2: Diets and Deficiency Diseases, *Atlas of Diseases*, Plate 9 (New York: American Geographical Society, 1953). . . . .

containing vitamins and minerals. Desire for prestige foods strengthens the demand for sweets and may lead also to increased consumption of white flour and polished rice. As people give up their old subsistence agriculture and buy their food in markets, white flour and polished rice, which are more easily preserved than whole-grain flour and rice rich in vitamins and minerals, tend to take the place of the more nutritious cereals, and to some extent also of vegetables and plantains, which contain elements essential for balanced consumption. Prestige value attaches itself not only to white flour products, but also to food in packages and cans, which increase the cost of the diet without necessarily improving it.[5]

Where workers employed away from home eat in large numbers in commissaries run by employers, considerable attention has been paid to giving them food that will increase their productivity. A diet worked out in detail to every calorie and every established protective element is fed to workers in the copper mines of the Rhodesias and the gold mines of the Witwatersrand, and whether they like it or not they have no choice but to take it. I know of no evidence, however, indicating that such diets influence food consumption in the homes of the workers when they return to them; on the contrary, there is evidence to show that, since the women of the family are those who prepare the food, changes in the diets of men in mining and industrial establishments

have little effect on family nutrition.

The first impact of a money economy is typically accompanied by the introduction of new diseases, but in many cases there is a good record of improvement later, when doctors, nurses, and hospitals for native people are introduced. Satisfactory figures on change, however, are lacking.

Housing

In the area of housing the weight of evidence is not so strongly on one side as it is in the case of food. According to circumstances, both improvement and deterioration take place. So long as people can live in their own native habitat, changes tend to be for larger space, better construction, and more amenities; but these changes come slowly. On the other hand, deterioration comes rapidly when workers move themselves, and especially their families, to centers of industry. There is no worse housing in the world than in the slums of many Asian and African cities. Flimsy construction, as of cardboard and tin, terrific crowding, the absence of elementary sanitation, and the presence of insects and rodents—all these distinguish the kind of houses in which many workers have to live when industry expands. A great deal has been written on experiments in good housing for underdeveloped peoples as they come to new centers of labor, and there are many such experiments under municipalities and employers, but compared to the need for them they are numerically unimportant. What is also little recognized is the fact that employers of labor in providing "good" housing often pay little attention to what workers want; for example, they substitute identical rows of rooms for separate huts, thus depriving families both of privacy and of the opportunity to have in their homes a little variety and expression of personal taste. So the values gained

---

[5] Considerable research has gone into the preservation of whole cereals and to the restoration of vitamins and minerals to commercially prepared foods. This can be done, and sometimes quite inexpensively. The problem now is chiefly to insure that the more nutritious products are on the market and are the ones actually used by the people. Such groups as the United Nations Food and Agriculture Organization are trying to bring this about.

by better construction and equipment, when these are given, may be more than offset by the fact that the new houses do not accord with the families' living habits and interest in their home.

Clothing

So far as clothing is concerned, when a money economy is initiated, direct effects on welfare are generally not very important, though the introduction of new kinds of clothing needs to be accompanied (as it sometimes is not) by understanding of ways to use it hygienically and keep it clean. The indirect effects may be considerable, however, because clothing makes one of the earliest appeals to consumer interest, and after absolute necessities are met, it attracts expenditures more rapidly than objectives which, like housing, require more experience and education. It is of interest that in underdeveloped societies in general men change their styles of clothing before women change theirs, that for both sexes the ages where change comes first are from twelve to twenty, and that for both sexes the forms of outerwear are generally changed before underwear. This is in accordance with what we should expect from the facts that women are held to be culturally the more conservative sex, that disposition to change in general is more marked at adolescence than at other periods of life, and that outerwear, being more visible than underwear, is more subject to the influence of emulation.

Recreation

It is difficult to generalize on the effects of a money economy on recreation, since influences which may be much more important than those of money economy enter into the picture. Recreation, moreover, is closely related to adjustment in the pattern of consumption as a whole. Motion pictures of certain types (in my experience the most popular types are animated cartoons and Wild Wests) are greatly desired and extend the horizon in various ways. But much of the change in the recreation area is due not so much to the availability of new commercial forms of entertainment as to the lapse of old forms of tribal recreation, sometimes related to tribal religion, and to their suppression or discouragement by the authorities, and, in some cases, to the provision by those authorities of new forms of recreation free or at low cost. In British East Africa, for example, the government has encouraged the institution of social halls where beer or tea can be obtained, and in some cases the beer hall plays a major part in the recreation of the community.

Social Participation

Social participation, which is a part of the pattern of consumption, is related in some way to all the categories of consumption, particularly to recreation and to contributions to religion, organizations and movements, and gifts to other people. Most people in economically underdeveloped societies have more of a large-family system than we, and under the impact of a money economy this tends to break up. But the need of social participation, the willingness and desire to contribute to others, remains, and seeks other outlets. I know of no study which deals with the nature and amount of contributions among underdeveloped peoples under the impact of change, but I know that sometimes the amount, in proportion to income, is very great. I have spoken of the large contributions to schools made by the Kikuyu. Contributions to organizations are likely to be especially great if the people see a means to bolster their morale through a religious, educational, or political organization of their own. The rapid growth of what to our eyes are peculiar religious movements among underdeveloped peoples is a good example of this. Some of these movements or churches operating as Christian introduce old magic under new guises, represent Christ as an Indian or a Negro, and make a great economic show which serves to compensate the members for the sense of personal inferiority they may have received from the outsiders who are the agents of economic change. Members live vicariously in the splendors of this organization.

The Total Pattern

This latter part of our discussion has indicated that what may happen to the pattern as a whole is much more important than what happens in any single category of consumption. We need a word on the nature of total patterns,[6] which are made up of parts in-

---

[6] Our subject might include discussion of changes in proportions given to different categories of expenditure as a money economy comes in. For example, a money economy tends to increase real income, and it is as true as it ever was that, as incomes increase, a smaller proportion of income is usually spent for food (Engel's law); indeed, this should be obvious. Also, as income increases, it is likely that for a considerable time a larger proportion goes for durable goods. . . . In services, too, proportionate expenditures of underdeveloped peoples tend to increase with income, though this does not mean that such proportions increase indefinitely. For example, people in underdeveloped societies who are very poor by our standards may employ a servant as their means increase; but as they step out of the category of "underdeveloped," expenditures for servants may decline and greater proportionate expenditures for household equipment be made. A considerable body of data on family expenditures has been collected among various underdeveloped peoples, and it might seem at first that we could compare proportions of expenditure made by less developed groups with those made by the more developed. But since the background conditions of the different societies are very

terrelated and to a considerable degree interdependent. Any influence which disturbs any part greatly is likely to react on the rest; and the whole may be disturbed also by any over-all conditions which increase or decrease available resources in any major way, or which (particularly in the case of standards of living) introduce new concepts of the values of life.[7]

As has been said, if change comes slowly to underdeveloped peoples and they can set their own pace, no very serious problems may arise. But people who find themselves precipitated into a new situation of greatly increased purchasing power may go beserk with it. They may not know what to do with the new money, and the transitory delights of sensory and emulative spending may take it all before a wider range of alternatives comes into the picture. Not only may the people throw away their money for almost any new object, but unaccustomed spending of a sensory and emulative nature may lead to decay of morale and permanent loss. The willingness to follow any leader who promises prestige and security and the increase of crime found in societies in process of very rapid change are symptoms of this.

Obviously, more than consumption patterns are involved in the tensions and attitudes toward life which arise under the impact of a money economy. The problems call for understanding from many disciplines besides eco-

---

different, and since the studies vary greatly in selection of families and in classification and interpretation of data, as well as in accuracy, it would be dangerous to use them for this purpose.

[7] The *locus classicus* for discussion of standard of consumption and standard of living is Joseph S. Davis, "Standards and Content of Living," *American Economic Review*, 35 (March, 1945), 1-15. Among other things, this stresses the importance of balance in the whole.

nomics, and a whole complex of related values must be understood. Consumption patterns are the most tangible part of this complex.

The Market and Other Means of Constructive Change

Little thought has been given to the nature and organization of markets in underdeveloped societies as an appeal to new purchasing power and as an encouragement to increase this power. In the earliest stages of development of money economies among underdeveloped peoples in modern times, a good deal of emphasis was placed on compelling the people to work by force or by laws requiring every man to give evidence that he had been employed so many days out of the year or by taxes that could not be met except by new forms of labor At a later or higher stage, attention was paid to trying to make the conditions of employment pleasant, as by giving prizes for regular work. Very little attention indeed has been, or is being, given to motivating the people by giving them a new and greater choice of goods. The value of the spread of wants to stimulate economic development has been for the most part unperceived. One can look through whole shelves of books on the economics of underdeveloped areas without finding reference to the importance of incentive through development of wants or the importance of markets as a means by which this incentive can be given. This silence contrasts oddly with the emphasis on aggressive salesmanship and advertising in our own economy. It might be assumed that we need to have our imaginations stimulated, but that underdeveloped peoples have imagination enough already.

The general assumption has been that if the profit motive of traders is given relatively free play, the problems of supplying new goods and services through markets will be taken care of by itself. In my experiences in Central America and British East Africa, the markets show cultural lag. Indeed the traders themselves are in general unfamiliar with the wide range of inexpensive goods which we in the United States take for granted, as a result of the competition of five-and-ten-cent stores, mail-order houses, and other merchandising agencies which offer mass-produced goods at low prices. Also, particularly in Central America, tariffs interfere with imports for popular consumption, and in both Central America and East Africa there is little manufacture of such goods within the countries themselves.[8] On the other hand, in these countries or areas there appears to have been no lack of effort to supply the people with goods and services of an elementary sensory nature such as I spoke of earlier—sweets, proprietary medicines, tobacco, soft and hard drinks—and prostitutes and temporary wives are readily available for wage earners away from home and for some who have their families with them. Governments fight such sensory amenities in some cases, but are less active in providing a range of alternatives which might take their place.

---

[8] That offerings of inexpensive consumer goods are neglected in underdeveloped countries which have been under the impact of a money economy for some time is suggested by W. H. Nicholls in "Domestic Trade in an Underdeveloped Country—Turkey," *Journal of Political Economy*, **59** (December, 1951), 463-480. Not only was there inadequate attention to consumers' wants or needs in Turkey, but "in so far as . . . the consumer-goods industries have . . . been developed, the government has frequently followed a high-price policy to produce the profits necessary to offset losses" incurred elsewhere (465). The author of the article believes that his conclusions are "probably applicable to other countries in approximately the same stage of economic development as Turkey" (478).

Two Examples of Market Development

In contrast to this negligence or lethargy, I should like to mention two approaches to the development of markets, one by a colonial and the other by an independent government. The first is in Danish Greenland, where the colonial government has for many years put emphasis on the development of the trading post as an agency for bringing modern civilization to Eskimos. In the second case, at the request of the government of India, Professor Lincoln Clark of New York University conducted in the summer of 1955 a marketing experiment to see what consumer response would be to a variety of inexpensive goods sold through mobile stores in different types of regions. To finance this the Indian government set up the National Small Industries Corporation. It is significant that private capital was unwilling to take the risk. The government hopes, however, that after it has demonstrated that selling a variety of inexpensive goods is good business, private investors will buy stock in the corporation.

Our assumption that private capital will take the risks involved in such new undertakings arose at a time of great economic expansion, during and following the commercial and industrial revolutions in western Europe and the United States, when large risks were taken by men inoculated with the spirit of enterprise and selling primarily to their own people. Very different conditions are involved in the development of new consumer markets among underdeveloped peoples, either by members of those societies or by businessmen from without. For our businessmen to see opportunities of profit in our own society by selling to our own people calls for less imagination than to see such prospects far afield, especially as the opportunities at home are now very great.

Other Contributions to Integrated Consumption

It is obvious of course that a wide range of goods offered through markets, important as it is, is not by itself enough to take care of the development of incentive in an intelligent way. Consumers would still need protection from harmful or deleterious products, and although the offering of a wide range of alternatives is far better than the offering of a narrow range, there could still be disorganization in consumption patterns. The subject is too large to be treated here with any completeness, and I shall not discuss education, which in its broad sense is the foundation of constructive and integrated consumption. I should, however, like to mention two efforts made by native people themselves to deal with the problems involved in incorporating new goods and services into their consumption patterns.

The first example is Japanese. At least as early as the Meiji period, the rulers of Japan began to send some of their own people abroad to examine and bring back elements of foreign culture which appeared to them desirable. These elements were then further examined in Japan, and if they passed the test were modified as necessary and introduced into the home culture under the aegis of the emperor, who was also the cultural high priest.

The second example is from modern Kenya. I have mentioned earlier the passion for school building which I saw in the Kikuyu territories in 1950-51. Some of these schools were "independent" schools and had as one of their objects to bridge the gap between the old cultures and the new as a money economy came in. Important elements both of the curriculum and of extracurricular activities were the peoples' own efforts toward easing the cultural transition. But when Mau Mau troubles broke out in 1952, these schools were closed on the grounds that they were contributing to Mau Mau; they were not permitted to reopen under their former direction; and their constructive and positive contributions to consumption adjustment were not examined. In this case the money necessary for such a study was offered to the British Colonial Office, the Colonial Office itself to appoint the personnel for the study. It was said that tensions were too great to make study possible, and the offer was declined.

Too Little Explored

In relation to their great importance, consumption patterns and adjustment within them have received little attention, and little research has dealt with them directly. Consumption problems in general have been less studied than those of other main areas in economics, partly because the consumer's interest is everybody's interest, not that of a special group. In addition, consumption requires a considerable appreciation and some knowledge of social sciences other than economics; in fact, it is the economic example par excellence of need for collaboration among the social sciences. And the problems of consumption, difficult enough at home, become even more difficult when our concern is with the consumption patterns of underdeveloped peoples. We need to acquire a new set of facts and we need to enter into the minds of others, understanding why a condition of wants or lack of wants which seems to us completely unreasonable may not be unreasonable in view of the background against which the condition occurs. Only with such understanding can we see the most intelligent ways by which we can help in providing adequate substitutes for what is passing and in enlarging the range of alternatives for choice. Only with such understanding can we help the people to see their own situation in relation to others, so that they themselves can lay the foundations for their own balanced development.

Leisure and Prestige

ALFRED C. CLARKE

Lundberg's observation, made twenty years ago, that social scientists have paid little attention to the problems of leisure,[1] holds true today with few ex-

Alfred C. Clarke, "The Use of Leisure and Its Relation to Levels of Occupational Prestige," *American Sociological Review*, **21** (1956), 301-307.

[1] G. A. Lundberg, M. Komarovsky, and M. A. McInery, *Leisure: A Suburban Study* (New York: Columbia University Press, 1934), p. 8.

ceptions, even though living habits have been altered by the further reduction of the work week.[2] Much of the

[2] American leisure is obviously a broad subject with many facets and many definitions. In this study the term is used essentially in the same manner as conceptualized in the following statement by Lundberg: Leisure is "the time we are free from the more obvious and formal duties which a paid job or other obligatory occupation imposes upon us. In accepting this definition we are not overlooking the interdependence of work and leisure. Such terms are merely pragmatic ways of designating aspects, rather than separate parts, of life. It remains a fact, however, that nearly

previous research has been approached from a recreational, community, or welfare point of view. Many of these studies appeared in the middle 'thirties when the enforced leisure of the depression years stimulated communities to become increasingly concerned with the way in which people spent their hours away from work. Moreover, few studies have attempted to consider leisure in terms of the larger cultural context. For example, are the dominant values of the culture reflected in the differential use of leisure time? Is there a systematic relationship between social status and leisure styles? Does the occupational structure influence the ways in which work-free time is spent? Research evidence bearing on these and similar questions is extremely limited. In addition, the question can be raised whether present leisure-time patterns are accurately portrayed by past research. It would appear probable that in recent years increasing amounts of spare time, accompanied by rising income levels, might tend to equalize the frequency of participation in many spare-time activities among different segments of the population. Perhaps certain alleged differences in leisure behavior are more apparent than real. It may well be, as Denney and Riesman suggest, that mass leisure has emerged so suddenly that we tend to interpret it by drawing on the stereotypes of an earlier era.[3]

The present research views leisure activity as an aspect of social stratification. It focuses on the role of leisure as a part of the life styles of individuals occupying different prestige levels.

The Study Design

Although levels of prestige have been delineated in varied ways, it was felt that an occupational referent would provide a meaningful standard upon which leisure behavior could be based.[4] The North-Hatt Occupational Prestige Scale was selected as the instrument best suited to the requirements of the present study.[5] Through the use of this scale it was possible to translate the prestige level of individuals into a numerical score. A second instrument was constructed to measure certain configurations of leisure behavior. It included a section on frequency of participation in different types of leisure activities, a set of questions concerning preferences and attitudes, several items pertaining

all people can and do classify nearly all their activities according to these two categories in a way that is deeply meaningful to themselves. . . . As such the categories are . . . useful for our purpose" (*ibid.*, pp. 2-3).

There are, however, other researchers who feel that leisure should also be considered as an attitude of mind rather than merely spare time. For a discussion of this point of view, see Reuel Denney and David Riesman, "Leisure in Urbanized America," in P. K. Hatt and A. J. Reiss, Jr., eds., *Reader in Urban Sociology* (New York: The Free Press of Glencoe, Inc., 1951), p. 470.

[3] *Ibid.*, p. 315.

[4] Occupational prestige is generally regarded as the most satisfactory and probably the most valid index of social status. For example, Warner and his associates found a high correlation between occupation and other measures of "social class." A multiple correlation of occupation, source of income, house type and dwelling area, with subjective judgments of community informants (Evaluated Participation) was .972. A zero-order correlation of .91 was obtained between occupation alone and Evaluated Participation. W. Lloyd Warner *et al.*, *Social Class in America* (Chicago: Science Research Associates, 1949), pp. 35 ff.

[5] This scale was based on ratings of occupations by a cross section of the American population interviewed by the National Opinion Research Center. There were of course some occupations encountered in this study which did not appear in the North-Hatt scale. Final ratings of all occupations not mentioned on the scale were the average of individual ratings made by five sociologists asked to compare and equate these occupational titles with those in the scale and to assign corresponding prestige ratings to them.

to membership in voluntary organizations, and a section of relevant background items. This instrument, in questionnaire form, was pretested on one hundred male respondents randomly selected from the Columbus city directory.

Since this study sought to delineate the nature of the relationship existing between different prestige levels and leisure styles, rather than focusing on the stratification system of a particular community, a sampling technique providing similar numbers of cases at different occupational levels was chosen. A design of this type would appear to have broader applicability for the study of social stratification in general, and could enable research findings to transcend local configurations with greater ease.

The selection of respondents was confined to urban, adult males, in order to increase the homogeneity of the sample so that significant differences in leisure among the strata studied could be more readily identified. Cutting points were established along the continuum of occupational scores, dividing them into five prestige levels, and within these categories five separate random samples were selected. These samples encompassed the total range of occupational prestige. It should be noted that the term "prestige level," as used in this study, was defined as a category of persons with occupations of somewhat similar prestige status. They do not, therefore, represent "social classes" in the sense of clearly distinguishable categories "set off from one another." The limits of the categories were determined by the investigator and were chosen to facilitate analysis of the data.[6]

---

[6] The range of scores in each of the five prestige levels include: Level I, 82-96; Level II, 75-81; Level III, 67-74; Level IV, 55-66;

The Samples

The basic plan of the sampling technique was to obtain a random sample of at least one hundred respondents at each of the five occupational levels. It was necessary at this point to estimate how many cases would have to be selected in order to yield these one hundred respondents at each level. The distribution of occupational scores of respondents in the pretest offered a basis for this estimate. The smallest number of returns occurred at the lowest prestige level. Only four persons from this group in the pretest sample of one hundred returned the questionnaire. Thus in order to obtain one hundred returns in the lowest prestige category, at least 2500 cases would be needed in the total sample. In order to allow for partially completed returns, approximately 3000 potential respondents were systematically selected from the Columbus city directory, and the name, address, and occupation of each was placed on a separate card.[7] The cards were then sorted by occupations into five prestige levels, yielding the distribution shown in the first row of Table 1.

Level V, 44-54. The chief factor underlying the choice of the intervals was an effort to reflect major occupational groupings. Thus the scores represented by Level I include, for the most part, professional persons. Level II encompasses largely managers, officials, and proprietors, while Level III includes sales and clerical workers as well as white collar employees generally. Skilled craftsmen and kindred workers comprise the major portion of Level IV, while service workers, semi-skilled and unskilled laborers make up most of the lower prestige level.

[7] It should be noted that several factors restricted the city directory from yielding a random sample in the strict sense of the term. For example, the directory was over a year old. Obviously, the population had changed to some extent during the interim. Also, some names may have been initially omitted. The representativeness of the sample is therefore decreased to the extent that these and similar factors were operative.

Pattern of Questionnaire Returns

In order to satisfy the requirements of the sampling design, two mailings were necessary. In the first mailing, questionnaires were sent to persons at each level. As the returns of this mailing were received, it was noted that the frequency of completed returns varied directly with occupational prestige level. In other words, the higher the prestige level, the higher the frequency of returned questionnaires. Due to the operation of this factor, the first mailing did not produce the needed one hundred cases at Levels IV and V. Additional names were then randomly drawn from the replacements in these levels. The returns from the second mailing were sufficient to produce the number of cases needed at these lower levels and increased the total sample to 574 usable cases, as summarized in Table 1.

When the specific occupational information contained in the returned questionnaires was evaluated, it was found, in some instances, that the initial prestige rating, based on a brief occupational description in the city directory, no longer applied. This necessitated a reassignment of some cases to either a higher or lower prestige category.[8] Although the research design called for limiting arbitrarily the number of cases in each level to one hundred, it was later thought best to utilize every completed questionnaire returned. Thus the number of respondents varies from one level to another, and the total frequencies exceed one hundred cases in each of the five prestige levels.[9] It should also be noted that throughout the classification of the data, the five initial prestige categories were kept separated. The several samples were never combined and never treated as representative of a single universe.

The Findings

In the analysis of the data the first area of concern involved two related questions:

1. Is the frequency of participation in specific leisure-time activities significantly associated with occupational prestige levels?

2. If such association exists, in which prestige level is participation in a given activity most frequent?

For this analysis the chi-square test of significance was applied to relative frequencies of participation of the five samples. The results are summarized in Table 2.

---

[8] The final totals after this reassignment were: Level I, 128; Level II, 102; Level III, 133; Level IV, 109; Level V, 102.

[9] Additional details concerning the sample and its logic are presented in the writer's unpublished doctoral dissertation, *The Use of Leisure and Its Relation to Social Stratification*, Ohio State University, 1955.

TABLE 1   Questionnaire Returns, by Occupational Prestige Level

Sample Procedure	PRESTIGE LEVELS					
	I	II	III	IV	V	Total
Number in sampling population	192	348	1113	789	568	3010
Number of questionnaires sent	192	250	250	375	550	1617
Number delivered to addressees	180	234	226	331	475	1446
Number returned	134	128	112	117	108	599
Per cent returned*	74.4	54.7	49.5	35.3	22.7	41.4
Number of usable cases	130	122	110	109	103	574

* Percentages are based on the number of questionnaires returned which presumably were received by potential respondents. The percentages do not include questionnaires which were returned because of faulty addresses.

Activity	PRESTIGE LEVEL PARTICIPATING MOST FREQUENTLY					Level of Significance
	I	II	III	IV	V	
Attending theatrical plays	X	....	....	....	....	.001
Attending concerts	X	....	....	....	....	.001
Attending special lectures	X	....	....	....	....	.001
Visiting a museum or art gallery	X	....	....	....	....	.001
Attending fraternal organizations	X	....	....	....	....	.001
Playing bridge	X	....	....	....	....	.001
Attending conventions	X	....	....	....	....	.001
Community service work	X	....	....	....	....	.001
Reading for pleasure	X	....	....	....	....	.001
Studying	X	....	....	....	....	.001
Entertaining at home	X	....	....	....	....	.01
Attending motion pictures	X	....	....	....	....	.05
Out-of-town weekend visiting (overnight)	....	X	....	....	....	.001
Attending football games	....	X	....	....	....	.001
Attending parties	....	X	....	....	....	.001
Playing golf	....	....	X	....	....	.001
Working on automobile	....	....	....	X	....	.01
Watching television	....	....	....	....	X	.001
Playing with children	....	....	....	....	X	.001
Fishing	....	....	....	....	X	.001
Playing card games other than bridge and poker	....	....	....	....	X	.001
Playing poker	....	....	....	....	X	.01
Driving or riding in car for pleasure	....	....	....	....	X	.01
Attending auto theater	....	....	....	....	X	.01
Spending time in tavern	....	....	....	....	X	.01
Spending time at zoo	....	....	....	....	X	.05
Attending baseball games	....	....	....	....	X	.05

As an inspection of this table indicates, significant differences were found to exist between occupational prestige and leisure use.[10] Most of the relationships were linear or near-linear in nature, that is, individuals with higher scores were more likely to participate frequently in some types of leisure pursuits and infrequently in others.[11]

Several relationships, however, were curvilinear. For example, the number of times a year the respondents played golf increased along with their prestige ratings—until the middle-status group was reached. At this point the frequency of participation began to decline with higher occupational scores. Within this middle group the highest degree of participation occurred among

[10] Eight activities included in the questionnaire were not significantly related to occupational prestige. They were: hunting; bowling; working in garden; out-of-town visiting (not overnight); listening to radio; loafing; doing odd jobs around home; attending picnics, fairs, exhibitions.

[11] The direction of these relationships was examined by assigning arbitrary weights to the frequency categories as follows:
Almost daily, 4; about once a week, 3; about one to three times a month, 2; less than once a month, 1; rarely or never, 0.

Obviously, participation in certain activities, such as baseball, fishing, and so on, depends largely upon the season of the year. In such cases the respondents were asked to "place an X in one of the columns to indicate how often you usually do these things *during the regular season.*"

Mean scores on all activities were computed for each prestige level. Using this procedure it was possible to estimate if differential participation varied directly or inversely with prestige level.

those who classified themselves as "salesman." This would appear to be consistent with the widespread conception that golf offers an excellent opportunity for pursuing business relations under informal and pleasant surroundings. It should also be noted that among the participant sports, golf represents perhaps the most pertinent example of how an activity is being transformed from the exclusive pastime of a few wealthy individuals to a popular pastime for many, representing diversified backgrounds in income and social status. The possible instrumental nature of this activity suggests, however, that membership in the "right" golf club could still be accepted as an important index of social status.

While examination of individual spare-time activities is useful in understanding leisure behavior, the design of this study also permitted an analysis of certain broader dimensions of leisure use. At this point the focus will shift to a consideration of these configurations.

Spectator Type Activities

Although value judgments differ considerably regarding the desirability of certain forms of amusement, the passive spectator nature of some leisure pursuits has probably received more widespread criticism than any other facet of contemporary leisure behavior. While few people dispute the merits of participation in physical activities, there are those who seem to consider "spectatoritis" as a new national affliction. The idea is current that most Americans spend most of their spare time in a spectator role.

Information collected in this study, however, does not substantiate this observation. The respondents were asked to indicate the spare-time activities taking up most of their leisure time. An analysis of the responses when classified as "spectator" and "nonspectator"

types,[12] revealed that the majority of respondents at each level devoted most of their leisure time to nonspectator activities. The data in Table 3 show

TABLE 3 Percentage of Respondents Devoting Most of Their Leisure Time to Spectator Type Activities, by Prestige Level*

Type of Leisure Activity		PRESTIGE LEVEL				
		I	II	III	IV	V
	N	120	96	126	98	96
Spectator		25.7	22.9	41.3	36.1	23.9
Nonspectator		74.3	77.1	58.7	63.9	76.1
Total		100.0	100.0	100.0	100.0	100.0

* Percentages are based on the number of respondents giving the necessary information. No data cases were excluded.

the nonlinear nature of this relationship. The largest proportion of respondents who spent most of their leisure hours as spectators (41.3 per cent) occurred at the middle occupational level. This percentage decreased markedly as the upper and lower segments of the prestige continuum were approached. Only about 25 per cent of the respondents at Levels I and V devoted most of their spare time to activities that could be classified as constituting "spectatoritis." These findings appear to cast serious doubts on the validity of current conceptions concerning the allegedly ominous portions of time consumed by such activities.

Commercialized Leisure

Another criticism frequently leveled at the American leisure pattern is an alleged dominance of commercialized amusements. Hollywood movies, night

[12] Among the activities included in the "spectator" category were: watching television; attending motion pictures, lectures, plays, and musical events; attending various sports events, e.g., football, baseball, basketball, boxing, wrestling, and auto races.

clubs, and dance halls are sometimes defined as threatening the "basic values of the society." However, the empirical basis for this observation seems to be indeed limited. The surprisingly small proportion of respondents for whom commercial types of recreation occupied most of their leisure hours is shown in Table 4. It will be noted

TABLE 4   Percentage of Respondents Devoting Most of Their Leisure Time to Commercial Type Activities, by Prestige Level

| | | PRESTIGE LEVEL | | | |
Type of Activity N	I	II	III	IV	V
	124	98	130	104	99
Commercial	3.8	4.2	7.7	7.9	10.1
Noncommercial	96.2	95.8	92.3	92.1	89.9
Total	100.0	100.0	100.0	100.0	100.0

that the percentages representing these respondents varied inversely with prestige level.[13] As little as about 4 per cent of the persons in Level I specified activities which could be included in the commercial category. The proportion of respondents in this category increased to about 10 per cent at Level V. Even though commercialized recreation has become one of the nation's largest business enterprises, it still does not occupy a large share of the leisure time of the adult population.

Craftsmanship

In his provocative book, *The Lonely Crowd*, David Riesman advances the hypothesis that competence in craftsmanship during leisure hours may have

___

[13] Some of the activities included in the "commercial" category were: bowling, attending theatrical plays, motion pictures, playing pool or billiards, spending time in a cafe or tavern, attending a night club, dancing, attending sports events. If the event or activity generally involved the payment of a fee, it was classified as "commercial."

developed new meanings in contemporary American society.

The man whose daily work is glad-handing can often rediscover both his childhood and his inner-directed residues by serious craftsmanship. An advertising man, involved all day in personalizing, may spend his weekends in the craftsman-like silences of a boatyard or in sailboat racing. . . . But the craft-skill is valued more than ever before for its own sake, as in the case of the Sunday painter. . . . Certainly many people now have the leisure and encouragement to pursue crafts who never did before. . . .

There is a widespread trend today to warn Americans against relaxing in the featherbed of plenty, in the pulpy recreations of popular culture, in the delights of bar and coke bar, and so on. In these warnings any leisure that looks easy is suspect, and craftsmanship does not look easy.[14]

Some of the data collected in this study bear upon these observations, and perhaps in some measure support them. Craftsmanlike activities, which appeared throughout the list of leisure pursuits consuming most of the respondents' spare time, were separately tabulated.[15] The results of this analysis are shown in Table 5. These data

TABLE 5   Percentage of Respondents Devoting Most of Their Leisure Time to Craftsmanlike Activities, by Prestige Level

| | | PRESTIGE LEVEL | | | |
Type of Activity N	I	II	III	IV	V
	124	98	130	104	99
Craftsmanlike activities	19.9	21.4	21.9	23.2	30.3
Other types of activities	81.1	78.6	78.1	76.8	69.7
Total	100.0	100.0	100.0	100.0	100.0

___

[14] David Riesman, *The Lonely Crowd* (New York: Doubleday & Company, Inc., 1953), pp. 333-336.

[15] Among the activities classified as "craftsmanlike" were: model building, sculpting, painting, and various forms of woodworking.

suggest that craft interest tends to vary inversely with prestige level. An interesting relationship appears when these frequencies are compared with the percentages of respondents devoting most of their time to commercial types of recreation (see Table 4.) The proportion of respondents who frequently participate in craftsmanlike activities is greater than the per cent who participate chiefly in commercial forms of amusement. This relationship holds for each occupational level studied.

It is difficult of course to know how much significance should be attached to this emphasis on craftsmanship, because comparable data indicating the percentage of those who engaged in this activity in previous years are not available. Therefore little can be said concerning a possible trend in this direction. Even though increased sales of home workshop equipment and the phenomenal increase in "Do-It-Yourself" literature may be partially explained by such correlative factors as the increase in home ownership and certain characteristics of suburban living, it may well be that competence in craft skills has developed new meanings for many persons.

Use of Added Leisure Time

It was thought that additional insight into the use of leisure would be attained by analyzing responses to the question: What would you do with an extra two hours in your day? An analysis of these responses may reflect both an individual's attitude toward the appropriate use of leisure time as well as certain subcultural differences regarding the proper use of leisure. These choices were readily classified into eight categories. The findings are summarized in Table 6.

An inspection of the data shows that the respondents in the higher and lower

TABLE 6   Response to the Question, "What would you do with an extra two hours in your day?" by Prestige Level, in Percentages

| | | | PRESTIGE LEVEL | | |
| | | I | II | III | IV | V |
Activity	N	128	102	133	109	102
Relax, rest, loaf, sleep		24.7	31.1	26.7	32.9	39.7
Read, study		27.9	18.7	14.8	11.2	12.8
Work at job		19.8	13.8	14.0	8.3	9.1
Work around house		8.5	7.9	12.3	18.4	15.7
Spend time with family, play with children		4.3	11.8	7.3	7.5	4.9
Watch television		0.0	1.9	2.5	5.6	6.9
Other leisure activities		7.1	4.1	10.8	6.1	3.2
Don't know		2.3	5.8	8.3	6.4	3.9
No answer		5.4	4.9	3.3	4.6	3.8
Total		100.0	100.0	100.0	100.0	100.0

groups would use this extra time in quite different ways. For example, the modal response category for the highest status group indicates that these persons would use the time to read and study, while the highest proportion of those at the other extreme of the prestige continuum replied they would use the extra two hours to rest, loaf, and relax. The proportion of persons at Level I who would use this time to work at their jobs is almost as great as the percentage who would relax and rest. It would seem that for a somewhat greater proportion of the higher than the lower prestige groups, an extra amount of leisure would serve largely as an extension of the main activities of life.

Further analysis of these responses reveals that the amount of time which would be spent "working around the house" also tended to vary inversely with prestige level. The percentage of persons who stated they would watch television increased as occupational level decreased. Interestingly, no one in the higher group would use this time to watch television.

Many of the above responses would seem to support the conclusion that a substantially greater proportion of the higher prestige groups would use this hypothetical increase in leisure time largely to implement their business and professional interests. While many interpretations of this pattern are perhaps tenable, it would appear that differential levels of aspiration might account for some of these differences. Perhaps other differences reflect the fact that unlike occupations place widely different demands and expectations upon the role incumbent. It may well be that through the process of attaining higher occupational status, it becomes increasingly difficult to dissociate business interests from leisure pursuits. At the extreme, this process would seem to be most clearly demonstrated in those cases where the practice of a man's profession becomes so important to him, aside from pecuniary considerations, that it becomes his avocation as well as his vocation.

Summary

This study sought to delineate some of the relationships between prestige levels and leisure behavior. Systematic differences were found between the frequency of participation in certain types of leisure activities and levels of occupational prestige. Most of the relationships were linear or near-linear.

Some of the preceding data strengthen the findings of earlier research regarding relationships between social status and leisure use. However, other data suggest the emergence of new patterns. Perhaps competence in certain leisure pursuits, notably craftsmanship, has developed new meanings for many persons. Perhaps the alleged domination of spare-time activities by commercial forms of recreation needs to be re-evaluated. Furthermore, the conception of the man at leisure as chiefly a spectator—a nonparticipant—may be a major distortion of fact.

In spite of much current research directed toward the delincation of different life styles, most investigations have largely overlooked the institutionalization of leisure. Since it is highly probable that the amount of leisure will continue to increase in the future, this aspect of present-day life in American society assumes increasing proportions and significance. This would seem to indicate that social scientists must eventually recognize that it is as important to understand the leisure-time aspect of American society as it is to understand the economic, familial, religious, or political aspects.